Rescaling Urban Poverty

RGS-IBG Book Series

For further information about the series and a full list of published and forthcoming titles please visit www.rgsbookseries.com

Published

Rescaling Urban Poverty: Homelessness, State Restructuring and City Politics in Japan
Mahito Hayashi

The Urban Question in Africa: Uneven Geographies of Transition
Pádraig R. Carmody, James T. Murphy, Richard Grant and Francis Y. Owusu

Theory and Explanation in Geography
Henry Wai-chung Yeung

Decolonising Geography? Disciplinary Histories and the End of the British Empire in Africa, 1948-1998
Ruth Craggs

How Cities Learn: Tracing Bus Rapid Transit in South Africa
Astrid Wood

Defensible Space on the Move: Mobilisation in English Housing Policy and Practice
Loretta Lees and Elanor Warwick

Geomorphology and the Carbon Cycle
Martin Evans

The Unsettling Outdoors: Environmental Estrangement in Everyday Life
Russell Hitchings

Respatialising Finance: Power, Politics and Offshore Renminbi Market Making in London
Sarah Hall

Bodies, Affects, Politics: The Clash of Bodily Regimes
Steve Pile

Home SOS: Gender, Violence, and Survival in Crisis Ordinary Cambodia
Katherine Brickell

Geographies of Anticolonialism: Political Networks Across and Beyond South India, c. 1900-1930
Andrew Davies

Geopolitics and the Event: Rethinking Britain's Iraq War through Art
Alan Ingram

On Shifting Foundations: State Rescaling, Policy Experimentation And Economic Restructuring In Post-1949 China
Kean Fan Lim

Global Asian City: Migration, Desire and the Politics of Encounter in 21st Century Seoul
Francis L. Collins

Transnational Geographies Of The Heart: Intimate Subjectivities In A Globalizing City
Katie Walsh

Cryptic Concrete: A Subterranean Journey Into Cold War Germany
Ian Klinke

Work-Life Advantage: Sustaining Regional Learning and Innovation
Al James

Pathological Lives: Disease, Space and Biopolitics
Steve Hinchliffe, Nick Bingham, John Allen and Simon Carter

Smoking Geographies: Space, Place and Tobacco
Ross Barnett, Graham Moon, Jamie Pearce, Lee Thompson and Liz Twigg

Rehearsing the State: The Political Practices of the Tibetan Government-in-Exile
Fiona McConnell

Nothing Personal? Geographies of Governing and Activism in the British Asylum System
Nick Gill

Articulations of Capital: Global Production Networks and Regional Transformations
John Pickles and Adrian Smith, with Robert Begg, Milan Buček, Poli Roukova and Rudolf Pástor

Metropolitan Preoccupations: The Spatial Politics of Squatting in Berlin
Alexander Vasudevan

Everyday Peace? Politics, Citizenship and Muslim Lives in India
Philippa Williams

Assembling Export Markets: The Making and Unmaking of Global Food Connections in West Africa
Stefan Ouma

Africa's Information Revolution: Technical Regimes and Production Networks in South Africa and Tanzania
James T. Murphy and Pádraig Carmody

Origination: The Geographies of Brands and Branding
Andy Pike

In the Nature of Landscape: Cultural Geography on the Norfolk Broads
David Matless

Geopolitics and Expertise: Knowledge and Authority in European Diplomacy
Merje Kuus

Everyday Moral Economies: Food, Politics and Scale in Cuba
Marisa Wilson

Material Politics: Disputes Along the Pipeline
Andrew Barry

Fashioning Globalisation: New Zealand Design, Working Women and the Cultural Economy
Maureen Molloy and Wendy Larner

Working Lives - Gender, Migration and Employment in Britain, 1945-2007
Linda McDowell

Dunes: Dynamics, Morphology and Geological History
Andrew Warren

Spatial Politics: Essays for Doreen Massey
Edited by David Featherstone and Joe Painter

The Improvised State: Sovereignty, Performance and Agency in Dayton Bosnia
Alex Jeffrey

Learning the City: Knowledge and Translocal Assemblage
Colin McFarlane

Globalizing Responsibility: The Political Rationalities of Ethical Consumption
Clive Barnett, Paul Cloke, Nick Clarke & Alice Malpass

Domesticating Neo-Liberalism: Spaces of Economic Practice and Social Reproduction in Post-Socialist Cities
Alison Stenning, Adrian Smith, Alena Rochovská and Dariusz Świątek

Swept Up Lives? Re-envisioning the Homeless City
Paul Cloke, Jon May and Sarah Johnsen

Aerial Life: Spaces, Mobilities, Affects
Peter Adey

Millionaire Migrants: Trans-Pacific Life Lines
David Ley

State, Science and the Skies: Governmentalities of the British Atmosphere
Mark Whitehead

Complex Locations: Women's geographical work in the UK 1850–1970
Avril Maddrell

Value Chain Struggles: Institutions and Governance in the Plantation Districts of South India
Jeff Neilson and Bill Pritchard

Queer Visibilities: Space, Identity and Interaction in Cape Town
Andrew Tucker

Arsenic Pollution: A Global Synthesis
Peter Ravenscroft, Hugh Brammer and Keith Richards

Resistance, Space and Political Identities: The Making of Counter-Global Networks
David Featherstone

Mental Health and Social Space: Towards Inclusionary Geographies?
Hester Parr

Climate and Society in Colonial Mexico: A Study in Vulnerability
Georgina H. Endfield

Geochemical Sediments and Landscapes
Edited by David J. Nash and Sue J. McLaren

Driving Spaces: A Cultural-Historical Geography of England's M1 Motorway
Peter Merriman

Badlands of the Republic: Space, Politics and Urban Policy
Mustafa Dikeç

Geomorphology of Upland Peat: Erosion, Form and Landscape Change
Martin Evans and Jeff Warburton

Spaces of Colonialism: Delhi's Urban Governmentalities
Stephen Legg

People/States/Territories
Rhys Jones

Publics and the City
Kurt Iveson

After the Three Italies: Wealth, Inequality and Industrial Change
Mick Dunford and Lidia Greco

Putting Workfare in Place
Peter Sunley, Ron Martin and Corinne Nativel

Domicile and Diaspora
Alison Blunt

Geographies and Moralities
Edited by Roger Lee and David M. Smith

Military Geographies
Rachel Woodward

A New Deal for Transport?
Edited by Iain Docherty and Jon Shaw

Geographies of British Modernity
Edited by David Gilbert, David Matless and Brian Short

Lost Geographies of Power
John Allen

Globalizing South China
Carolyn L. Cartier

Geomorphological Processes and Landscape Change: Britain in the Last 1000 Years
Edited by David L. Higgitt and E. Mark Lee

Rescaling Urban Poverty

Homelessness, State Restructuring and City Politics in Japan

Mahito Hayashi

WILEY

This edition first published 2024
© 2024 Royal Geographical Society (with the Institute of British Geographers)
This Work is a co-publication between The Royal Geographical Society (with the Institute of British Geographers) and John Wiley & Sons Ltd.

All rights reserved. No part of this publication may be reproduced, stored in a retrieval system, or transmitted, in any form or by any means, electronic, mechanical, photocopying, recording or otherwise, except as permitted by law. Advice on how to obtain permission to reuse material from this title is available at http://www.wiley.com/go/permissions.

The right of Mahito Hayashi to be identified as the author of this work has been asserted in accordance with law.

Registered Office(s)
John Wiley & Sons, Inc., 111 River Street, Hoboken, NJ 07030, USA
John Wiley & Sons Ltd, The Atrium, Southern Gate, Chichester, West Sussex, PO19 8SQ, UK

Editorial Office
9600 Garsington Road, Oxford, OX4 2DQ, UK

For details of our global editorial offices, customer services, and more information about Wiley products visit us at www.wiley.com.

Wiley also publishes its books in a variety of electronic formats and by print-on-demand. Some content that appears in standard print versions of this book may not be available in other formats.

Limit of Liability/Disclaimer of Warranty
The contents of this work are intended to further general scientific research, understanding, and discussion only and are not intended and should not be relied upon as recommending or promoting scientific method, diagnosis, or treatment by physicians for any particular patient. In view of ongoing research, equipment modifications, changes in governmental regulations, and the constant flow of information relating to the use of medicines, equipment, and devices, the reader is urged to review and evaluate the information provided in the package insert or instructions for each medicine, equipment, or device for, among other things, any changes in the instructions or indication of usage and for added warnings and precautions. While the publisher and authors have used their best efforts in preparing this work, they make no representations or warranties with respect to the accuracy or completeness of the contents of this work and specifically disclaim all warranties, including without limitation any implied warranties of merchantability or fitness for a particular purpose. No warranty may be created or extended by sales representatives, written sales materials or promotional statements for this work. The fact that an organization, website, or product is referred to in this work as a citation and/or potential source of further information does not mean that the publisher and authors endorse the information or services the organization, website, or product may provide or recommendations it may make. This work is sold with the understanding that the publisher is not engaged in rendering professional services. The advice and strategies contained herein may not be suitable for your situation. You should consult with a specialist where appropriate. Further, readers should be aware that websites listed in this work may have changed or disappeared between when this work was written and when it is read. Neither the publisher nor authors shall be liable for any loss of profit or any other commercial damages, including but not limited to special, incidental, consequential, or other damages.

A catalogue record for this book is available from the Library of Congress

Hardback ISBN: 9781119690979; Paperback ISBN: 9781119691020; ePub ISBN: 9781119691105; ePDF ISBN: 9781119691044; oBook ISBN: 9781119691051

Cover Image: © Mahito Hayashi
Cover design by Wiley

Set in 10/12pt Plantin Std by Integra Software Services Pvt. Ltd, Pondicherry, India
Printed and bound by CPI Group (UK) Ltd, Croydon, CR0 4YY

C9781119691020_261023

For Shoko and Kenjiro, with love

Contents

List of Figures	xii
List of Tables	xiv
List of Abbreviations	xv
Series Editor's Preface	xvi
Preface and Acknowledgements	xvii

Part One Theory, Method, Context   1

1. Introduction and Theoretical Framework   3
   Urban Political Economy: For Homelessness?   7
   State Rescaling: The Central Concept of this Book   9
   Subcomponent 1: National States   13
   Subcomponent 2: Public and Private Spaces   17
   Subcomponent 3: Urban Social Movements   21
   The Method of Theorisation in this Book   26
      Step 1: Theory Making   28
      Step 2: Theory Specification   28
   Postcolonial Urban Theory   30
   Between Abstract and Concrete   30
   The Structure of this Book   32

2. Japanese Context and the Regulationist Ethnography   37
   Theory Specification 1: National States   38
   Theory Specification 2: Public and Private Spaces   40
   Theory Specification 3: Urban Social Movements   44
   Regulationist Ethnography   45
   Sites of Participatory Observation   49
   The Nature of Data   53
      Data on Homelessness   54
      Data on Regulation   55

  Data on Social Movements   55
 Subaltern Materials   56
 Conclusion   59

Part Two National States and Public and Private Spaces   61

3. Scales of Societalisation: Integral State and the Rescaling of Poverty   63
 Theory and Its "Deviants"   64
 Theoretical Framework   67
  The Nationalised Space of Poverty Regulation   67
  Crises of the Nationalised Space of Poverty Regulation   70
  Rescaling   72
  Comparisons to Brenner's Meso Model   76
 Mobilising the Theory for Japan   77
 Nationalised Space of Poverty Regulation in Japan   79
  High Growth, c. 1950s–1972   79
  1970s World Crisis and Its Aftermath, c. 1973–1985   83
  Bubble Economy, c. 1986–1991   85
  Postbubble Crisis, c. 1992–2007   87
  The World Financial Crisis, Mass Disasters, and Their Aftermath, c. 2008–2010s   89
  Overview   91
 New Regulatory Spaces in Japan   93
  New Regulatory Spaces   93
  Round One: Ground-Up Rescaling   95
  Round Two: Picking-Off Rescaling   96
  Round Three: Unfolding Rescaling   99
 Conclusion   100

4. Rescaling Urban Metabolism I: Homeless Labour for "Housing"   103
 The Urban Matrix and the Housing Classes   104
 Metabolism, Societalisation, Rescaling   107
  Metabolism and Societalisation   107
  Rescaling and Reregulation   111
 Specification of Theory   116
  Theory for Japan   116
  Late Formation of the Housing Classes in Japan   116
  Small Use Values Attached to Japan's Urban Matrix   117
  State-Saturated Societalisation and Consumption in Japan   118
  Ground-Up Rescaling in Japan   120
 Metabolism and Regulation I: Locational Ethnography   122
  Background for Ethnographic Narratives   122
  Small Public Parks   123

  A Municipal Sports Park and a Gymnasium   126
  A Railway Station   126
  The Coast   128
 Metabolism and Regulation II: Multicity Ethnography   130
 Conclusion   132

5. Rescaling Urban Metabolism II: Homeless Labour for Money   135
 Homeless Recyclers: A Regulationist Approach   136
 Homeless Recyclers in Japan   139
 Regulationist Ethnography I: Regulating the Recycling Metabolism   143
  Regulation in the City of Yokohama   143
  Regulation in the City of Hiratsuka   145
  Summary   147
 Regulationist Ethnography II: New Recycling Strategies   147
  Regulation or Escape?   147
  The First Strategy of Recyclers: Find the Spots   148
  The Second Strategy of Recyclers: Change the Target   149
  The Third Strategy of Recyclers: Etiquette for Neighbourhoods   149
  Summary   149
 Regulationist Ethnography III: Movements for Homeless Recyclers   150
  Any Social Movements?   150
  A Movement in the City of Yokohama   150
  A Movement in the City of Hiratsuka   152
  Summary   153
 Conclusion   153

Part Three Urban Social Movements   155

6. Placemaking in the Inner City: Social and Cultural Niches of Homeless Activism   157
 The Inner City: Beyond Regulation   158
 Lefebvre in the Inner City   159
  Revisiting Lefebvre   159
  Expanding Lefebvre   162
  Inclusive Urban Form   163
 Japanese Contexts   166
  Attuning the Theory to Japan   166
  The Kotobuki District   167
 Placemaking in Yokohama's Inner City: From Run-Ups to the 1970s   170
  Summary   175
 Placemaking in Yokohama's Inner City: The 1980s   176
  Summary   180
 Placemaking in Yokohama's Inner City: The 1990s   180
  Summary   183
 Conclusion   183

7. Commoning around the Inner City: Whose Public? Whose Common?   186
    Commoning, Habiting, Othering   187
    Commoning against Othering   189
    Japanese Parameters of Commoning   191
    Commoning in Yokohama in the 1970s   192
        The Start of Commoning   192
        From Radicalism to Downright Oppression   194
        A National Scale of Commoning?   196
        Disarmament   197
        Summary   198
    Commoning in Yokohama in the 1980s   198
        Between the Two Cycles of Homelessness   198
        Commoning by the Union   199
        Commoning by Housed Citizens   201
        Summary   202
    Commoning in Yokohama in the 1990s–2000s   203
        Commoning Public Spaces   203
        Commoning Public Provision   207
        Discommoning   210
        Summary   213
    Conclusion   214

8. Translating to New Cities: Geographical and Cultural Expansion   216
    Outlying Cities   217
    Brokerage and Translation   220
    Placemaking in the Outlying Cities   224
        Kotobuki: A House of Brokerage   224
        Placemaking in the City of Sagamihara   225
        Placemaking in the City of Fujisawa   227
        Placemaking in the City of Hiratsuka   229
    Commoning in the Outlying Cities   229
        Early Attempts at Commoning   229
        Successes in Commoning   231
    Solidarity against a New Rescaling   234
        Linking the Cities   234
        Learning the Rescaling   235
    Conclusion   236

Part Four   Towards the Future of Rescaling Studies   239

9. New Rescalings in Japan   241
    Upscaling of Homeless Politics in the Late 2000s   241
    Neoliberalisation and Workfarist Reform in the 2010s   246

Rescaling for All 249
When Public Spaces Are Closed 251
Repoliticising the Urban 253
The Inner City against Gentrification 254
COVID-19, Rescaling, Recommoning 256

10. Conclusion **258**
Urban Theory and Ethnography 261
Remapping Urban Political Economy 262
Habitat and Urban Class Relations 263
Integral State Rescaling 264

References 265
Index 294

List of Figures

Figure 1.1	Overarching theoretical framework of this book.	12
Figure 1.2	A geographical approach to methodological abstraction.	27
Figure 1.3	Three layers in each "empirical" chapter.	35
Figure 2.1	Kanagawa Prefecture.	51
Figure 3.1	Rounds of rescaling.	74
Figure 4.1	People's two metabolic circuits in public space.	112
Figure 4.2	Regulation of urban encounter and societalisation in public space.	115
Figure 4.3	Comparative view of Japanese public space: a policy discourse.	118
Figure 4.4	A bench in Shinshuku Park, 25 August 2004.	124
Figure 4.5	A signboard in Shinshuku Park, 28 August 2004.	125
Figure 4.6	A site of homelessness in Hachiman Yama Park, 28 August 2005.	125
Figure 4.7	Belongings of a homeless person at the stadium, 11 August 2004.	127
Figure 4.8	A notice at a homeless site beside the gymnasium, 3 April 2004.	128
Figure 4.9	A notice at the railway station, 2 December 2005.	129
Figure 4.10	A house and farm of a homeless person in the coastal area, 18 April 2004.	130
Figure 5.1	Double-edged metabolism of recyclers and its regulation.	138
Figure 5.2	Homeless people's cash income from labour, 2003–2012.	140
Figure 5.3	Homeless people's income-generating activities, 2003–2012.	140
Figure 5.4	Bicycle of a homeless recycler in Yokohama, 1 January 2019.	141

Figure 5.5	Public notice displayed at Yokohama's public dumping sites in 2004.	144
Figure 5.6	Notice board at Hiratsuka's public dumping site, 17 September 2004.	146
Figure 5.7	Homeless recycler's notes on the days of official garbage collection, 28 August 2005.	148
Figure 5.8	Yokohama's limited "acceptance" of homeless recyclers.	151
Figure 6.1	Inclusive urban form and its urban effects.	164
Figure 6.2	The Kotobuki district, 1965.	168
Figure 6.3	Undated handbill distributed in Kotobuki in the mid-1970s.	173
Figure 6.4	Handbill distributed in Kotobuki on 4 September 1976.	176
Figure 7.1	Handbill distributed at Yokohama's junior high schools in 1983.	201
Figure 7.2	Handbill distributed to homeless people in Yokohama on 21 January 1993.	204
Figure 7.3	Handbill distributed to homeless people in Yokohama on 1 July 1994.	206
Figure 7.4	Letter from the City of Yokohama to the movement on 9 August 1994.	209
Figure 7.5	Yokohama's food and hotel vouchers issued in the 1990s.	210
Figure 7.6	Handbill distributed to homeless people in Yokohama on 21 September 1994.	210
Figure 7.7	Yokohama's food and hotel vouchers issued in the 2000s.	213
Figure 8.1	Handbill distributed by activists in Yokohama on 27 December 1977.	223
Figure 8.2	Mayor of the city of Hiratsuka listening to activists, 28 November 2005.	233
Figure 9.1	Households on public assistance between 1976 and 2014.	245
Figure 9.2	Decline in "countable" homeless people in the Tokyo–Yokohama metropolitan region, 2003–2012.	251
Figure 9.3	Public spaces of central Yokohama, 1 and 2 January 2019.	252

List of Tables

Table 3.1	Japan's nationalised spaces of poverty regulation, 1950s–mid-2010s.	92
Table 5.1	Ordinances that criminalise nonpublic recyclers in Kanagawa Prefecture.	142
Table 7.1	Key movement actions in and around the Kotobuki district in the 1970s.	195
Table 7.2	Murders and injuries of homeless people in Yokohama during winter 1983.	200
Table 7.3	Information-gathering tours for public space commoning.	206
Table 8.1	Groups for homeless people in Kanagawa Prefecture.	219

List of Abbreviations

KLH	Kotobuki Livelihood Hall
KSMA	Kotobuki Self-Management Association
MHLW	Ministry of Health, Labour and Welfare
NSPR	Nationalised Space of Poverty Regulation
NUP	New Urban Poverty

Series Editors' Preface

The RGS-IBG Book Series only publishes work of the highest international standing. Its emphasis is on distinctive new developments in human and physical geography, although it is also open to contributions from cognate disciplines whose interests overlap with those of geographers. The series places strong emphasis on theoretically informed and empirically strong texts. Reflecting the vibrant and diverse theoretical and empirical agendas that characterize the contemporary discipline, contributions are expected to inform, challenge and stimulate the reader. Overall, the RGS-IBG Book Series seeks to promote scholarly publications that leave an intellectual mark and change the way readers think about particular issues, methods or theories.

For details on how to submit a proposal please visit:
www.rgsbookseries.com

Ruth Craggs, *King's College London, UK*
Chih Yuan Woon, *National University of Singapore*
RGS-IBG Book Series Editors

David Featherstone
University of Glasgow, UK
RGS-IBG Book Series Editor (2015–2019)

Preface and Acknowledgements

My first encounter with homelessness took place in Tokyo. A domestic economic crisis that had begun in 1992 was striking the population hard. In 1997, big firms and banks suddenly started to collapse. Japan was sliding into a double-dip recession. I entered university that same year, and to get there I travelled via big railway stations such as Shinjuku and Tokyo. On each journey, I witnessed sites of homelessness encroaching deeper and deeper into spaces of public transportation, like water endlessly springing up and soaking the ground. The scenes lingered in my heart.

I found a group of homelessness activists on the internet and started to get involved. It only took a short while before I knew that this small group was the most radical organisation for homelessness in Japan, seeking to free up for roofless people every park and alley of Tokyo's Shibuya Ward. My task in the group was relatively modest: to engage in frequent visits to homeless sites, to distribute meals to homeless people, to sell secondhand clothes at flea markets with homeless youths, and to take part in street demonstrations. This first encounter lasted three years, and the experience taught me how intolerant public spaces can be for people without housing.

The second encounter took place in Kanagawa Prefecture, just south of Tokyo. This place left me with more colourful memories. In Tokyo, I was struggling to adapt to the worlds of homelessness and activism and the tense political situations that surrounded them. In Kanagawa, I had already finished my "socialisation" into the street-level worlds of homelessness and had decided to conduct social research and fieldwork on these worlds. In Tokyo, a lack of clarity about this issue had given me, an undergrad student, somewhat uncertain feelings. In Kanagawa, I was a graduate student, and more forward looking. I worked with different local groups but most frequently took part in groups in two cities, Yokohama and

Hiratsuka. The timing was definitive because it was the moment when, for the first time in history, the Japanese state was stepping up its regulation of homelessness. Under the state's vigorous intervention, the hidden "structure" of homelessness, regulation, and activism was becoming apparent.

Tokyo and Kanagawa, two sites of my unusual urban encounters, form the ontological basis of my research, though only Kanagawa Prefecture provides conjunctural information for this book. Using the same site of fieldwork, in fact, I published a book in Japanese in 2014. This work won an important prize and is considered a unique contribution to the study of urban poverty, social movements, homelessness, and the day labourer population in Japan. All along, my work on homelessness has had a core claim and a specific attribute. Foremost has been the assertion that homelessness can be conceptualised in terms of labour-mediated relations of deprived people to urban nature, of metabolic processes of production and consumption in public spaces, which provoke "normal" (domiciled) society to intervene into the spaces of homelessness. A specific attribute of my work has been a thorough depiction of the long-term history of social movements for homeless people and day labourers in Yokohama's Kotobuki district and its outskirt areas, which researchers previously had not entirely depicted.

Though my Japanese-language book was successful, I was motivated to write an original book in English, an ambition prompted by Neil Brenner. After publication of the Japanese book in 2014, I started to think deeply about how I could write things differently. Writing a useful scholarly book in English demanded that I construct a comprehensive theoretical and methodological framework that could deliver my message to international audiences. The task was to create a new, large-scale research programme with theoretical rigour and methodological clarity, logically linking various dimensions of my materials and observations. This must guide my narrative for international readers in an intelligible and attractive way.

Rescaling Urban Poverty is the outcome of this multifaceted struggle. Compared to my previous efforts, the present book is more theoretically and methodologically sophisticated, more conscious of the meanings of regulationist and critical literature on the issue of "homelessness plus Japan". The book was created around a carefully woven network of Lefebvrian, Gramscian, Harveyan, and other Marxian concepts. New materials are used widely, and old information is reexamined. For better or worse, throughout the process of production, I was almost completely confined to one unimpressive area of Japan that is remote from centres of Japan's national dynamics. I believed that this confined status would be very productive and that it might help my creative endeavour to reach international audiences beyond local milieus.

In this struggle, my companion was Antonio Gramsci's *Prison Notebooks*, rather than other, canonical texts. Gramsci gleaned many new ideas from his famous experience of "being enclosed". This reflection of my own situation onto the work of the canonical author now looks far more naive and indefensible than it seemed at the time. The truth is that I needed this and other myths to maintain my morale during the extended period of this book's preparation and writing. In the late days of the writing, someone who shared time with me in New York City made me aware of the city's old poets, and their works were quickly added to my bookshelf's mythmaking section.

I hope that a variety of readers will find this book interesting. While the book commits to particular strands of critical urban and capitalism studies, my intention is to make its core debates interesting and intelligible to various kinds of reader—including those who are not very familiar with these discourses. I believe that the modes of argumentation employed here are useful for many audiences who are interested in issues related to policy, poverty, social movements, and the (re)scaling dynamism of state/urban space.

My special thanks go to Neil Brenner, who has given me limitlessly generous support since we met. At the departments of Sociology and Social and Cultural Analysis at New York University, where I conducted research as a visiting scholar, he completely internationalised my scope and persuaded me to write for an English audience. I hope I can now demonstrate that Neil's long-lasting commitment to me—as a researcher and as a person—was not misplaced. Nik Theodore reminded me that I should create, and not just use, theory, and his words have affected the form of this book. David Fasenfest powerfully encouraged me to complete this project during the final few years of the writing by locating my scholarship in active networks of international scholars.

My research has been helped by many scholars in Japan, including Yukihiko Kitagawa, Tan'no Kiyoto, Takashi Machimura, Masao Maruyama, and Akihiko Nishizawa. I remember how generously Yoshiharu Kishi, a teacher of modern German literature, made time for me—someone who had just entered university. At his cosy office, we read classics, with an intention to nurture my ability to read text *as text*, which Kishi thought to be the only way to "intellectualise" what he called my "turbulent" (*sōzōshī*) world, a world that was being saturated by Tokyo's not-so-cosy politics. I am grateful to Kazushi Tamano, an urbanist with whom I started the earliest version of this project when I was an undergrad. Communication with him has inspired my interest in Japanese urban policy and its historical background.

The sustained enthusiasm that Chih Yuan Woon, Ruth Craggs, and David Featherstone—the present and past editors of the RGS-IBG Book Series—have shown for this project in the past several years has incited me to broaden the readership and intellectual basis of this book. I am grateful for anonymous reviewers' feedback and for the assistance of Durgadevi Shanmugasundaram, Kilmeny MacBride, Giles Flitney, and Todd Manza who helped me with the final processes of this publication. I appreciate the financial support provided by the Japan Society for the Promotion of Science (KAKENHI JP21K01931 and JP22H00909).

I deeply thank activists working in and outside of the Kotobuki district. These spirited and thoughtful people have stood with homeless people despite the sometimes difficult consequences of their actions. There were times when mere "compassion" for homeless people could result in difficult relations with municipal workers, security staff, service providers, or local communities. The activists did not preclude collaboration with them. They would, however, emphatically defend homeless people's survival milieus in public spaces when the "regulators" aspired to flatten these appropriated spaces of homeless people.

This book fundamentally develops arguments that appeared in my previous publications. These include the following:

Theorizing regulation-in-city for homeless people's subaltern strategy and informality: societalization, metabolism, and classes with(out) housing. *Critical Sociology* 48 (2): 323–339. [2022; Chapter 1]

Times and spaces of homeless regulation in Japan, 1950s–2000s: historical and contemporary analysis. *International Journal of Urban and Regional Research* 37 (4): 1181–1212. [2013; Chapter 3]

Toshikūkan ni sumikomu nojukusha: 'tsukaeru jimen' eno shin'nyū to kūkan kanri [Homeless people inhabiting urban space: intrusions into "usable spaces" and spatial control]. *Nenpō Shakaigaku Ronshū* 18: 182–191. [2005; Chapter 4]

Kenzō kankyō de tashaka sareru jyūtaku kiki: toshi no shizen o meguru rōdō to kanri to yume [Housing crisis being othered at built environments: labour, control, and myths around urban nature]. In: *Toshikūkan ni Hisomu Haijyo to Hankō no Chikara* [Forces of Exclusion and Resistance within Urban Space] (ed. T. Machimura), 25–60. Tokyo: Akashi Shoten. [2013; Chapter 4]

Hōmuresu no hitobito no "kyojyū" to kōkyōkūkan [Homeless people's "habitation" and public spaces]. In: *Hōmuresu to Toshi Kūkan* [Homelessness and Urban Space], 60–81. Tokyo: Akashi Shoten. [2014; Chapter 4]

Sēsē suru chīki no kyōkai: naibuka shita "hōmuresu mondai" to sēdo henka no rōkaritei [Emerging boundaries of regional society: geographical diffusions of homeless people and institutional changes at the local level]. *Soshioroji* 52 (1): 53–69. [2007; Chapter 5]

Hōmuresu no hitobito no "shigoto" to kōkyō kūkan: toshizatugyō no "ika" ni yoru haijyo [Homeless people's "labour" and public space: the exclusion of urban small works by "othering"]. In: *Hōmuresu to Toshi Kūkan* [Homelessness and Urban Space], 82–109. Tokyo: Akashi Shoten. [2014; Chapter 5]

Public space excludes homeless workers in Japan: regulating the "recyclers" for hegemonic habitat. *Social Theory and Dynamics* 2: 3–17. [2018; Chapter 5]

1970 nendai kara 1980 nendai no kotobukichiku [Kotobuki in the 1970s and 1980s]. In: *Hōmuresu to Toshi Kūkan* [Homelessness and Urban Space], 110–167. Tokyo: Akashi Shoten. [2014; Chapters 6 and 7]

1990 nendai no kotobukichiku [Kotobuki in the 1990s]. In: *Hōmuresu to Toshi Kūkan* [Homelessness and Urban Space], 172–216. Tokyo: Akashi Shoten. [2014; Chapter 8]

2000 nendai no kotobukichiku [Kotobuki in the 2000s]. In: *Hōmuresu to Toshi Kūkan* [Homelessness and Urban Space], 220–225. Tokyo: Akashi Shoten. [2014; Chapter 9]

Rescaled "rebel cities", nationalization, and the bourgeois utopia: dialectics between urban social movements and regulation for Japan's homeless. *Antipode* 47 (2): 419–441. [2015; Chapter 10]

Opening up the welfare state to "outsiders": pro-homeless activism and neoliberal backlashes in Japan. In: *Civil Society and the State in Democratic East Asia* (ed. D. Chiavacci, S. Grano, and J. Obinger): 269–298. [2020; Chapter 10]

Mahito Hayashi
Nagoya
June 2023

Part One
Theory, Method, Context

Chapter One
Introduction and Theoretical Framework

As I sat down to write this introduction, the media was telling heart-wrenching stories about homeless people in Tokyo, about how "they" experienced a gigantic typhoon—which claimed the lives of one hundred Japanese people in October 2019—differently from "us". The first report was about two homeless men who tried to enter an evacuation centre set up at a public gymnasium but were immediately rejected by its operator—a municipal government of Tokyo's Taito Ward—and thrown out into the turbulent weather (Aoki 2019). The second concerned an individual who disappeared in the elevated waters of the Tama River, which runs through the middle of Tokyo; he was swept away by the currents and (according to the media) became the only victim of this typhoon in the Tokyo Metropolis (Adachi and Wada 2019).

Once the typhoon had passed, the Tokyo Metropolitan Government justified the rejection of homeless people from local evacuation centres on the grounds that it has to operate these centres for the benefit of official ("registered") citizens in Tokyo. Homeless people are not such citizens under Japanese law, although the national government claims that it wants local evacuation centres to be more open to all. On TV and radio, comedians voiced sarcastic and unsympathetic reactions to these events, claiming that homeless people normally avoid public services anyway, and that "we" don't want to see "them" using the same evacuation centres, even in an emergency. Finally, a small web media agency offered a contrasting picture, focusing on activists working for homeless people. Participants in such homeless-supporting activism, with roots in inner-city areas called *yoseba* that are historically inhabited by day labourers who can easily end up homeless, denounced the administrators and clamoured for the opening up of evacuation centres to homeless people in the future.

Rescaling Urban Poverty: Homelessness, State Restructuring and City Politics in Japan, First Edition. Mahito Hayashi.
© 2024 Royal Geographical Society (with the Institute of British Geographers). Published 2024 by John Wiley & Sons Ltd.

Disasters like this are increasingly common in the early twenty-first century. Global warming is heating up the Pacific, creating larger rain clouds, making Japan highly vulnerable to the climate crisis and increasing the risk for the already disadvantaged.[1] At the same time, what we are witnessing in the current phase, according to many scholars, is the *longue durée* construction and destruction of the environment by capitalism (e.g., Moore 2015). Against this backdrop, these Japanese stories reveal everyday dimensions of homelessness under the capitalist urbanisation of our age.

First, extant forms of the commons for people—emergency reliefs, municipal facilities, community-run services, commonly used urban amenities, inclusive frameworks of citizenship, and the like—can exclude some of the most impoverished people. By locating homeless people within the spaces of arbitrariness, abandonment, and uncertainty, the state and society might be absolved from maintaining impoverished people's access to the commons.

Second, in our age of generalised poverty, when even middle-class people think of themselves as poor (Lawson et al. 2015), the stigma attached to the "dangerous" class—*the* homeless as the outsiders of the housed—preserves the integrity of society from the ravages of internal strife; this is, indeed, the externalisation of class antagonism to the wild space of nonhabitat. Homeless people, or the non-housing class, are not just excluded from the "homogeneous risk communities" (Offe 1996, p. 165) but also constitute its internal consistency by *being* excluded and so delineating its edges from without.

Third, in the face of this difficulty, homeless people try to survive the life-threatening conditions of exclusion and regulation, sometimes with the support of activists, volunteers, and a few municipal workers who are striving to open up the commons to homeless people.

Ultimately, these orthodox and heterodox actors—policymakers, municipal regulators, police officers, housed citizens, homeless people, and activists/volunteers—advance sociocultural actions (framing, placemaking, and translating) through which we may co-construct and counter-construct "homelessness" on different spatial scales.

Rescaling Urban Poverty addresses these currently marginalised homeless-related processes and spaces, revealing that the marginality of "homelessness" owes much to its peripheral relations with normative urban settlement centred on city dwellers who are housed. To unpack this marginal position, this book situates homelessness within urban and territorial contexts of regulation that are intrinsically spatial, social, and multiscalar. In this book, the state and society—*domiciled* society— denote important nodes of regulation around which these urban/territorial features take observable shape. Hybrid devices, knowledge mobilities, and instantaneous instrumentations are found in abundance within the state–society spectrums, and they also fall within this book's extensive conceptualisation of regulation. These milieus may normalise malregulated, deregulated, or crisis-prone elements that are rampant in capitalist urbanisation, through precipitating micro spaces and capillary networks of regulation across the state and social sectors.

Geographers already provide spatially informed agendas of regulation theory that are fruitful for this line of research (e.g., Amin 1994; Brenner 1998, 1999; Brenner and Theodore 2002; Collinge 1999; Cox 1997; Goodwin and Painter 1996; Hudson 2001; Jonas 1994, 1996; Jones 1997; Jones and MacLeod 1999; Krätke 1999; MacLeod 1999; MacLeod and Goodwin 1999; Mayer 1994; Painter 1997; Peck 1996; Peck and Tickell 1992, 1995; Swyngedouw 1997; Tickell and Peck 1992). These and other papers, book chapters, and books—many of them published in the 1990s—created a *torrent* of spatially attuned regulationist research agendas in geography.

With the help of this literature, and through refreshing its concepts in relation to nearby (Lefebvrian, Gramscian, Harveyan, or other Marxian) theoretical lineages, I argue that homelessness as a sociospatial phenomenon presents a major opportunity to reassert the relevance of these existing understandings of regulation in line with new topics and geographies. These regulationist literatures are used constructively in this book, not only to disclose the urban/territorial centres of the hegemonic landscape but also to reorient critical urban studies thematically to the sociospatial margins of the city (Heynen 2009). Specifically in this book, these margins are the sites where (de)contestation takes place in uncertain and inconclusive ways around the housing crisis of deprived people. The Japanese case is beneficial for this work because it displays both unique patterns and notable similarities to discussions on regulationist approaches (Amin 1994; Boyer and Yamada 2000; Jessop and Sum 2006; Peck and Miyamachi 1994).

By remobilising inherited Lefebvrian, Gramscian, Harveyan, and other Marxian methodological discussions, and by using them to reframe the central claims of regulationist authors, this book seeks to fill important voids that may be identified within and between different literatures. The essential ideas of classical continental regulationists will be scrutinised carefully (Aglietta 1979 [1976]; Boyer 1990; Boyer and Saillard 2002 [1995]; for influential reviews, see Jessop and Sum 2006). Central to this book, however, is the more recent concept of state rescaling (Brenner 1999, 2004a; Jessop 2002; Peck 2001b, 2002; Swyngedouw 1997), which has been applied to a variety of theoretical and empirical contexts (Boudreau et al. 2007; Brenner 2019; Hayashi 2013a; Keil and Mahon 2009; Li, Xu, and Yeh 2014; Lim 2017; MacKinnon and Show 2010; MacLeavy and Harrison 2010; Park 2013; Sonn 2010; Tsukamoto 2012; Ward and Jonas 2004; Wu 2016; Zhang and He 2021). This *spatially* regulationist concept will be mobilised intensively in this book to interpret various dimensions of homelessness.

The discussion of "homelessness" in this book can inform the literature in unique ways, in light of my fieldwork experience in Yokohama's inner-city district (Kotobuki) and its surroundings. In this urban geography, and in urban Japan more generally, there was a conspicuous growth of homelessness within and around inner-city areas during the 1970s. In turn, in the 1990s and 2000s, larger numbers of homeless people began to appear in public spaces. Homeless people came to live side by side with housed citizens, more constantly and more closely, and this created regulatory ruptures in public spaces, which took the form of what I understand as the homeless–housed divide (Cloke, May, and Johnsen 2010; Gowan 2010). I will apply this cyclical understanding to two cycles of homelessness in postwar Japan: the "inner-city cycle" of homelessness, from the mid-1970s to the early 1980s, and the "widespread cycle", beginning in the 1990s.

This cyclical spatialisation of homelessness has stimulated state rescaling dynamics that produce new scales and spaces of regulation. In Japan, an earlier moment of rescaling started in the 1970s, moulding new spaces of homeless regulation in bottom-up ways by deploying locational means of assistance and policing. A newer phase of rescaling began in the 2000s, when the Japanese state provided a national framework for localised regulation and managed rampant interscalar tensions in territorial poverty regulation through selective power devolution to municipalities. There are therefore also two rounds of rescaling in postwar Japan—one starting in the 1970s, which I understand as a haphazard, "group-up round" of rescaling, and another beginning in the 2000s, which I conceive as a more concerted "picking-off round" of rescaling.

My geographically focused and socially entangled fieldwork reveals hidden connections between these cycles of homelessness and rounds of rescaling. The ruptures that homelessness creates in urban society have repeatedly incited Japan's multiscalar experiments with rescaled/rescaling homeless regulation. Furthermore, these ruptures have been addressed not just by regulating actors but also by homeless people and their supporters. Homeless people's own practices have complicated all of these processes because homeless people are not unspoken "shadows" of regulation but *people* who can actively reconstitute Japan's "well-regulated" urban landscape for living and joy. Activists and volunteers also have formed their own spaces and cycles of urban social movements around—and increasingly *beyond*—inner-city areas, unlocking public spaces and programmes and producing new urban commons such as liveable shelters, tasty food, reliable information, homeless–housed solidarities, and accessible political opportunities, which may help homeless people's economic/sociocultural/political life.

In this book, I make an extensive effort to develop robust urban narratives by carefully attending to these multiple aspects of Japanese homelessness. This introductory chapter will mainly embark on substantial theoretical and methodological discussions. I begin by outlining some of the key works in geography that directly address homelessness, detailing a series of urban geography discussions about the utility of political economy concepts for homelessness. My hope is that examination of these debates can steer diverse readers, including those who do not share similar backgrounds, towards the theoretical and methodological core of this book.

Urban Political Economy: For Homelessness?

By using US contexts and highlighting urban policy in New York City, Neil Smith (1996) presented the grand idea of revanchist urbanism, which contributed much to the regulationist explanation of homelessness. His primary task was to produce an anatomy of gentrification, which transforms areas of affordable housing into areas of (conspicuous) consumption for the rich. In this discussion, Smith found homelessness to be an avenue for developing a new paradigm of urban political economy. The gentrification-driven destruction of affordable housing aggravated the housing crisis and relegated many to homelessness. In public spaces, the resulting growth of homelessness dialectically exhibited what Smith (1996, p. 3) calls a "class struggle on Avenue B", in which homeless people and their supporters aggressively challenged gentrification. Smith argues that these dialectical tensions are what finally drove New York City to its notoriously harsh policing of homeless people.

Building on Smith's work, Don Mitchell (1997, 2003) presents a more analytic view of homeless regulation under the banner of the "annihilation of space by law", a play on words from Marx. Mitchell found that the local authorities had a key legislative lever to advance antihomeless policing and to make cities "attractive to both footloose capital and to the footloose middle and upper classes" (Mitchell 1997, p. 305). The utility of this thread of urban political economy is implied in scholarly work emerging from another country in North America, Canada (Blomley 2009).

Subsequent geographical works eloquently questioned what they regarded as the overt simplicity lurking in these neo-Marxist formulations. According to Geoffrey DeVerteuil and his coauthors, US cities are characterised by homeless people's own efforts to survive. The omission of this aspect by Smith and by Mitchell represents a pitfall in urban political economy perspectives, which characterises the "dominant perspective on homelessness since the 1990s" that ended up in a "singularly punitive framework that downplays, if not wholly ignores, homeless agency" (DeVerteuil, Marr, and Snow 2009, p. 636; see also, DeVerteuil, May, and von Mahs 2009). DeVerteuil (2006, p. 118) develops a similar argument on homeless shelters, another space of homelessness marked by "contradictory tendencies and motivations". Homeless shelters internalise a spectrum of regulatory inconsistency, even in Los Angeles, where regulation is harsh, which makes these shelters into potential sites for homeless people's purposive practices.

An even more direct criticism of the Smith–Mitchell line of argument appears in the work of Paul Cloke, Jon May, and Sarah Johnsen (2010). These geographers use the British case of homelessness—its "messy middle grounds" (p. 11)—as an antidote to the "theory-led neo-Marxist critiques" (p. 36). They enumerate the divisions suffered by homeless people and volunteers: the "faith/non-faith divide" (p. 46), the "boundaries between the public and private sector" (p. 25), and the divide "between homeless people and members of the housed public" (p. 67). This enumeration is followed by extensive arguments about the ways in which these divides can be healed. Voluntary actors nurture the "ethical impulses of love, joy, peace, charity, equality" (p. 46), which can overcome such divides. Also, the "maps of the homeless city drawn up by homeless people themselves" (p. 62)—homeless people's own sensemaking about the spatial distribution of useful/harmful sites in city space—enable homeless people to overcome, though within certain limits, "the hegemonic meanings and mappings of the city" (p. 85).

In short, volunteers (and, to a certain point, homeless people) can co-construct with regulators the local outcome of what Jamie Peck and Adam Tickell (2002) call rollout neoliberalism (Cloke, May, and Johnsen 2010, pp. 35–36). They see this possibility as a chance to *push back* the domain of revanchism, and its theorisation by neo-Marxist scholars, to the North American continent. This stance is reasonable because "the response to this crisis in Britain was more complex [than in the United States]" (p. 30).

All in all, DeVerteuil and his coauthors relativised the urban political economy of Smith and Mitchell from within US cities, while Cloke and his colleagues drew a strong line between Britain and the United States. These geographers established a key debate over political-economic modes of theorisation on homelessness and its urban politics. My own position is that the Smith–Mitchell line of argument—when used as a theory for homelessness—is not immune to criticisms. However, I also argue that the punitive revanchist critiques still offer possibilities for next rounds of critical homeless studies.

Why did the neo-Marxist approach—to homelessness, to regulation, to counterpolitics—provoke such critiques? One reason may be the existing criticism that the approach is too strongly focused on punitive forms of urban regulation and is separated from broader interscalar contexts and in-scale consequences that are not logically or empirically punitive. Critics of Smith and/or Mitchell subscribe to this view, seemingly identifying Marxian streaks in homeless studies with the Smithian theory of urban revanchism (DeVerteuil 2006; DeVerteuil, May, and von Mahs 2009; Johnsen and Fitzpatrick 2010).

My view is that the main components of the Smith–Mitchell line of argument are not entirely free from this criticism. I note, however, that the two authors signalled ways to overcome this criticism when they explored wider scalar contexts of urban regulation or struggle—i.e., when Smith (1993) examined a scale jumping possibility for urban prohomeless politics and when Mitchell (2003) analysed the nested structure of the US court system and the extent to which this legal structure can penetrate actual city space. I develop these scale-sensitive arguments of Smith and Mitchell with regard to homelessness by reconnecting them to more recent conceptual vocabularies that can systematically unpack the scaled/scaling construction of urban regulation.

Furthermore, this book's approach can address a tricky ambiguity that I find in urban political economy: its lack of clarity about the levels of methodological abstraction in political-economic exploration. Which levels of abstraction should the researcher use, and how are his/her multiple anchors in the abstract–concrete continuum constructed into a research project when the main focus of the study is placed on "urban affairs"? As Cloke, May, and Johnsen (2010) implied in their study of British homelessness, this obscurity of urban political economy in terms of the level(s) of methodological abstraction may foster its alleged appearance of unboundedly ballooning its "applicable" geographies without fetters, beyond the birthplace of political economy concepts (see also Robinson 2006).

However, even this second line of criticism may not hinder urban political economists in engaging with difference/diversity/alterity. A helpful thread of argument for this purpose lies in rescaling theory, which nurtures acute methodological sensitivity to differentiated layers in the abstract–concrete spectrum (Brenner 2004a). I will revive some such layers in abstract–concrete (dis)continuums, not just to tweak existing concepts but also to "sink" political economy theory into the most concrete aspects of the urban lifeworld. This sinking and entrenching of political economy theory within the *concrete* urban entails a vast use of my ethnographic experience as an ontological springboard for a topical/geographical extension of urban political economy, which will register (not efface) a radical incommensurability of the ethnographer "in the field" (for this methodological discussion, see Chapter 2).

It is hoped that this research programme, drawing upon Euro-American geographical debates, can make theoretical, methodological, and empirical contributions to existing works in Japan. Geographers, in particular, have discussed municipal policy conditions of homelessness (Mizuuchi 2002), have applied Euro-American geographical conceptions (including those of Neil Smith and Don Mitchell) to Japanese homelessness (Kiener and Mizuuchi 2018), and have analysed local histories of day labourers for homelessness research (Haraguchi 2010). By building a broad interpretational framework based on the state rescaling concept and using it to construct robust urban narratives, this book may help to make these and other discussions about Japan more theoretically intelligible, internationally situated, and empirically multifaceted.[2]

I will begin my efforts to centre the book's various arguments on the concept of state rescaling. A further exploration of this concept is beneficial at the outset, for it is a main organising pillar of different research agendas in the book.

State Rescaling: The Central Concept of this Book

According to Neil Brenner's *New State Spaces* (2004a), national states that historically entered the era of Atlantic Fordism have undergone, since the late 1970s, the major process of what he understands as state rescaling.[3] For Brenner, state rescaling is about the spatial scalar restructuring of state power that destabilises "the primacy of the national *scale* of political-economic life".

In this process, "we are witnessing ... a wide-ranging recalibration of scalar hierarchies and interscalar relations throughout state apparatus as a whole, at once on supranational, national, regional, and urban scales" (pp. 3–4, original emphasis).

If one focuses on phenomena and processes *within* national boundaries, state rescaling has created waves of devolutionary politics that delegated various regulatory tasks from national to subnational regulatory units. This development is at once a response to and a catalyst for the intensification of globalisation and global city formation, which posed serious threats to the spatial unity of national states. This devolutionary politics of rescaling did not completely undo national states' responsibilities for their territorial space. National states withstood the "erosion, withering, or demise" (p. 4) even amid the intensification of global city formation.

And yet Brenner thinks that the crisis-induced, crisis-prone, experimental character of state rescaling destabilises our inclinations to "ontologically prejudge" what *the* state is. So the story is not a return to national states as we know them. The argument can be best depicted as the collapse of "spatial Keynesianism", which can be defined as a geographical mode of redistribution policy that offset the uneven development of capitalist urbanisation until the 1970s, and its ongoing replacement by "metropolitanized" forms of urban planning (pp. 172–256). Under rescaling, locality-sensitive modes of policymaking and their attraction of local–global networks grew across city regions and saturated national territorial space, making spatial Keynesianism obsolete. The driver of capitalist urbanisation now came largely from fluid, spontaneous, creative socio-economic relationships in urban society and markets that overwhelmed the fixed, inflexible parameters of Keynesian policymakers (pp. 114–171). As such, state rescaling meant fundamental realignments in the state's scalar organisation, which remoulded relations between the spatial scalar categories underpinning the capitalist geopolitical economy, but without undoing national states as organisational scaffoldings of urban restructuring.

Brenner (2004a) situates this state rescaling theory against the "end of the nation state" debates (e.g., Ohmae 1995). Instead of being disempowered, national states can reassemble new state capacity from diverse globalisation experiences. This state capacity is understood to redefine state space in more porous, flexible, resilient terms so that national states can collaboratively shape globalisation, with multiple socioeconomic forces residing at different spatial scales. This concept is linked to contemporary arguments about the political economy of scale and multiscale governance (e.g., Jessop 2002; Peck 2002; Smith 1993; Swyngedouw 1997), while Brenner (2004a, p. 75) bases his thesis fundamentally on Henri Lefebvre as a state *and* urban theorist. This dual reference to Lefebvre allows Brenner to stay deeply engaged with the urban spatialities of state rescaling. As such, his theory of rescaling has provided a broad, postdisciplinary interface through which urbanists can interpret forms and scales of urbanisation with reference to the new geographies of political economy, the de-/re-territorialisation of capital, and the ongoing restructuring of state space.

To use this theory, I will consistently subscribe to what Jamie Peck (2002, p. 357) has discussed as the "scale manager" role of national states, considering this role to be a key platform for national states when these states reconstruct state capacity amid rescaling dynamics. Peck's suggestion is that national states can discursively and institutionally rearticulate and rephrase the territorial layers of different spatial scales and their interscalar tensions so that national states can perform the strategic role of coordinating rescaling dynamics. I shall interpret this scale manager role, a form of state capacity concomitant with and generative of rescaling, by connecting it to Bob Jessop's (1982, pp. 123–124; 1990, pp. 8, 268) conception of the unity of the state. If, as Jessop suggests, a certain level of substantive actual unity (compared to formal legal unity) is always required to sustain the state, the national state's scale-managing role can be understood as functional to the sustaining and rebalancing of this unity under the dynamics of rescaling.

How then can we explain the emergence of this new state capacity in different national regimes? For one thing, there are the famous "path-dependent" mechanisms. These mechanisms can guide the process of rescaling within the relative continuity of regulatory elements (formal and informal). This guiding effect of relative regulatory fixities should persist, to a certain degree, maintaining the territorial form of multiscalar coherence and its substantial unity even in the age of intensive globalisation and rescaling, when disruptions become "normal". In this light, the Japanese pathways of state rescaling should provide interesting cases for theory. In addition, the uneven emergence of the state's scale-managing role can also be explained more conceptually with reference to the multiple *theoretical* terrains of rescaling. As Peck (2002, p. 331) argues, there are "different forms of rescaling". These include "the hollowing out of the national state, the emergence of localized economies of association, the rescaling of labor organization and regulation, the globalization of economic flows, the formation of territorialized production complexes, the reorganization of governance hierarchies, or the reanimation of agglomeration economies".

I understand that these different theoretical realms create comparable but uneven geographies of state rescaling in different national regimes. In addition to Peck's list of "different forms of rescaling", I shall argue that national welfare regimes and their spatial scalar "workfarist" restructuring, which can take place in the face of new forms of poverty (Peck 2001a, 2002), become a fruitful theoretical arena for rescaling studies. Urban poverty can place significant tension on the interscalar unities of national welfare statism (understood as a territorial rule regime for welfare delivery) in different countries. New regulatory rules, norms, codes, and practices—which emerge in response to new forms of poverty and cohere around subnational scales—destabilise the inherited interscalar balance of national welfare statism, making for the ground-up dynamics of rescaling. This bottom-up drive can push national states to take on the scale management role so that an acceptable level of state space unity can be reconstructed, or at least reperceived, amid the experiences of rescaling that can be highly disruptive to the substantive/actual unity of state space.

Recent work on rescaling has rightly addressed the diverse spaces and processes of state rescaling within the Euro-American world (Boudreau et al. 2007; MacKinnon and Show 2010; MacLeavy and Harrison 2010; Ward and Jonas 2004) and beyond (Hayashi 2013a; Li, Xu, and Yeh 2014; Lim 2017; Park 2013; Sonn 2010; Tsukamoto 2012; Wu 2016; Zhang and He 2021). At the same time, the need now emerges to gauge the extent to which the general—even "strong"— mode of theorisation in the earlier regulationist literature can remain the basis for contemporary rescaling studies. My choice of homelessness for this clarification is sound. Due to their profoundly marginal position vis-à-vis the territorial homogeneity and inclusive hegemony envisioned by spatial Keynesianism, urban poverty and homelessness can powerfully delineate the emergent contours of rescaling dynamics and advance rescaling studies theoretically.

Chapter 3 in particular will closely examine the discussions of continental regulationist thinkers such as Michel Aglietta and Robert Boyer so that background arguments and theoretical scaffoldings supportive of the concept of state rescaling, including "mode of regulation" and "accumulation regime", can be dovetailed into my research agendas. However, this introductory chapter focuses on more recent strands of regulation theory—the spatialised paradigms.

Figure 1.1 presents the three theoretical arrangements—subcomponents— through which Chapters 3–8 of this book address homelessness by using the concept of state rescaling. These components are national states, public and private spaces, and urban social movements. These three subtheories are appropriate as building blocks because they can accommodate, interrelate, and integrate the book's various theoretical slants—arguments from a wide range of literature— and organise them around the state rescaling concept.

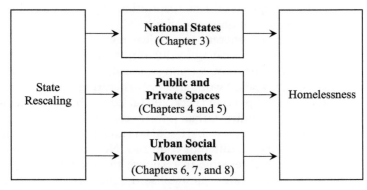

Figure 1.1   Overarching theoretical framework of this book.

I would stress that these three subcomponents allow the state rescaling concept to capture various urban/territorial dynamics around homelessness without reducing the complexity of the issue. Indeed, these three subcomponents constitute this book's central device to render the state rescaling concept sensitive to the social, cultural, and political complexities that we find in homelessness (Cloke, May, and Johnsen 2010; DeVerteuil, May, and von Mahs 2009; Johnsen and Fitzpatrick 2010). Ultimately, in this book, these complexities will steer me towards the exploration of state rescaling as *integral* state rescaling, the study of which focuses equally on state, *quasi*state, and *non*state spaces as (mis)integrated fields of urban regulation and its territorial scalar contexts.

Subcomponent 1: National States

The National States box in Figure 1.1 denotes the initial set of theoretical arrangements that this book brings to the concept of state rescaling. Chapter 3 applies and develops this argument. It emphasises that different postwar societies formed similarly nationalised spaces of poverty regulation (NSPR). The NSPR organised the three spheres of poverty alleviation—public provision, the labour market, and social fabric (family plus community)—on the national scale so that people who experienced impoverishment could remain on the economic, social, and cultural horizon of citizenship and living standards.

This is the locus of the so-called welfare state. However, NSPR is a more appropriate term for my purpose—I've used it in this book because it helps to shift the focus from relatively stable centres of society to its impoverished peripheries. Seen from these margins, the promises and outcomes of welfare statism look highly inconclusive, unstable, and malleable. Impoverished people who cannot fully enjoy the wealth streams of welfare statism can escape the economic, social, and semiotic horizon of citizenship, trigger the open politics of exclusion/inclusion, and build up pressure for the restructuring of the NSPR. Studies about different national regimes suggest that the NSPR in each country had to manage this restructuring pressure constantly throughout the long postwar era (on the United Kingdom and United States, see Fraser 2003; Trattner 1999; for Japan, see Estevez-Abe 2008).

The historical dynamics of the NSPR can be theoretically understood with reference to the concept of societalisation, as refined by Bob Jessop (1990, 2002) with Ngai-Ling Sum (Jessop and Sum 2006; Sum and Jessop 2013). Partly building upon the well-known French regulationist literature (for classical overviews, see Boyer 1990; Boyer and Saillard 2002 [1995]), Jessop and Sum have developed a broad-based argument about regulatory social milieus and processes as societalisation. Jessop and Sum have employed the concept in unique ways, reframing the notion of social cohesion that is more conventional in regulationism in order to make the central notion of regulation theory more sensitive to social cohesion's dynamic, contingent, strategic, and ephemeral traits.

Jessop (2002, p. 56) succinctly defines societalisation as "a pattern of institutional integration and social cohesion that complements the dominant accumulation regime and its mode of economic regulation, thereby securing the conditions for its dominance in the wider society". On this basis, I use the concept of societalisation to refer to a territorial pattern of overall/sectoral social orders, and their sociological regulatory milieus, which can maintain the various "reproduction requirements of capital accumulation" (Jessop 2002, p. 23), especially on the national scale, including the consumptive reproduction of labour force, the penetration of capitalist principles into extracapitalist realms, and overarching accumulation strategies.

For these matters, according to Jessop, there can be no finished forms of societalisation. Instead, societalisation is prone to trials, errors, crises, and challenges, because "interstitial, residual, marginal, irrelevant, recalcitrant and plain contradictory elements that escape subordination" (Jessop 2002, p. 22) are concomitant and coeval with any given paradigms of societalisation, resulting in the persistence of "potential sources of disorder" as a substrate of societalisation dynamics.

In fact, this contingency of societalisation has prompted Jessop and Sum (2006, p. 85) to remind readers to "simply explore the uneven development of modern social formations", without looking for any coherent fixities of "post-Fordist societalization". I note the somewhat agnostic connotation of such caveats (for more recent statements in this vein, see Sum and Jessop 2013). However, I wish to do more than find yet another case of unevenness, contingency, and fragmentation/localism by using the case of homeless and poverty regulation. This book represents my effort to theorise—without belittling complexity—the multiscalar patterns of societalisation from a unique perspective on the periphery of urbanisation. Seen from this peripheral angle, the NSPR discloses some rampant reformation—not just deformation—of a structure, semistructure, or "form" of social regulation.

All in all, the arguments on societalisation enable me to frame social cohesion as rooting (and repeatedly re-rooting) in different principles and logics, different spaces and temporalities, of societalisation. Social cohesion in this sense is a net effect of various organisational, cultural, and urban milieus of social regulation that are contingent, contextual, and even emergent and experimental, full of trial-and-error dynamics, delays, and disruptions. This conceptualisation is a dynamic one—one that allows us to grasp social cohesion as being perpetually "in movement" (Aglietta 1979 [1976], p. 12). A capitalist society and its class relations/divisions, even once societalised, still meet with a lot of irregularities, disjunctions, and "failures". A project of societalisation can be disrupted by various local/national/global restructuring moments at the interface of these irregular (deregulating) elements and events.

In all, in the places where Jessop's text emphasises the contingency and dynamics of societalisation, he pays equal attention to both sides: systemic and countersystemic. Disrupting forces/groups do not just elude but also creatively challenge a pregiven form of societalisation, calling into question the terrains of a "hegemonic bloc" in a societalised society. In this sense, societalisation can be construed as open processes of societalisation and *de*societalisation; this dynamic conception provides a promising inroad into a reconstruction of political economy around contested urban geographies. Languages, epistemologies, agencies, and spaces that are involved in desocietalisation (and in *re*societalisation) can be used as a window on emergent or disrupted contours of social cohesion that are elusive. This perspective shows a possible way to make a late (but not belated) response to Peck and Tickell's (1995) call for a social turn in regulation theory, and to their caveat that "regulationist theorists have been at pains to stress the relative autonomy of forces of social regulation" (p. 17; see also Gough 2002).

I argue that the NSPR's primary role is to delineate, surveil, monitor, and sustain the fringes of societalisation on the national scale by coordinating the wealth streams to impoverished people via the three spheres of welfare delivery: public provision, the labour market, and the social fabric (family plus community). At these margins, economic crises and downturns are acutely felt, deteriorating the living standards of wage labourers and their families. Without the sound capacity of the NSPR, societalisation on the national scale can be highly unstable and even unsustainable, for acute forms of poverty can threaten the realms and spaces in which the "reproduction requirements of capital accumulation" (Jessop 2002, p. 23) must be achieved for current and new rounds of capitalist development.

Around the late 1970s, Western societies started to witness a major decrease in the societalising capacity of the NSPR at its meeting points with extreme forms of impoverishment. These points were peripheries—meaning, in effect, the spaces of homelessness and ghettoisation—that sociologists have examined as the new urban poverty (NUP; Mingione 1996; Wacquant 2008; Wilson 1997). Homelessness and ghettoisation were central to the NUP, but slightly more socially tolerable forms of "welfare dependency"—long-term welfare recipients considered able to work—were also included in this category (Wilson 1997). In the face of the NUP, national societalisation decreased previous levels of social cohesion, especially when and where the three realms of the NSPR were destabilised. This rise of poverty met the eruption of antipoor public discourses addressing desocietalisation. Diagnostic labels such as "the underclass", "the undeserving poor", and "welfare dependency" (aforementioned) were invoked and critically scrutinised (Fraser and Gordon 1994; Hague, Thomas, and Williams 1999; Hamnett 2010; Pahl 1988; Woodward 1995). In Japan, a new phase of poverty growth started in the 1990s, when homelessness was greatly increased, and this phase was followed by antihomeless sociopolitical backlash (for the Japanese case, see Hayashi 2020; Kasai 1999).

The NSPR entered the major process of restructuring in the face of acute poverty growth. In the context of the NUP, regulatory agencies often repeat strategies of "omission", "avoidance", and "grouping" vis-à-vis homelessness, ghettoisation, and other forms of poverty deemed to be outside or on the margins of sound housing classes. This can lead to various haphazard patterns of devolutionary politics—the disconnecting of urban regimes from the NSPR—for achieving flexible forms and mixtures of welfare delivery, its conditional delivery, and its nondelivery. As a result, national states reduce their scale-dominating effect over welfare statism in favour of the local scale's "adjustment without resource", and thus the rescaling of the NSPR can potentially emerge in the spontaneous forms of state space restructuring, promoting the decentralisation of interscalar balance within welfare statism. However, this initial ad hoc (haphazard) phase of rescaling can be followed by more systematic phases of rescaling in which national states' role of "scale manager" (Peck 2002, p. 357) comes to the fore. National states do not necessarily remain bystanders to haphazard dynamics; rather, they can actively rebalance, mediate, and manage emergent interscalar tensions and connectivity by discursive and institutional means.

For example, British homelessness was met with the national state's effort to recode and streamline homeless-related interscalar tensions by regrouping homeless people and navigating them to scale-sensitive measures and nonmeasures. That is, boundaries between inclusion and exclusion—"deserving" and "underserving"—were mainly drawn at the local scale because much of the management of this border politics was transferred to local regulators (Burrows, Pleace, and Quilgars 1997; Watson 1986). As a result, deciding who among homeless populations in society will be helped and who will not became an utterly local matter. Rather than nationalising homeless policy, British rescaling rephrased these fragmented local practices in legal terms, allowing "local authority housing departments [to] adopt a gatekeeping role between the homeless and the limited stock of council housing" (Watson 1986, p. 13). The consequence was rampant devolutionary politics in which local authorities had "considerable discretion" (Pleace, Burrows, and Quilgars 1997, p. 4), and this in turn resulted in "local practices [that] varied very considerably" (Lowe 1997, p. 21). In this lineage, it is said that the UK's Homelessness Act of 2002 animated "a complex *rescaling* of responsibilities" (Cloke, May, and Johnsen 2010, p. 34, original emphasis).

In the United States, known for its historically loose nationalisation of welfare statism (Skocpol 1992), national administrators responded to homelessness by mobilising extant frameworks and creating new ones. These frameworks rephrased the local regulatory tensions of homelessness in legal terms without significantly easing them at the national scale, and they submerged regulatory tensions of homelessness, which could have played out more strongly at the national scale, into the inherited parameters of decentralisation (for local variations of US homeless policy in this context, see, e.g., Baumohl 1996; Blau 1992; Stoner 1995; for a multiscalar analysis, see Hayashi 2014a). Japan developed its own approach to rescaling, which streamlined interscalar tensions, eased state space fragmentation, and justified ground-up regulatory practices for homelessness. A paradigmatic example is the 2002/2003 system, with which the Japanese state called for municipalities to address "local homelessness" in more formal and programmatic ways, against the previous tendency of scale informalisation that had fragmented the scalar construction of territorial poverty/homeless regulation in Japan.

Overall, accepted notions and institutionalised forms of citizenship, right, and welfare delivery were redefined in relation to this new form of poverty. I add the adjective *new* because, although homelessness has a long history in each country (Daly 1996), the regulatory situations and tension of homelessness have added to this "old" question nuances and characteristics that were little expected by policymakers before the 1970s. In more recent years, cities under rescaling have developed the new governance fields of urban poverty by cultivating state, quasistate, and nonstate actors/resources for its different dimensions. As a result, the gap between regulated/deregulated areas of policy, between "deserving" and "undeserving", are now ever more powerfully measured, calculated, framed, subdivided, mapped out, abandoned or selected, and strategically tolerated within scale-sensitive and scale-relativising measures, discourses, and consequences.

Subcomponent 2: Public and Private Spaces

The Public and Private Spaces box in Figure 1.1 gives a sense of why homelessness in particular matters to societalisation and drives the rescaling of the NSPR. Chapters 4 and 5 of this book are focused on explicating this subcomponent. The central argument is that public/private spaces (as a set and as a matrix) form a powerful milieu of societalisation by smoothing out spaces of consumption, which organise urban settlement and produce the housing classes as its generalised dwellers. The societalising power of public and private spaces is based on their capacity to inclusively accommodate people's lives. Streets, alleys, avenues, pavements, parks, community fields, railway stations, and other spaces/means of transportation and amenity consumption are the public spaces that urban dwellers can use. Equally, private spaces are internally differentiated—into flats, apartments, row houses, mansions, bungalows, inns, hotels, and the like. These different housing types compose an urban housing regime that is geographically situated and spatially pigeonholed, so that the city—and, in fact, *urbanisation*—can house different groups and classes beyond social strife, class antagonism, and desocietalisation.

Societalisation through private spaces is well recognised. Urbanisation has given birth to various types of housing, which have secured the social reproduction of dwellers (Lefebvre 1991 [1974]; see also Hanson and Pratt 1995). A major result was less distinct class relations in cities—the formation of housing classes

(Harvey 1976; Rex and Moore 1967) out of classical class relations (i.e., worker–employer relations). Neil Smith's (2000) incisive question "What happened to class?" finds interesting twists around the housing classes. The argument is that the historical formation of the housing classes tamed classical class relations—potentially antagonistic employer–worker relations—by overlapping them with mutually acceptable or indifferent relations among households and by filling each household with intimate (familial) relationships. These households were constituted by the geographically situated, socially pigeonholed space of housing. As Lefebvre (1991 [1974], p. 319) argues, the space of reproduction is the space that is broken up, but this character "makes it possible for urban workers to live side by side with other social classes". The material quality of housing is diverse; its semiosis, highly local—hence, housing class*es* (plural). Yet people in this category still share the trait of possessing housing units, which makes housing a key domain of societalisation.

By contrast, societalisation through public spaces has attracted perhaps less theoretical attention, although this process is also suggested by the same classical theorists (Harvey 1976; Lefebvre 1991 [1974]; 2003a [1970]). However, public spaces, by accommodating and representing various people's open consumption of a public good, can in fact actively construct the material, semiotic, normative horizon of "our" urban world, thereby bringing the "users" into a reciprocal expectation of the same (or similar) "relations in public" (Goffman 1971). Each public space hosts different types of consumption and denotes different sets of rules/norms for that consumption. In this context, public spaces (in their entirety) become an inexhaustible ladder of social norms (so-called consumption norms) that define the public types of urban encounter. When making public spaces "definitive" in this way, the consumption norms assume one important thing: that the users of public spaces have already acquired housing units outside of those public spaces and therefore can unproblematically leave the most private elements of life (elements of "reproduction") in their housing. In other words, *the users of public spaces must be the housing classes*—according to the dominant consumption norms.

In a nutshell, public and private spaces (as a set) can be an important platform for societalisation. This platform is what the book generally calls the public/private matrix (or "grid"). The matrix can keep the housing classes as the self-societalising users of cities, making them into a collective body of urban societalisation (for a feminist perspective on public/private spaces in reference to classical class relations, see McDowell 1983). This recognition is not to deny that the housing classes are internally differentiated; its pluralisation is rather inevitable. This also is not intended to obscure the fact that people in the housing classes have developed progressive (even radical) politics in/through public and private spaces, in defence of liveable urban neighbourhoods and housing (Castells 1983; Cox and Mair 1988; Harvey 2012; Hou 2010; Logan and Molotch 1987). Differentiating, reappropriating, or revolutionising efforts of the housing classes have fuelled new struggles and encounters beyond the horizon of the given urban matrix (Goonewardena et al. 2008; Merrifield 2013; Valentine 2008). Yet relations within the housing classes could still be patterned by the societalisation capacity of the public/private matrix, arguably, in spite of popular struggles that rise up from within local residents, public-space users, and their communities.

It might be tempting to say that the societalisation power of the public/private matrix has declined due to the long-term tendencies towards public-space enclosure and gated neighbourhoods (Graham and Marvin 2001; Kohn 2004; Low 2003) as well as the recurrent cycles of urban marginalisation and intensive ghettoisation (Wacquant 2008). However, we do not have to identify the societalisation role of the public/private matrix with the specific period of Keynesian urban policy and imagine that its historical role is over. Public/private spaces do not abandon the role of societalisation in the extended era of neoliberalisation. In fact, neoliberal urbanisation actually increases the need for social organisation and cohesion because it entails escalation in poverty, inequality, segregation, and class division. A reasonable theoretical understanding would be that the neoliberal era increases the systemic necessity of public/private spaces to societalise the housing classes against neoliberalisation's own desocietalising effect.

Homeless people can occupy the position of special "outsiders" in this picture. They wittingly or unwittingly redefine public spaces as private spaces (Mitchell 2003; Snow and Anderson 1993; Wagner 1993)—that is, they use public spaces for developing the most private elements in life, such as sleeping, eating, drinking, and in the most unfortunate cases, suffering disease. Furthermore, this privatisation of public spaces can be exhibited directly to the view of the housing classes. It is worth mentioning that for the housing classes, the pleasant construction of public spaces presupposes the concealment of privacy (the core elements of reproduction) behind the doors and walls of housing. In this context, the mere *presence* of homeless people in public can be a symbol of desocietalisation and incite regulation.

Against this backdrop, antihomeless gentrification, which Neil Smith (1996) and Don Mitchell (1997, 2003) found in abundance in New York City, can be understood as a broader phenomenon intrinsic to contemporary urbanisation. Indeed, as shown by "not in my backyard" (NIMBY) arguments and how NIMBYism arises against homelessness (DeVerteuil 2013; Takahashi 1997; Wagner 1993), housed citizens *themselves* can form a breeding ground for antihomeless regulation; their "social" imaginaries of the urban become a major driver of regulating activity by "political" agencies.

The rescaling formation of homeless regulation is a key process of neoliberalisation (its late variants) through which to rehabilitate the societalisation matrix of public/private against neoliberalisation's own desocietalising ("dehomogenising") impact. Of course, this systemic explanation needs an adequate understanding about process—about how the thrust and agency come into being. Regarding this point, it should be fruitful to show the complexities through which the housing classes and political regulators create a powerful epistemological plane of homeless regulation for *re*societalisation.

In the rest of this book, I will unpack this production of homeless regulation, with a focus on public spaces, conceiving them as the central domain of resocietalisation vis-à-vis homelessness. It is within public spaces that unhoused and housed people meet, where their conflicting actions/imaginaries are visualised and take the form of homeless–housed divides and where housed people and political regulators can possibly be lined up against homeless people. On this basis, I understand that these public spaces are a major site where urban class politics—the politics of the housing classes—are visualised, vitalised, contested, and defended.

Key authors have explained how easily homelessness can touch off serious divides between homeless and housed people and how deeply this division is rooted in the generic public/private construction of modern urban space (Snow and Anderson 1993, p. 332). Comparable homeless–housed divides in public spaces are reported from different empirical settings in Western Europe and North America (Cloke, May, and Johnsen 2010; Gowan 2010). The power of public spaces to assemble homeless regulation in situ can be explained by the "resource-rich" character of contemporary public spaces—the broad availability and networks of police officers, security staff, and various other social control agencies, as well as the monitoring strategies and legal codes that can widely cover/tackle urban irregularities (Amaral 2021; Herbert 1997; Robinson 2019; Stuart 2014). I understand that homeless–housed divides, shown or suggested by many of these authors, represent the locations of urban struggles fought for/around the societalised form of public spaces.

For this book, this antihomeless situation in public spaces denotes the starting point of state rescaling. A "new urban frontier" (Smith 1996) of social crisis emerges from it, and this critical zone soon brings about the form of social crisis management that is fundamentally "street-ised". Repetitive encounters between housed and unhoused people trigger the emergence of new regulatory spaces around public spaces. The new meshes of regulation coming from the streets, parks, alleys, and pavements are remaking the local scale into the central scale of homeless regulation. This "streetisation" of the societalisation crisis and its management leads to a significant consequence for the theory of state rescaling. That is, the "recalibration of scalar hierarchies and interscalar relations throughout the state apparatus as a whole" (Brenner 2004a, pp. 3–4) now starts from within public spaces—theoretically, well before policymakers adopt the "scale manager" role (Peck 2002, p. 357) and begin the official narration of the ground-up complexity. In this context, the NSPR vigorously decouples local initiatives for homeless people in the streets and parks, letting urban policy move "freely" across public spaces. This coagulates various local variants of homeless regulation, which decreases national vigilance power over territorial poverty regulation.

In order to theorise homelessness itself and the subaltern strategies that homeless people develop in the ambit of regulatory power, the Public and Private

Spaces subcomponent of this book's theory taps into, and uniquely elaborates, the notion of metabolism that has broad resonance with conceptions in Marxism (Burkett 1999; Foster 2000; Heynen, Kaika, and Swyngedouw 2006; Moore 2015; Swyngedouw 1996; 2015; for urban theoretical conceptions beyond Marxism, see Angelo and Wachsmuth 2015; Gandy 2004; Wachsmuth 2012). I use *metabolism* in this book to underscore the idea that homeless people purposefully rework urban spaces, including public spaces, before and during their daily use, amid the reign of consumption norms practised and activated by users, guardians, and policing manoeuvres (Hayashi 2013b, 2014b, 2022). The essence of this argument resides in a key recognition that homeless people's use (consumption) of public spaces entails their production of housing spaces through labour processes. Marx (1976 [1867]) and Marxian authors largely use the term *metabolism* to denote human beings' labouring capacity, directed towards (urban) nature, which can produce useful materials (use values) for life. Seen from this metabolic angle, homelessness—particularly its key processes being developed in public—can be grasped as metabolic relations with public spaces qua urban nature, through which homeless people produce new housing use values in the streets, parks, pavements, and so on.

The setting up of cardboard shelters, tents, and encampment sites are the significant signs of homeless people's reworking of and labour-mediated struggle with public spaces. However, even homeless people's minimalist approach to accommodation—*lying on the ground*—entails a vast labour expense. To lie on the ground demands construction of a unique form of the homeless metabolism: people living this form of homelessness must defend themselves against (often unpleasant) open encounters with pedestrians and security staff, secure reliable storage space for belongings to prevent theft, calculate available time for a safe sleep, keep other places for emergency evacuation, and "kill" a lot of time outside of their sleeping site even after dark. All of this labour is needed to make their one-night sleep (or, rather, brief period of rest) possible.

Finally, the homeless metabolism can aim for more than the production of housing and its safe consumption. For instance, homeless people can grow vegetables and raise livestock in public spaces when these spaces are not strongly regulated (Hayashi 2005, 2014b). Homeless people can also gain exchange value (money), for instance, by gathering wasted materials from public spaces (Gowan 2000, 2010; Hayashi 2007, 2014b).

Subcomponent 3: Urban Social Movements

The Urban Social Movements box in Figure 1.1 is the third subcomponent tying the state rescaling concept to homelessness. Chapters 6, 7, and 8 use this subcomponent to make sense of the transformative spaces and agencies that can emerge under rescaling. Jamie Peck (2001a, p. 363) suggests that social movements for poor people are tendentiously localised, that this localisation of social movements reflects localised regulation, and that we should not mythologise these social movements and their "local victories". The reason is that propoor social movements in a context of rescaling can hardly have a large impact if they enclose themselves within localities without upscaling efforts. In relation to this, Peck and Tickell's (2002) concept of rollout neoliberalism suggests that volunteers working at the local scale hold remote, prosystem coalitions with local regulators in which even their best intentions are entangled in the "partnership-based modes of policy development and program delivery" (p. 390).

While it is important to heed these caveats, I find that local victories (and local failures) should be a new target of regulationist accounts. The reason is that when local activism triggers improvements for the apparently "deviant" outsiders of mainstream (housed) society, its localising strategies are creatively using up the "weak parts, voids" that can be "revealed only in practice" (Lefebvre 2009a [1966], p. 144) within rescaled geographies. Moreover, these victories (and failures) give regulation theory insights for better understanding systemic tendencies and their limits.

Habiting is the most general term that I employ in this book to denote social movements for homeless people. Habiting is about the places, processes, geographies, and sociocultures through which activists and volunteers stand with homelessness and promote (more) prohomeless or homeless-friendly forms of urban society. Henri Lefebvre (2003a [1970], p. 81) pitted the term habiting against *habitat*—"dwelling machines" and their functionalised environments—to assess the chances of urban revolution recommencing in neo-Fordist cities. What is a "new" form of dwelling? How can it overcome habitat? Lefebvre's answer was rather pessimistic. According to Lefebvre, after passing the critical point that emerged around the 1960s, urbanisation achieved the main part of habitat production (in a stable urban form) and absorbed various urban dwellers across classes.

In the face of this gloomy view from Lefebvre on the prospect of habiting, I suggest that social movements for homeless people can be a new vessel for Lefebvre's habiting to relativise, destabilise, and potentially overtake the reign of habitat, whose evolutionary stalemates are now apparent in terms of society-organising capacities of public/private spaces (Graham and Marvin 2001; Low 2003). At no point do I mean that homelessness is a "finished form" of habiting. Nor do I think that these movements can fully disclose the contemporary meanings and possibilities of "urban revolution". Its trajectories and consequences are deeply constrained by pregiven urban form, urban metabolism, and housing class relations and their societalisation. Yet by fighting for the Other of habitat—in the streets or in buildings—activists and volunteers can develop unusually radical (form-destabilising) ideas about urban nature and societalisation. This can productively divorce ("declass") social movements from the hegemonic housing classes and allow the movements to leap the formidable homeless–housed divide, in order to communicate with homeless people and promote a (more) homeless-friendly urban society.

Now, it should be clear that the Urban Social Movements box mobilises my general understanding of habiting to denote the overall feature of social movements for homeless people. For the purpose of operationalisation, however, I need to break down this broad understanding of habiting into three subcategories: placemaking (Chapter 6), commoning (Chapter 7), and translating (Chapter 8). Each of these notions meets with limits and constraints in relation to their counterhegemonic enunciation and contestation of a given paradigm of societalisation centring on the housing classes. In varying degrees in practice, however, homeless-supporting and prohomeless social movements are somewhat "structurally" driven to develop spatial strategies in these three dimensions, so that they can enunciate, critique/criticise, and possibly contest a given geography of societalisation that negates homeless people as the mere disturbers of the urban. For scholarly purposes, a consistent tracking of these three dimensions offers an opportunity to reveal the hidden milieus and deployments of state space and regulation.

Placemaking in this book is about the production of places that comprise homeless-friendly and/or explicitly prohomeless identities, imaginaries, discourses, and networks. Geographer Tim Cresswell (2015) emphasises that homeless people in public spaces are socially recognised as "out of place". Home/house is a basis of placemaking (Relph 1976; Tuan 1977), but homeless people lack it, and in public they are "evaluated as being in the wrong place" (Cresswell 2015, p. 190).

This book subscribes to a similar, if slightly more systemic and subaltern, interpretation of housing regimes qua habitat. In this vein, I emphasise that homeless people's difficulty with placemaking is also experienced by social movements. The importance of place for social movements is significant (Leitner, Sheppard, and Sziarto 2008; Martin and Miller 2003; Miller 2000; Nicholls 2009). For this book's social movements, placemaking can entail a search for margins of domiciled society where they may be able to construct their places. That is, these movements might find "spots" of placemaking, especially in those areas that Lefebvre (1991 [1974], 2003a [1970]) called peripheries and ghettos, which for him meant the margins of habitat that are internal to urbanisation but displaced from the regulated urban. These margins can be a hothouse of homeless-supporting and prohomeless placemaking, which can be achieved when/where activists and volunteers create thick cultural environments and extrovert relations as "porous" places (Massey 1994). Often called the inner city, these areas are peripheralised by public/private spaces and, due to this peripheralisation, can turn into spaces in limbo, partially immune to regulatory discourses and open to countersocietalisation or postsocietalisation struggles (for classical US cases, see Piven and Cloward 1971). By filling this limbo with new languages and imaginaries, activists and volunteers may break out of the sociocultural reign of habitat and start off its place-specific relativisations.

Commoning is theorised here as the opening up of the circuits and pools of urban use values (public spaces, urban amenities, means of transportation, municipal welfare provision, community-based service delivery, "waste" materials in the streets, and so on) to homeless people's subaltern metabolism, through regulatory change and new commons-form production. The urban pools of use values are otherwise restricted to the housing classes, at the expense of homeless people's access to these values. Commoning is said to entail the contestation of pregiven codes/practices around the commons (Harvey 2012; Linebaugh 2008, 2014). In this light, the starting point for this book can be particularly meaningful because spaces of commoning are uniquely circumscribed in the politics of homelessness. Homeless people's "right to the city" can be difficult to recognise, much less promote, because these people lack the distance-keeping use value—housing—which is a prerequisite for any need and right of urban residents to be recognised as valid.[4] As a result, in the case of homeless politics, those openings that sociologists of social movements call "political opportunities" (McAdam, McCarthy, and Zald 1996; Tarrow 1998) are downsized, fragmented, and rescaled into slippery (non)structures of urban governance.

The notion of commoning, when adapted to homelessness, reveals these difficult contexts and how they can be conquered purposefully. Activists and volunteers, once they are effectively placed at the margins of habitat, can have power to struggle towards commoning. Strategies of commoning include both direct action (such as street-level resistance and occupation) and more lively communications with local agents in the state and civil society sectors, which entail active framing strategies (for framing practice by homeless movements, see Croteau and Hicks 2003). Altogether, these movements might alter or suspend antihomeless rules/norms over the commons and, even further, produce new forms of the commons fitting homeless people's specific needs—their street-based economies and their post–public space lives. This commoning becomes realistic when placemaking can sustain it.

Translating denotes the transplantation of place-specific transformative ideas to new sites and scales, which invigorates habiting beyond its birthplace and "birth scale" (original scale). Social movements merely working at and around the pockets of poverty can be reduced to extremely minoritarian and spatially limited forms. Even when welfare offices and neighbourhoods create "progressive" rules, regulation can remain unchanged in the rest of the city. In this case, movements can translate the inherited language of placemaking and commoning to new sites and scales.

Translation is the keyword of contemporary Gramscian scholars who try to illuminate the linguistic side of Gramsci's philosophy of praxis (Ekers et al. 2013; Ives 2004; Ives and Lacorte 2010). A people's language to rearticulate their worlds for possible change, once originating in the "centre" of a historical movement, may mutate and hybridise with other sociocultures so that it can sustain the movement's transformative capacity at diverse geographies beyond the original site and scale. Through this translation, activists may be able to reform the inherited language in multisited, multiscalar ways. Horizontally, it can spread and connect movements' placemaking activities in interlocal and intralocal manners (Leitner, Sheppard, and Sziarto 2008; Martin and Miller 2003; Miller 2000; Nicholls 2009), breeding commoning actions at these levels as well. Vertically, translation can allow activism to leap local constraints and become communicative to national society and the national state. In the case of the vertical translation, translation can foster the scale jumping of the habiting movement (on social movements' scale jumping, see Herod 1997; Leitner, Sheppard, and Sziarto 2008; Martin and Miller 2003).

Placemaking, commoning, and translating can be more vividly demonstrated by borrowing examples from the literature. These examples reveal not just possibilities but also rampant difficulties of social movements for and with homeless people at ground level. First, in relation to placemaking, Geoffrey DeVerteuil (2015, p. 32) suggests that different inner-city areas have similarly turned into social places of supportive agency "through hallmarks such as density, concentration, proximity, solidarity, collectivism, irreplaceability and motivation to preserve previous gains". A stripe of similar placemaking is also reported for one US city in New England, where "the streets ... constituted a community, and many service providers are a part of that community" (Wagner 1993, p. 36), so that prohomeless (housed) individuals can stand with homeless people and halt the "widespread 'not-in-my-backyard' movements against shelters and even against soup kitchens" (p. 2). In David Wagner's case, these facilitative hot spots for placemaking are even implied to have allowed housed citizens—those who "sleep at home at night" (p. 36)—to overcome homeless–housed tensions. In turn, homeless advocacy groups on the national scale, richly discussed in the US context (Blau 1992; Hopper 2003), may be understood as a nationalisation of local places. And yet these places still can repeatedly face contradictory moments (DeVerteuil 2015; Wagner 1993).

Second, commoning has ensued from placemaking histories. The very maintenance of prohomeless places includes liminal but essential forms of commoning against discommoning—that is, everyday renegotiation with entrepreneurs and regulators who try to impose the regulatory urban matrix on the sociospatial niches of poverty for profit-making or societalising purposes. These liminal forms of commoning do not necessarily lead to durable mobilisation. Rather, sustainable forms of commoning can be difficult. According to Wagner (1993, pp. 138–142), "a majority" in his homeless community once participated in a "self-styled indigenous organization", fiercely struggled against the municipality, and succeeded in "improving the situation of the homeless". Yet such political activity remained episodic, due to homeless people's scarcity of resources and their reluctance to act under a political leadership (p. 140). Carolyn Stevens (1997, p. 18), commenting on Yokohama's Kotobuki district, a Japanese inner-city area, suggests another possibility, that commoning for homeless people can instead be based on service provision by "middle-class volunteers". Similar outcomes of homeless-supporting activism have improved regulatory and service-providing contexts in multiple cities (Cress and Snow 2000).

Third, translation can be a highly elusive part of the habiting movement. Neil Smith (1993) has provided an inspiring argument that a piece of public art in New York City—a mobile installation called *Homeless Vehicle*—opened a scale jumping (upscaling) possibility for prohomeless politics. This argument gives not only a theoretical but also a contextual clue as to how the reworking of local culture can help to create new scales of politics for homeless people. In Smith's case, the homeless population in New York City was large, "at between 70,000 and 100,000 people" (p. 87), and their presence had been gathering national attention. In addition, New York City is a well-known haven for radical artists. The idea to "visualise" the hardship of homeless people in the form of public art for a wider audience would be suitable for this brand of New York City and for the city's cultural attraction. At no point does Smith's narration tell us that scale jumping by translation is an easy matter. Far from it, the outlook is that the translation across scales is a highly contextual and complex process. It is about utilising given prohomeless/propoor sociocultures developed in situ, remaking them into forms understandable at a new scale, and creating a far larger resonance beyond the locality.

These three realms of urban social movements (placemaking, commoning, and translating) have been articulated in Yokohama's Kotobuki district and its surroundings—the site of my fieldwork—in unique ways (see Chapter 2).

The Method of Theorisation in this Book

The plan for this book is to steer the state rescaling concept towards homeless studies by using three theoretical subcomponents—national states, public and private spaces, and urban social movements as depicted in Figure 1.1—as entry points. The problem is that the linkages between the abstract and the concrete can sometimes seem highly complicated. The issue of homelessness comprises many undertheorised topics—such as capitalist/noncapitalist spaces of survival, relations of regulatory and counterregulatory agencies in urban governance, interscalar political contexts, and state space that may construct these contexts into territorial homeless regulation—that can make this complexity overwhelming. Equally daunting is that later chapters examine the Japanese case in depth by using concepts, notions, and logics derived largely from Anglophone theoretical literature. How can this book make sense of the probable confusions?

In order to extend regulationist theory to "homelessness plus Japan" in a reliable manner, I construct and employ a two-step method of theory making and theory specification. The purpose of attaching this twofold method to regulationist theory is to extend the scope of theoretical understanding beyond original geographical underpinnings and topical interests, but without denying the inherent regional character of a constructed theory. The essence of this method is illustrated in Figure 1.2.

STEP 1

Theory making

Empirically informed, thought-level construction of a more inclusive theoretical model that can summarily describe a set of paradigmatic forms of capitalist geographical development in the Euro-American world (meso-level abstraction)

STEP 2

Theory specification

Readjustments of theory (from step 1) for "new" or "marginal" (undertheorised) territorial areas in the non-Euro-American world, which can enhance the theory's mobility to margins and outsides of its main (Euro-American) geographies currently under methodological abstraction

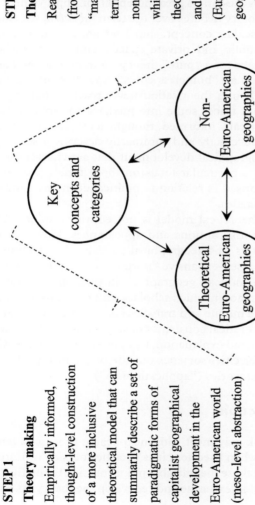

Enhanced theory mobility beyond Euro-American geographies

Figure 1.2 A geographical approach to methodological abstraction.

Step 1: Theory Making

By gleaning useful concepts, categories, and theories from North American and Western European social science literatures, mainly but not exclusively from political economy literatures, I broadly theorise homelessness as a set of phenomena deeply related to the dynamism of state rescaling regulation under capitalism. Some critics argue that issues related to urban informality have been marginalised in political economy approaches (Roy 2005, 2009). In this context, I would state that the (re)inclusion of homelessness—its regulation, contestation, and subaltern strategy—within these approaches offers great potential for improvement (for this book's approach to contemporary debates over the term *subaltern*, see Chapter 2).

Starting with the state rescaling concept, step 1 advances it around the three pillars of national states, public and private spaces, and urban social movements. This step does not make for a "pure" theory—a transcendental argumentation intended to encompass all "homeless cities" regardless of their different time-space envelopes. This book's theorisation never reaches that highest level of abstraction. Instead, step 1 traces some intermediary patterns in meso-level abstraction. This is an empirically informed, thought-level (re)construction of a theoretical model that can succinctly and summarily describe a set of paradigmatic forms of capitalist geographical development that are characteristic of the Euro-American world, with a particular focus on those topics (e.g., homelessness) that are still undertheorised in relation to political economy concepts even for Euro-American cities/societies.

This construction of a theoretical model is not entirely "unbiased" as it is tinged with Euro-American assumptions and appearances. However, this theoretical model clearly registers this geographical partiality by claiming to be a meso-level abstraction (not a self-expansive "pure theory"), marking its relative borders vis-à-vis *non*-Euro-American geographies, in turn opening for the next step (step 2) a new working space in which scholars with political-economic ideas can make their theories more mobile and transferable to margins and outsides of "the West". Although the theoretical constructs of step 1 may have implicit power for international comparison and explanation, this power can decrease when they are straightforwardly used for cities/societies outside of the birthplace and birth scale of political economy categories ("applicationism").

Step 2: Theory Specification

The theory behind this book may meet with inexplicable processes, tendencies, and sociocultural elements when used for cities/societies outside of Euro-American experience. By targeting these inexplicable points outside of the Euro-American world, however, I can recontextualise and redevelop the theory. As part of this effort, the process in step 2 reweighs the concepts and theoretical claims in the context of "new" or "marginal" (e.g., Japanese) territorial areas and histories. As a result, the theory can revive its explanatory capacity when used for non-Euro-American geographies.

This step, which I call theory specification, does not have to have a brand-new construction of theory as its aim. The main aim of step 2 can possibly be a relatively modest level of recontextualisation that targets the "necessary minimum". This specification entails selective readjustments of the step 1 theory for "new" or "marginal" territorial areas that lie outside (or on the fringes of) the Euro-American domains of capitalist geographical development and urbanisation.

In step 2, the researcher is asked to delineate the relatively unique and under-theorised geographies of non-Euro-American capitalist geographical development and urbanisation in comparison to the theoretical constructs in step 1. Even though it can decrease explanatory power in context-specific realms, the theoretical model of step 1 has potential for more global explanation, but again the power of explanation can be decreased for those areas that lie outside (or on the fringes of) the Euro-American world. The step 2 specifications for a relatively few (targeted) aspects can possibly enhance the explanatory power of the step 1 theory for non-Euro-American areas and assist the step 1 theory to become more "mobile" across various territories. The following chapters endeavour to discern these specifications by using a range of Japanese contexts with regard to the national state, public and private spaces, and urban social movements.

To be sure, steps 1 and 2 presuppose the fundamental role of the ethnographer in reorienting existing concepts to those subjects and territories currently submerged in the shadows of theoretical paradigms. The ethnographer can play a fundamental role in facilitating the extension of concepts to hitherto marginalised topics (e.g., homelessness) and applying existing theoretical paradigms to relatively new territorial areas (e.g., Japan). This role of the ethnographer becomes a driver for my conceptual reworkings during steps 1 and 2. In this venture, the intake of fresh field-level ontology from the emergent urban, via the ethnographer, can inspire the whole theoretical project during theorisation (step 1) and specification (step 2).

Ethnographic details might seem redundant to theory when the selection and logical simplicity sustain steps 1 and 2; abstraction is an act of selecting those elements that the theorist thinks necessary (Sayer 2010). However, this book will repeatedly test the theorist–ethnographer rapprochement so that it can locate the margins of the theoretical realm by using political economy concepts. These margins are the domain of the ethnographer's ontological and even incommensurable experience, where the ethnographer encounters—and may be overwhelmed and bewildered by—meanings, events, and contestations that are unexpected (or less expected) in political economy theory (for further discussions on this "regulationist ethnography" methodological approach, see Chapter 2).

Postcolonial Urban Theory

It is hoped that this approach will lead to a manageable response to postcolonial urbanists' methodological reflections on urban-level theorisation. Concerned by the predominance of Western concepts in the research on "third world" cities, Jennifer Robinson (2006, p. 3) requests urbanists to practise "parochialisation" of Western knowledge for the purpose of promoting more cosmopolitan urban research and subduing "the ambitious scope and sometimes dominating authorial voice of a universalizing theoretical practice" (Robinson 2016, p. 8). Ananya Roy takes a perhaps less resolute position with regard to Western concepts but wishes a radical displacement of the current strongholds of theory production in the West. This entails disseminating new nodes of theorisation in various non-Western cities and "produc[ing] a new set of concepts in the crucible of a new repertoire of cities" (Roy 2009, p. 820).

I would emphasise that the approach used in the present book registers this intrinsic regional character of (political economy) theories. From this position, I seek to reopen pregiven Western concepts to "a more cosmopolitan engagement with experiences and scholarship elsewhere" (Robinson 2006, p. 3). With this in mind, I will, in a self-restricting manner, apply Western concepts to the contrast that Roy (2009, p. 820) detects between theory's geographical situatedness (in the phase of production) and theory's increased autonomy (in the phase of appropriation).

This book thus strives to revitalise political economy perspectives in relation to the criticisms from postcolonial urbanists so that it can engender a wider theoretical/comparative connectivity around these concepts. This response operates within three major parameters. First, along with some political economy theorists (see the next section), I fully recognise the "local and limited origins" (Robinson 2006, p. 3) of my key concepts. However, I will systematically counterweigh these concepts through repetitive specifications in the theoretical realm (steps 1 and 2). Second, this research design asks the ethnographer to play a fundamental role in "soaking" the given concepts in "new" urban worlds of marginalisation, regulation, and politicisation that are currently less accommodated in political economy paradigms (see Chapter 2). Third, although the book involves some "de-Westernisation" of concepts, this is not calling for a radical separation of the non-West from the West, nor is it attempting a reductionist universalisation. Rather, it marks a dialectical opening of international theoretical connectivity and comparative urban research agendas.

Between Abstract and Concrete

What is a meso-level theorisation? Theory making through an abstraction can be understood as a process to critically decipher the "being abstracted" character of the real world, or the world we live in and coproduce, by using the enlightening power of key concepts and categories, which is itself a historical consequence of actual abstraction processes happening in our world (for discussions about "real" or "concrete" abstraction, see Brenner 2019; Jappe 2013; Loftus 2015; Stanek 2011; Toscano 2008). But how can the prefix *meso-* characterise my position in terms of *methodological abstraction*, that is, methodologically sound attempts at theory making using such concepts and categories? Neil Brenner (2004a) has elaborated this methodological standpoint for urbanists, defining *meso* as a strategic arena for regulationist methodological abstraction programmes. According to Brenner, the meso level denotes "relatively durable institutional arrangements, regulatory frameworks, and territorial configurations" (p. 20). As such, the meso level in abstraction

> differs from the abstract level because it illuminates the historically specific, regularized forms in which the system's underlying social processes—such as commodification, capital accumulation, urbanization, and state regulation—are articulated. It is on this [meso] level, therefore, that periodizations of capitalist development are most commonly developed. ... The meso level reveals the underlying regularities that tie together these variegated contexts within a shared historical-geographical configuration. ... It is on this level that fundamental questions regarding the character of contemporary large-scale social, political, and economic transformations can be posed. Insofar as the meso level refers to certain entrenched but potentially malleable institutional arrangements, regulatory practices and developmental tendencies, it involves the analysis of secular trends over a medium-term time scale, generally a period of several decades. (p. 20)

In this sense, meso-level abstraction for theory making registers (and even emphasises) the regional character of the theoretical claim. Brenner "parochialises" his regulationist theorisation, apparently with the awareness that what Western Marxists talk about under the banner of abstraction sometimes tacitly includes elements of meso recognition oriented to Euro-American geographies. Writing in the early 2000s, Brenner enumerates key instances of such meso objects as Atlantic Fordism and its accumulation crisis, what Jessop dubs the Keynesian welfare national state and its regulation crisis, world-regional consolidations such as the European Union, and the like.

A set of topics related to homelessness also can be conceptualised at the meso level of methodological abstraction. Any critical analysis must entail the researcher's constant movement between the abstract and the concrete, which Andrew Sayer (2010, p. 87) calls a "double movement". Presumably, the meso level, "a 'middle ground' between theory and empirics" (p. 54), becomes a busy zone—a crossing point—visited and traversed by many theoretical and empirical scholars who dare to "move doubly". Apart from this general recognition, there is a scarcity of meso conceptions among scholars on homelessness, urban marginality, and social movements. This lack, in my view, has seriously obscured the abstract–concrete linkage in these literatures and their international scope.

This book's method, which maps out the meso level in abstraction and the deeper levels of historical conjunctural analysis, and the ways in which these two are related in a broader scheme, is my critical engagement with the assumption of some major neo-Marxist approaches: that theory can create "pure" abstract recognition that fits into various time-space envelopes of modern capitalism without reconsiderations at different levels of abstraction. On this basis, I argue that the ambiguous position of Japan in international theoretical paradigms—having both the anomalies and the veritable similarities to the Western patterns—can effectively disclose a differential time-space envelope of capitalist modernity outside of the West. This difference of Japanese capitalist modernity can be used for a nuanced internationalisation of political economy approaches.

Japan-based contextualisation and comparison thus can reveal the meso contextuality and regional scope of political economy theory as well as highlight the ways in which the theoretical appears differently at different levels of abstraction. The rich anomalies of Japan—which suggest Japan's unique angle of insertion into world capitalist modernity—can be viewed as a strength, not a weakness, for Japan-based (or non-Western-based) researchers. If critical literature in the West sometimes conflates pure abstract arguments with intermediary ones, the Japanese case can clarify this conflation and unravel the tangled threads, due to its differential insertion into the theoretical–international context.

The Structure of this Book

Chapter 2 is entitled "Japanese Context and the Regulationist Ethnography". First, the chapter locates the theoretical framework outlined in the introduction within the Japanese context of national states, public and private spaces, and urban social movements. In this book, these three core arguments are reconsidered within the ambit of Japanese modernity, state formation, and urbanisation so that the theory can be tailored to Japan's own time-space envelope. To that end, I centre the historical features of the Japanese "developmental state", which still has repercussions and ramifications. Second, Chapter 2 explains my ethnography methodology approach under the rubric of "regulationist ethnography". This is a theory-informing *and* -generating type of ethnographic endeavour that uses territorial/urban regulatory dynamics as a locus for both regulationist theorisation and the observation of how the theory appears in concrete territorial/urban contexts. Third, this chapter shows how I (as an ethnographer) observed and engaged with urban processes in Kanagawa Prefecture, which provides this book with subaltern materials and perspectives on homelessness.

Chapter 3, "Scales of Societalisation", employs this book's overarching theory by grabbing its first handle: national states and their restructuring. Not many urbanists today employ state theory when studying diverse geographies of urban policy. This chapter shows that the redeployment of state theory in urban studies can powerfully locate urban and local processes within the larger context of regulation, crisis formation, and capitalist development. State theory is also informative for regulation theory, as some continental strands of regulation theory only weakly incorporate the dynamics of the state. I note that Keynesian–Fordist national states saw the NUP after the 1970s crisis and that dialectical relationships between national/local rule-setting and the NUP—including homelessness—formed "rounds" of rescaling. The chapter makes this theory specific to Japan by highlighting the developmental state context that created the Japanese character of rescaling. Japan's rescaling is prone to localisation, but it occasionally experiences strong interventions from the managing national state.

Chapter 4, "Rescaling Urban Metabolism I", holds the book's overall theory by its second handle: public and private spaces. The rubric thus shifts from national territory to cities and urbanisation. The understanding is that urban metabolism, being distilled through the public/private matrix, generalises the housing classes qua urban hegemonic classes, that this housing class formation marginalises homeless people and their sociometabolism, and that it incites rescaling reregulation. Homeless people produce and consume the use values of housing *in public*, which distorts dominant land-use patterns of the housing classes and their societal construction. As a result, homeless people and their metabolic process are recognised as the Other of normative urban settlements and their metabolic circuits. Homeless people become "noncitizens", who are counterposed to housed citizens, and in doing so coconstitute homeless–housed divides (with other urban actors) and accelerate rescaling reregulation. Specifically, in Japan, developmentalism has made public spaces a narrow locus of use values for residents, which results in a high intolerance of public space homelessness.

Chapter 5, "Rescaling Urban Metabolism II", continues to employ the public space–centred approach. Whereas Chapter 4 considers the use value dimension of metabolic class relations, this chapter shifts the focus to the exchange value dimension. In making this shift, I highlight the particular part of homeless people's subsistent economies: the collection of waste materials from dumping sites. The collection of such materials from public spaces is a major source of income for homeless people, but this side of homeless labour incites regulatory practice. This dynamism proceeds in a rescaling manner, breeding new regulatory spaces outside of the national standards of citizenship. In Japan, a unique form of neighbourhood community (*chōnaikai*) has societalised urban residents in developmentalist urban contexts; this community form is revitalised into a moral leader for the regulation of homeless recyclers. Thus, public spaces offer another instance to analyse the ground-up (haphazard) dynamism of rescaling.

Chapter 6, called "Placemaking in the Inner City", begins to use the third handle of the theory: urban social movements. The discussion starts with the hidden understanding of Henri Lefebvre's examination of peripheries. Lefebvre hinted that urban peripheries can be favourable sites for valorising the heterodox, beyond-habitat imaginaries and actions (habiting). This chapter reshapes this understanding into a theory of prohomeless placemaking. Historical pockets of poverty, often called the inner city, breed positive and compassionate understandings about homelessness, which become structurally scarce in the middle of the regulated urban. This, I theorise, facilitates the placemaking activity of activists and volunteers, allowing activism to leap the homeless–housed divide. Using this theory, I interpret Yokohama's inner-city area known as the Kotobuki district. Day labourers and supporters in Kotobuki created movement strongholds in the 1970s. Until the 2000s, this formative history was followed by multiple prohomeless and homeless-supporting groups in the Kotobuki district.

Chapter 7, under the heading of "Commoning around the Inner City", investigates the actual ways in which movements redress antihomeless regulation. Because they are locked in the metabolic and sociopolitical hegemony of the housing classes, homeless people's interests in public spaces, goods, and provision are seen as detrimental to urban governance. Borders of the commons are entrenched, surveilled, and policed on behalf of societalisation. Even in this hostile environment, activism can struggle against and communicate with the rescaled gatekeepers of the commons. This can lead to the opening up of public spaces, goods, and provision for homeless people. My ethnography reveals that Kotobuki's activists in the 1970s engaged in a fierce struggle with the municipality for commoning. In the 1980s, when neighbourhood residents fomented antihomeless feeling, new groups engaged in the commoning of urban use values for homeless people. After the early 1990s, activists/volunteers united in issue-specific coalitions and improved Yokohama's regulation over the commons.

Chapter 8, "Translating to New Cities", concludes my movement-centred approach by addressing the geographical expansion of social movements. The key concept here is translation, a neo-Gramscian reworking of Gramsci's linguistic theorisation over the philosophy of praxis. Homeless activism can extend the geographical scope of placemaking and commoning by translating the periphery-born sociocultures into new guises tailored to cities away from the periphery. The chapter examines how this translation helped Kotobuki-born activism to reach the outlying areas of the prefecture's metropolitan centre. Central to this was activists' reworking of historical values and beliefs, whereby they remained critical of the urban system of public/private spaces at its most stable points, namely, in cities away from Yokohama's inner city. Consequently, Japan's new round of rescaling, in the 2000s, was accompanied by the geographical expansion of activism. Attempts of translation made a broader area—Kanagawa Prefecture, comprising many cities—a new battlefield for prohomeless and homeless-supporting people.

Chapter 9 deciphers more contemporary phases of homelessness, state rescaling, and urban social movements between the late 2000s and early 2020. The ending of the 2000s was a rare positive situation for homeless advocacy groups, as Tokyo's movement elicited from the national state an unusual acceptance of progressive claims for the citizenship and rights of homeless people. However, the resulting inclusion was soon followed by formidable processes of neoliberal reversals, through which conservative political/social agents tried to exclude the "undeserving" poor from the national terrains of citizenship. This trend has fomented a major buildup of Japan's workfare state, which, by redeploying rescaling logics, is powerfully realigning and marginalising impoverished people in general around Japan's nationalised system of citizenship. In this context, public spaces have gained a new capacity to surveil, police, and depoliticise urban poverty and homelessness, while activists are fighting back.

Chapter 10 reemphasises that the conception of rescaling is a powerful weapon for synthesising, unpacking, and comparing multiple dimensions of homelessness, regulation, and social movements. Finally, I flesh out the theoretical, methodological, and empirical contributions and signal future research agendas that can come out of the present study. I schematically show possible ways to improve and make the theories, methodologies, and practices of urban political economy more sophisticated in response to some key criticisms from geographers and urbanists.

It should be noted that the "empirical" chapters in parts 2 and 3 have a similar organisation, comprising three layers of argumentation, as shown in Figure 1.3. The first layer is the place where my theoretical ambition for homelessness is highlighted, by targeting the meso level of abstraction and theory making. In the second layer, the chapters specify, retheorise, and "Japanise" these large theoretical arguments in order to avoid the simplistic and reductionist process of "applicationism", which can subdue the historicity of Japanese capitalist modernity and urbanisation in the name of abstraction. In the third layer, the chapters make it clear that my ethnographic engagement is not the finishing point of my theoretical practice but a creative site to revitalise and reontologise the theory in relation to new geographies and research topics.

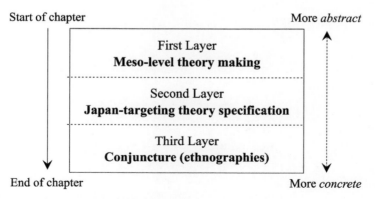

Figure 1.3 Three layers in each "empirical" chapter.

Notes

1 At the COP25 climate change conference, a famous climate nongovernmental organisation based in Germany announced that, in 2018, Japan was the most vulnerable country to natural disasters induced by climate crisis (Eckstein et al. 2019).
2 These works of geographers in Japan can be located in the interdisciplinary body of Japanese homeless studies in which sociologists, political economists, and social policy researchers have played key roles since its formative years (e.g., Aoki 1989; Eguchi, Nishioka, and Kato 1979; Iwata 2000).
3 Regarding the concept of scale, I've focused in this book on its specific usage in a spatialised strand of regulationist political economy. This strand employs the scale concept in reference to the repetitive vertical differentiation/reordering that is generally understood as the process of (re)scaling (Brenner 2004a, 2019; Collinge 1999; Jessop 2002; Keil and Mahon 2009; Peck 2001b, 2002). In this strand, scale is conceived as intrinsically relational (Brenner 2004a, 2019; Peck 2001b). That is, no "roles" of a scale are analysable independently from the entire architecture of *all* scales and their relationalities relevant for the understanding of a territorial geography under scrutiny.
4 Lefebvre (1991 [1974], p. 339) says that living in the city is possible for various city-dwellers only by purchasing "a particular distance—distance from the purchaser's dwelling-place to other places". As homeless people lack this distance-making use value (housing), and as their production of alternative "distance" cannot easily be admitted as such in the given form of the urban, the prospect would be that homeless people's right to the city is difficult to justify and to support in cities. This justification and support, however, might happen in the unique geographies of urban social movements.

Chapter Two
Japanese Context and the Regulationist Ethnography

In this chapter I move from the theoretical discussions of Chapter 1 and demonstrate how these are modified to fit Japanese contexts. Denser specifications will take place in each of the more "empirical" chapters from 3 to 8. This chapter gives the reader a shorthand understanding of these specifications. The Japanese "developmental state" is the connecting thread through this series of theory specifications. In geography, the scalar formation of the developmental state has been discussed at great length using the South Korean case (Park 2005, 2008, 2013; Park, Hill, and Saito 2012). This chapter reconsiders the scalar formation and rescaling of territorial regulation in Japan by using this concept of the developmental state (for Japan's rescaled urban policy in developmental state contexts, see Tsukamoto 2012).

Chalmers Johnson's (1982) influential arguments on the Japanese developmental state are useful in order to excavate and align various Japanese contexts. However, he may have too sharply contrasted the developmental state with the regulatory state (as the US pattern). This dualistic conception is systematically mitigated in this book because I employ the developmental state notion to make my meso-level theory—the composite theory of state rescaling—more "mobile" from the original geographies of theory making (step 1) to the new (Japanese) geographies of specification (step 2) (Figure 1.2).

After summing up this book's theory specification processes, the present chapter constructs my method of "regulationist ethnography". One purpose of the discussion of regulationist ethnography is to explain my focus on state space as a territorial context of ethnographic endeavour. This chapter brings territory—which

Rescaling Urban Poverty: Homelessness, State Restructuring and City Politics in Japan, First Edition. Mahito Hayashi.
© 2024 Royal Geographical Society (with the Institute of British Geographers). Published 2024 by John Wiley & Sons Ltd.

can be "thought of as the extension of the state's power" (Elden 2013, p. 322)—back to ethnography, so that this book can enhance the ethnographer's role to reshape political economy concepts with reference to territorially specific processes of urbanisation. Under the rubric of regulationist ethnography, I argue that political economy theories can fundamentally benefit from the ethnographer's take-up of new urban ontology from the emergent urban worlds. Following these discussions, the chapter explains my fieldwork sites and my materials—what I understand as "subaltern materials"—in relation to preceding ethnographic works on Japan and contemporary debates over the term subaltern.

Theory Specification 1: National States

As introduced in the overall framework in Chapter 1, the theoretical component of National States is intended to focus on the nationalised space of poverty regulation and relate it to the theory of the accumulation regime. By overlapping the three societalising spheres (public provision, the labour market, and the social fabric), Western versions of the NSPR advanced the integrity of society on a national scale, which can be highly class-divided under capitalism. After the early 1980s, Fordism entered a crisis period and the NSPR was hampered by a growth of poverty. The new urban poverty saw an increase of less-consenting ("undeserving") social groups and individuals at the margins of the NSPR and fomented (mini)crises of societalisation.

The rise of poverty led to the rescaling production of new regulatory spaces that powerfully activated spontaneous actions of local regulators, which tipped the balance of interscalar relations of territorial regulation towards the local scale. On the one hand, new regulatory spaces in cities developed regimes of "moralisation", intended to incentivise impoverished people and drive them towards more spontaneous acceptance of (re)societalising logics around the labour market. On the other hand, this also ran into the process of policing-cum-surveillance of the most "undeserving" populations. All in all, the increased autonomy of (semi) coercive and moralising spaces of reregulation on the local scale shortchanged national standards of citizenship to be maintained by the NSPR.

This theoretical argument can be tailored to fit the Japanese context. First, Japan showed stronger tendencies towards the national-statist regulatory process than did the Euro-American states. This national state emphasis was highly capable of tempering crisis formation and inserting a national time-space envelope in the US-led arena of global capitalism (Cumings 1999; Desai 2013; Heller 2011; Itoh 1990; Panitch and Gindin 2012). As a result, Japan wallowed in (rather than suffered from) the wave of profit squeezing during the early phase of globalisation in the 1970s and escaped a major crisis of the accumulation regime during the 1980s, when Euro-American states incurred a severe crisis of capital accumulation (Arrighi 1994; R. Brenner 2002).

Due to this success, the national-statist character of Japanese interscalar relations did not simply wither away, even after the onset of globalisation-cum-rescaling. As Japanese cities gained increasing autonomous power, a significant pull towards rescaling also came from the national state's lawmaking activity, which paradoxically reactivated some level of the national resistance against local haphazard rules and nonrules—an inheritance from the developmentalist past—in various regulatory fields. In Japan, the theoretical role of the national state under rescaling, its role as "scale manager" (Peck 2002, p. 357), was connected to this inherited developmentalist character, which drove the Japanese state to achieve a higher level of state space unity.

Second, the developmentalist state can remould the concept of the NSPR for Japan by explaining the weaker character of the welfare state and the NSPR's poverty-regulating capacity in the country. This developmentalism once steered vast national resources towards the costly process of initiating the "catching-up" economy. The resources and wealth handled by the national state were predominantly allocated to infrastructure building, technological enhancement, and industrial expansion, which translated into the state's insignificant provision to people (Esping-Andersen 1997; Kwon 2005). Worse still, developmentalism also sacrificed the poverty-regulating role of the labour market and wages (Itoh 1990), which is another theoretical pillar of poverty regulation, thereby assuring the persistent existence of "working poor" populations at the apogee of developmentalism (Eguchi 1979, 1980a, 1980b).

Acute urban poverty was rampant well before the major crisis of Japan's developmentalist statism. The deregulation of poverty typically emerged in inner-city zones called yoseba. The yoseba zones were spaces of labour-power reproduction for day labourers—meaning here the less skilled casual workforce sent to manual labour sites such as docks, construction sites, manufacturing lines, and elsewhere—which, on behalf of Japan's postwar industrialisation, demanded a vast number of precarious labourers whose wages hardly compensated for hazardous working conditions (on day labourers' regulation beyond Japan, see Theodore 2003).

Third, the rampant deregulation of poverty under developmentalism, while geographically concentrating on yoseba zones, persistently created homelessness in these inner-city areas. Day labourers living in yoseba zones ran into episodic/chronic homelessness even before the 1990s. I call this early form of homelessness prior to the 1990s the "inner-city cycle" of Japanese homelessness. This cycle of homelessness was, in large measure, geographically contained in and around yoseba zones (see Aoki 1989; Eguchi, Nishioka, and Kato 1979; Nishizawa 1995), which forged Japan's urban societalisation and its well-ordered character outside of the inner-city areas.

In the 1990s, however, the accumulation crisis finally caused crisis moments in the NSPR and vastly increased homelessness all over urban spaces (Aoki 2000; Hayashi 2006; Kariya 2006; Kitagawa 2001; Nakane 1999; Yamaguchi 1998), thereby replacing the past (inner-city) cycle with the "widespread cycle" of homelessness, which was a Japanese version of the NUP in its clearest form. The rescaling of the NSPR and the production of new regulatory spaces became most intense in Japan during this widespread cycle of homelessness after the early 1990s and into the 2000s. It is true that precursory, less systematic forms of rescaling reregulation appeared in and around yoseba zones before the 1990s, which managed the geographical containment of homelessness in yoseba zones. Nonetheless, multiple rounds of rescaling were unleashed when Japanese cities were amid the second, widespread cycle of homelessness, when the effects of deregulation were more powerful and threatening to urban societalisation based on the housing classes.

It was in this context that the Japanese state produced an overall rescaling framework—the 2002/2003 system—which is comparable to the McKinney-Vento Homeless Assistance Act and its aftermath in the United States (Hayashi 2014a). Japan's 2002/2003 system contained powerful normative prejudgements that described homelessness as a potential danger for housed citizens and justified its control on this basis. On its face, the 2002/2003 system called for municipalities to produce a workfare-like apparatus in which homeless people were categorised based on work ethic and placed at the fringes of nationalised citizenship (which in the Japanese case is strongly nationally centred).

Through this system, Japan programmatically rescaled the NSPR in highly concerted ways. To some degree, this process reconstructed the historical centrality of the national scale in Japanese statecraft, a product of Japan's developmentalism. In Japan, the state's theoretical capacity as a "scale manager" (Peck 2002, p. 357)—which is about assembling new state capacity from fragmentary rescaling experiences—coincided with a strong reassertion of the national state/scale's dominance over the local state/scale within Japanese statecraft.

Theory Specification 2: Public and Private Spaces

Public and Private Spaces, the next theoretical component covered in Chapter 1, is a general matrix of sociometabolic life in support of the housing classes. Public and private spaces satisfy people's needs for urban use values, and their consumption of these use values becomes a semiotic base of urban societalisation. Core private elements are hidden in housing, which opens streets and parks to publicness, or public forms of consumption. This material–semiotic framework of consumptive societalisation never precluded progressive politics from arising in/through urban habitat (Castells 1983; Cox and Mair 1988; Hou 2010; Logan and Molotch 1987). Yet, as a tendency and almost as a rule, people shaped into the housing classes eagerly consumed the realm of publicness without witnessing symbols of acute (deregulated) poverty. Empty stomachs, untreated diseases, and accidental deaths were concealed behind doors and walls and unobservable from public spaces. As such, the public/private matrix almost limitlessly extended the housing classes by guarding the consumptive and semiotic life of the urban populace, who were classified as "worker" or "producer" in traditional vocabularies but now strongly recognised themselves as "dweller" or "consumer" *of the matrix*, against capitalism's continual ballooning of poverty and class division. While so doing, the matrix provided capitalist urbanisation with a spatial framework of societalisation.

Yet this expansive mode of urban societalisation based on the matrix became more problematic in the era after the watershed years around the 1970s. The "militarisation" of public spaces, the gating of neighbourhoods, and the intensification of gentrification all suggest that societalisation based on the generalisation of public and private spaces increasingly became less straightforward (Davis 1992; Graham and Marvin 2001; Low 2003). Cities became a breeding ground for rescaling, especially where public spaces pitted homeless people against the housing classes, activated antihomeless semiosis, and hastened the formation of new regulatory spaces. In this context, public spaces deteriorated the capacity to integrate the impoverished margins of society, as homeless people were excluded from the public/private matrix and society was besieged by homeless–housed divides. Nonetheless, homeless people still try to survive within the rescaled spaces of regulation, which often ensued from a local increase in homelessness, by opening new metabolic circuits of production and consumption in/around public spaces.

This theory of public and private spaces also can be specified for Japan by using the developmental state idea. The point here is that the developmental state sacrificed people's use values in cities and that public and private spaces in Japan did not fully adhere to the pattern hypothesised by Euro-American literatures. By the early twentieth century, Japan's early state-led approach to the urbanisation of capital caused slums to appear in big cities (Ishizuka 1977). Impoverished people in these slums were called *saimin* (small people), which included those without a roof or a house.

Even in the early twentieth century, the public/private distinctions and homeless–housed divisions were still vague. The "modern" categories of habitat were not a generalised condition, and the housing classes were still undeveloped (see Nakagawa 2000). After World War II, the Japanese developmental state started to acknowledge social needs for urban planning based on the notion of public and private spaces (Sorensen 2002). Even at this late date, however, the priority of urban planning was still placed on industrialisation, and this once again restricted the formation of habitat. It is true that public and private spaces became the basic framework of urban planning after World War II, that urban slums were relegated to the inner-city zones (yoseba), and that the housing classes and public/private distinctions were generalised. Yet even by the 1970s, when the housing classes grew, the use values of public and private spaces remained highly unsatisfactory for the working class's consumption. Because the vast pools of wealth and space were reserved for industrialisation, housing was small and public amenities were undeveloped; moreover, environmental pollution significantly degraded the living conditions of urban workers (Miyamoto 1976).

Suffering this dearth of pleasant urban environments in developmentalism, the Japanese housing classes could have been politicised and might have embraced radicalism. Contemporary Japanese urbanists repeatedly voiced this expectation (Matsubara 1974; Shoji and Miyamoto 1964; Ui 1974), and residential neighbourhoods indeed saw the expansion of social movements in the 1960s (Matsubara and Nitagai 1976). Yet the housing classes remained for the most part relatively silent politically. This was partly due to the subjugation of local initiatives by national political elites, which is very typical of developmentalist urbanisation. At the same time, Japanese urban regulation was semiotic and, to be clearer, organisational. In this regard, Japan's traditional framework of community formation enlisted within developmentalism—called chōnaikai (neighbourhood associations), which historically hybridised local society with state power for Japan's "state-saturated" urbanisation—functioned as a major plane of developmentalist societalisation. Since the recent phase of community fragmentation in Japan, this domain of community formation has had decreased societalisation power (Nakamura 2011). However, as I will show in some detail in this book, the traditional sites and process of neighbourhood-based solidarity also can revitalise the historical societalisation role when meeting with those outside of the housing classes, that is, homeless people.

Run by residents themselves but with involvement from administrators, the chōnaikai units of community multiplied in postwar Japanese cities, obtained formal positions in administrative frameworks, and powerfully guided housed citizens and their local societies (Akimoto 1971; Sorensen 2002; Tamano 1993; Yoshihara 1989). In this context, Japanese public spaces also were filled with symbols and slogans produced by public regulators and community leaders, who thereby defined the "appropriate" forms of consumption and social relations (Fujita 2006). Pedestrians willingly upheld the rules of public space consumption (Pele et al. 2017). These codes and forms of consumption, while they were guided by administrators (Matsubara and Nitagai 1976), were deeply elaborated by housed citizens, who used chōnaikai as the main arena of such elaboration (Iwasaki et al. 1989).

In later chapters, I argue at greater length that this traditional character of neighbourhoods also forged a well-organised and highly conformist (hyperconformist) type of societalisation in Japan. While allowing elaboration by residents, Japan's local society formation, led by community leaders and administrators, often tightly guided the sense-making and consumption of the housing classes in accordance with the specificity of Japan: state-led urbanisation in favour of industry, the state's lesser support of people's use values, and the enlargement of the housing classes under these conditions.[1]

Located in this conformist type of societalisation, any volume of street homelessness could be disruptive to the housing classes and their political guardians. Until the 1980s, the possibility of this urban disruption was in large measure managed by local regulators and their relatively minor rule making on the local scale. This sowed the seeds of new regulatory space in and around yoseba zones because under the inner-city cycle of homelessness, the geography of homelessness was concentrated in those zones and their small radius. However, homeless people started to make huge deregulating impacts when they increased in number and when they encroached into "normal" public spaces.

To be sure, even during this cycle of widespread homelessness, starting in the 1990s, the number of homeless people was generally smaller than in many Euro-American countries. The number of Japanese homeless people did not compare to that of the United States in the early 1980s, for example, when that country was experiencing the terminal crisis of Fordist–Keynesian urbanisation and the federal government's Department of Housing and Urban Development estimated the number of homeless street people at between 250,000 and 300,000 (Rossi 1989, p. 37). According to official statistics compiled by the Ministry of Health, Labour and Welfare (MHLW), the number of homeless people in Japanese public spaces was below 30,000 at its peak during the early 2000s (MHLW 2003). The number seems insignificant even after considering Japan's smaller national population and how homelessness is defined (including a widely used definition of homeless people in Japanese statistics, which counts as homeless only people visible in public spaces).

However, these statistics seriously underestimate Japanese homelessness. In Japan, homeless people were inserted into the hyperconformist mode of societalisation. Because this societalisation needed to achieve the difficult feat of integrating the housing classes around small use values in cities (Miyamoto 1976), even the relatively minor appearances of homelessness raised concerns of a societalisation crisis among residents and pedestrians, security staff and municipal workers, nearby shopkeepers and landowners—that is, a broad spectrum of the housing classes and their guardians (Hayashi 2014b; Kasai 1999). This generated haphazard waves of antihomeless regulation at ground level, and eventually such local events were followed by the Japanese state's production of the 2002/2003 system.

In this context, Japanese public spaces must be seen as a real breeding ground for state rescaling in which homeless people were treated in substandard and violent ways in favour of Japan's well-regulated public spaces (for the case of Tokyo, see Kasai 1999; Sakokawa 2013; Shinjuku Renraku Kai 1997). If homelessness can still exist in this well-organised (hyperconformist) type of societalisation, then the actions of homeless people to produce new spaces, values, and meanings—the homeless metabolism exhibiting material–semiotic versatility—are their real attempt to survive and rework Japanese urban society at its margins.

Theory Specification 3: Urban Social Movements

The third subcomponent of theory in this book, Urban Social Movements, concerns the ways in which social movements for homeless people create their environments on the periphery of normative urban settlement (habitat). Spatial niches of poverty can amass ideas and actions for homeless people. Their relative separation from the epicentre of societalisation, from habitat and the housing classes, allows activists and volunteers to escape the disciplinary imaginary of habitation so that they might conceive of cities differently. This is what I call "habiting". The danger is that prohomeless actions can sometimes be seen as antihabitat and antihousing insofar as they—whether wittingly or unwittingly—relativise the "normal" world of public/private spaces, which is a powerful semiotic (meaning-making) space of the housing classes. In this context, activists need to withstand the sheer moralising and normalising power of public and private spaces before, during, and after making claims for homeless people.

This theory of habiting is divided into three themes: (1) activists/volunteers may overcome the colonising power of reregulation by producing their own places at the margins of habitat (placemaking); (2) activists/volunteers may change regulatory frameworks and create a homeless-friendly (and even prohomeless) form of urban commons whose use value circuits are otherwise closed to the housing classes (commoning); and (3) activists/volunteers may spread these transformative environments to new sites, cities, and scales beyond their birthplace and birth scale, through cultural reworking (translating).

Habiting and its relationship with placemaking, commoning, and translating had unique twists in Japan. In the Japanese case, habiting had to combat the pervasive, organisational, highly depoliticising type of societalisation—hyperconformist societalisation—that was a sociological layer for developmentalism to establish social cohesion with small urban use values. Because the housing classes and their urban spaces had long been co-opted into this type of social cohesion, it was difficult for activists and volunteers to problematise those who suffer this urbanisation at the furthest fringes of the housing classes, their use values, and their society. Simply put, any voices *for* homelessness could be erased from urban public spheres and governance. In this context, yoseba zones, the inner-city districts of day labourers, provided rare geographies that hosted placemaking actions of activists/volunteers wishing to work for homeless people. Ethnicity and race were not the prime levers for collective placemaking in the early years. Until the 1970s, the placemaking framework often dominantly deployed Marxian class vocabulary. However, yoseba zones also cultivated more diverse views for prohomeless placemaking in later years.

Commoning—regulatory change in favour of prohomeless or homeless-supporting urban commons—was distinctively articulated in Japan. Commoners often focused on a particular legal thread of the national citizenship framework, that is, *sēzon ken*, or the right to livelihood, which is detailed in article 25 of the constitution and in the Public Assistance Act of 1950. These laws ideally determine the livelihood right broadly and inclusively, as a right of all Japanese citizens to a basic living standard, but this standard often was not maintained due to the meagre spending of welfare statism constrained by developmentalism (for these constraints, see Kwon 2005). In this national context, some commoners framed "homeless politics" as a politics towards more genuine forms of the livelihood right, and in part they spelled out the requirements by using law-related terms, while others favoured more anarchic ideas for framing commoning action and eschewed almost any kind of engagement with formal policy (for varieties of framing, see Hasegawa 2006; Hayashi 2015).

Despite such framing activity, it was often difficult to open up public spaces and goods. Public spaces were probably the part of the urban commons that experienced the least regulatory change. In part, that was a reflection of Japan's extremely conformist variant of societalisation, which became highly intolerant of "outsiders" in defence of Japanese public spaces, which were—and still are—comparatively small. Even the relatively small population of homeless people was met by aggressive policing, which commoning fought against.

The translation of sociocultures, preserved at the margins of normal public/private spaces, to external areas and larger scales of societalisation was possible in Japan due to the efforts of a few devoted activists and volunteers who moved back and forth between inner-city areas (yoseba zones) and the remote areas/scales where homelessness had newly appeared. In postwar Japan, areas and scales remote from the inner city were often unreached by apparent forms of homelessness, typically until the mid-1990s. Due to this "newness", the translation of language to new areas or scales required groundbreaking action. Despite this difficulty, the translating attempts to spread local cultures compassionate to homeless people to broader areas/scales resulted in successful processes. Aerial (horizontal) expansion through translation started in the 1990s (for a famous case in Tokyo's Shinjuku Ward, see Kasai 1999; Shinjuku Renraku Kai 1997). In the late 2000s, translation for scale jumping expansion (upscaling) succeeded in advancing commoning and placemaking on the national scale (Hayashi 2015).

Regulationist Ethnography

This book's theory makings (step 1) and specifications (step 2) fundamentally benefit from my ethnographic experience. This ethnographic side of the book has a unique name—*regulationist ethnography*. I shall explain this regulationist ethnography methodology approach by describing its three pillars. First, ethnographic engagement in concrete research fields can catalyse, enhance, and make mobile extant political economy theories in relation to the emergent urban margins, or to the non-West. This is achieved by providing these extant theories with "new" or "marginal" topics and geographical areas that can revitalise pregiven political economy notions. Those topics (such as homelessness) and territorial/local areas (such as Japan/Japanese cities) that currently are *not* on the main radar of political economy approaches are beneficial in this sense.

Second, this ethnography-led extension of political economy theory can productively use the territorial form of *integral* state spaces (political, social, or hybrid) as an arena for a broad-based recontextualisation of ethnographic information. Seen from this angle of state space, regulationist ethnography is understood as a territorial practice through which the ethnographer equipped with thoughts on political economy diversely relates his/her place-specific information to integral state space as a territorial whole.

Third, these two arguments come down to my ontological claim that an amalgamation of the "theorist" and the "ethnographer" within one and the same individual—in this case, me acting as both—can effectively advance these two practices. That is, the extension of political economy theory and the exploration of integral state space can be based on the existential ground of the ethnographer—on his/her incommensurable experience "in the field".

Let us move from a summary of regulationist ethnography to its more substantial assessments. If ethnography usually values the complexity of urban lifeworlds, simplicity is a key to theorisation by abstraction. Andrew Sayer (2010, pp. 86–87) contends that "an abstract concept, or an abstraction, isolates in thought a *one-sided* or partial aspect of an object", noting that the theorist "must 'abstract' [a theoretical claim] from particular conditions, excluding those which have no significant effect in order to focus on those which do" (original emphasis). Indeed, this book makes a sustained effort to maintain the theoretical realm—steps 1 and 2, discussed in Chapter 1—to be focused on the targeted topic (homelessness) and the geographical area (Japan). The abstraction here is conducted at the meso level, "a 'middle ground' between theory and empirics" (p. 54), not at the highest level of abstraction. However, the theory's focus on logical simplicity and logical flows is not compromised even at the meso level of abstraction. Here arises a key question of how to broach the theory's logical simplicity, given the uneven and plural forms of urbanisation—marginalisations, societalisations, contestations—that deeply underlie urban society.

My working hypothesis is that this conundrum can be manageably answered by the ethnographer. In pursuit of this goal, this book is guided by what Clifford Geertz (1973) calls care for the "thickness" of description, evaluating the ethnographer's existential relation to the field. A study of rescaling needs to articulate wider contexts and environments of regulation; this role of rescaling studies goes "beyond 'thick descriptions' of state restructuring" (Peck 2003, p. 222). Even in relation to this caveat, however, it would not be paradoxical for this book to attempt a "thick" anchoring of the ethnographer in local space. I suggest that this local anchor can facilitate the enlisting of political economy concepts within the new geographies of marginalisation, societalisation, and contestation, which the ethnographer can observe but the theorist may be unprepared for. While the theorist can make political economy concepts topically and geographically mobile in steps 1 and 2, the ethnographer, focused on the locality, can assist the mobility of a theory by making it (more) sensitive to the topic-specific and locality-specific patterns of capitalist urbanisation.

Geertz's application of thickness has been criticised by postmodern anthropologists. Such critics have argued that the label reveals Geertz's naive understanding of the ethnographer's privileged positionality in relation to a field—to the "text" that comprises various relational webs of the local world—and that this positionality perpetuates the ethnographer's nonreflexive ideas about an ethnography's constructedness (Clifford and Marcus 1986; Erickson and Murphy 2013; Gardner and Lewis 1996). Crucially, George E. Marcus (1998) has advanced a major postmodern relativising of thick description. In his conception, the ethnographer should be sensitive to the demise of capitalist modernity's "master narrative" (p. 46)—which Marcus probably considers to be a hidden scaffolding of Geertz's unmediated relationality to the field—and to how the master narrative is "plurally resisted and accommodated" (p. 40). Marcus's strategy is to compromise the ethnographer's commitment to a single place by collating it within a broader circuit of places that the same ethnographer may construct across the globe.

Marcus calls this strategy a "multi-sited research imaginary" of the ethnographer (p. 14). The present book does not contravene the ethnographer's multi-sitedness per se. A regulationist ethnography can imagine, and use, many sites. To some degree, however, this book's ethnography recalls the ethnographer's existential relation to the field from its postmodern hibernation, i.e., from the "anti-thickness" attitude recommended for ethnographers to relativise and question their incommensurable experience in a specific field of study (for this tendency in postmodern anthropology, see Appadurai 1996).

By using his/her ontological commitment to the field as thrust, the ethnographer possibly can join the "simple" connotation of theoretical concepts, which may be understood as a marker of good methodological abstraction (Sayer 2010), with the complexity of urban lifeworlds. This theory–ethnography rapprochement may allow him/her to handle the dilemma that repeatedly emerges between the theorist's necessary simplicity and the ethnographer's incommensurable experience as an "everydayness" of the theorist–ethnographer, finding certain points of compromise in between for ongoing descriptive, analytical, and conceptual practice. It is in this sense that I understand the ethnographer as having the capacity to make political economy concepts more strongly committed to specific research fields.

This position marks the rationale for this book's regulationist ethnography methodological approach, but the ethnographer can play another role in making regulationist ethnography functional, by situating local descriptions within state space. In this dimension of regulationist ethnography, the ethnographer's goal is to reembed the obtained urban perspectives within the territorial form of state power that constructs, if remotely, the ethnographer's local experience. This ethnographer can observe state space from its margins and outsides, and not from its centres and "strong points", where state space restructuring powerfully masks "voids", "ruptures", and "lacunae" (Lefebvre 2009a [1966], pp. 140, 144). When "the existing State is grounded upon these strong points" (p. 144), the ethnographer's relative autonomy from these strong points can negate them, see state space from subaltern or peripheral locations, and develop new theoretical connectivity around ruptures and peripheries.

This situatedness of the ethnographer in state space can be compared to Michael Burawoy's (2000) proposal for "global ethnography". Burawoy presents his celebrated ethnography paradigm as a necessary method to grapple with the "*transnational* connections" (p. 34, original emphasis) of globalisation. Under globalisation, field observation is "detached and redirected across national boundaries" (p. 34). For Burawoy, globalisation demands that ethnographers be free "from solitary confinement, from being bound to a single place and time" (p. 4). In overcoming the national confinement, ethnographers must make sense of "the lived experience of globalization" (p. 4) and pursue "extensions of observations over time and space" (p. 27).

Yet I would argue that Burawoy's global ethnography can be effectively complemented by regulationist ethnography, which seriously considers the embeddedness of ethnographic observation in the inherited contexts of state space, which I define as *integral* state space. The notion of state space in this book is based on Neil Brenner's (2004a, p. v) fundamental interpretation of this term, which he appropriates from Henri Lefebvre. This key idea is intended to register internal sociopolitical complexities of state space through my understanding of *integral* state space having the three subspaces of *political*, *social*, and *hybrid*.[2]

The theory–ethnography linkages can be secured by using territorial imaginations and histories of these different state spaces as a medium and a connecting thread. In fact, Burawoy rightly (but only briefly) refers to this aspect as "the strong magnetic field of nation states" (p. 34). Regulationist ethnography offers a way for the ethnographer to examine how and why this "magnetic field" remains so alluring not just to highly theoretical but also to grounded social research.

Tellingly enough, a later work by Burawoy (2009, pp. 178–179) on multisited ethnography cites Trotsky's thesis of combined and uneven development, and it claims, "Capitalism continually expands and transplants itself onto foreign soils and combines with different social structures", producing "distinctive national characters". Burawoy thus implies the possibility that a territorial amalgam of different milieus of state space (political, social, or hybrid) becomes a basis for the ethnographer's deciphering of how capitalism is rooted and rerooted in the "different social structures" that can be captured between the most abstract and most concrete levels.

In keeping with these traits of regulationist ethnography, this book calls for the reactivation of regulationist political economy by anchoring it in the complexity of urban lifeworlds and their territorial state space contexts. We live in an urban world where sites, processes, and (mal)functions of regulation perpetually oscillate. This is what Jamie Peck and Nik Theodore (2015) call "fast policy", continually moving back and forth "between fixity and motion" (Brenner 1998). In the face of this instability, the ethnographer equipped with regulationist vocabularies is in a good position to oscillate along with the real flux in regulation appearing in cities and to interpret the obtained urban perspective within the territorial arena of state space. As such, this work is greatly informed by ethnographic works conducted by authors who have committed to regulationist ideas (Fairbanks and Lloyd 2011; Peck and Theodore 2015; Wacquant 2008). At the same time, I hope to add to this literature a stronger sense of how political economy concepts can be fitted into specific research fields, and of the ethnographer's territorial imagination of state space as a dense informational arena for enhancing this concept–field fit.

In this sense, the ethnographer is not just someone who can make theory sensitive to complexities. Even more fundamentally, the ethnographer is expected to synchronise the theoretical literature itself with the perpetual moves at ground level. With the ethnographer's input of new urban ontology, theoretical concepts can be used to revive this synchronisation in process and to advance "incessant feed back between the conceptual framework used and empirical observations" (Lefebvre 1996 [1967], p. 151), enabling us to grasp the current limits and emergent forms of the urban as a "virtual" object. Thus, the theorist, through the ethnographer, may wage an intellectual fight to revive the explanatory power of key theoretical concepts, and through this process, to renew confidence in fundamental concepts with reference to "margins", which appear thematically (e.g., in the topic of homelessness) or geographically (e.g., in Japan).

The research described in this book systematically practises this theory–ethnography partnership, which might be called dual oscillation and which keenly traces the zigzag course of today's urban regulation. In so doing, it enlarges the scope of both ethnography and theory. By activating the capacity of the ethnographer in this way, today's regulationism can make sense of how fragmentary spaces for reregulation ("second-order" regulation) open up around more cohesive spaces of societalisation ("first-order" regulation); how this process alters the logics, meanings, and ramifications of urbanisation; and why the prevalent dynamic of regulation is experienced differently by different groups and in different geographical areas.

Sites of Participatory Observation

A large part of this book's empirical information was obtained through my participatory observation in multiple cities of Kanagawa Prefecture. This work was most intensively conducted between 2001 and 2009. I do not wish to downplay the utility of other fieldwork methods for regulationist ethnography projects. However, it seems that participatory observation is highly suitable to regulationist ethnography.

For one thing, the ethnographer who becomes devoted to a place-based observation through participation is more likely able to gather a diverse range of materials, including inevitably politicised ones, about the processes, consequences, and contexts of regulation. For another, participatory observation accommodates an ethnographer's sharp awareness that he/she is tracing a unique, academically and existentially important research object. These two dimensions can motivate the ethnographer (me as an ethnographer) towards a "thick" description of (de)regulation, allowing regulation/state theory to conceive various place-based actions, variegated strategies, and postregulatory imaginaries that otherwise remain in the background.

Kanagawa Prefecture is located in the Tokyo–Yokohama metropolitan region, which has a population of more than 29 million and forms the biggest metropolitan region in Japan. The metropolitan region has three prefectural units: the Tokyo Metropolis (14 million), Kanagawa Prefecture (9.1 million), and Chiba Prefecture (6.3 million). While the three prefectures are mutually interwoven into a largely unified space of economic geography and the global city dynamics of the Tokyo–Yokohama region (Sassen 2001), each prefecture retains socioenvironmental distinctions and political autonomies. The vitality of Kanagawa Prefecture stands out in Japan. By 2020, when forty out of forty-seven Japanese prefectures were seeing a decrease in population under Japan's massive birthrate decline, Kanagawa Prefecture was still increasing in population.

Kanagawa Prefecture combines thirty-three municipalities (cities, towns, and villages). The social, political, and economic centre of gravity resides in the relatively small area around Tokyo Bay (Figure 2.1), where Yokohama—the largest city—is located. Yokohama's central business district (CBD) begins roughly in the area of the railway station, around which are gathered the city's commercial sites and political organs. The Yokohama railway station is itself a huge complex of buildings and underground streets that not only connects various railway lines but also includes fashionable shops and restaurants. From the Yokohama railway station, the main CBD stretches southward for a few kilometres. Walking south, one finds the Sakuragi-chō area, where tall buildings form a commercial and business zone known as Minato-mirai, which brings together popular shops, amusement parks, and private firms that tend towards manufacturing and information and communications technology.

Going farther south, one finds another commercially attractive area, Motomachi, which houses tailors and jewellery shops and makes symbolic contributions to the city of Yokohama as a site for conspicuous consumption and the middle class. To the southeast of the CBD, one reaches Chinatown, known for its nice Chinese restaurants, the Yokohama stadium that is home to a professional baseball team, and political/administrative organs such as Yokohama city hall, the headquarters of Kanagawa Prefecture, and the Yokohama district court.

Figure 2.1 Kanagawa Prefecture.
Note: Shaded areas are the main locations that appear in this book's empirical discussions.

At the southern fringe of Yokohama's CBD lies the most impoverished zone in this region: the Kotobuki district. It is an inner-city area inhabited by disadvantaged day labourers and retired ex-labourers, many of whom originally came to this zone to find casual labour markets, affordable accommodation, and accessible welfare facilities. Similar inner-city areas—generally called yoseba—exist in virtually all Japanese urban centres; in addition to Kotobuki, Tokyo's San'ya and Osaka's Kamagasaki are the prime examples. These are the spaces of bodily and cultural reproduction for present and former day labourers. Yoseba zones, accommodating these labourers, have historically been despised, reviled, feared, and segregated from the "normal" urban dwellers and their guardians (Aoki 1989; Fujii and Tamaki 2003; Ikuta 2007; Nishizawa 1995).

The Kotobuki district's history as a yoseba zone is relatively recent compared to other cases, beginning in the mid-1950s, when it was entrenched as a well-defined yoseba zone. Its geographical production involved a political manoeuvre on the part of the municipality, an outcome of the city's "programmed segregation" (Lefebvre 2003a [1970], p. 144), through which policymakers after World War II tried to replace Yokohama's traditional geography of slums, which previously were more prevalent, with a highly concentrated form of geographical segregation by enclosing the urban presence of day labourers in the small area of the Kotobuki district.

When the Yokohama docks recruited and used a vast number of male unskilled labourers after World War II, the Kotobuki district became the place of workforce reproduction for these day labourers. It should be noted that the Yokohama docks were a late adopter of the container system, a labour-saving innovation for the operation of docks. The delay in its adoption was partly due to the abundance of day labourers pooled within proximity of the docks in the Kotobuki district. This economic nexus between the Kotobuki district and the Yokohama docks was suddenly disrupted in the mid-1970s, when a worldwide capitalist crisis stopped the operation of the docks and its day labourers were made redundant and became homeless. From this time onward, different kinds of activists, would-be activists, and less politicised volunteers started to gather in the Kotobuki district.

At the northern edge of the city of Yokohama lies another big municipality, the city of Kawasaki, which has the second-largest population in Kanagawa Prefecture. Together, the cities of Yokohama and Kawasaki compose the prosperous metropolitan area of Kanagawa Prefecture around Tokyo Bay, which also encompasses inherited geographies of segregation and impoverishment.

Other cities are less busy. I call these the "outlying" cities. These are satellite suburb cities spreading beyond the city of Yokohama, and while these outlying cities are well integrated into the metropolitan geography around the bay, their distinctions from Yokohama are clear enough. This is the area in which subcontracted production firms, smaller commercial agglomerations, large agricultural fields, calm residential neighbourhoods, and well-known tourist spots are located and create clusters.

While this area has thus played an important role in production, commerce, and community in the regional geography of Kanagawa Prefecture, these outskirt cities attract attention for a different reason: their different exposure to homelessness. That is, while the core metropolitan area around Tokyo Bay started to witness the rise of homelessness in the 1970s, meaning that the area experienced the inner-city cycle of the 1970s and early 1980s *and* the widespread cycle of homelessness in the 1990s and 2000s, the outlying cities only started to see homelessness after the mid-1990s. Hence, the outlying area of Kanagawa Prefecture underwent only the widespread cycle of Japanese homelessness, without encountering the earlier wave of homelessness. This spatially and temporally unique exposure to homelessness led to peculiar dynamics of rescaling reregulation there.

This book focuses on this intellectually rewarding region of Kanagawa Prefecture, as a whole, for its ethnographic endeavour. Owing to the differentiated exposures to the cycles of homelessness, the combined metropolitan area and outlying cities provide an ideal set of two geographies whereby I can effectively consider, from differential angles, the multiple issues related to homelessness. These issues include how a hegemonic urban society and its public and private spaces can be opposed to homelessness, why homeless–housed divides emerge from this contradiction, how regulatory agents and the housing classes scramble on antihomeless semiosis in the promotion of rescaling reregulation, and how heterodox urban voices advocating habiting can arise and expand its scope.

When I offer the most concrete form of urban narratives, I often employ key cases from the two cities in which my ethnographic experience has been the richest—Yokohama and Hiratsuka. One is situated in the metropolitan centre, the other in the outlying cities. The city of Yokohama has had a major yoseba zone (the Kotobuki district) and has experienced homelessness politics since the 1970s. In contrast, Hiratsuka is an important example among the outlying cities with the largest homeless population in this group, which began to see public space homelessness in manifest forms only in the late 1990s. My narratives utilise the vantage point of these two contrasting cities to reveal the unevenness of homelessness, its regulation, and its grassroots contestation within this area. This intralocal unevenness testifies to the highly emergent character of homelessness and its rescaling reregulation.

At the same time, this book's coverage of other cities in Kanagawa Prefecture is not incidental. I belonged to a homeless advocacy coalition that coordinates all homeless-prone cities at the prefecture level. This coalition framework enabled me to obtain a wide range of information from across the entire prefecture. I must note that my coverage is less detailed for Kawasaki, although this city had a significant number of homeless people. This is due to the relative separation of activists and groups in the city from the pan-prefectural coalition. Nonetheless, I can interpret processes and phenomena in the city of Kawasaki by using the historical information amassed by Yokohama's activists.

The Nature of Data

My participation in activism within Kanagawa Prefecture, which took place most intensively from 2001 to 2009, was my core avenue for gathering data. My participation in local activist groups provided me with an array of opportunities to obtain important materials on homelessness, its regulation, and its contestation. This position as an activist researcher could entail some empirical limits, but I worked to mitigate these challenges as much as possible.

Notable US sociologists have suggested the importance of forming a "team of researchers" to overcome the partiality of data that can be significant for homeless people (Snow and Anderson 1993, p. 28–29). In my case, however, a research team, had I organised one, would have hindered my research. It might have ossified the ontology of me as an ethnographer when my status had to be reflexive. Activism offered me, as a sole ethnographer, viable opportunities for data collection during homeless-visiting tours, in food-distribution programmes, at homeless–volunteer gatherings, in activism–municipality discussions, and during internal meetings. I also was able to practise interviews and gain access to historical materials (handouts, pamphlets, newsletters, notebooks, and more fragmentary sources) stored at the offices of social movements. The point is that this empirical window revealed its full possibility to me only thorough my continuous and reflexive commitment to the social worlds of this area's homeless activism.

Data on Homelessness

My firsthand knowledge about homeless people largely derives from my participation in social movement actions in the cities of Yokohama and Hiratsuka. In Yokohama, multiple homeless-visiting tours were organised through the Kotobuki Day Labourers' Union and the Kotobuki Supporters' Gathering Club (which jointly form multiple patrolling groups). Activists and volunteers visit Yokohama's homeless-prone areas, such as the Yokohama station buildings, the area around the Yokohama baseball stadium, the pavements along the Tsurumi River, and elsewhere. I most frequently participated in these tours in Yokohama during the early and mid-2000s, which gave me reliable opportunities to witness the location, forms of dwelling, actions, and opinions of homeless people, which I mainly recorded by means of field notes. In Hiratsuka, similar visiting tours are organised by a local group called the Hiratsuka Patrol, and I regularly participated in these tours between 2001 and 2008. There, too, I recorded the distribution of homelessness, the appearance of homeless people's lives, and their voices by taking notes and, when not disruptive, taking photographs as necessary. I will use pseudonyms to refer to homeless individuals throughout the book.

Because these local groups themselves gathered records on the whereabouts and state of homeless people, this book uses these sources as well. In addition, activists frequently held meetings with homeless people and municipal workers, which provided me with important data on homeless people. Finally, information about homeless people in cities other than Yokohama and Hiratsuka, as well as historical information about all these cities, was obtained from an overarching coalition of activists in the prefecture (the All-Kanagawa Assembly of Night-Walk Groups and Patrols), my interviews with key activists and volunteers, and my access to local archives.

Data on Regulation

My data collection examined two types of regulators, political and social, as well as their intermediary forms, coworking units, and knowledge transfer that easily occurs around Japan's public space and local community. My observation of the political regulators was directed at policymakers, rank-and-file workers, quasimunicipal agents, and their coworking frameworks with housed citizens. My knowledge about these agents was most detailed for the cities of Yokohama and Hiratsuka, where I participated in local activism. At the same time, activists repeatedly held meetings with these and other municipalities during the 2000s, in order to change the local trajectories of rescaling. I participated in many of these meetings, which enabled me to record the locational patterns of political regulation for the entire Kanagawa Prefecture.

I also collected data on the housing classes that exhibited or hinted at, both on and off the streets, many homeless-related messages, insinuations, and actions during my fieldwork. This data collection examined the ways in which different types of housed people—residents, shoppers, pedestrians, and travellers—responded to homeless people and how these responses of housed people motivated, collaborated with, and merged into the political regulators, both instantaneously and on a longer-term basis, at ground level. I acquired this information through street-level observation and archival work; the latter involved a wide range of materials preserved at the offices of social movement organisations.

Finally, this book's data on regulation includes information from the earliest phase of Japan's rescaling politics, dating back to the 1970s. My interviews with key activists and my access to local archives allowed me to aquire information relating to regulation in the 1970s and 1980s.

Data on Social Movements

My participation in social movements for homeless people during the 2000s ensures this book's rich data on multiple aspects of these movements. Because my exposure to activism for the narrative-making of this book happened in the 2000s, the memories and records of the activists and volunteers addressed by my research were most vivid for the recent phase of homelessness—what I call the widespread cycle of homelessness, which started in the 1990s. During this period, activists, groups, and coalitions were working on homelessness and homeless regulation across the extensive area of Kanagawa Prefecture. This timing thus enabled me to gather firsthand data on the ongoing process of social movement actions and how the groups spread and reformed themselves, reflexively, against the evolution of local regulation and the fluid pattern of homelessness.

My observation of activism was richest for Yokohama and Hiratsuka, but again, my data covered the entire area of Kanagawa Prefecture. I recorded the voices and actions of activists and volunteers. I kept materials distributed at the repeated internal meetings they held in each city and at the level of the prefecture. I took notes on the language and belief systems of activists and volunteers in action, which testified to the expansion of prohomeless sociocultural spaces that was characteristic of the period of my fieldwork. Importantly, my continuous participation in local activism put me in a suitable position to interview key activists and to look into their collections of pamphlets, newsletters, notebooks, and memoranda. These opportunities allowed me to investigate the periods dating back to the 1970s.

All this data gathering—on homelessness, regulation, and social movements—was achieved through everyday talks, dialogues, and encounters with the people inside and outside of activism, which typically took place during actions for homeless people, meetings with the municipality's branches, and a lot of walks with other activists. I conducted participatory observation with five homeless-supporting patrol groups: the Thursday Patrol (in the city of Yokohama), the Sagamihara Thursday Patrol, the Fujisawa Tuesday Patrol, the Hiratsuka Patrol, and the Odawara Communicating Patrol. I also frequently participated in actions and events held by the Kotobuki Day Labourers' Union and the Kotobuki Supporters' Club, which have been key mobilisation bases for patrols and other homeless-supporting actions in this area.

This book uses my interviews with eight activists (twelve times in total). Details on these interviews can be found in the book's reference section. Often, the main purpose of these interviews was to formally record activists' views and opinions that had already been made explicit in more informal exchanges or in other types of material. I kept the number of interviews relatively small because I felt the need to avoid too apparent devotion to "research" compared to "activism", even though I was clearly recognised as a researcher in the community. My colleagues' strong awareness of me being a researcher might have made my location in the community more "formal", rendering unreliable this book's coverage of the "informal" aspects of social movements, such as intricate cultural differences and relations between/within groups, which account for the great variety of movement groups and actions in this area. In addition to interviews, this book uses eleven printed or handwritten materials (pamphlets, leaflets, newsletters, notes, and memoranda) produced by movements and kept at their offices, which also are listed in the reference section. This book is also informed by flyers and handbills made by the movements, but this part of my materials is not listed in the references because their titles are often unclear.

Subaltern Materials

David Featherstone (2012, p. 55) suggests that in order to deeply decipher subaltern forms of solidarity, without mistreating them with any "disembodied or abstracted relations", ethnographic researchers can widely use materials created by and through subaltern movements. To this end, researchers can tap into "sources such as texts, political songs and activist testimonies as part of, not separate from, the conduct of political activity" (p. 64). In this light, social movements in which I have participated have been a major site of subaltern solidarities for homeless people since the 1970s, which offered me a range of subaltern materials. Because these materials can reveal long and dynamic histories of homeless-related activism in the locality and its national context, this book can make unique temporal and contextual contributions to two preceding ethnographies of the Kotobuki district (Gill 2001; Stevens 1997), both of which were based on the authors' fieldwork during the early 1990s.[3]

Readers might wonder whether my status as activist researcher has affected the nature of the gathered data. Perhaps it did. I would not want to justify my data-gathering interfaces by overtly politicising them. I would suggest, however, that this kind of partiality can be inherent in the fieldwork for "subaltern social groups", whose "history is necessarily fragmented and episodic" (Gramsci 1971, pp. 54–55). In this context, the activism interfaces were a realistic and reliable medium for gathering information about issues around homelessness in Japan. To mitigate the fragmentary tendency, I carefully checked the events and processes shown in the subaltern materials by collating them with existing chronological narratives, with newspaper articles, and with my interviews, so that this book can put the subaltern materials in a consistent historical perspective.

By using these subaltern materials, this book spotlights homeless people within public spaces, excluding from its central scope their post–public space lives—that is, the lives of formerly homeless people after leaving their "housing" in public spaces. By comparing Tokyo and Los Angeles, Matthew Marr (2015) has studied homeless people who have withdrawn from public spaces to improve their living conditions. As he emphasises, this mobility can entail highly positive processes for homeless people. Previously, I have published work on homeless people's struggle to get out of public spaces and reenter the housing classes (Hayashi 2003, 2006, 2014b; Kitagawa, Kawahara, and Hayashi 2003). The present book can contribute to this line of research by closely describing forms of provision for homeless people's post–public space life, which include shelters, public assistance, and a local voucher system, among others, but I still centre this book on public spaces, depicting these off-street spaces *in relation to public spaces*.

In this book's approach, key regulatory dynamics are understood to emerge from, and be mediated by, public spaces in which the subalternity of homeless people becomes most conspicuous to a societalised society and its class relations. For this reason, public spaces can provide highly useful materials and perspectives for homeless studies.

These discussions on subaltern materials reveal this book's hopefully productive relations with contemporary geographers who reconceive the term *subaltern* through repositioning it around poststructuralist literatures. According to one such effort, subalternist geographers should avoid "normative deployments of the watchwords 'subaltern' and 'subalternity'" (Jazeel and Legg 2019, p. 13), in order to rigorously work through the questions previously asked, in rather "forthright" (p. 12) ways, about the subaltern's autonomy from the elite realms and power relations (p. 10). In a comparable vein, geographers on subaltern geopolitics are to refrain from propagating "binary geopolitical structure" (Sharp 2011, p. 271) because "the language of the 'Other' establishes a dichotomy that reinforces the centrality of the hegemonic ('Western') world" (Woon 2011, p. 286).

These recent debates regarding the term *subaltern* help us to consider how/where the subaltern's own spatial practice can(not) outgrow the delimited status that has been stressed in analytical terms by previous subalternist authors (such as Gayatri Spivak), namely, "the famous analytical definition of the subaltern as he or she who 'cannot speak'" (Legg 2016, p. 793). To continue using Stephen Legg's words, it may be possible to say that my subaltern materials can effectively explore "empirically subaltern spaces" (p. 802), which for Legg means the yet analytically unknown spaces of the subaltern's everyday practices, with particular attention being paid to homeless people and their material–semiotic everyday practices.

A difference in my approach, however, is that the subaltern materials in this book are constantly joined by my careful but dense mobilisation of Lefebvrian, Gramscian, Harveyan, or other Marxian notions that are intended to situate subaltern materials within the broader contexts of state rescaling, urban metabolism, urban regulation, and overall capitalist urbanisation. Taric Jazeel (2014, p. 89) is critical of "geography's materialist turn" because this turn "has been embraced at the expense of a thoroughgoing engagement with representation itself" (see also Jazeel and Legg 2019, p. 13). In light of these comments, this book's intensive use of Marxian concepts for interpreting the subalternity of homeless people would benefit from some accountable characterisation.

Central to this book is the belief that my conceptual engagements can reveal how homeless people's material–semiotic spaces differentiate the regulatory urban landscape and (metabolically mediated) class relations in reflexive ways. Homeless people's subaltern struggles are based on their constant decipherment ("monitoring") of how regulatory agencies (i.e., police officers, welfare providers, housed residents, pedestrians, and so on) can powerfully entangle, but *not* determine, their everyday practice at the margins of housed citizens. It is *within* these entangled (but not determined) conditions that homeless people (and their supporters) start reconstructing the everyday relative autonomies—which need to be clearly distinguished from "independence" (Jazeel and Legg 2019, p. 10)—that may turn pregiven urban spaces (including public spaces) into viable survival spaces of homeless people.

My subaltern materials can broadly cover these capillary forms of power, and the urban geographies in which these power forms are reflexively compromised in situ through homeless people/supporters' constant search for everyday autonomies from regulators and their defence of pregiven class relations. This relative autonomy (autogestion) search by homeless people and their supporters in the ambit of regulatory power, as well as the autogestion–regulation entanglements that accentuate the peripheries of normative urban settlement, can be conceptually delineated by using my Lefebvrian, Gramscian, Harveyan, or other Marxian vocabularies that are relativist in character. As such, my conceptual engagements can powerfully augment subaltern materials to delineate these intricate power relations and their differentiation/relativisation in cities, particularly within those Western/non-Western cities where the margins of habitat (i.e., the housing classes' public/private spaces) have become the intensive site of rescaling politics managing the locational (mini)crises of societalisation.

Conclusion

This book's three meso-abstract theoretical arguments, organised in Chapter 1 around the state rescaling concept, can be systematically specified for the Japanese context. Attempts at denser specification will take place in the chapters to come. This present chapter, however, has shown rather systematically how theory specifications (step 2) can modify the book's meso-level theory making about national states, public and private spaces, and urban social movements (step 1), in light of Japanese territorial histories and geographies.

The meso-abstract space of theorisation presented in Chapter 1 is a concisely constructed space. This "simplicity" is mostly necessary insofar as the logical flows and relations among the key concepts should be clearly shown as theoretical models for political economy approaches. In order to sustain these logical flows and relations, however, this chapter has shown that this book can advance step 2, theory specification, which dovetails the meso-abstract theory with the Japanese context. The original integrity of this book's theory can be reconstructed around the threads of "the Japanese developmental state" during this specification stage.

In this process, the ethnographer's ground-level ontology—his/her incommensurable experiencing of the urban lifeworld as it is—can facilitate the effective reshaping of pregiven Western concepts. Regulationist ethnography is about increasing this urban imaginary of the ethnographer, using it for conceptual reworking with/in the field, and reinterpreting both the local ethnographies and conceptual explanations by locating them in the territorial information of state space. Based on my long-term fieldwork, as well as various subaltern materials obtained from it, I am attempting to develop a set of robust urban narratives for this methodological venture.

Notes

1 Adopting this "systemic" understanding of chōnaikai (as a developmentalist case of urban societalisation) may enhance existing research relating to this topic as it can encompass the subaltern perspectives of extrahabitat people and geographies. This does not deny that chōnaikai has played vital roles for housed citizens and their welfare in Japan. This mainstream context has been well-documented by Japanese scholars from the perspective of local residents.
2 Antonio Gramsci famously conceptualised "state" in the broader sense of "integral state" that encompasses both political and social forces/processes. I am extending Gramsci's integral state conception by incorporating the middle ground between the political and social—i.e., the various state–society hybrids and networks that are characteristic of contemporary state space—and the question of how this middle ground nurtures emergent regulatory fields. This theoretical manoeuvre finds a basis in Bob Jessop's (2002) neo-Gramscian state theory in which he understands governance as a scaled mixture of political and social forces.
3 Carolyn Stevens (1997, p. 17) engaged in fieldwork in the Kotobuki district from 1992 to 1994. Her research focused on middle-class volunteers who arrived in the district from Yokohama's mainstream society and became active as service providers. Tom Gill (2001, p. 7) notes that his book uses a fieldwork experience in the Kotobuki district that spanned the years 1993 to 1995, with particular focus on the Kotobuki Day Labourers' Union, local labourers, and the local contexts that surrounded them.

Part Two
National States and Public and Private Spaces

Part Two

Chapter Three
Scales of Societalisation: Integral State and the Rescaling of Poverty

This chapter will elaborate the overall framework outlined in Chapters 1 and 2, with a particular emphasis on a state-centred approach. Intensive forms of globalisation have driven influential urbanists to enhance theoretical approaches that bypass state space when addressing urban policy (McCann and Ward 2011). These approaches are useful, but I argue that it is valuable to subscribe to the assertion that national states can still play key roles in updating and sustaining urban policy geographies through rescaling (Brenner 2004a; Peck 2001b).

To examine the possibility of state space for the study of urban policy, this chapter begins the construction of my major conceptual apparatus: the nationalised space of poverty regulation. After tracing historical arguments, I will show that regulationist strands can be revitalised by a careful theorisation of how a territorially constructed form of society can be sustained through the national state's maintenance of territorial institutional integrity and its restructuring. The concept of the NSPR is intended to reveal the ways in which each national state uniquely coordinates multiple institutions of poverty regulation so that urban poverty is managed into forms less inimical to the level of social cohesion that facilitates capitalist urbanisation and accumulation.

I then theorise that this national form of poverty regulation can meet with an acute rise of poverty that is unmanageable by inherited regulatory institutions and their territorial integrity on the national scale. This regulatory crisis qua poverty crisis increases the local and urban crises of societalisation. New urban dynamics of state rescaling set in when the poverty crisis calls for local assemblage of new regulatory agencies that can develop various forms of regulatory activity between

Rescaling Urban Poverty: Homelessness, State Restructuring and City Politics in Japan, First Edition. Mahito Hayashi.
© 2024 Royal Geographical Society (with the Institute of British Geographers). Published 2024 by John Wiley & Sons Ltd.

the two poles of the political and the social, coercion and consensus. The ground-up restructuring of the NSPR thus opens new regulatory spaces of poverty on the local scale, at the fringes of the citizenship, rights, and welfarist entities already organised on the national scale. In the early round of rescaling, national states are likely to remain bystanders to the haphazard, ground-up dynamics arising from cities. National states, however, can grow more tolerant of, and proactive with regard to, this ground-up process of rescaling by increasing their role as "scale manager" (Peck 2002, p. 357).

This theory of the NSPR and its rescaling is a meso-abstracted theory focusing on North American and Western European geographies. The theoretical exposition is that the new urban poverty grew especially in the 1970s and 1980s and that this rise of urban poverty touched off social crises that triggered regulatory experiments on multiple spatial scales. This initial increase in local regulatory dynamics in turn led to expanded forms of rescaling in relation to the national state's role as scale manager.

The chapter then tailors this meso-theoretical construction to Japan by aligning its unique contexts around the "developmental state". I argue that the Japanese state, because it emerged out of its developmentalist past, was willing and able to hold a considerable degree of power even during the rounds of rescaling (on the rescaling of the developmental state, see Park 2013; Sonn 2010). The result was a unique pattern of rescaling in which the meso-theoretical parameters were mediated by Japan's developmental historicity. The bottom-up impetus made significant impact on developmentalist urban policy (Tsukamoto 2012). Nonetheless, the Japanese state rehabilitated its historical dominance over local regulatory affairs and regained the national-scale focus from the denationalising impetus of rescaling.

Theory and Its "Deviants"

I have two objectives in interrogating gaps in the main writings on regulation theory. One objective is to examine "homeless regulation", a term that might sound odd to many regulationist thinkers. The other objective is to focus on Japan—whether and how regulation theory can help us understand Japan, because the theory emerged out of the Western experience of modern capitalism. By developing the theoretical and methodological apparatus of regulation theory, I situate these two tensions at the heart of the literature. This entails a major reworking of regulationist political economy, which will result in the expanded reconstruction of regulation theory to cover wider issues and geographical settings, beyond previous exclusive or exceptionalist treatments.

I initiate this discussion with the influential Parisian school of regulation theory as a guiding thread. If early Parisian writings favoured a more heuristic use of concepts for recollating historical records, later works have derived well-articulated analytical tool kits (Boyer 1990). In particular, Robert Boyer and Yves Saillard's (2002 [1995]) seminal volume presents a broad overview of the "mode of regulation", a domestic system of institutions and norms that can serve as a powerful mechanism of socioregulatory guidance capable of organising national economic activities into a relatively closed circuit of production and consumption. In this view, a mode of regulation comprises a monetary regime, a wage–labour nexus, a form of competition, state relations with the economy, and an insertion into the international regime. When successful, regulation on the basis of these five institutional mechanisms organises anarchic streams and multifarious sites of domestic economy into a national system of accumulation best described as an "accumulation regime".

Within this framework, homeless regulation would be best located under the rubric of the wage–labour nexus, which is the conceptual locus originally intended to accommodate various working-class interests. Yet deviation becomes clear immediately. While the Parisian concept of the wage–labour nexus presupposes a working class that is reproduced through waged labour and wage-based consumption, this regulatory scope of the wage–labour nexus is *already* exhausted in the case of homeless regulation, because such regulation typically comes into play when and where liveable wages disappear from society. Homeless people are those who are marginalised from waged labour.

Furthermore, when the wage–labour nexus seeks the first-order regulation of the working class and its consumptive life on behalf of capitalist consumption, production, and accumulation, the immediate target of homeless regulation changes. The main target becomes the reregulation of the redundant—i.e., extra–labour market and extracapital—population, in order to prevent the deregulating appearance of this "unsubsumed" population from embarrassing a dominant (wage-based) society. I call this "second-order" regulation, which should be distinguished from "first-order" regulation once achieved by national projects of societalisation under the welfare state.

A society that forms its cohesiveness around consumption norms—and, by extension, *social* wages capable of sustaining normative consumption—is understood to be a wider environment of sound capitalist regulation and the accumulation regime (Aglietta 1979 [1976]; Boyer 1990; Boyer and Saillard 2002 [1995]). The problem is that eminent scholars in regulationism little imagined actual societal strata in which the normative consumption can easily become unstable and even inconceivable; this situation, however, has occurred with the NUP, which is inimical to the integrity of urban consumptive society (see Chapter 4).

To be sure, Michel Aglietta (1979 [1976]) provided a rare suggestion that regulation theory has the potential to address spaces of *de*regulation where deteriorated conditions of "industrial slums" and "working-class housing" (p. 84) contravene normative consumption in the city. His own spatial-regulationist vision on normalised urban settings is that "the *standardized housing* ... is the privileged site of industrial consumption" (p. 159, original emphasis). Even in Aglietta's case, however, social cohesion and its normative character are too safely assumed: "The mode of social unification [is] engendered by the accumulation of capital" (p. 18).

Homeless regulation unravels this kind of safe assumption, and the concept of "societalisation" now looms as an appropriate term sensitive to *crises* (and by implication minicrises) of social cohesion. Homelessness decreases the probability of societalisation, which is a matter of ongoing process and chance discovery in contemporary capitalism, far from being a safe condition of accumulation. In this context, I define homeless regulation—rescaling reregulation—as a new regulatory movement towards the reconstruction of societalisation by narrating, seizing, subduing, and possibly filtering out the deregulating appearances of impoverished people on the national horizon. Furthermore, the concept of the state is perhaps not well fitted with the main theoretical apparatus of classical regulation theory. Although Aglietta (1979 [1976], p. 27) started his canonical volume with a call for state theory, the main thrust is discernibly to downsize the state into one among many institutional compromises (Aglietta 1979 [1976]; Boyer 1990, 2004; Boyer and Saillard 2002 [1995]; Boyer and Yamada 2000).

In my own theory, homeless regulation broadly traverses the full spectrum of the state qua the "integral state". For Antonio Gramsci, this term means a combination of the state (the political) and civil society (the social), to which this book would add the assemblages, instrumentations, and knowledge mobilities that can be found abundantly between these two poles. This "integral" conception of the state makes the present book state-centred without losing a grip on political and social sectors and their nuanced middle grounds, considering that these together can constitute a *relatively* unified state space on the national horizon (for regulationist reworkings of Gramsci's state theory, see Jessop 1990, 2002; Jessop and Sum 2006). This vision gives the book a useful perspective on multiscalar and multi-institutional processes in which the mosaics of regulation are generated but managed into a viable state form with the help of social, political, or hybrid leaderships. Localised forms of homeless regulation, while they place some unravelling pressure on this integral state space, also hasten efforts to reconstruct the state, quasistate, and nonstate spaces/milieus into a (slightly more) streamlined state form of "government + governance" (Jessop 2002, p. 239). In this way, the form (unity) of state space can be rehabilitated in a second-order fashion, even after rescaling dynamism sets in.[1]

Finally, Japan itself reveals oddities, as well as commonalities, within regulation theory. Scholars in the Parisian school have made prolific examinations of Japanese capitalism, seeking to show the theory's unproblematic applicability to Japan (Boyer and Yamada 2000). At the same time, the historicity of Japanese capitalism has prompted some regulationists in geography to seriously reappraise the theory's utility for interpreting the Japanese case (Peck and Miyamachi

1994). These critical reflections do not necessarily have to be taken as a negation of careful efforts to expand the theory's scope to Japan, which offers a lucrative laboratory for comparison and theoretical extension (Amin 1994, p. 23; Gottfried 2000; Jessop and Sum 2006, p. 69; Sayer 1989). I use Japan—its oddities and commonalities—as a productive space for rethinking regulation theory's parameters in "other" geographical contexts and settings. This particular chapter intends to show that some of the most classical premises of regulationism, in combination with more contemporary expositions, can apply in Japan, without diluting the theory's original cohesiveness.

Theoretical Framework

The Nationalised Space of Poverty Regulation

Bob Jessop and Ngai-Ling Sum (2006, p. 124) formulate "national mode of growth" as the "pattern of production and consumption of a national economy in the context of its role in the global division of labor". In this definition, national modes of growth—also referred to as growth patterns—describe the more abstract concept of the accumulation regime for each country (p. 42). In what follows, I will periodise Japanese history based on this territorial understanding of capitalism. Simplistic attempts at periodisation by using an accumulation regime might sound deterministic. However, careful treatments of national growth modes and their chronological succession have proven useful for recoding specific histories and geographies of regulation (see, for instance, Amin 1994; Brenner and Theodore 2002; Jessop et al. 1988; McDowell 1991; Peck and Tickell 1995).

Following in these footsteps, I use information about national growth patterns to generate period-specific analysis. This procedure is based on the following premises: First, a growth pattern of a given period sets some constraints on how well a certain national state can regulate poverty. Then, when a national growth pattern is undermined in an economic crisis, the regulatory space of poverty can be destabilised, which potentially leads to conventional and novel forms of poverty. Subsequently, the regulatory space of poverty is reorganised and restructured through trial-and-error processes and strategies.

I advance this method of theorisation further by using two central concepts: societalisation and the nationalised space of poverty regulation. The notion of societalisation in this book is based on the grander idea that the capital (value) circuit—a series of production, exchange, and consumption—needs viable social scaffolding to emerge around it. There, crisis tendencies of capital might be socially embedded and provisionally "fixed". This idea of societalisation, virtually speaking, is to push the right hand of this formula—an "accumulation regime + its mode of regulation" (Jessop 2002, p. 5)—far back to the social and semiotic outskirts of capital. In these outskirts, the sociorelational, normative, aesthetic, and epistemological frameworks remote from accumulation can remain relatively autonomous and can facilitate the self-reproduction and self-governance of the working class. Whether the regulationist formula of capitalism—an accumulation regime + its mode of regulation—can find such extended webs of society is a matter of chance discovery (for a use of this notion of chance discovery in geography, see Peck and Tickell 1995, p. 17).

However, the theory finds key sites and milieus wherein labourers/citizens can potentially enjoy relatively autonomous forms of societalisation. Jessop (2002, pp. 57–58) briefly explains several key milieus of societalisation: "an individual and/or social wage to satisfy their [workers'] needs from cradle to grave; growth in the consumption of standardized, mass commodities in nuclear family households and in the provision of standardized, collective goods and services by the bureaucratic state".

Jessop is enumerating wage relations, family, and state provision as the key scaffolding of societalisation. The first pillar, wage relations, is strongly affected by the commodified form of the wage–labour nexus. We would expect that societalisation based solely on wage relations would not be very autonomous from capital. The limited societalising capacity of wages is due to capital's sheer dominance over labour at the production point, which Marx vocally criticises: "He who was previously the money-owner now strides in front as a capitalist; the possessor of labour-power follows as his worker. The one smirks self-importantly and is intent on business; the other is timid and holds back, like someone who has brought his own hide to market and now nothing else to expect but—a tanning" (Marx 1976 [1867], p. 280).

Up to a point, even this business-dominated realm of wages, found at the heart of Marx's "accumulation for accumulation's sake, production for production's sake", can be compromised.[2] Wages in the postwar period took the socially renegotiated form of Fordist wages (Davis 1986; Jessop 2002, p. 57; Schmitter and Lehmbruch 1979). The relative autonomy of "social wages" kicked in and partially altered the capitalist logics of wage formation in favour of societalisation.

The second and third pillars of societalisation raised by Jessop are the production of the family and the provision of the state. These two can move more freely beyond the narrow parameters of "accumulation for accumulation's sake". Indeed, the autonomy of these spheres from capital has attracted much attention in comparative welfare state studies (Esping-Andersen 1990; Huber and Stephens 2001). All in all, wages, the family, and state provision can have some level of freedom from the bare bones of economic relations at the production point. Hence, multiple "societalising autonomies" open up, at the social outskirts of accumulation, new space of theorisation for regulationist thinkers.

I construct my own conception, the NSPR, around these arguments. The convergence of civil society on national territorial space was visited and theorised by Nicos Poulantzas (1978 [1978]) and Henri Lefebvre (2009b). By the same token, the spatial-scale selectivity of societalisation, its nationalising character, can be emphasised in the theory of societalisation. The point is that the margins of societalisation's "nationality" (its national-scale integrity) must be made legible, evened out, and reintegrated in the face of the destructive, disintegrating tendencies inherent in capitalism and capitalist urbanisation. For the working class, these tendencies appear as poverty, as a decline in living standards and consumption norms, and as resulting difficulties in the bodily (self-)reproduction of people, which gnaws at societalisation during moments of regulatory/accumulation crisis. For societies to survive this overdetermined formation of societal crisis, societalisation needs the preventive space of national-scale poverty regulation, which is a mechanism of crisis management that should be equipped for any territorial project of societalisation.

By distilling and remoulding the appearances of poverty, the NSPR can flatten the marginal, uneven zones of national society into patterns (more) suited to societalisation under capitalism. To invoke Michel Foucault (2003 [1997]), society must be defended. In my conception, it will be defended not just for the intrinsic, almost universal (that is, modern) nature of "bourgeois society" but also for its spatio-temporal societalisation, for the achievement of society's broad resonance with the accumulation regime, against and beyond the regime's destructive tendencies, which cyclically erode societalisation and its resonance with "accumulation for accumulation's sake". This statement avoids teleological, determinist, reductionist, or finalist assumptions, for it leaves to chance discovery, amid the repetitive experiences of the regulatory/accumulation crisis, the question of whether the filtering effects of the NSPR can really rehabilitate the *form* of the state—can really manage state, quasistate, or nonstate spaces/milieus into a (little more) streamlined pattern of "integral state".

It is possible to achieve this "defence" of society vis-à-vis poverty by constantly redeploying around the impoverished margins of civil society different logics and spaces of societalisation, to counter disrupting tendencies and thereby perpetually reestablish normalised civil society's extended coverage of impoverished people. This chapter has already noted that Jessop enumerates the three pillars of societalisation. Accordingly, the NSPR performs its role by reassembling these three pillars at the margins of national civil society.

To explain more clearly how these pillars can function, I invoke Karl Polanyi's historical analysis and derive from it the three spheres of public provision, labour market, and social fabric. Together, these three realms manage poverty for societalisation, though their individual processes and logics should be distinguished from one another. *Public provision* is the sphere of redistribution that provides directly for impoverished people who cannot obtain sufficient means of subsistence through the labour market or through social fabric (Polanyi 1957, pp. 50–51, 92, 232). *Labour market* is the sphere of exchange for impoverished people who earn wages in exchange for their labour, which subjects them to the price mechanism as a basis for selling labour as a commodity (pp. 46, 71–72, 81, 110, 142). And finally, *social fabric* is the sphere of reciprocity that, on the basis of mutual assistance, provides a means of subsistence to impoverished people who are embedded in families as well as local kinship and neighbourhood relations (pp. 48–51, 92, 136, 156; for the utility of Polanyi's notions for geographical political economy, see Peck 2013).

In the Fordist era, it seems that these spheres had relatively clear-cut gender implications (McDowell 1991). Public provision provided housing (Bratt, Hartman, and Meyerson 1986; Schwartz 2010) or it supported consumption in the household (Fraser 2003; Trattner 1999). Either way, Fordist public provision presumed and strengthened the domestic labour of women in the family. As for the family itself, feminist geographers in the 1970s demonstrated that capitalism and its urban form re-create the family, and social fabric in general, into a highly gendered domain in which women's domesticity is increased and naturalised (Burnett 1973; Hayford 1974). Feminists also sparked incisive arguments about how the labour market accompanied the gendered geographies of wage work (Hanson and Pratt 1995). Various authors noted that these regulatory areas could not be understood separately, as they were structured into a relative coherent form of mutuality in history (Hanson and Pratt 1988; MacKenzie and Rose 1983). All these arguments suggest that a historical consolidation of the NSPR was based on the gender articulations of societalisation, which gathered the different spheres of the NSPR into a territorial fixity of gender selectivities (Jessop 2004).

Crises of the Nationalised Space of Poverty Regulation

While the orthodox literature on welfare states understates the peculiar roles and processes of poverty regulation that appear in relation to acute poverty, my conception of the NSPR registers these roles and processes and how they are deployed at the *margins* of normalised society. At these margins of mainstream society, the vigilance of welfare states over national populations can be exhausted. As a result, a dynamic of regulation becomes central to the interpretation of the NSPR, while welfare state studies might be able to remain more stable even when the "transition" of welfare states is discussed (Esping-Andersen 1996).

By and large, my own view of the NSPR is based on the regulatory failure that the NSPR has incurred. This failure, which is failure in societalisation, occurs more frequently in the margins than in the centre of a so-called welfare state. At these margins, impoverished people's subsumption into the capital (value) circuit can be extremely unstable, and the failure of societalisation repeatedly spawns the impoverished "deviants" as the outsiders of hegemonic social relations (such as the urban relations among the housing classes). In history, the societalisation capacity of the NSPR typically precipitated this crisis situation—and crisis-induced restructuring—after the watershed moments that developed in the mid-1960s and the 1970s (for precrisis and crisis phases of Fordism, see Aglietta 1979 [1976]; Lipietz 1994).

My theory locates the NUP at the heart of this crisis formation in societalisation. Sociologists use the notion of the NUP when they address the rise of mass homelessness and massive ghettoisation during, and more typically after, the mid-1960s to 1970s. The new forms of impoverishment are said to have been cultivated by a deterioration in wages, social ties, and public welfare provision (Mingione 1996; Wacquant 2008; Wilson 1997). I understand this growth of the NUP as a form of regulatory (mini)crisis in the NSPR that disrupts and encumbers societalisation. To the degree that the Keynesian consensus of the welfare state has declined (Esping-Andersen 1996), societies experienced the rise of the NUP as a failure of societalisation. This decline in the postwar social form also meant that the social rights of citizenship—what Marshall (1964, p. 103) classically called "an absolute right to a certain standard of civilization", and which actually had been institutionalised as a national regime of the welfare state in different Western countries (Pierson 2006)—partially lost their institutional capacity as a social contract.

Karl Polanyi (1957) helps us to understand this period of regulatory failure and how it leads to evolution. First, the regulatory space of poverty fails and creates regulatory crises in a cyclical fashion. The labour market fails when the "trade cycle fail[s] to ... restore employment" (pp. 215–216). But even when a boom revitalises urban labour markets (p. 97), social fabrics fail because they tend to become ineffective or dislocated, or may even be destroyed (p. 136). Public provision fails not only when it is ineffective in itself (p. 83) but also when the "scope of any policy of relief or public works will be limited by the requirements of budgetary equilibrium" (p. 219), that is, by fiscal crisis.

Second, the regulatory space of poverty evolves through crises. On the one hand, it evolves through spontaneous attempts to resolve the crises, undertaken by social groups such as trade unions, communities, villages, landowners, or industrialists (pp. 162, 184, 194, 213). On the other hand, it evolves through the legislative practices of the state, whose "intervention [is] necessarily aimed at reducing the flexibility of wages and the mobility of labour, giving stability to incomes" (p. 225; see also p. 223). According to Polanyi, the three spheres of poverty regulation—public provision, the labour market, and the social fabric—cyclically face crisis, and in times of crisis they both evolve spontaneously and are changed deliberately by various economic, political, and social actors. This Polanyian interpretation allows us to analyse the NSPR specifically from the angle of two temporalities: crisis and evolution.

Even during periods of regulatory crisis, the NSPR does not abandon the national scale as an arena for poverty regulation. The essence of poverty regulation is supplied by the mystic character of the nation, in which various vested, competing interests can possibly turn into a legible, transparent, *almost* harmonious society (Poulantzas 1973 [1968]). In large measure, this argument corresponds with that of some contemporary geographers who assert that national states—and their nationally constructed state space—can resist erosion even during the most intensive phases of globalisation (Brenner 2004a; Peck 2002). My conception of the NSPR emphasises that this process animates national restructuring efforts, especially at the points where mainstream society is frustrated by the NUP—by its new (deregulating) form of poverty against societalisation. It is at these actual meeting points, between spaces of societalisation (the housing classes) and spaces of desocietalisation (the NUP), where the demand for more flexible use of the citizenship criteria vis-à-vis impoverished people is experimented with, encouraged, and endorsed. On the national scale, up to a point, the NSPR internalises new techniques for body politics that rework and downplay the classical distinctions between consensus and coercion, between the social and the political, in search of actually functional forms of poverty regulation.

Rescaling

On the other hand, damage done to the NSPR can widen, deepen, and recur. The loss of control over impoverished people can lead not just to the internal restructuring of the NSPR but also to new spatial strategies for the production of scale. Here a drive towards rescaling reregulation kicks in, which opens localised spaces of poverty regulation at the margins of the NSPR. When regulatory failure is repeated at the margins of the NSPR, these marginal areas become a focal site of multiscalar restructuring, rescaling, and new regulatory spaces. First-order regulation espoused by the NSPR dwindles, and the goal to societalise impoverished and deprived people fades on the national horizon. Increasingly, then, the goal is about second-order regulation, about filtering out the impoverished "deviants" from the NSPR, depriving these frustrating individuals/groups of rights and citizenship, and keeping this institutionally created "dangerous class" in politically, socially, and culturally docile forms both locally and in cities.

This method of poverty regulation may not be well understood merely as exclusion from the mainstream sociopolitical spheres, or as "social exclusion" (although I agree with the importance of emphasising the perspective). Rather, the desocietalising poor—themselves an institutional creation—create dialectical tensions with the societalised "us", and these tensions are reregulated, *in process* and *in probability*, through the production/relativisation of scale (for processual reflection on rescaling, see Brenner 2019). The NSPR is thus associated with locally instrumentalised "shock absorbers" that may (not) contain the desocietalising impacts of "them" within the local scale and within urban milieus, without critically damaging the NSPR. The "autonomisation" of local processes, agents, and responsibilities are the crucial aspects of this politics of scale.

This rescaling production of new regulatory spaces typically is spearheaded by the unorganised ground-up eruption of local reregulating process. Eruptive episodes of local reaction lead to the bottom-up form of reregulation, which tries to assemble almost any regulatory resources in the locality.

The point is that the NUP looks "dangerous" to societalisation, to the society-integrating logics of public provision, the labour market, and the social fabric. Society must be defended, it is true, but in this context it will be defended only in substandard ways in which regulators tendentiously curtail rights and citizenship benefits that are accepted as standard in civil society. These standards may still be emphatically mobilised for the "core" members of a societalised society, less so for the outsiders of societalisation.

New regulatory spaces thus can start with coercive and punitive measures on the local scale, forming something akin to the "workhouse regime" (Peck 2001a, p. 46) of the nineteenth century, an old model that achieved the regulation of impoverishment by means of coercion, intimidation, and closure. However, as Peck's workfare theory implies, the new dynamics of rescaling also can cultivate the vast uncultivated area between coercion and consensus. Almost everywhere, new types of poverty regulation can emerge, and proliferate, by traversing and cross-fertilising the spaces of coercion and consensus, disagreement and agreement, eviction and acceptance.

Sooner or later, however, the "creativity" of these haphazard eruptions—the anarchic, episodic, localised form of rescaling against the NUP—comes to threaten the legal integrity of state space and the more institutional form of regulation. The unity of state space can be sustained, in theory, even under rescaling (on the unity of the state, see Jessop 1982, pp. 123–124, 1990, pp. 8, 268). By and large, regulators come up with new written and unwritten codes of regulatory behaviour. These codes and rules, against the backdrop of the rule of law, can possibly streamline, justify, and discursively rephrase—"trope on"—the fragmentation and informalisation of territorial poverty regulation that is constantly facilitated by the ground-up eruption of new regulatory spaces. States, especially national states, can have significant coordinating power to make new regulatory spaces legally rational and institutionally cohesive.

Based on these fundamental arguments, I conceptualise the dynamics of rescaling as having three theoretical phases: the *ground-up* round, the *picking-off* round, and the *unfolding* round (Figure 3.1). The ground-up round of rescaling starts with the emergence of the NUP and its related societalisation "failure", which opens new governance fields and regulatory spaces at the local scale. Already in this round, systemic "logics" of NUP regulation can be detected. For one thing, the three spheres of the NSPR—the national form of poverty regulation—have been eroding societalisation power and loosening its grip on impoverished populations, pushing them towards the margins of the NSPR. For another, on subnational scales, the ground-up emergence of the NUP and the national background of deregulation spawn new devolutionary politics. In this round, social movement actors may be able to intervene in local regulatory crises and change the local trajectories of NUP regulation on behalf of impoverished people. This social movement intervention can form collaborations with, not just oppositions to, local authorities. For such collaborations

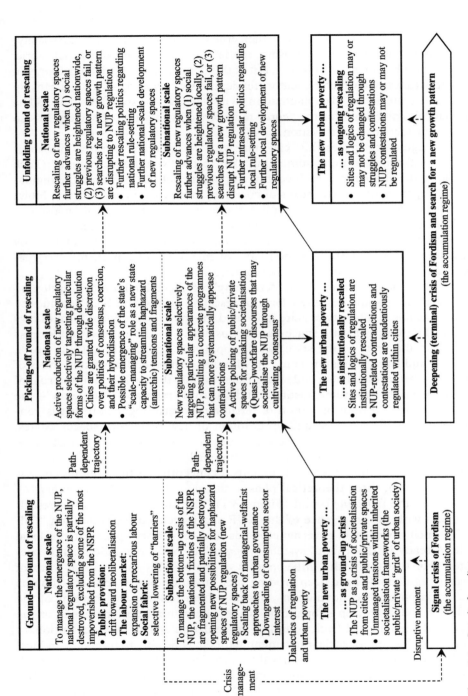

Figure 3.1 Rounds of rescaling.

to happen, however, social movements must nurture the reliable (and compassionate) attitudes of social workers, municipal staff, and policymakers from the initial episodes of contestation.

After the moment of rampant ground-up politics, the picking-off round can start, with a major decrease in the national state's vigilance over the NUP. Regulators can respond to this situation by designing policy programmes more consciously and "rationally", especially by denoting who is "dangerous" and who is less so, and by assigning different means/logics of regulation to different categories and subcategories of the NUP. While local agencies can advance this picking-off process, this round enables national states to acquire a new state capacity—the role of "scale manager" (Peck 2002, p. 357)—to construct the fragmentary patterns of state, quasistate, and nonstate spaces into a (slightly more) streamlined state form of "government + governance" (Jessop 2002, p. 239). Through this, (quasi-)workfare discourses can emerge and manage impoverished people's tacit agreement—or, rather, lack of disagreement—with societalisation, though this often entails allowing them smaller, substandard resources from public provision, the labour market, and the family.

During this round, social movements can experience fragmentation, as they face the same picking-off pressure as the NUP. The "radical" can be divided from the "progressive", and the former can be picked off from the rescaled arenas of poverty governance. Even so, viable radical–progressive coalitions can defend the diversity, versatility, and political vitality of activism against this multiscalar restructuring pressure towards "postpolitical" urban governance (for the latter, see Swyngedouw 2009; see also Chapter 9).

The unfolding round of rescaling emphasises the malleable character of rescaling that can still emerge even during the mature stages of decentralisation. In fact, the previous rounds of rescaling bring some powerful regulatory fixities to the local governance fields, which could in turn ensnare the initiatives of policymakers, social movements, and impoverished people. However, the tendency is for the mature forms of NUP regulation to continue redefining the codes of behaviour and ethics in the local governance fields—with regard to regulating actors, activists/volunteers, and impoverished people. In this context, the rescaled form of NUP regulation can at any time present opportunity for change. During the unfolding round of rescaling, such opportunity may emerge in the interplay of several key contexts: propoor and prohomeless struggles that can attract new audiences on different or even multiple spatial scales; loose regulatory rules or norms that can "postpone" strict forms of societalisation; and the restructuring of the accumulation regime (a growth pattern) that can illuminate the limits of societalisation in a given form.

Figure 3.1 stresses that the accumulation regime can be seen as an underlying context. The accumulation regime (forming a growth pattern) can create repercussions in historical rescaling regulation. For this reason, a historical analysis (periodisation) of the NSPR and its rescaling can be based on the historical rhythms of the accumulation regime (while allowing for other ways of periodising, of course). Accumulation crisis and evolution do not "determine" regulatory crisis and evolution—that is, rescaling strategies addressing NUP-driven desocietalisation show their own tempos and spatialities. Nonetheless, the NSPR and its rescaling can be well understood and periodised from the angle of the accumulation regime because societalisation is a territorialised pattern of the wider social conditions of the accumulation regime, which must receive wealth streams from the economic vitality of the same regime (via public provision, the labour market, and the social fabric).

Comparisons to Brenner's Meso Model

In Neil Brenner's meso-level theory, the rounds of state rescaling can share a specific sequence, which emphasises the territorial locus of capital accumulation and its crisis tendencies as the powerful driver of rescaling. First, there is a wave of initial crisis management that is geographically attuned to overcome a system-wide crisis through a reterritorialisation of capital within and beyond national borders (Brenner 1998; 2004a, pp. 36–47, 54–65). This crisis—often described as a crisis of Fordism—can be understood as having already started developing early forms and signals by the mid-1960s (Aglietta 1979 [1976]; Lipietz 1994).

Second, in this context, the devolution of regulatory tasks to localities produces a new, multiscalar, state-institutional "mosaic" within territorial borders, which departs radically from the territorial regulation of Fordist capitalism—the strategy of "homogenizing" (Brenner 1998, p. 476; see also Brenner 2004a, pp. 42, 121, 136, 160, 258)—that once targeted "national territorial equalization and sociospatial redistribution" (2004a, p. 3).

Third, this devolutionary politics does not diminish the centrality of national state institutions; rather, it often presupposes, and is presupposed by, national states as the "major locus" (p. 30) of political economy.

Fourth, the previous rounds of rescaling often result in regulatory failures and fissures, which prompt further rounds of rescaling to alleviate these fissures or postpone the effects, providing new thrust through rescaling dynamics with diverse path-dependent and uneven geographies (pp. 110, 115, 118, 295). Through this sequence, rounds of scale politics produce a "multilayered territorial mosaic in which political geographies established at different moments of historical time are tightly interwoven" (Brenner 2004b, p. 455).

In relation to this meso-level theorisation provided by Brenner, my own modelling would add that the effects of rescaling come down to the full parameters of integral state formation in the current era. Both political and social power, as well as their mobile networks and hybrid forms, are rescaled into urban regimes, in which the NUP—as a genre of regulation—is relocated and more or less "fixed" at the margins and outside of national standards and responsibilities. What the rise of urban poverty (the NUP) brings about is sociocultural crisis and "moral panic" (Peck 2001a, p. 40), in addition to the constant pressure for state space realignments and metabolic circuit reconstruction (the latter is discussed in Chapters 4 and 5).

To reregulate the recalcitrant section(s) among poor people, political power must be ever more coeval with social power in urban governance, where "government + governance" (Jessop 2002, p. 239) is rescaled into urban regimes at the end point of national societalisation under the NSPR. This may explain the "defensive" reformation of neighbourhoods against impoverished people, which accelerates antihomeless "NIMBYism" (DeVerteuil 2013; Takahashi 1997; Wagner 1993). It also supports the view that volunteers and nongovernmental organisations in civil society, for various reasons, can be mobilised to combat impoverishment during the rollout phase of neoliberalism (Peck and Tickell 2002), allowing homeless-supporting actors to reorient the rollout process towards nondisctructive trajectories at a local scale (Cloke, May, and Johnsen 2010; see also Chapters 6, 7, and 8) and a national scale (Chapter 9).

Mobilising the Theory for Japan

I have theorised the NSPR and the ways that it is rescaled under NUP-driven crisis. The question remains: How can we apply this theory to Japan? One way is to blur the meso character of theory and straightforwardly dovetail it with the Japanese case. In this case, the theorist is assuming that the meso theorisation rooted in Euro-American contexts can immediately gain an international scope beyond the theory's birthplace. As Chapters 1 and 2 have explicated, however, this book eschews this universalising mode of abstraction. One runs the risk of diluting the international scope of critical state theory and regulation theory if one applies them to Japan uncritically. One needs good theory specification in order to unleash the meso theory's potential for this non-Western formation of the integral state.

To advance this specification, this book will evoke debates associated with the Japanese "developmental state" (Johnson 1982). Especially germane to my argument has been the view that the Japanese state vigorously intervened in civil society and promoted well-disciplined and harmonious processes of late industrialisation (see also Woo-Cumings 1999). I have, however, emphasised that this explanation can methodologically define the "developmental state" as separate from Western states—from the "regulatory state", to invoke Johnson's (1982, pp. 10, 114, 306) notion. Though this book is informed by this literature on Japan, it uses the developmental state context to specify the meso theory of the NSPR and its rescaling. In this procedure, Japan's developmental state space is used as a site for reworking the theoretical state space I have already discussed by using Euro-American literatures, not as a space separated from Euro-American patterns. This is what I understand as the *non*separatist use of the developmental state concept. This nonseparatist use contrasts with the dichotomising understanding that is inherent among mainstream authors on developmental states (Hayashi 2021). It also boils down to some key revisions of regulation theory to suit the Japanese context.

First, the theory presupposes that Atlantic Fordism hinged on a sound national connection between mass production and mass consumption. Japan, however, found less buoyancy in the mass consumption of the working class and more strength in industrial investments driven by the state and state-related firms. This character of the accumulation regime, originally appearing during the 1950s, further evolved around the turbulent years of the 1970s and successfully delayed the accumulation (growth pattern) crisis to the 1990s. After the early 1990s, though, the Japanese accumulation regime started to face serious problems of malfunctioning policy, profit squeeze, and a loss of leading sectors.

Second, due to the curtailed material inputs from the catching-up economy, Japan's NSPR remained weak in terms of state provision. This resulted in Japan's heavy reliance on the other pillars of the NSPR, the labour market, and the social fabric. Until the 1980s, this strategy succeeded, and it contributed to Japan's high social cohesion and vigilance over poverty deregulation, due to the labour-absorbing capacity of the labour market and the cultural integrity of the social fabric. However, the NSPR met with major disruption in the 1990s, which led to a decline in the NSPR and poverty deregulation.

Third, the decline of the NSPR in the 1990s grew "homelessness without ghettoisation" as the Japanese version of the NUP. Before the 1990s, cities maintained a homogeneous, well-regulated form of urban society by segregating (nearly) homeless labourers in inner-city areas. During the 1990s, homelessness not only grew but also spread into "normal" public spaces, thereby unravelling the inherited pattern of ghettoisation as a barricade of societalisation.

Fourth, the rise of the NUP triggered bottom-up eruptions of new regulatory spaces, which played up the autonomous power of localised agents. In line with the theory's presupposition, Japan's rescaling of new regulatory spaces mobilised both state and social sectors on the local scale. However, this early round of rescaling in Japan—which utilised vast local actors and their "spontaneity" for grassroots rescaling, as this chapter's theory anticipates—was soon followed by very strong interventions by the Japanese state to streamline, recode, justify, and "trope on" the fragmentation and informalisation of territorial poverty regulation that is constantly facilitated by ground-up rescaling episodes. This leads us to revise the theoretical role of "scale manager" (Peck 2002, p. 357) for Japan. Having inherited from its developmentalist history the strong centrality of the national state and scale, seemingly, the Japanese state became a far stronger scale-managing agency than the theory anticipates. The relatively small number of homeless people in Japan thus prompted the national state to implement a powerful rescaling initiative in the early 2000s.

Fifth, the number of homeless women is relatively small in Japan—for example, in the year 2003, when public homelessness was at a peak, according to national records, only 3% of homeless individuals were women (MHLW 2003; on female homelessness in Japan, see Maruyama 2013; Moon 2006). This very minor presence of homeless women in public spaces might be understood in relation to the gender construction of the NSPR. A reasonable explanation would be that the realms of the NSPR prioritise the prevention of female homelessness over the prevention of male homelessness. Similar gender biases are reported elsewhere (Watson 1986), but I suggest that the gender pattern in homelessness prevention became significant in Japan and resisted obsolescence (Iwata 2005; Kawahara 2005) when its NSPR formed functional linkages (structured coherence) with the developmental state.[3]

All in all, the theory outlined here indicates robust linkages between the meso theory of Euro-American regulationism and the specific nature of Japanese statism. This reworking innovatively puts the developmental state literature in the ambit of regulation theory while also expanding the theory's international scope, with some methodological caveats (Brenner 2004a; Jessop 2002; Peck and Miyamachi 1994). Even so, the retreat of more conventional regulationist scholars from state theory has subdued this method of elaboration. Key scholars in the Parisian school, for instance, when working on Japan, claim that the developmental state context can only be detrimental, because regulation theory should achieve "a shift from active State policies" (Boyer and Yamada 2000, p. 3) towards the overlapping of *various* institutional compromises. I glean much from these Parisian arguments about Japanese capitalism, yet I would argue that a more state-centred approach is warranted.

The next section interprets the historical development of the NSPR in postwar Japan by dividing the history into five periods: the high-growth period (c. 1950s–1972); the 1970s world crisis and its aftermath (c. 1973–1985); the bubble economy (c. 1986–1991); the postbubble crisis and its aftermath (c. 1992–2007); and the world financial crisis, mass disasters, and their aftermath (c. 2008–2010s). For each period, I assess how the national growth pattern was organised, how it led to a period-specific formation of the NSPR, and how this national field of poverty regulation underwent crisis and crisis-driven evolution. I also examine the spatialisation of urban poverty in each period with reference to the period-specific societalising capacities of the NSPR.

Nationalised Space of Poverty Regulation in Japan

High Growth, c. 1950s–1972

Some Parisian regulationists declare that Japan's accumulation regime followed a profit-investment-led pattern in the period from the 1950s to 1972 (Boyer and Yamada 2000). While Atlantic Fordism formed growth patterns on a strong macroeconomic circuit of mass production and mass consumption, this relationship was weaker in Japan. Domestic demand came less from the buying power of the working class and more from the profit-inducing investments of capital in industrial, transportation, commercial, and energy/electric infrastructures. The national state fostered this growth pattern by deploying an industrial policy that engineered national markets, production processes, and economic agents along with statist planning (Johnson 1982). This nurtured strategic industries and businesses that attained high gross domestic product growth and profitability, yet it did not include a high-wage policy (Itoh 1990), a key economic input to societalisation in the case of Fordism (Aglietta 1979 [1976]; Boyer 1990, 2004).

This mechanism was feeble. After the war, Japan suppressed wages and allocated its finite wealth to industrial reconstruction at the cost of the population's quality of life. If the developmental state literature tends to overemphasise the harmonising power of the state—its putative capacity to "speak for the national interest" (Johnson 1982, p. 38)—my account of the NSPR should avoid a somewhat *ex post facto* nuance inherent in this explanation. How did the early formation of the Japanese NSPR manage the crisis tendency of poverty that could detract from national-scale societalisation?

Public provision is said to have been weak in postwar Japan; the primacy of industrial development sacrificed welfare policy and minimised public provision (Kwon 2005). This argument, however, demands qualification up to a point, because the *legal* framework was extremely egalitarian, and this apparent egalitarianism created great gaps between law and reality. The constitution of 1947 firmly constructed social rights as "rights to livelihood" by declaring, "All people shall have the right to maintain the minimum standards of wholesome and cultured living" (article 25). The Public Assistance Act of 1950 strengthened the national programmes of public assistance, saying, "The minimum standard of living guaranteed by this Act shall be where a person is able to maintain a wholesome and cultured standard of living" (article 3), referring to the special needs of unhoused people (article 38) and of those who are in emergency situations (article 7).

As early as the 1950s, then, this egalitarian framework decreed that all needy people are entitled to nationalised living standards. In fact, this framework was limited internally by the laws themselves and externally by the judicial and administrative sectors. Consequently, the rollouts of public assistance were minimised, despite the benevolent clauses. First, the Public Assistance Act of 1950 *also* determined that the provision of the national programme is restricted to those who have already been assisted by various legal, institutional, familial, and individual means of support other than this programme (article 4). This idea, called the "capturing" (*hosokusē*) principle of the act, was vaguely written and nurtured a wide range of interpretations and implementations across municipal welfare offices, the actual provider of public assistance, especially for such groups as homeless people, but it generally played a preventive role in deterring new applicants.

Second, court cases powerfully constrained public assistance. In the famous case of *Asahi v. Bō* (1967), the Supreme Court established that the clauses of livelihood rights in the constitution created a mere "best-effort" target—not an immediate goal—for the Japanese state.[4] Third, the welfare office often declined applications when the requests came from households considered to be "morally inferior" or "unworthy". In the developmentalist context, the "unworthy" categories multiplied and became surprisingly broad in Japan.

The labour market and wage formation—as means of poverty regulation and societalisation—were comparatively weak in the early part of this period, a harbinger of Japan's developmentalist economy, and denied even "liveable wages". However, even though it did not really include a Fordist type of high-wage policy, the Japanese labour market subsequently absorbed the national workforce, evolving into a leading sphere of the Japanese NSPR. The profit-investment-led pattern of economic growth undoubtedly subdued wage levels; Japan rarely saw a rate of wage growth that was indexed to productivity growth (Boyer and Yamada 2000; Itoh 1990), the hallmark of Fordism (Aglietta 1979 [1976]; Boyer 1990, 2004). This lack, along with weak public provision, diminished the spending power of the working class. Hence, the problems of hunger, unemployment, and eventually job insecurity soared and repeatedly fuelled labour radicalism (Dower 1999; Gordon 1985; Hayashi 2021; Moore 1983; on Japan's "working poor" problem in this period, see Eguchi 1979; 1980a, 1980b).

Towards the late 1960s and early 1970s, however, the labour market elevated the power of social regulation. First, the labour-absorbing capacity of the labour market was high and sustained low unemployment rates (Nakamura 1993). Second, new labour-control techniques quashed radical unionism (Clump 2003), strengthened manageable forms of employment unionism (Gottfried 2013), and threatened workers' political autonomies during Japan's state-led process of deskilling/reskilling (Hayashi 2021). Third, labour market segmentation by corporation, by firm size, and by employment status—known as companyist, dualist, or tripartite construction of the Japanese labour market (Ando and Ishikawa 1980; Boyer and Yamada 2000; Sumiya 1964)—mitigated the solidarity of labourers and depoliticised the working poor.

Social fabric—the concept I have adopted from Polanyi to identify community and the family as a poverty-regulating realm—provided impoverished people with only fragile resources and were overburdened. Yet, owing to the strength of the labour market, the social fabric avoided crisis. The rural social fabric was overwhelmed by migration from areas previously colonised by Japan, extended war zones, and ruined metropolises; villages simply had too many people to feed (Kase 1997). After the mid-1950s, tensions in the rural social fabric were quickly reduced by the outmigration of workers to cities, though this then created tensions in the urban social fabric.

For newly migrated urban workers, forming a family was often difficult, and even for workers who managed it, the family was often relatively weak as a poverty regulator because the extended web of relatives and kinship ties was usually excluded in this accelerated model of family formation (Kamata 1999) and because family dislocation was frequent, especially among relatively poor workers (Kamata and Kamata 1983). Within the family, great tension was felt by females, who absorbed the contradictory position of male breadwinners in the labour market by supporting their reproductive life under the patriarchal household system (Kato and Steven 1993).

In terms of community, postwar state policy endorsed the rebuilding of Japan's traditional community form—chōnaikai—and made it into the spontaneously formed yet administration-oriented arena of local neighbourhoods run on a "democratic" basis (Akimoto 1971; Pekkanen 2006; Tamano 1993; Yoshihara 1989). State policy keenly encouraged social relations among city dwellers through this intrinsically hybrid community form (for more resident-centred analyses of chōnaikai, see Iwasaki et al. 1989). It functioned not just as a material regulator of poverty but also as a cultural stabiliser of social fragmentation around the political/social/hybrid leaderships of developmentalism. Through this device, the state was able to exercise great vigilance over (de)societalisation at the local scale.

While the NSPR was thus being established, conspicuous forms of urban poverty were being spatialised in a distinctive postwar pattern. In the early 1950s, absolute poverty was rampant in Japanese cities, taking the forms of homelessness and slum communities (Imagawa 1987). However, this spatialisation of urban poverty, which was deeply impacted by World War II, was gradually replaced by a postwar spatialisation with particular characteristics and processes. First, poverty began to be regulated by the urban labour market, a process that initially animated and then tamed the labour movement (Hayashi 2021; Sumiya 1964).

Second, absolute forms of poverty were geographically relegated to relatively small districts in metropolises—namely, yoseba zones—which were highly integral to Japan's developmentalist accumulation. There, marginalised strata of the male workforce were geographically pooled, economically reproduced, and politically contained (Eguchi, Nishioka, and Kato 1979; Nishizawa 1995; Yamaoka 1996). When Japanese development largely closed off new workforce inputs from overseas, the male workers in yoseba zones became a functional equivalent to the migrant workers of Fordist countries. Yoseba zones were institutionalised by means of policing (Imagawa 1987; Yamaoka 1996), social discrimination (Aoki 1989), and ideological urban planning (Nishizawa 1995), and it was also through these processes that homelessness started to grow in these areas (Eguchi, Nishioka, and Kato 1979). Internally, yoseba zones formed social worlds that absorbed newcomers around distinct cultural identities (Nishizawa 1995). Externally, mainstream citizens discriminated against these zones, disdaining the seemingly "unproductive" lifestyle of day labourers (Aoki 1989).

Third, Japan's postwar spatialisation of urban poverty emerged, concentrating acute forms of poverty (and their desocietalising moment) within and around yoseba zones. This in turn sustained more homogeneous city space outside of these zones, for urban societalisation based on the housing classes, whose consumptive lives and cultural interests increasingly animated Japan's urban society formation in public spaces and urban built environments.

1970s World Crisis and Its Aftermath, c. 1973–1985

Japan's developmentalist accumulation encountered serious problems after the early 1970s. This situation occurred in the context of an international crisis, which can be understood as a "system-wide crisis of profitability" (Arrighi 2007, p. 154–155). However, Japan experienced the crisis in a different way than did Fordist regimes. The initial oil embargo crisis hit Japan severely, but the Japanese economy quickly recovered, which surprised political economists in the West and drove some major reinterpretations of Marxist crisis theory (Arrighi 1994; R. Brenner 2002; Itoh 1990). This swift rehabilitation of profitability was due to Japan's new (and temporary) introduction of Keynesian deficit spending, the country's labour productivity growth, and its specific mode of insertion into the global economy, which facilitated exports (Itoh 1990, p. 170; Takeda 2008, p. 225). Through these adaptations in the face of the international context, Japan updated its developmentalist growth pattern to the export-led model. Though domestic demand was still important, the new driver of growth came from exports. This export-led growth underscored Japanese competitiveness in global markets (Uemura 2000, p. 139), more than ever treated labour as a cost rather than as a demand (Itoh 1990, pp. 192–198), and exploited peripheral workers to a greater extent (Kato and Steven 1993).

Chalmers Johnson (1982, pp. 297–298, 302–303) finds no serious threats to Japanese statecraft during this experience of the 1970s crisis and the resulting "extroverted" shift of the economy. However, the experience *did* pose serious threats to the NSPR as an apparatus of national-scale societalisation. For instance, public provision was reconfigured in a way that further excluded the working class from redistribution channels. This was accomplished through a series of trial-and-error processes, which finally downsized this already meagre sphere in Japan's NSPR through partial (and early) adoption of neoliberal principles.

In the early and mid-1970s, public provision expanded to moderate the crisis experience of labourers and households. As the labour market in this period decreased its labour-absorbing ability, the Japanese state enacted short-term measures to deflect this labour market problem (Shinkawa 2005, p. 293). However, public provision quickly shifted from this path and started on the process of neoliberalisation, reflecting the business class's bids to reduce the national "wage cost" for exports (Estevez-Abe 2008, p. 161; Shinkawa 2005, pp. 153, 292–295). Conservative intellectuals and businessmen began calling for the reduction of public budgets (Rinji Gyose Chosakai 1981). Around 1980, the government created a new framework of public provision (*fukushi minaoshi*), tinged with an early neoliberal tendency (Itoh 2000, p. 95; Shinkawa 2005, pp. 97, 152–153). As a result, at the dawn of the 1980s, public provision became compatible with the creed of the export-led growth pattern. Reducing the cost of labour reproduction was seen as an appropriate means of enhancing Japanese competitiveness during the international crisis of corporate profitability.

The labour market initially deteriorated during this period. The business community reduced labour costs by threatening the working class with sophisticated means of workforce management, such as systematic deskilling and pro-business unionisation (Yamamoto 1977), in addition to more classical tools of dismissals and policing (Clump 2003; Hayashi 2021). The rate of real-wage growth plummeted to 6.2% (in 1973), and even to 0.6% (in 1974), after reaching the height of 10.5% (in 1972).[5] This quick drop caused a reduction in households' buying power and the escalation of the "working poor" problem (Eguchi 1979, 1980a, 1980b), yet it did not unravel the societalisation power of the labour market. Most importantly, unemployment did not balloon; the rate of unemployment hovered around 2%. What emerged was a new type of business–labour compromise—or, rather, eager assertions of such a compromise by business and state sectors—in which businesses could purportedly provide secure employment if labourers stopped demanding high wages (Hasegawa 1981; Hyodo 1978; Nikkeiren 1971; Shimoyama 1982).

The state briefly embarked on Keynesian public works production (Ibori 2001, p. 53) and tried to revitalise the economy by reinserting the country into global markets, which increased the total number of jobs available in Japan while causing a significant reduction in wage growth (Hayashi 2021; Itoh 1990, p. 170). These processes in the labour market increased irregular employment (Itoh 2000, p. 67), dualism (Shinkawa 2005, p. 204), and neo-Taylorism (Isogai, Ebizuka, and Uemura 2000, p. 39). Nonetheless, the low unemployment rate suggests that the Japanese labour market did not unravel the power of societalisation.

The social fabric showed a great shock-absorbing capacity under the strain of the 1970s crisis. In particular, nuclear family households strategically multiplied their income streams by sending female family members and students into the labour market, thereby compensating for breadwinners' reduced wages. Yet this multi-income strategy also overwhelmed family structure. A partial merger of developmentalism and neoliberalism, a hallmark of this period, worsened this tension: the state financially supported family life less and less, putting forth its policy of "self-help" through participation in the labour market (Shinkawa 2005, pp. 97, 102–104). Even under these adverse conditions, the nuclear family structure was able to manage poverty by absorbing redundant wage workers (Itoh 2000, pp. 62–63, 67) and by sacrificing the well-being of females (Kato and Steven 1993, pp. 87–88). However, to make this possible, females in particular had to work hard. On the one hand, they had the difficult task of managing the traditional work of "reproduction", which was heavily dependent on women and girls in the home, while on the other hand they were required to supplement the household's decreased purchasing power through their part-time participation in the labour market (Itoh 2000).

The state tried to reactivate local community, thinking of it as "a basic unit for residents to live a pleasant and secure everyday life" (MHA 1983). It is possible to find in this new community policy the state's logical understanding—expectation, at least—that the community's role in promoting citizens' mutual support could be purposely restrengthened, even when the conventional community form (chōnaikai) experienced tensions in the aftermath of the 1970s crisis.

In short, Japan's developmentalist growth pattern survived the 1970s crisis and its aftermath, as did Japan's NSPR, both of which actively evolved with a selective internalisation of neoliberal logics, and this contributed to the outstanding resilience of Japanese capitalism in the wake of the 1970s crisis. The NSPR reconstructed its regulatory (societalisation) capacity. As a corollary, spatial containment based on the geographies of yoseba zones was able to manage the socially "inimical" forms of urban poverty, even amid the major crisis. This is not to say that Japanese yoseba zones were free from the theoretical pressure of the NUP, which was already destabilising societalisation in many countries in the context of the 1970s crisis. Japan, too, saw an increase in the number of "dangerous" poor—the harbinger of the NUP—in the form of homelessness in and around yoseba zones.

Thus, the inner-city cycle of homelessness started in the 1970s, though this early form of Japan's NUP was largely masked during this period. First, the normative spaces outside of yoseba zones experienced rising poverty rates among the majority group of wage workers—i.e., those hired by small and medium-size firms (Hashimoto 2009)—but this scarcely took clear forms of the NUP threatening societalisation. Second, the areas in and around yoseba zones showed real fluctuations. Homelessness grew among male day labourers as yoseba labour markets tailored to this group dwindled (Nomoto 2003; San'ya Rodosha Fukushi Kaikan Unei I'inkai 1992; Ushikusa 1988; Yamamura 1996). As we will see, this harbinger of the NUP embarrassed "normal" public spaces around the spatial niches of poverty. Yet, as the labour market and social fabrics revived, so too did the capacity for spatial containment.

Bubble Economy, c. 1986–1991

In 1986, Japan embarked on a speculative boom known as the bubble economy. By boosting the price of real estate and stocks, this boom boosted the profitability of Japanese capitalism (Itoh 2000, pp. 81–82; 1990, pp. 178–179). The growth pattern of this period can be characterised as speculation-led because the expansion of the economy at this time was strongly influenced by the asset-inflated economy, particularly by investments in the real estate sector. Under this growth pattern, the asset-inflated economy surged ahead of the "real" economy (which was largely equivalent to traditional industrial sectors of developmentalism) as the locus of profit making.

The inrush of abundant capital in the asset market relaxed looming tensions in Japan's developmentalist accumulation, which during the mid-1980s had been confronting a glut of productive capacity and a decline in profitability. The developmentalist type of state policy—the industrial policy that previously had curbed economic competition through vertical integration—was formally sustained but increasingly detached from the actual locus of profit making: the asset market. At the same time, the external character of the asset-inflated economy was not perceived as a problem for the developmentalist state until the early 1990s, when the bubble economy ended abruptly and unleashed a major economic crisis. Though developmentalism as a regulatory and accumulation paradigm started to become obsolete, the historical paradigm of developmentalism still avoided a crisis. The NSPR was conditioned by this transitory situation.

Public provision rarely advanced in its capacity to regulate poverty. Yet, during this period, this unsatisfactory condition instead functioned to push working-age people and their families into the labour market, which increasingly exhibited workforce shortages under the strong economy and its labour-absorbing capacity. In this way, the sound performance of the NSPR during this period centred on the labour market. As a result, the weakness of public provision did not lead to the growth of poverty.

In the late 1980s and early 1990s, the government introduced new programmes to decrease the financial burdens of elderly people who were in need of special treatment (Estevez-Abe 2008, p. 228; Shinkawa 2005, p. 297). While these programmes did not change the problematic nature of Japan's public provision, that is, the historical neglect of workers and their families despite the benevolent law, neither did it lead to major disruptions of Japan's NSPR as a system.

During this speculation-led economic growth, then, the labour market acquired a strong capacity to regulate poverty by commodifying the old, the young, and female household members to mitigate the labour shortage. The unemployment rate decreased from an already low 2.5% (in 1988) to 2.1% (in 1991).[6] This strong trend towards labour commodification was backed up by the state, which tried to create better working environments and to push uncommodified family members into the labour market (Nagayama 2000, pp. 19–20). Even in this boom, however, real-wage growth stagnated, hovering just around 2%. The reduced "wage cost" of Japanese capitalism never returned to the heights of the late 1960s and early 1970s, yet the labour-absorbing power of the labour market was able to hide the gap between rich and poor through the intensive workforce commodification of impoverished people.

The social fabric continued to support the labour market. The realm of community did not incur a major loss in its societalisation capacity, even though new tendencies of neighbourhood-level fragmentation and individualisation began to spread in the wake of the 1980s (Tamano 2005; Yamada 2004). Families' capacity was perhaps more problematic. Because the labour market in this period commodified family members more intensively than before, nuclear families were increasingly overburdened. Social reproduction, especially for those in the external labour market, relied more heavily on the housework of married women. While serving family members, many of these females also had to participate in the labour market as part-time labourers (Itoh 2000, pp. 62–63).

The NSPR in this boom period sustained its poverty-regulating and societalising power through the labour market, and in this context the postwar spatialisation of urban poverty was no longer clearly articulated. Although socioeconomic gaps between the relatively rich and the relatively poor widened in terms of wealth distribution (Tachibanaki 1998, 2005a, 2005b), these gaps only meant different levels of consumption within mainstream society (Hashimoto 2009, p. 174), which suggests that, in relative terms, the societalisation of the working class remained intact amid the new socioeconomic divides. Moreover, homelessness and other forms of acute poverty decreased even in the yoseba zones of metropolises (Yamaoka 1996). Because the asset-inflated economy increased labour shortages among construction workers, for instance, the labour market absorbed even some of those who were the most disadvantaged in yoseba zones (Aoki 2000, p. 40).

Postbubble Crisis, c. 1992–2007

The asset-inflated economy crumbled in 1992. A "structuralist" explanation might be that a speculative economy can only temporarily solve problems inherent in capitalism and is "destined to collapse" (Itoh 2000, p. 87). Be that as it may, the time after overspeculation was spectacularly painful. Gross domestic product growth, employment, and domestic consumption all collapsed (Hutchison, Ito, and Westermann 2004; Uemura 2000); the financial system could not solve the problem of huge nonperforming loans for a prolonged period (Amix 2004; Hutchison and Watermann 2006); state interventions remained ineffective and only accumulated debts (Itoh 2000); and Japan's international competitiveness dwindled (Coriat, Geoffron, and Rubinstein 2000).

In this context, Japan had the twofold difficulty of restoring its accumulation regime (growth pattern) while also reviving new regulatory fixes of social regulation around accumulation. Japan *did* succeed in establishing an export-led growth pattern in the mid-2000s, but exports never produced the same distributive effects as they had earlier; instead, they unleashed real-wage reduction (Itoh 2009). This trajectory questioned the society-leading ability of the developmental state, which promoted its ongoing restructuring and, failing that, possible reification. In this course, the NSPR was reworked and, while being reshuffled, its three spheres grew tendencies of desocietalisation.

During this period, many national programmes for public provision remained unchanged in legal and institutional terms. Yet these programmes became less effective because irregular and impoverished workers increased in number and escalated the traditional problem of their exclusion from public provision. For one thing, the public assistance programme continued to externalise labourers who were deemed "able to work". For another, national unemployment benefits poorly covered irregular workers because employers shirked their legal responsibility to pay insurance premiums for irregular workers and because the number of these workers increased (Yuasa 2008, pp. 24–25). Worse still, in the 1990s the Japanese state reduced its role as the provider of public housing to impoverished people, a role that was already relatively small compared with its role as a granter of mortgages and credit to enable middle-class citizens to become homeowners (Hirayama and Ronald 2007). While so doing, the Japanese state once again emphasised the regulatory capacity of the market to ameliorate poverty.

However, the labour market was essentially at the epicentre of poverty growth and the breakdown of the NSPR in this period. Most importantly, in 1999 and 2004, the Japanese state revised the Worker Dispatch Law of 1985. The revisions significantly increased the range of occupations to which temporary staffing agencies could allocate dispatched labourers. Added to the increased numbers of dispatched labourers was the more spontaneous growth of temporary workers in conventional categories. Through this course, Japan came to have the most "dualistic" labour system among the Organisation for Economic Co-operation and Development countries (Vogel 2006, p. 81). While major firms rushed to the new sources of temporary workers, even those working at large corporations lost access to company-based welfare systems (Tachibanaki 2005b). In consequence, Japan saw a general deterioration in distribution rates for labour (Itoh 2009, p. 172). In all, this was a period of significant loss in the poverty-regulating ability of the labour market.

At the same time, in the 1990s and 2000s, the social fabric was no longer able to support this decreasing poverty-regulating capacity. As material inputs from the labour market were reduced, and as wages were less and less able to integrate the working class, the societalising vitality of the social fabric was overburdened and even becoming exhausted. Remaining unmarried became increasingly common in this period. The rate of those unmarried at age fifty (which is considered "lifetime nonmarried" in Japanese statistics) skyrocketed from 1990 to 2005, rising from 5.6% to 16% for men and from 4.3% to 7.3% for women (Cabinet Office 2018, p. 16). As this growth of the unmarried population continued and deepened, it contributed to Japan's notoriously low birth rate, which would soon affect the societalisation capacity of the NSPR at both the family and community levels. Furthermore, during these years, familial disruptions proliferated (Tachibanaki 2005a) and divorce rates soared (MHLW 2009a). The family was said to no longer be a stable source of reciprocal support (Yamada 2004, pp. 136–139).

As the NSPR trended towards crisis in its three spheres, the widespread cycle of homelessness started—always a clear manifestation of the NUP in Japan.[7] In the 1990s, homeless people were mostly elderly men who had been employed in yoseba zones; the unemployment of these disadvantaged labourers led to their mass homelessness (Aoki 2000; Nakane 1999; Yamaguchi 1998). Homelessness in the 1990s and 2000s accompanied the reduced role of the yoseba zones—segregated areas for day labourers' "reproduction" and once highly useful for Japan's developmentalist accumulation. Once unemployed, however, many of these male labourers became homeless and started drifting around the cities. This effectively resulted in the progressive disappearance of inherited spaces of ghettoisation in the yoseba zones, and the Japanese type of the NUP took the peculiar form of "homelessness without ghettoisation".

After the late 1990s, the homeless population diversified. First, there were now more young people and women among the homeless population (Aoki 2000; Hayashi 2006; Maruyama 2013; Moon 2006). Second, there emerged numbers of homeless people who were not visible on the streets but were living in precarious housing conditions, such as in twenty-four-hour internet cafés (MHLW 2007; TMG 2018). By taking the unique form of homelessness without ghettoisation, the NUP increased tensions within societalisation.

The World Financial Crisis, Mass Disasters, and Their Aftermath, c. 2008–2010s

The world financial crisis of the late 2000s started affecting Japan in autumn 2008. Gross domestic product growth rates dropped to −5.4% in 2009, a shocking number for Japan. Moreover, before it was able to fully recover from the late 2000s crisis, Japan was hit by several devastating mass disasters: the 2011 Great East Japan earthquake and tsunami and the subsequent Fukushima Dai-ichi nuclear power plant disaster. While the earthquake and tsunami killed more than 15,000 people, the nuclear plant released a huge amount of radiation and derailed the economy.

To bring the damaged areas out of jeopardy and to create effective demand, the Japanese state in 2011 began directing a vast quantity of its national budget to disaster recovery. According to one newspaper article, the spending totalled 29 trillion yen (US$270 billion) as of 2015 (Sekiya 2017). The sum of these expenditures far exceeded the amount needed for the official purposes of recovery (Saito 2015), and this spending played a key role in pulling the economy out of a severe postdisaster downturn, at least temporarily (Development Bank of Japan 2016). If any leading sector can be detected in this period, it was this state spending for the official purpose of disaster recovery. Hence, I dub this period's growth pattern the "disaster recovery–led" pattern, a short-lived model that materialised around the mid-2010s.

Although the accumulation regime only just escaped disintegration by employing this disaster recovery–led pattern, the NSPR still faced the severe pressure of deregulation and desocietalisation, as the economy had already experienced such developments by the late 2000s. Almost for the first time in Japan's postwar history, however, the sphere of public provision in the NSPR took a central role in preventing an economic crisis from turning into a societal crisis. The national programme of public assistance, which had long been operated in a harsh manner, with the excluding of "unworthy" households and "morally inferior" individuals, began to act more favourably towards these marginalised groups. In Chapter 9, we will see that this major "social inclusion" of the late 2000s and early 2010s was an outcome of the activism that had clamoured for the radical opening up (commoning) of public assistance. For the moment, it is sufficient to say that the public assistance programme began to have strong societalising and "decommodifying" effects in the late 2000s, which strengthened Japan's NSPR in this regard.

The Japanese labour market also was hit by the world financial crisis of the late 2000s, and this was especially damaging to precariously situated manual workers participating in the lower tiers of the labour market. As effective demand in the manufacturing industry evaporated, electric and automobile companies suddenly stopped relying upon temporary staffing agencies to fill job openings. The contraction of the labour market spread from manufacturing to nonmanufacturing sectors, and unemployment reached 5.6% in 2009—the worst rate for postwar Japan previous to that date.

Equally bewildering was the constant deterioration of working conditions. The low productivity of Japanese industries increased two antilabour tendencies in the labour market: the extension of working hours, which were already long by international standards (Konno 2012; Morioka 2013), and the reduction of the total "wage cost" through further advancing the use of temporary workers (MHLW 2017). The latter represented the realisation of a long-standing desire on the part of businesses (Nikkeiren 1995).

The supporting role of the family and local community was in jeopardy. The number of single people soared. The lifetime nonmarried rate reached 23.4% for males and 14.1% for females in 2015, a significant increase from the 2005 figures of 16% and 7.3%, respectively (Cabinet Office 2018, p. 16). This surprising rise made the formation of nuclear families less attainable for individuals (especially men) who were already suffering precarious working conditions, low wages, and unemployment (Cabinet Office 2019; MHLW 2017). Life inside the family was no better. The rate of children living below the poverty line reached an all-time high of 16.3% in 2012 (MHLW 2016), and the increase in poverty among women is considered a major contributor to this growth in child poverty, as it impoverished single-mother households (Abe 2014). With regard to the community, decreasing birthrates and the population decline that has already begun, and is expected to increase in the future, is prompting a significant contraction of local community and residential neighbourhoods, making this communitarian locus of societalisation more and more unreliable for policymakers (Masuda 2014; MLIT 2014).

The overall tendency is that the NSPR faced serious shock waves from the repetitive accumulation crises. As the national track of "accumulation for accumulation's sake" was continually derailed, it undercut the NSPR. Although one sphere in the

NSPR (i.e., public provision) gained a new vitality in the wake of the world financial crisis, the deteriorated conditions overall could not help but impoverish the entire society. The poverty rate hovered around 10%, but when society in general is impoverished, this rate does not indicate the true magnitude of generalised poverty.

The characteristic (period-defining) feature of Japanese society today is that average households have lower standards of living, that society in general has become poorer, and that the frequent dropping of individuals through the social ranks exacerbates social uncertainty (Hashimoto 2018a, 2018b). In short, the Japanese (developmentalist) type of Keynesian social contract—that all citizens will belong to the middle class (*ichioku sōchūrhyū shakai*) at the end of statist industrialisation—has disappeared.

Miraculously, this loss in the capacity of the NSPR has not led to a crisis in societalisation. Most tellingly, the Japanese NUP—homelessness without ghettoisation—has declined because homelessness has been reduced in public spaces. The number of homeless people officially recognised by the state's statistics declined to 4,555 in 2019 (MHLW 2019), which relaxed the pressure of desocietalisation even amid the generalised growth of poverty. Until the late 2000s, a major contributor to this statistical decline was the rescaling production of new regulatory spaces (discussed in the next section). Even as poverty became more generalised, Japan saw a paradoxical reduction of the *appearance* of the NUP.

Overview

Table 3.1 summarises growth patterns, the NSPR, and the spatialisation of poverty as they appeared in postwar Japan. First, a national growth pattern historically evolved through profit-investment-led (c. 1950–1972), export-led (c. late 1970s–1985), speculation-led (c. 1986–1991), a second export-led (c. early 2000s–2007), and disaster recovery–led pattern models (c. 2010s). The thrust of developmentalism was especially strong until the 1970s, but the aspiration of the national state to supervise domestic regulatory affairs continued even after the zenith of developmentalism.

Second, the NSPR evolved under these growth patterns, forming period-specific amalgams of public provision, the labour market, and social fabrics on a national scale. Even with the characteristic (developmentalist) weakness of public provision, the NSPR overcame the 1970s crisis without exacerbating urban poverty, due to the absorbing capacity of the labour market and the resilience of social fabrics.

Third, the NSPR was weakened in the 1990s, leading to street homelessness. Japanese societalisation had been based on the extreme vigilance of sociopolitical agents, who watched the "deviants" and waited for them to do damage to social harmony. In this context, even the relatively small number of homeless people were thought to be detrimental to societalisation.

Table 3.1 Japan's nationalised spaces of poverty regulation, 1950s–mid-2010s.

	Growth pattern	Nationalised space of poverty regulation			Spatialisation of poverty
		Public provision	Labour market	Social fabric	
c. 1950–1972 High growth	Investment-led	Meagre expenditures; immature welfare policies; no demand to create policies for wage workers	Rising wages; low unemployment rate; absorption of labourers in newly opened urban labour markets	Emerging nuclear families; patriarchal family relations to support the breadwinner; remaining agricultural villages	Production of homogeneous urban society; concentration of acute poverty in yoseba
c. 1973–1985 World crisis and its aftermath	In crisis	Minor roles in poverty regulation amid economic crisis	Relative stability of employment; a start of "wage cost" reduction and "working poor" problems	Multi-income generation within family; increasing burdens on women in the home	Rising homelessness in yoseba
	Export-led	Soaring spending for safety nets (1970s); emphasis on self-help (since the 1980s)	Keynesian spending for public works (1970s); introduction of female workers	Reemphasis on nuclear families and community building; further integration of women	Reduced poverty within and beyond yoseba
c. 1986–1991 Bubble economy	Speculation-led	Neoliberalisation without turmoil; sharp emphasis on self-help	Good performance of the labour market; low unemployment rate	Continued emphasis on nuclear families; community building under strong economy	Diminishing homelessness in yoseba; heightened urban economic affluence
c. 1992–2007 Postbubble crisis	In crisis		Regulatory crisis		Rising homelessness among disadvantaged workers; reduced size of yoseba; NUP with a deghettoisation tendency; subsequent reduction in homelessness
	Export-led	Reduced efficacy of public safety nets; increased roles of the housing market and "self-help"	Worsening conditions for temporary workers; reemergence of the "working poor" problem	Increased instability of nuclear families; increased number of the nonmarried	
c. 2008–2010s World financial crisis, mass disasters, and their aftermath	In crisis		Regulatory crisis		Homelessness among more typical workers; general increase in poverty
	Disaster recovery-led	Opening up of public assistance to homeless and destitute people	Exploitive labour relations in low-productivity sectors; deepening of the "working poor" problem	Major loss of poverty-regulating capacity in family and community	Absorption of acute poverty by public assistance; general increase in poverty

Note: Shaded squares denote significant reduction or crisis of poverty-regulating capacity.

Finally, the highly deregulated form of poverty according to this book's understanding, public space homelessness, decreased after the late 2000s. Urban poverty in its acutest form constantly met multiscalar regulating efforts on the local and national scales, which modified the threatening appearance of the "dangerous poor" for society. This is the story that I develop in the next section.

All in all, Japan's NUP has displayed rhythms and patterns that are different from those predicted by the meso theory based on Euro-American literature, according to which the departure from a Fordist regime generally intensifies poverty in cities, and this poverty takes both dispersed *and* concentrated forms—homelessness *and* ghettos (Marcuse 1996). Atlantic Fordist countries saw major deterioration into homelessness and ghettoisation during the late 1970s and early 1980s (Daly 1996; Rossi 1989; Wacquant 2008). This situation in turn prompted experimental forms of regulatory activity by national states, the overall effects of which were often to (further) relativise the dominant scale of poverty regulation and to heighten the localising tendency of regulatory regimes (Baumohl 1996; Blau 1992; Burrows, Pleace, and Quilgars 1997; DeVerteuil, Lee, and Wolch 2002; Watson 1986; for a Japan–United States comparison, see Hayashi 2014a).

In light of this, three tendencies are unique to the Japanese case. First, the Japanese NUP has so far predominantly assumed the form of homelessness with a lesser manifestation of ghettoisation—whether in yoseba zones or other poverty niches. Second, the major moment of the Japanese NUP came after the early 1990s, in the context of a domestic accumulation-regime crisis, rather than in the late 1970s and early 1980s in the context of a worldwide accumulation-regime crisis. Third, the Japanese NUP—homelessness without ghettoisation—seemingly decreased towards the 2010s despite the fact that over these years Japan saw the generalisation of poverty among its people.

New Regulatory Spaces in Japan

New Regulatory Spaces

The NSPR is a societalising filter equipped to protect any Fordist versions of the accumulation regime against the acute manifestation of poverty at the social fringes. This theoretical role of the NSPR took on a unique pattern in Japan, with heavy reliance on the labour market and the social fabric and not on public provision, for Japan's developmentalist economy reserved finite national wealth for industrial expansion. This historical trajectory, while spawning formative types of the NUP in the 1970s, led to the unprecedented growth of homelessness in the 1990s.

As I have repeatedly suggested, however, the formation of the NUP in postwar Japan was increasingly reregulated at the margins of the NSPR and societalisation.

The multiscalar and scale-producing process of NUP regulation constructed and evolved new regulatory spaces of homelessness on the local scale and in cities, which blunted, ensnared, and dispersed the acute form of homelessness. In this section, I will unpack this rescaling dynamism around homelessness—around desocietalisation—in terms of the three rounds of rescaling described in the chapter's theoretical exposition. The central question becomes this: How and to what degree did the rescaling succeed in defending societalisation from regulatory failure and the moral panic brought about by homelessness?

The answer is that state and social sectors as well as their coworking capacities were vigorously scaled back into (half-)autonomised urban regimes through addressing homelessness. At first, local political and social actors responded to homelessness in ad hoc ways, and the ground-up process propelled the haphazard production of new regulatory spaces. Later on, the Japanese state determined national rules of rescaling, which powerfully reconstructed state space unity and to some extent rehabilitated a national focus against the anarchism of urban regulation. The three rounds of rescaling outlined in this chapter are fully applicable to the Japanese process of rescaling, though two points of theory specification are warranted.

First and foremost, as I have suggested, Japanese developmentalism previously had made the central locus of bureaucratic rule-setting national by curtailing the autonomy of local and urban regulators; this had been a hallmark of developmentalism in postwar Japan. In this context, the Japanese version of rescaling dynamism elicited stronger efforts from the national state to play the theoretical role of "scale manager" (Peck 2002, p. 357). In Japan, this role was linked with the keenness of the Japanese state to repeatedly make the "self-autonomising" cities and their haphazard dynamics and fluidities, a characteristic feature of rescaling in its early phase, into legible and calculable processes for national policymakers.

Second, the magnitude of rescaling became large and actually threatened the historical centricity of the national scale in Japan. This intensity of rescaling may look mysterious because the number of homeless people remained comparatively small. The quantitative dimension cannot be compared, for example, to the United States after Fordism—in the mid-1980s or thereabouts—when that country saw 250,000 to 300,000 roofless people in public spaces (Rossi 1989, p. 37). According to national counts, there were fewer than 30,000 homeless people living in Japanese public spaces even at the peak (MHLW 2003). One might interpret these numbers, which remain proportionately smaller even after taking into account the size of the population, as a sign of Japanese nonsignificance, or intrinsic benevolence, or separation from international patterns.

I, however, eschew any such separatist interpretation. Instead, I reframe the issue by asking: Why did the relatively small occurrence of homelessness incite the gigantic dynamism of rescaling in Japan? A possible answer is that Japan's societalisation, which received only limited material (use value) inputs from the developmentalist economy, became extremely intolerant of "disorder". These limited use values for people's societalisation historically drove developmentalism to look carefully at the contours and inner processes of societalisation—to prevent disruption—by vigorously patronising/absorbing/endorsing urban democratic leaderships and by multiplying state–society coworking or hybrid units, around the centricity of the national. Thus, Japan was highly prone to rescaling regulation even though the quantitative aspect of homelessness remained smaller.

Round One: Ground-Up Rescaling

In the ground-up round of rescaling (c. 1970s–2002), Japan's rescaling dynamism arose locally and from the cities, and the Japanese state remained in many ways an onlooker and bystander. This ground-up round was already prefigured during the 1970s crisis. When the oil embargo hit the Japanese economy, homelessness surged in (and around) the yoseba zones of metropolises. Breakdowns in societalisation took locational (but not pan-urban) forms. The municipality and local society engaged in antihomeless attacks and harassment, though some officials and activists began services and claims making for homeless people.

The earlier manifestation of homelessness in Japan—the inner-city cycle of homelessness—decreased towards the mid-1980s and ended during the asset-bubble boom, before the early 1990s. In the 1990s, when Japan ran into a severe economic downturn, public space homelessness resurged and took a completely new form—the widespread cycle of homelessness. Homeless people in the 1990s spread across public spaces, far beyond the historical niches of poverty (yoseba zones). In response to this widespread homelessness, the ground-up (haphazard) construction of new regulatory spaces intensified, which rescaled the Japanese integral state space in ad hoc ways.

It should again be noted that the legal frameworks in Japan define citizenship very inclusively in order to ensure the "right to livelihood" for all. The Public Assistance Act of 1950 has clauses that guarantee the flexible mobilisation of the public assistance programme—a key benefit system covering such areas as housing, medical care, and income maintenance—for those who are in emergency situations (article 7) and for unhoused persons (article 38). In fact, however, this inclusive idea in the law was never realised. While the NSPR prohibited the NUP from increasing in Japan *without* public provision (see the previous section), the widespread cycle of homelessness in the 1990s made the gap between law and reality fully apparent.

This also was the period in which the ground-up round of rescaling became highly intensive. Local regulators in the state and society were deployed to address widespread homelessness. Policing, harassment, and dispersal were the three basic processes in this haphazard reaction, which intensified the autonomous activities of state and social regulators on the local scale (Hayashi 2014b; Ikuta 2007; Kasai 1999; Sakokawa 2013). The court sector facilitated this ground-up rescaling. The decision was reached that homeless people who seemed able to work must live without public assistance. The courts thus endorsed the haphazard dynamism of Japan's rescaling reregulation.[8]

Round Two: Picking-Off Rescaling

In the picking-off round of rescaling (c. 2003–2007), the Japanese state was no more than an onlooker with respect to local dynamics, as the national government and ministries developed a coherent regulatory framework that legally codified the ongoing rescaling process. Homeless people were decreed to be an object that could be regulated outside of the NSPR and outside of the minimum living standards determined by law. This state-led rescaling elaborated regulatory roles for the municipality and for local civil society, embellishing them with new codes and rules. The net effect was the justification and coordination of rescaling reregulation through national policy, which propelled the devolutionary politics around homeless people in a systematic way.

This picking-off round of rescaling thus stabilised the ongoing transfer of regulatory tensions from the national to the local scale. This highly state-driven pattern of dominant-scale relativisation in Japan was partly due to the historical strength of the national state/scale, which emerged out of the country's developmentalist experience. Even after rescaling dynamism set in, the Japanese state was eager to sustain its interscalar dominance, seeking to reestablish Japanese state space that should be tightly unified around the national scale.

The legal framework of the national state in question is what I call the 2002/2003 system, which comprised two parts. One is the Act on Special Measures Concerning Support for Homeless People's Self-Help, or the Self-Help Act. The other is the Guidelines Concerning Support for Homeless People's Self-Help, or the 2003 guidelines. The Self-Help Act determined the general purpose of Japan's rescaling reregulation, while the 2003 guidelines delineated intricate protocols and codes. The 2002/2003 system specified the roles that should be performed by the two sectors (state and social) in the locality, which systematically rescaled the whole integral state into local patterns of "government + governance" (Jessop 2002, p. 239). The 2002/2003 system thus cultivated the vast fertile area between coercion and consensus, as well as purely coercive measures themselves, into new regulatory spaces covering homelessness.

First, the 2002/2003 system introduced a new understanding of homeless regulation, to be advanced through workfarist programmes that, through educating and "moralising" homeless people, could relocate this most "recalcitrant" part of deprived people from the streets to the labour market. In practice, the 2002/2003 system asked larger municipalities to open new public facilities such as self-help assistance centres and to use them to assess and cultivate the self-support capability of homeless people in the labour market (chapter 3, section 2 of the 2003 guidelines; see also articles 3 and 8 of the Self-Help Act). As the system granted wide discretionary power over how the municipality enacted workfarist policy and operated these facilities, homeless people's access to citizenship and public assistance became powerfully blurred. It was officially said that this approach would "rehabilitate" homeless people's labouring capacity through training, but it often failed in the sustained "commodification" of homeless people's labour power, due to the fragmentation of their labour markets, and ended up merely cramming homeless people's bodies into temporary shelters.

Second, the 2002/2003 system defined public spaces as the privileged turf of the housing classes, which must be secured by antihomeless policing that decreed that the municipality and the police could remove homeless people and their belongings from public spaces for the "safety" of housed citizens. These "eviction clauses" included some conditions for implementation (to be discussed in Chapter 7). Nonetheless, homeless people were deemed a danger to "local residents" (*chīki jūmin*) by creating "fear and harm" (*huan ya kigai*) among them (chapter 3, section 2 of the 2003 guidelines). In this way, homeless people were legally defined as potential challengers to the housing classes, local society, and public spaces. Though the same perception—that the homeless are the "dangerous" poor—had emerged during the ground-up round of rescaling (c. 1970s–2002), the 2002/2003 system integrated this tendency into the Japanese legal system, with reference to homeless people as a danger to the "proper use" (*tekisetsu na riyō*) of public facilities and as the special target of policing and supervision (*torishimari*) (article 11 of the Self-Help Act; chapter 3, section 2 of the 2003 guidelines).

Third, the 2002/2003 system encouraged municipalities to communicate with nonprofit organisations and volunteer groups, to use them as knowledge resources and useful partners in advancing homeless regulation and provision. The lack of local knowledge on the part of the municipality was suggested, and the system called for this information deficit to be overcome by forming partnerships and coworking units with social agents, civil society, and nongovernmental organisations (article 12 of the Self-Help Act; chapter 3, section 2 of the 2003 guidelines). The use of social actors (including social movement actors) for municipal homeless regulation, and the formation of rescaled governance fields to assemble political and social powers into "government + governance" (Jessop 2002, p. 239), was a preexisting tendency in some localities. The 2002/2003 system legalised this tendency and advocated it for all municipalities.

Finally, the 2002/2003 system called for municipalities to publish a so-called implementation plan (*jissi kēkaku*), which is a catalogue of programmes, facilities, services, and networks available in each locality (article 9 of the Self-Help Act; chapter 4 of the 2003 guidelines). By asking municipalities to publish this policy document, the Japanese state made *formal* the autonomous, rescaled regulatory spaces of municipalities. The 2002/2003 system also made the rescaled regulatory spaces *legible* to the Japanese state's close surveillance of municipal regulatory affairs. Both were the inertia of developmentalism, whose "path dependence" within Japanese state space was vigorously revitalised in this second round of rescaling.

In response to the 2002/2003 system, major municipalities evolved their previous versions of rescaling to adopt more streamlined and explicable models, which entailed the publication of implementation plans to formalise the local grounds of rescaling (City of Kawasaki 2004; City of Nagoya 2004; City of Osaka 2004; City of Yokohama 2004; Tokyo Metropolitan Government [TMG] 2004). For example, the Tokyo Metropolitan Government and its wards opened five emergency centres and five self-help assistance centres in the 2000s, absorbing a large number of homeless people in these facilities.[9] Through these facilities, Tokyo responded to the national state by constructing an urban workfare apparatus for homeless people. The official aim was to re-create the able-bodied homeless as "wilful" labour commodity owners adapted to the neoliberal labour market, to make public spaces "clean and safe" for the housing classes, and to reregulate the impacts of homelessness at the fringes of citizenship. Tokyo created new programmes for means-testing homeless people, enhancing their job search techniques, and condemning those who remained in the streets (see Kitagawa 2006).

Tokyo and its wards also reclaimed their control of public spaces. From 2004 to 2007, they implemented the Programme for the Facilitation of Community-Based Lives and transferred about 1,200 homeless people from five targeted parks to the private housing sector, providing a housing unit to each person for up to two years (TMG 2007, 2009). This "housing first" programme afforded homeless people new opportunities for housing, albeit temporarily, which was a positive development (Bando 2005; Kasai 2005; Yamamoto 2005). This programme, however, was accompanied by harsher surveillance-cum-policing in public spaces. The Tokyo Metropolitan Government and its wards contracted private security companies, had them visit homeless people every three hours throughout the night, and virtually banned the practice of sleeping in many public parks (Yamada 2005). Through these efforts, the Tokyo municipality decreased the visible homeless population in public spaces from 5,521 in 2000 to 3,402 in 2007, according to official counts (TMG 2007).

Finally, nongovernmental organisations and activists became tightly enmeshed in Tokyo's homeless regulation during this round of rescaling. Many homeless-supporting organisations had already existed well before the Japanese state promulgated the 2002/2003 system. By the mid-2000s, these organisations were interwoven into Tokyo's "self-help system". Up to a point, this absorption meant that Tokyo's local governance helped homeless-supporting activists to achieve their own progressive goals (see Mugikura 2006).

Round Three: Unfolding Rescaling

In the unfolding round of rescaling (c. 2008–present), new regulatory spaces in Japan widely internalised the transformative moments of homeless activism. This redressed the inherited terrains of antihomeless regulation on behalf of homeless people, thereby creating more supportive conditions for homeless people in some cities and on the local scale (see Chapters 7 and 8). When Japan plunged into the world financial crisis of the late 2000s and a number of workers confronted an increased risk of homelessness, the past experiences of social movements for homeless people, which had accumulated a lot of achievements on the local scale by the late 2000s, led to a nationwide transformative process of activism. A movement that started in Tokyo forced the Japanese state to improve national regulation over public assistance. However, this nationwide improvement of homeless policy was soon affected by the concerted efforts of politicians, bureaucrats, and conservative intellectuals to subdue prohomeless and propoor initiatives, spaces, and languages and to scale them back, once again, to uncertain urban regimes and their (partial) autonomy constructed at the fringes of the NSPR.

I will analyse these newer dynamics more closely in Chapter 9. For the moment, let us explore the key events and turning points. To begin with, the integration of nongovernmental organisations and activist groups into local systems of "government + governance" (Jessop 2002, p. 239) had greatly advanced under the 2002/2003 system. This was an internalisation of transformative pressures in the rescaled fields of integral state governance, and the localised pressure finally formed a nationalising politics to redress antihomeless regulation nationwide. In the late 2000s, activists in Tokyo embarked on a major confrontation with the national state and society. These activists occupied Tokyo's central business district, which was very close to national ministries and the Diet Building—the centre of the Japanese state. The movement cunningly used the economic crisis of the late 2000s to promote progressive homeless-related initiatives to national politicians and the general public (the societalised "us"). This succeeded in improving operational rules for a national citizenship programme (public assistance), leading to the inclusion of homeless people and "undeserving poor" in the NSPR.

However, politicians soon launched antipoor campaigns to rescale poverty and its regulation, not only for those without a roof or home but also for the entire population. Haunted by the desocietalising ethos against homelessness and "welfare dependence", new national and local institutions of workfarist regulation were now under vigorous construction, in order to minimise the rolls of public assistance and to redirect (potential) welfare recipients to fragmented labour markets. Even more important, this process entailed the overall remilitarisation of Japanese public spaces against homelessness across cities, so that the increased poor populations would not threaten urban societalisation (which was now increasingly possible). Japan's rescaling dynamics, originally adopted on behalf of homeless people, are thus in the process of expansive reproduction and new experimentation, in order to treat virtually all impoverished people in a similar rescaling manner (see Chapter 9).

Conclusion

After World War II, many Euro-American countries strengthened poverty regulation under what is usually understood as the banner of the "welfare state". I have conceptualised from a different angle the nationalised space of poverty regulation, which assembles the three regulatory spheres of national society (public provision, the labour market, and the social fabric) against the disruptive tendencies of capitalism. The role of the NSPR is to support societalisation by blunting acute appearances of poverty, which are inimical to social cohesion around consumption norms.

This ability of the NSPR developed crisis tendencies during the 1970s. Impoverished and deprived people were "set free" and deregulated, leading to the NUP, a post-Fordist genre of poverty that was detrimental to mainstream society and to the societalisation that had been firmly constructed in the era of Fordist accumulation. At the speed of "fast policy" (Peck 2002; Peck and Theodore 2015), rescaling dynamics made local regulators responsible for handling the NUP; these regulators, too, were set free from national fetters of citizenship.

Building upon the innovative conceptions of Neil Brenner and Jamie Peck, my chronological view of rescaling is that local regulators initially tried to achieve the reregulation of poverty in haphazard ways and that this local anarchism was later streamlined and conditioned by formal and informal rules. Up to a point, it achieved the consistency of new regulatory spaces and rescaling processes with the overall unity of state space.

This theory of the NSPR and its rescaling is useful for the Japanese case. However, we need to specify the theory by focusing on the Japanese context. To increase the explanatory capacity of regulation theory for Japan—a "deviant" and ambivalent location for regulationism—I have modified the theory and shown that the Japanese NSPR was deeply conditioned by the Japanese character of the "developmental state", which used national wealth on behalf of late industrialisation at the expense of public provision. As a result, the labour market and social fabric became overburdened spheres in the Japanese formation of the NSPR. This contradiction was subdued and masked until the 1980s, but it burst out in the 1990s and 2000s, taking the form of homelessness without ghettoisation.

As anticipated by the theory, Japanese rescaling dynamics was spearheaded by local eruptions of rescaling activities for reregulation. In Japan, with its developmentalist history, this anarchic pattern of rescaling met very strong efforts on the part of the national state to legitimate, streamline, and recode the new ground-up regulatory spaces/crises. This renewed involvement of the Japanese state, I have argued, was due to the inherited centrality of the national state/scale in the Japanese type of integral state space that emerged out of developmentalism.

Finally, the gender selectivity of the NSPR may explain why homeless women are difficult to enumerate in Japanese public spaces. The Japanese case suggests that there are different approaches to the gender selectivity of the NSPR and, by extension, to the gendered construction of homelessness as marginal and outside of a national societalisation.

Notes

1 These multiscalar dynamics of state space (re)construction may suggest some tendency of the Parisian regulationist thinkers to mythologise and naturalise the national scale as an extremely privileged (even solely functioning) spatial scale in territorial capitalist regulation (for a major exception, see Lipietz 1994, p. 39).
2 The English edition of *Capital* used here translates this phrase as "accumulation for the sake of accumulation, production for the sake of production" (Marx 1976 [1867], p. 742). I have changed this translation slightly throughout this book.
3 Japanese developmentalism enlisted men in long-term wage labour and amplified a patronising ideology vis-à-vis women's intensive domestic labour (Kato and Steven 1993; Morioka 2013). From this emerged the societalising norm that "good" women in the family remain unexposed to hazardous external contexts; men were mainly seen as responsible for economic failures. In Japan, this gendered pattern effectively resisted obsolescence and reification, because structured coherence materialised between developmentalism and this norm. This may explain why public provision in Japan has "selectively" supported women and prevented female homelessness, and why this tendency seems to persist. By contrast, the most precarious labour markets, such as those in yoseba zones, assembled men without citizenship, and it was these male day labourers who became a major source of the homeless population (on historical gender patterns in Tokyo's yoseba zone San'ya, see Nishizawa 1995).
4 In this court case, the Supreme Court declared that "Article 25 of the constitution declares [livelihood rights] only as the liability of the state, and it is not intended to provide each Japanese citizen with rights in a concrete sense." The irrationality of this judgement in light of the constitution has evoked waves of propoor litigation, but these have not led to a major withdrawal of this declaration by the courts.
5 Data obtained from the Monthly Labour Statistics organised by the Ministry of Health, Labour and Welfare.
6 Data obtained from the Labour Force Survey organised by the Ministry of Health, Labour and Welfare.
7 According to the first nationally organised statistics on homeless people, in 2003, there were 25,296 street homeless people in Japan (MHLW 2003). Though these numbers would be less impressive to an international audience, even this level of homelessness

was deemed "threatening" because Japanese public spaces have been constructed in a highly orderly way (see Chapter 4).
8   In the case of *City of Nagoya v. Hayashi* (1997), for instance, the Nagoya District Court promulgated the markedly antihomeless decision that the plaintiff was expected to "help himself" in the labour market, even though he was actually ill. The Supreme Court supported this decision in 2001.
9   Emergency centres, whose total resident population reached 13,727 by February 2007, are places where homeless people are sheltered for up to one month, means-tested, and then directed to the next step. Subsequently, 46.6% go to self-help assistance centres, 19.1% begin receiving public assistance, 11.5% leave "voluntarily/without permission", and 11.0% leave upon term expiration. Self-help assistance centres, whose total resident count was 7,057 by February 2007, accommodate, discipline, and train homeless people for up to two months, aiming for their reinsertion into the local labour market. Of these, 51.3% achieve "self-support by employment", 35.2% leave "voluntarily/without permission", and 12.6% leave upon term expiration, without achieving employment (TMG 2007).

Chapter Four
Rescaling Urban Metabolism I: Homeless Labour for "Housing"

Jamie Peck (2001a) suggests that a society hit by acute poverty growth moves from an initial crisis phase of "moral panic" (p. 40) to a regulatory phase of "moral crusade" (p. 10). But why is homelessness *in particular* distracting to society, for whom is it so, and in what sense? In answering these questions, this chapter reconceptualises public and private spaces with reference to critical notions about sociometabolism, Lefebvrian arguments on housing, and Marxian interpretations of "metabolically mediated" class relations in cities, all of which are interwoven with this book's central concept of rescaling.

City dwellers—both rich and poor—are established as the housing classes through their consumption of public and private spaces. Public spaces serve as a key milieu in which members of the housing classes can recognise one another as more or less homogeneous occupants of cities. This does not stop the politicisation of public spaces and publicness (Fraser 1990; Hou 2010; Low and Smith 2006; Nicholls, Miller, and Beaumont 2013), but contained and regulated types of public (and private) spaces can guide the housing classes into a series of "normal" encounters/consumptions, which in turn sustains the basic integrity and cohesion of urban society. Homeless people are marginalised in this societalisation process and yet are forced to survive in public spaces, against all the norms of consumption and encounter to which the housing classes adhere.

The result is the proliferation of homeless–housed divides (Cloke, May, and Johnsen 2010; Gowan 2010), a spatialisation of significant tensions between the homeless and the housed. Public spaces not only provoke this contradiction between "us" and "them" but also prompt new regulatory spaces at parks and

---

Rescaling Urban Poverty: Homelessness, State Restructuring and City Politics in Japan, First Edition. Mahito Hayashi.
© 2024 Royal Geographical Society (with the Institute of British Geographers). Published 2024 by John Wiley & Sons Ltd.

playgrounds, in streets, pathways, and alleys, by the riverside and the seaside, and in other locations, in order to manage "them". In this chapter, I attempt to elucidate why this dynamism of being torn apart and yet amended—i.e., being relegated to discrete (non)homeless spaces and yet reunified into a functional urban matrix—generates significant tensions in urban consumption and the "commons". I locate this question in the broad context of capitalist urbanisation. Using Lefebvre as an inroad, I invoke Marx's concept of metabolism (the circuits of production and consumption in nature).

That which homeless people produce and consume in public spaces is the new use value of housing; they create it from, and appropriate it within, public spaces. This value-producing aspect of the homeless metabolism seems like a "disturber" of the normative metabolism of housed citizens, which is consumptive. The "encounter" of these two metabolisms—one is production oriented and the other consumption oriented—can reduce the society-organising (societalising) effect of public spaces. In this context, public spaces, with private spaces, develop new ways to sustain their societalisation effect on behalf of urban society at large. At the same time, homeless people have powerful agency. In both material and cultural spheres, they can renegotiate this ground-up spur for reregulation and resocietalisation.

To unpack regulation itself, I tap into Antonio Gramsci's argument that "state" must be conceived as a combination of "political society + civil society" (Gramsci 1971, p. 263). I elaborate upon this famous "integral state" concept by locating various intermediary points, knowledge mobilities, and hybrid forms in the same integral state space. This extension is warranted because these regulatory "middle grounds" or "grey zones" frequently emerge between the political and social sectors, move flexibly along the coercion–consensus spectrum, and crystalise micro milieus of regulation around malregulated, deregulated, or crisis-prone elements that are rampant in the geographies of "fast policy" (Peck and Theodore 2015).

The Urban Matrix and the Housing Classes

By considering antihomeless policing in public spaces and by situating it in gentrification theory, the urban revanchist thesis of Neil Smith (1996) and Don Mitchell (1997, 2003) spurred an epistemological turn in the study of homelessness. The impacts subsequently incited sociocultural geographers to find "something more"—complexity, diversity, unevenness—that could not be obscured by the theory of revanchism (Cloke, May, and Johnsen 2010; Cloke, Milbourne, and Widdowfield 2002; DeVerteuil 2006, 2015; DeVerteuil, Marr, and Snow 2009; Johnsen and Fitzpatrick 2010). As mentioned earlier, this debate in geography is germane to the present book. Particularly relevant to this chapter is the point that neo-Marxist and post-Marxist arguments exhibit a similar unresolved issue: both treat public space regulation separately from private space regulation and hardly locate the two in an overall matrix of urban regulation. However, Lefebvre was eager to treat public and private spaces as a matrix and a "grid" that can powerfully facilitate urban-level regulation. In his words, "Private space is distinct from, but always connected with, public space" (Lefebvre 1991 [1974], p. 166).

It is this matrix—not public spaces per se—that makes homeless people into the outsiders (the "Other") to housed citizens, breeds the homeless–housed divide, and engenders new regulatory spaces. Homelessness—an experience of being thrown into the streets without housing goods—drives homeless people to the production and consumption of housing. Homeless people are injected into the matrix of public and private spaces differently and, due to this difference, appropriate public spaces differently than the housing classes. This demarcates spaces of homelessness as a clear target of rescaling reregulation on behalf of the housing classes and their cities.

The public/private grid delineates different urban spaces by endowing them with distinct (but mutually related) use values, consumption norms and rules, and attendant symbolisms and hierarchies. According to Henri Lefebvre (1991 [1974], p. 271), this manner of material–semiotic demarcation of urban space already loomed in sixteenth-century Europe. However, Lefebvre also suggests that the modern *form* of the public/private matrix became powerful more recently. It took a long time for the grid of modern capitalist urbanisation to stably normalise the lifestyle, encounters, and consumption of urban dwellers (pp. 338–339). In this process, the enclosure of privateness within housing was definitive: "As for the bodily 'functions' of eating and drinking, sleeping and making love, these are thrust out of sight" (p. 315). For the wealthiest, housing offers multiple rooms, floors, and corridors in which to carry out these functions intimately and discreetly. For the less wealthy, housing represents a more basic version that he calls the "minimal living-space" (p. 316).

Lefebvre's tone occasionally turns pessimistic, especially when he says, "Suburban houses and 'new towns' came close to the lowest possible threshold of sociability" (p. 316), or "It [urbanism] controls the consumption of space and the habitat" (Lefebvre 2003a [1970], p. 164). When the enclosure of privateness into housing increasingly involved the production of new towns, these also began to take a broad form of built environment, which "extends outwards in the surroundings of the housing itself—into those [public] areas variously represented as the environment, transitional spaces, means of access, facilities, and so on" (Lefebvre 1991 [1974], pp. 338–339).

Lefebvre's interesting discussion finds (remote) echoes and reworkings in David Harvey, a Lefebvrian thinker who contributed an afterword to the English edition of Lefebvre's *The Production of Space*. Indeed, Harvey (1989a, 2006) located a key argument—that the (use) values of the city grew under the expansive phases of Keynesian (and pre-Keynesian) urbanisation—in exactly this type of discussion. Harvey's definitive addition was the concept of the housing classes. Harvey's 1976 article suggested that the use value enlargement under Keynesian urbanisation was something that generalised the twin formation of public and private spaces, facilitated the generalisation of the housing classes as the dominant consumers of public and private spaces, and in so doing, vastly advanced the all-encompassing capacity of urban society formation and societalisation against capitalism's class-antagonising tendencies.

Here, the Weberian theory of the housing classes (Rex and Moore 1967) was creatively redefined in relation to the system of public and private spaces and the very form that this system took under Fordist–Keynesian capitalism. In short, the Weberian theory of the housing classes was turned into a regulationist/Marxist theory of the same classes as the consumer of public/private spaces and the body of societalisation. He wrote, "We are concerned here with housing, transportation (to jobs and facilities), amenities, facilities, and a whole bundle of resources that contribute to the total living environment for labour. Some of these items can be privately appropriated (housing is the most important case) while others have to be used in common (sidewalks) and in some cases, such as the transportation system, even used jointly with capital" (Harvey 1976, p. 267).

The power of public and private spaces to remould the working class into forms less inimical to societalisation (the housing classes) was apparent. Indeed, the whole dynamism involved the "fragmentation of the working class into 'housing classes' of homeowners and tenants" (p. 272). After writing this article, Harvey more or less skirted around this formulation of the housing classes, public and private spaces, and their society-forming power.[1] More recently, Harvey (2006) presented a comparable view on public and private spaces, but it no longer uses the housing classes as a lens for deciphering class relations in the city. Nonetheless, organising urban research in this way is still promising. In Neil Smith's (2000) question "What happened to class?" one can find unexploited room for revitalisation around the housing classes, which is a line of research that is implied, though perhaps in a roundabout way, by Edward W. Soja (1989).[2]

Harvey's perspective resonates with Marxists who have revitalised Marx's understanding of metabolism from the side of the working class (Burkett 1999; Foster 2000). Harvey's argument remains unique because he suggests that the metabolic nature may take the form of public and private spaces, that its systemic effect is to fragment and regroup the working class into the housing classes at the level of urban metabolism, and that societalisation gains from this process its important underpinning of consumptive urban imaginaries. Harvey in this respect appears to be close to Manuel Castells (1983) and to John R. Logan and Harvey L. Molotch (1987), who have observed an outburst of new ontologies and actions in the locus of residential neighbourhoods (see also Cox and Mair 1988). Harvey's (1976) approach is distinctive because he thinks that the increased use values of public and private—and people's struggle for that increase—share co-shaping (that is, self-regulating) dynamics with Keynesian state policy and capitalism.

In this book, I attempt to dovetail Harvey's critical arguments on public/private spaces, the housing classes, and their Keynesian expansion with a theory of spatial Keynesianism mobilised by Neil Brenner (2004a). I argue that "homelessness" occupies a key position in this Lefebvre–Harvey line of discussion. Theoretically, homeless people are the one and only type of urban dwellers who are fundamentally alienated from the urban grid, from public and private spaces, and from the "normalized lifestyle" (Lefebvre 1991 [1974], p. 338) that these spaces constitute. Without having housing spaces, homeless people have to insert themselves in the urban grid differently than those who are housed. Inevitably, this distinct insertion drives homeless people to develop a "less-than-normal"—or, as it were, "more-than-normal"—lifestyle that contravenes and overwhelms the modern history of urban societalisation based on public and private spaces.

At the sites of homelessness, urban abstraction in action faces ruptures that are unabstracted and unconcealed. This provokes endemic local efforts towards reregulation (masking) in defence of the matrix of cities, its main consumers (the housed), and their norms and symbolic/hierarchical apparatus. The homeless–housed divides thus proliferate, an effect which sociologists and geographers find all-important (Cloke, May, and Johnsen 2010; Gowan 2010; Snow and Anderson 1993).

It should be noted that homelessness is a source of fundamental instability for the housing classes. The housing classes can be strongly inspired to struggle to defend existing public and private spaces from the "invasion" of homeless people. When this happens, homeless people become an antithetical reference point for urban society reinstating actions of the housing classes, known as NIMBYism (DeVerteuil 2013; Takahashi 1997; Wagner 1993).

Metabolism, Societalisation, Rescaling

Metabolism and Societalisation

It should now be clear that the urban matrix of public and private spaces encloses the plight, deficiencies, and misery of city dwellers within housing and—to follow Lefebvre's nomenclature—within "dwelling machines" (Lefebvre 2003a [1970], p. 81). Through this enclosure, the failure of consumption (such as empty stomachs, untreated diseases, or unexpected deaths) is hidden from the sight of publicly behaving citizens. This enclosure makes citizens (qua the housing classes) ready to perform "relations in public" (Goffman 1971) outside of the privatised, enclosed life. In turn, public spaces are separated from private and are endowed with distinct norms of consumption that advance spatial functionalism around housing, with an essential role in gentrifying and normalising urban consumption/encounter by letting "people (the 'inhabitants') move about in space which tends towards a geometric isotopy" (Lefebvre 1996 [1967], p. 128).

The net effect of this whole urban matrix, this isotopy, is what Lefebvre understood as "habitat", which can mask alienation, dispossession, and exploitation inherent in class-divided and class-dividing urbanisation and can achieve the feat of social cohesion and societalisation against recursive disruptive tendencies. In this theory, public spaces are a powerful arena of societalisation. Regulationist thinkers have understood consumption norms to be a key condition of Fordism (Aglietta 1979 [1976]; Boyer 1990; Boyer and Saillard 2002 [1995]; Jessop and Sum 2006). Urban space has been discussed as a major site for the realisation of this consumption (Aglietta 1979 [1976]; Amin 1994; Brenner and Theodore 2002; Dear and Scott 1981; Harvey 1989b; Jessop 2002; Soja 1989). Public spaces, and their position in the matrix of public and private, play a pivotal role in ensuring that "normal" consumption dictates the very normative outlook in urbanisation.

Homeless people are those who are filtered out of the grid of public and private spaces. Homeless people, after experiencing this filtration effect and suffering a loss of housing (private) space, are then forced to reinject themselves into public spaces to survive, but this reinjection is seen as "abnormal". Homeless people must find housing in public, and this powerfully fuels rescaling dynamism in and around public spaces. In theorising this dynamism, I employ the two notions of *societalisation* and *metabolism*. This book has greatly elaborated the notion of societalisation, which concerns the wider social conditions of late (late) capitalism, but what is metabolism?

In this book, *metabolism* refers to a material–semiotic substrate of societalisation, in which the social consolidation (societalisation) of people can find a physical and cultural foundation. As explicated here, the construction and agglomeration of public and private spaces in cities plays this fundamental role. By providing the urban built environment in the material sense (Harvey 1982), public and private spaces also promote the vast meaning-making, reappropriating, and placemaking work of "users" and "consumers" that actively define who they are, how they live, what they defend, and against whom they defend it (Castells 1983; Hou 2010; Logan and Molotch 1987; Low 2003; Relph 1976; Tuan 1977).

While the notion of metabolism attracts much attention from geographers and urbanists from different fields and perspectives (for a useful review, see Heynen 2014; Newell and Cousins 2015), I follow the Marxist line, which focuses on the labouring process of people. Marx locates labour at the heart of society–nature dialectics (Ekers and Loftus 2013; Smith 1984). The Marxist stock of metabolism theory seeks to decipher labour, or the use value producing ability of human agency (Burkett 1999; Foster 2000; Heynen, Kaika, and Swyngedouw 2006; Swyngedouw 1996, 2015).

Homeless people's lack of housing pushes them into a unique, minoritarian pattern of urban metabolism in public spaces, and this metabolism hinges on the reemancipation of their labour capacity (reskilling) from its systemically subdued status (deskilling). Only through this labouring capacity and its reskilling can homeless people produce, and immediately consume, new housing (private) spaces in public spaces vis-à-vis all the rules and norms of consumption promulgated among, and practised by, the housing classes during their everyday consumption. The net effect of this minoritarian metabolism is profound: the mere *existence* of homelessness in public spaces can be perceived and interpreted as aggressively challenging the common semiotic system of the housing classes.

This production-oriented (labour-intensive) process of metabolism thus becomes threatening to normative public spaces.

Marx (1976 [1867], p. 283) states, "Labour is, first of all, a process between man and nature, a process by which man, through his own actions, mediates, regulates and controls the metabolism between himself and nature. ... He sets in motion the natural forces which belong to his own body, his arms, legs, head and hands, in order to appropriate the materials of nature in a form adapted to his own needs." In this thread of metabolism theory, Marx argues that metabolism is the labour-mediated relations of people to nature that are widely found and ubiquitous in both capitalist and noncapitalist spaces (for urban political ecology on this thread of Marx, see Swyngedouw 2015; Swyngedouw and Heynen 2003).

In homelessness, this argument in Marx's metabolism theory takes on a unique dimension. For one thing, homeless people produce the use value of housing by labouring in public spaces. Homeless people can consume the use value of private spaces (to sleep, talk, eat, cook, and socialise) through this production of housing out of public spaces—the particular portion of the second nature (Lefebvre 1976 [1973]; 1991 [1974]; 2003a [1970]). In addition, the consumption of the product—housing goods—is itself labour; homeless people achieve this consumption by constantly managing and dodging regulatory pressure, which the housing classes and their guardians generate in defence of consumption norms. This labour-intensive view of metabolism applies to homeless people more than it does to the housing classes (whose metabolic relations are more consumptive).

Now let us reconsider the urban metabolism in public spaces from the other side, that of the housing classes. I theorise that the existence of the housing classes in public spaces, and their consumption of public spaces, can render the homeless metabolism "abnormal" and politicised. Generally, where a vigorous formation of homeless regulation is occurring in public spaces, homeless people have already essentially formed their *labour-intensive* metabolism, demonstrating and opposing it to the housing classes' *consumption-intensive* metabolism. Marx gives us a clue to understand this situation when he says that "production ... is also immediately consumption, consumption is also immediately production" (Marx 1973, p. 91). If this statement sounds somewhat circular, let us follow it a little further and we will find a clearer understanding about the circuit of metabolism and how consumption is located in the circuit.

> Consumption creates the need for new production, that is it creates the ideal, internally impelling cause for production, which is its presupposition. Consumption creates the motive for production; it also creates the object which is active in production as its determinant aim. If it is clear that production offers consumption its object, it is therefore equally clear that consumption *ideally posits* the object of production as an internal image, as a need, as drive and as purpose. It creates the objects of production in a still subjective form. (Marx 1973, pp. 91–92; original emphasis)

Here is an angle that is, by and large, discernible from Harvey's (1982) famous and much-discussed "circuits of capital" thesis, and his definition of urban amenity and housing as the "secondary circuit of capital" (Harvey 1989c, pp. 64–65). My argument in this chapter owes much to Harvey, but here, to Marx. In this quote, Marx says more than that someone's production needs someone else's consumption in order to advance the balanced expansion of commodity society and the motion of value chains. Even further, Marx acknowledges that consumption has a *generative* role distinct from production per se, that is, it gives production (and society based on it) an "image", an imagined "need", and a shared "purpose". We may find here Marx's anticipation of postmodern thinkers who redefine consumption as an autonomous field of semiotic political economy (Baudrillard 1998 [1970]).

This image-generating process in consumption is also central to urban metabolism. In this sense, metabolism is understood as not just a material but also a semiotic process, in which the consumers can enrich, rearticulate, and broaden the image of urban nature through every bit and piece of everyday consumption. This theoretical elaboration allows us to give a regulationist explanation for how and why the housing classes can so powerfully relegate the homeless metabolism in the semiotic process of consumption, through the cultural construction of NIMBYism (DeVerteuil 2013; Takahashi 1997; Wagner 1993).

The housing classes are people who *can* consume urban nature without producing it. The housing classes cultivate this consumption *ontologically*, not as something given by the grid or the "structure" but as something that they purposefully and spontaneously construct. Here lies the answer to the question of why public spaces become the platform of societalisation. Public spaces can fulfil this fundamental role in capitalism because public spaces prompt the housing classes—through consumption—to develop various images of "public" away from the experiences and hardships of private life and waged labour (which remain turbulent in capitalism).

This explains why "behavior in public places" can be so limitlessly gentrified, as sociologist Erving Goffman (1963) seems to have believed it is, and why the participants can imagine these gentrified relations as meaningful and attractive. These participants, the housing classes, can enrich public spaces during material–semiotic consumption as they are spatially separated from the extra-public spheres (private life and waged labour) that still can remain wild and de-societalising. By organising the consumptive side of metabolism, cities achieve the feat of accommodating mutually competing (or even antagonistic) populations, classes, and class fractions side by side (Lefebvre 1991 [1974], p. 319). In particular, people's metabolism in public spaces can generate a robust semiotic layer of consumption that allows the housing classes to share common images and meanings of how the city *should* be, beyond the alienating and exploitative effects that still characterise urbanisation.

Capitalism—while advancing metabolic subsumption—can still find increases and upticks in noncapitalist or postcapitalist economies and urban nature production (Gibson-Graham 2006; Roelvink, Martin, and Gibson-Graham 2015). Noncapitalist economies have repeatedly appeared at the fringes of the capitalist world system and have supported its core–periphery relation from its vanishing points (Wallerstein

1979). However, what we see here is a unique type of noncapitalist economy that frustrates the majoritarian metabolism at its heart and is immediately retaliated against—avenged—by the hegemonic classes, their guardians, and their societalising coalitions.

This tension is rather reminiscent of Rosa Luxemburg's (2003 [1913], p. 397) notion of noncapitalist environments—the "aid of non-capitalist organizations"—whereby she conceptualised that the "accumulation of capital is a kind of metabolism between capitalist economy and those pre-capitalist methods of production without which it cannot go on". Luxemburg observed acute contradiction between capitalist forms of metabolism and their outside (noncapitalist) spaces, the latter also entailing metabolic milieus in their own way: "Although this non-capitalist milieu is indispensable for accumulation, the latter proceeds at the cost of this medium nevertheless, by eating it up. ... Capital cannot accumulate without the aid of non-capitalist organizations, nor ... can it tolerate their continued existence side by side with itself."

A similar if distinct contradiction between two metabolic relations can grow by taking the form of homeless–housed divides at the heart of urbanisation—not somewhere peripheral or concealed from our "normal" urban life. This *contradictory simultaneity* of two metabolic circuits is shown in Figure 4.1. On the left is the circuit of minoritarian metabolism attempted by homeless people. On the right is the circuit of majoritarian metabolism engaged in by the housing classes. There is a material and semiotic contradiction between these two metabolisms. In this book, I define the homeless–housed divide as this material and semiotic cleavage that can open at the level of metabolism and its semiotic auspice.

Rescaling and Reregulation

We have seen that the homeless–housed divide emerges between the two circuits of urban metabolism. But there is more to this story. Because the homeless–housed divide is rooted in the fundamental contradiction of urban metabolism, "regulation" arises to address the contradiction. This homeless regulation—an aspect of societalisation—has some interesting affinities with Marx's "forest regulation".

According to Marx, a noncapitalist pattern of people's metabolism with nature—the "gathering of fallen wood"—provoked the Prussian state's novel attempts to outlaw such metabolic practice, which the state defined as "thefts of wood" (Marx 1996 [1842]). Contemporary homelessness might analogously be defined as a theft of public space. Yet the difference is profound. In Marx's era, forest regulation was the state's legal effort against many people in defence of a few (Linebaugh 1976). By contrast, today's homeless regulation is action against the minority in defence of the majority (the societalised "us"); what this context evokes is not only political formation but also society formation and their collaboration/hybridity, which can mobilise the vast imaginaries and resources of the housing classes for the sake of "homeless regulation". To invoke a Gramscian concept, public spaces can serve as a hegemony-valorising

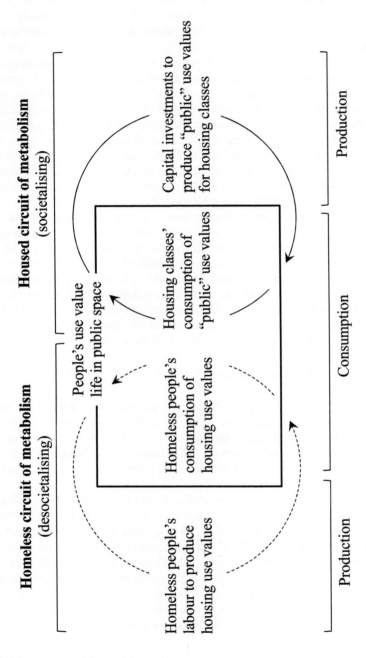

Figure 4.1 People's two metabolic circuits in public space.

site because, in these spaces, "the citizenry come to believe that authority over their lives emanates from the self" (Morton 2007, p. 93). This bottom-up imaginary (self-belief) of the housing classes, accumulated in public spaces, can drive *integral* state rescaling.

As a theoretical framework for this regulation in public spaces, I will use Antonio Gramsci's theory of the state and civil society as two mutually dependent defenders of hegemony (for interpretations of this theory, see Ekers et al. 2013; Jessop 2002; Morton 2007; Thomas 2009). For Gramsci, the state (in the narrow sense) is about law, government, and sanction-backed guidance (Gramsci 1971, pp. 261, 267). As such, the state has the power of coercion, compulsion, and guidance. Civil society is the locus of spontaneous consent among citizens and moral leaders grounded on their religious/institutional bases; it is the site for the "evolution of customs, ways of thinking and acting, morality" (p. 242; see also p. 12). Gramsci presents the view that different societies developed these two sectors without a complete overlapping, achieved processual unity and a partial amalgam in the histories and geographies of the two (the "integral state"), and in so doing regularised trajectories of civilisation.

Gramsci uses the term *hegemony* to describe a well-balanced state–society relationship; this good balance must be predominant if there is to be a stable hegemony in civilisation. Up to a point, the state can withdraw coercion in the expectation that civil society will build consensus around moral leaders. At this point, hegemony arises as "a combination of force and consent which balance each other so that force does not overwhelm consent but rather appears to be backed up by the consent of the majority" (1992, p. 156). As such, hegemony is a "balance between political society and civil society" (1971, p. 208) and is "protected by the armour of coercion" (p. 263). The expression of "political society + civil society" (p. 263) usefully denotes historical ways in which the integral state is repeatedly reformed through combining the two sectors, in relation to concrete-level contexts of regulatory crisis.

This is Gramsci's famous formulation of the "normal" type of hegemony. For my purpose, this discussion is important because Gramsci never leaves the normality as it is. Instead, he dovetails hegemony with *non*hegemony or *less* hegemony, with times and spaces of regulatory crisis (or waning) and reconstruction. A "crisis of hegemony" (Gramsci 1971, p. 210) can be autonomous from the economy. He does, however, recognise that beneath the times and spaces of hegemonic crisis lies the fertile ground for the material, the "world of the economy or of production" (p. 263). For example, it was laissez-faire capitalism that disturbed an established equilibrium between social forces and prompted new regulation by "legislative and coercive means" (p. 160).

Yet he is keen to distinguish himself from economic determinism. It is only within *certain* relationships with the economy that the coercion–consensus balance can be lost in hegemonic fields, which leads to nondeterminist, nonteleological courses for new regulatory dynamics. What arises is an ongoing process that must assemble available regulatory elements to keep a hegemonic civilisation on track. In such times and spaces of regulatory crisis, the bare bones are apparent: "Hegemony [is] protected by the armor of coercion" (p. 263) and a "field is open for violent solutions" (p. 210; see also pp. 160, 261).

Gramsci's thought is foundational to my theory. The idea of "normal" hegemony is useful in thinking about the "normal" pattern of public spaces as a good state–society balance, in which coercion retreats into the background and consensus looms in the foreground. Because urban encounters in public spaces can powerfully cultivate and stabilise public codes (Goffman 1963, 1971), public spaces play the bottom-up role to valorise hegemony.

Harvey's theory of urban public spaces partly follows this Gramscian vein, adding to Gramsci's theory the unique angle of the housing classes. According to Harvey (1976, p. 278), public spaces and amenities—"streets and sidewalks, drains and sewer systems, parks and playgrounds"—can regulate labour-side interests because they are "collectively consumed".[3] Public spaces—through their collective consumption—can form the "techniques of persuasion" (p. 277). We have already seen that this hegemony-valorising (consensus-building) role of public spaces becomes possible because public spaces—when coupled with private spaces and forming the urban matrix—have the power to organise city dwellers into a civil society of "housing classes" (p. 272). These classes can "share a common romantic image of nature" (p. 286).

Homeless people (their "distinctive" lifeworlds) come to exist outside of, but side by side with, these hegemonic imaginaries and forms of urban encounter that are valorised by the housing classes through their consumption of public spaces. In response, the state and civil society assemble tools, networks, and units of regulation that are deemed "suitable" to these "outsiders"—or, more precisely, to the "wild" encountering points of the housed with homeless people's lifeworlds. In this context, civil society—a conspicuous site of consent-making—can respond coercively to the homeless "outsiders" of the housing regime, its public/private matrix ("grid"), and its attendant urban imaginaries, which all affect (if not determine) the forms of urban encounter that are acceptable for the housing classes. As Gramsci (1971, p. 266) implies, a society that is rehabilitating social consensus can develop coercive regulatory methods, especially when the "consented citizens" are faced with the "non-consented Other".

The extent to which "pure coercion" is mixed up with elements of consensus and materialises as interpenetrating arenas of homeless regulation should vary from one city to another, one location to another; hybridisation is contextual. At any rate, however, the basic appearance of public spaces can adopt a more regimenting tone. The impact is immense: homelessness drives the production of new regulatory spaces, thereby hastening the entire rescaling of the NSPR and its integral state subspheres. Public spaces come to assemble various (semi) coercive mechanisms on the borders of rights and citizenship. Amid the "crisis of homelessness", which is a particular form of hegemonic crisis, public spaces thus become a breeding ground for *integral* state rescaling.

Figure 4.2 illustrates the dynamics I have demonstrated. First, the hegemonic relationship of the state, civil society, and public spaces is indicated in the top

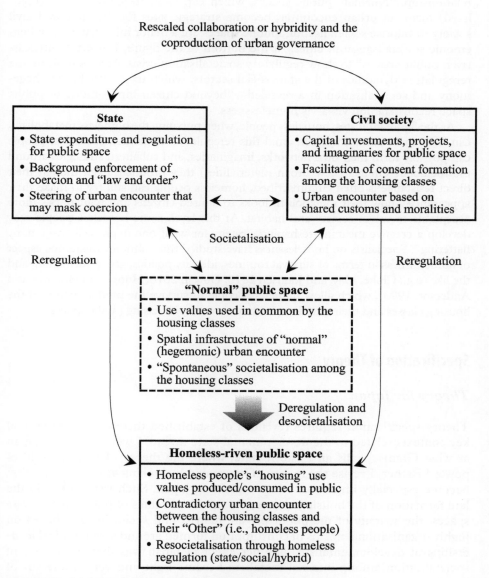

Figure 4.2 Regulation of urban encounter and societalisation in public space.
Note: Dotted lines denote realms/relations being deregulated under homelessness.

three boxes. Bidirectional arrows link the three boxes, representing the tripartite relationship. "Normal" public spaces, which can facilitate conventional (regulated) forms of urban encounter, become strategic sites for the state and civil society to valorise societalisation; public spaces are a major infrastructure of hegemonic societalisation in cities. At the bottom of the figure, I insert "homeless-riven public spaces" to show regulatory/societalisation crisis. Arrows indicate the reregulation dynamics of the state/social sectors, which try to rehabilitate hegemony and societalisation in a rescaled—"beyond citizenship"—mode of public space reconstruction vis-à-vis homelessness.

As the figure indicates, homeless people, when pursuing the homeless metabolism, can hold some autonomy even amid this reregulation dynamics. Homeless people can possibly form their own networks, imaginaries, and subaltern strategies around the metabolic circuits (new urban materialities) they produce. Even though their direct resistance is often circumscribed, homeless people can still try to make their appearance—how their metabolism looks to housed citizens and regulators—more acceptable to urban society and habitat. At this level, some homeless people may develop a creative meaning-reshaping strategy for what one might call "hegemony flattering". Specialists on homelessness have studied this culturally dexterous aspect of homelessness in terms of survival routines, identity politics, group formation, and the like (e.g., Cloke, May, and Johnsen 2010; Gowan 2010; Hopper 2003; Snow and Anderson 1993), which allow homeless people to survive the predominance of the housing classes and their guardians without overtly politicising public spaces.

Specification of Theory

Theory for Japan

Theory specification requires revisions of established theory by using several key contexts related to the developmental state thread. I would *not* treat Japan as what Gramsci calls an Eastern state, where the theory of hegemony loses power.[4] Rather, I revise the theory of hegemony by looking at those issues that become especially important when explaining Japan. Such issues include the late formation of the housing classes, the small use values of public and private spaces, the sparsity of the public/private matrix, and societalisation based on highly organisational norms of consumption formed around sociopolitical leaderships of developmentalism. The net effect in Japan was that the nature of societalisation among internal members became tight and very intolerant of those on the outside (i.e., the homeless people).

Late Formation of the Housing Classes in Japan

Even in the early twentieth century, the housing classes were not a perceivable type of urban dweller in Japan; the formation of the housing classes came late to the nation. Rural populations suffering the crisis of the agrarian economy flooded into big cities in the interwar period, and the new arrivals were accommodated in a premodern type of dwelling called *kyodō nagaya*, onestory buildings made up of multiple small rooms, or worse, in shared lodges called *kichinyado*, in which the distinction of each room was even weaker (Yokoyama 1994 [1903], 1994 [1912]). These rooms only had space for a few tatami mats, the dwellers had no more possessions than "goods for travel", and they often rented sleeping mattresses rather than owning them (Nakagawa 1985, p. 31). Even in the best case, the tiny rooms enclosed only a small area of household "private" space. Cooking, washing, bathing, parenting, and excretion were conducted outside of each private unit, when there was such a thing, and relationships among different households were not clearly delineated by walls.

It is suggested that half of the total urban population was outside of the modern housing classes at the end of the nineteenth century (p. 27). In the early twentieth century and thereafter, more of the populace became able to form a discrete family unit and to move to more enclosed types of private housing (p. 399; see also Sorensen 2002, p. 59). Even after the beginnings of this late formation of the housing classes, however, more than a few households found it difficult to maintain their stable position within the housing classes (Kamata 1999).

Small Use Values Attached to Japan's Urban Matrix

Japanese state policy deeply influenced the late formation of the housing classes. Policymakers' adoption of the public/private matrix happened only relatively recently. Rather, the Japanese state emphasised the technological enhancement of new industries, and national wealth was allocated to the catching-up economy (Johnson 1982). Just as Japan's minimalist approach to the so-called welfare state ensued from developmentalism (Kwon 2005), so too did Japan's avoidance of producing built environments for popular consumption (Miyamoto 1976). Paris—its "magnificent boulevards and public structures, recently renovated by Napoleon III and Baron Haussmann" (Sorensen 2002, p. 50)—amazed Japanese policymakers, but they did not fully adopt the notion of the public/private matrix as a doctrine of urban policy. Instead, the state "largely ignor[ed] spending to improve quality of life", taking a minimalist approach to "social infrastructure such as parks, sewer systems, and local roads" (p. 90), as well as to "new housing that would be affordable for working people" (p. 88).

During the 1970s, the small, malfunctioning, or highly polluted use values of public and private spaces under Japan's developmentalist urbanisation precipitated local societal crises in the form of environment crises (Miyamoto 1976). More recently, the housing question worsened under repeated neoliberal

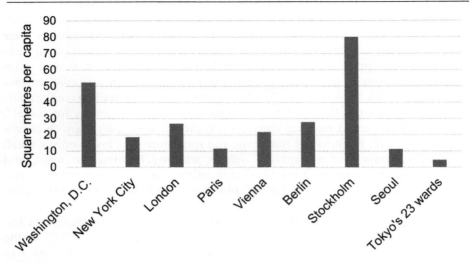

Figure 4.3 Comparative view of Japanese public space: a policy discourse.
Note: This graph, which is reproduced from a report by the Ministry of Land, Infrastructure, Transport and Tourism, a key national regulator, compares public parks and green spaces in Tokyo to parks and green spaces in other global cities. Similar international comparisons of Japanese public space are repeatedly made by policymakers in Japan (e.g., MLIT 2003; TMG 2014). It indicates that these policymakers are aware of and concerned about the small use values of Japanese public space and how that can make Japanese cities unattractive to urban consumers and visitors.
Source: MLIT (2015).

adjustments (Hirayama and Ronald 2007). As for public spaces, the historical smallness of parks and public green spaces is something that worries today's policymakers (MLIT 2003, 2015, 2018; TMG 2014). International comparisons, such as that in Figure 4.3, "prove" to Japanese urban planners how few parks and green spaces there are in their cities.

State-Saturated Societalisation and Consumption in Japan

In theory, public spaces, after being separated from the private and workplace spheres, become a site of material–semiotic consumption that can powerfully support societalisation. Public spaces in this sense offer formative opportunities to the semiosis of the housing classes—their worldview production and its generalisation into shared urban meanings. Use values are consumed, and they become more meaningful with every bit of consumption as it is filtered through the public/private grid. This theory appeared uniquely in Japan, where the use values of urban spaces (both public and private) remained small. In the early modern era, this smallness drove authorities to the policing of a riotous local social climate.

In the postwar era of democratisation, this authoritarian societalisation took on a more consensual pattern, moving beyond mere coercion. This brought about clearer borders between "state" and "society" in accordance with Japan's postwar democracy building (Hirata 1969). Even after contriving this modern situation, however, democratic societalisation was regimented and state–society distinctions were blurred. Following into the path of prewar Japan (Moore 1967), administration-oriented residential communities reemerged under the aegis of state policy, strategically mixing state and social sectors in the municipality to achieve depoliticised local governance. In the 1950s and 1960s, when Japan was launching and deploying its "industrial policy" (Johnson 1982) by targeting areas of industrialisation and their hinterlands, this form of local community circumscribed—without overtly rejecting—people's democratic spontaneity in local neighbourhoods.[5] This trajectory facilitated a mode of urban societalisation in which residents would not be politically frustrated by the small use values permitted to them, or would not disagree with the state's preference for elitist industrialisation over people's use values and collective consumption (Matsubara and Nitagai 1976).

The key mechanism in this trajectory was provided by the chōnaikai (neighbourhood association), a type of local community group endorsed by administrators and widely distributed in localities. These groups directed the public meanings of consumption towards the narrow, functional purposes of child care, garbage collection, security maintenance, and so on (Pekkanen 2006; Yoshihara 1989). André Sorensen (2002) articulates,

> The chōnaikai are ... clearly part of the answer to the question why the middle class was not more active in municipal politics. The fact is they were very active at the local level, co-opted into government-directed local activities such as providing most of the local social welfare and community services as well as garbage collection and street-cleaning, and providing their own street-lighting. This relieved local governments of the need to provide a range of costly local services, as well as providing a direct conduit for central government information and directives to reach every neighborhood and ultimately every family in the country. (p. 106)

In point of fact, some Japanese sociologists depict chōnaikai as an embodiment of residents' spontaneous power to produce local community qua "association mediated by housing" (*jyūen asoshiēshon*) (Iwasaki et al. 1989), while others recognise that neighbourhoods around chōnaikai became democratic when residents negotiated with regulatory agencies (Tamano 1993; Yoshihara 1989). While these sociological complexities are obscured in Sorensen's articulation, it rightly highlights the structural roles of chōnaikai, which are also underscored in Japanese-language works (Akimoto 1971; Matsubara and Nitagai 1976; Tamano 1993; Yoshihara 1989). Building on these works, my account seeks to emphasise that this administration-oriented locus of local society facilitated the narrow and methodical societalisation of people's consumption life in urban settlements. One ramification of this is that Japanese public spaces in and around neighbourhoods have become filled with many notices, slogans, and unspoken rules of administrators and leaders who elaborate the codes of consumption for residents (Fujita 2006), and these codes are keenly followed in public spaces (e.g., Pele et al. 2017).

All in all, the small use values of public spaces, which mirrored Japan's developmentalist approach to urbanisation, came to be consumed in a highly orderly fashion by the housing classes throughout the postwar years. This methodical, historically state-saturated, and organisationally elaborated mode of societalisation—what could be called hyperconformist societalisation—decreased the likelihood of radical revolts and progressive movements against policymakers in local neighbourhoods, although such popular struggle is emphasised by international theorists (e.g., Castells 1983) as a driver of urban politics. In Japan, community social movements became more prominent for a relatively brief spell after the mid-1960s (Matsubara and Nitagai 1976), but this growth in local activism soon subsided. In short, the "progressive will" of residents was steered towards the narrow, state-saturated functionality of community formation, which—through the tight consumptive norms—helped the depoliticisation of the Japanese housing classes and their public/private matrix as a grid of societalisation.

This utility of Japanese communities as a plane for developmentalist societalisation should be emphasised, because the housing classes in Japan actually experienced the smallness of use values. If we apply the international (regulationist) theory straightforwardly, the housing classes should have erupted in more neighbourhood-rooted activism throughout the postwar decades. The regional mode of consumption norms—the methodical, administration-oriented tone that these norms adopted via mediums such as chōnaikai—explains this theory–reality gap in the Japanese case. In fact, in more contemporary periods, community groups such as chōnaikai have shrunk in Japan (Nakagawa 2011). However, this historical locus of community relations may be revitalised, especially when they meet with the "repugnant" outsiders of the housing classes. Amid this housed–homeless encounter, groups such as chōnaikai can strengthen their moral leadership for the housing classes, delineating their borders vis-à-vis the subaltern group and *reactivating* Japan's conformist type of societalisation in the cities.

Ground-Up Rescaling in Japan

Homelessness challenges the Japanese pattern of societalisation and promotes the urban dynamics of rescaling. As I noted earlier, homeless and near-homeless populations existed well before the 1990s, in and around the yoseba zones of the metropolises, which were a type of inner-city phenomenon distinct from but comparable to the patterns of racialised ghettos. When Japan launched postwar developmentalism, yoseba zones, a geography of segregation tailored to each metropolis, were highly supportive of developmentalist urbanisation.

Most importantly, yoseba zones accommodated the cities' mostly male day labourers and their "deviant" process of social reproduction without disrupting the integrity of mainstream society and societalisation. These precarious labourers, whose wages hardly compensated their intensive work and hazardous working conditions, were essential for Japanese developmentalism; they became a functional equivalent to international migrant labourers in Atlantic Fordism. The problem was that the labourers' living conditions were too unstable to be safely incorporated into the housing classes. In this context, yoseba zones offered a half-institutionalised space of segregation in which the bodies and relations of day labourers were "pooled" outside of mainstream society (and its spaces of societalisation) but still kept in an accessible form for urbanised capital.

Homeless people existed among this population of day labourers well before the 1990s. The inner-city cycle of Japanese homelessness had already emerged in the 1970s, which drove the ground-up (haphazard) process of reregulation and created localised, locational rules of homeless regulation relating to public spaces and welfare-providing programmes. However, the more recent, widespread cycle of homelessness, starting in the 1990s, has spawned larger societal impacts far beyond the inner city. When homeless people became increasingly ubiquitous in "normal" public spaces, the prevailing perception was that homeless people's metabolic relations with urban nature were no longer filtered through the grid of public and private and that they were challenging the basic distinctions and categories of societalisation held by the housing classes. Because Japanese societalisation was historically underpinned by (quasi)formal leadership and regimented norms of consumption based on the organisational mode of residential neighbourhoods, Japanese societalisation turned out to be highly intolerant of the "Other" of hegemonic urban consumption—homeless people.

In consequence, the widespread cycle of homelessness during and after the 1990s hastened vigorous formations of homeless regulation as the integral state; the multiscalar production of new regulatory spaces mobilised both state and social agents, who formed numerous coworking units and knowledge-transfer networks in cities. In many cases, these urban regimes tried to preserve hegemonic public spaces by defining homeless people as the mere disturbers of the collective consumption. In fact, homeless people were not just "consumers" but also "producers", and the local regulatory complexes aspired to downplay this versatile formation of the homeless metabolism in defence of quotidian consumption. Extensive homeless roundups occurred, clearly intended to rebuff the metabolic and hegemonic impact of homelessness. Large-scale roundups were planned or undertaken mainly in metropolitan areas and these processes mobilised both state and social sectors (Fujii and Tamaki 2003; Hayashi 2014b; Kasai 1999; Sakokawa 2013). There also were small-scale evictions that were sporadically reported but equally effective in removing homeless people (Hayashi 2005, 2014b).

More nuanced—sometimes "homeless-friendly"—policies were created in many localities, and the local and national states did create forms of regulation other than violent ones (see Fujii and Tamaki 2003; Mizuuchi 2002; Yamasaki et al. 2006; also Chapters 7, 8, and 9). However, the basic pattern of homeless regulation *in public spaces* was coercive, and it remains so. In reaction, homeless people tried to reconstruct viable survival strategies both on and off the streets (Hayashi 2005; Kitagawa 2001; Maruyama 2013; Yamaguchi 1998; Yamakita 2006).

In terms of numbers, Japanese homelessness even during this major crisis period does not compare to that of the United States during the extended crisis of Fordism. The number of homeless street people in that country was estimated at between 250,000 and 300,000 in the early 1980s (Rossi 1989, p. 37). The number of homeless people living in Japanese public space was just below 30,000 at its peak in the early 2000s, according to official counts (MHLW 2003). Yet even this relatively small volume of homelessness spawned a significant homeless–housed divide, antihomeless built forms and symbolisms, and rescaling regulatory dynamics in postcrisis Japan.

This Japanese solution looks paradoxical to the theory of rescaling but it is in fact fully explainable: the historically small use values of Japanese public spaces for the housing classes, the tight societalisation of these classes that had depoliticised (the lack of) consumption, and the deep surveillance of public spaces by state/quasistate/nonstate agents made Japanese urban metabolism very susceptible to urban "disorder" brought about by homeless people. Even though their number was relatively small by international standards, this homelessness promoted the major dynamics of rescaling reregulation.

Metabolism and Regulation I: Locational Ethnography

Background for Ethnographic Narratives

This section and the next develop a series of ethnographic enquiries into ground-up rescaling as it appears in Japanese public spaces. When homeless people started dwelling in public spaces and engaging in new metabolic relations, the sociometabolic process of the hegemonic (housing) classes was fundamentally affected, for what homeless people created out of (and within) public spaces is housing. When this homeless metabolism eluded the filtering effects of the public/private grid, the housing classes became alarmed and started antihomeless meaning-making. Led by the semiotic power of public space users, state and social regulators began to deploy effective antihomeless rules and practices. In order to defend the "normal" metabolic relation, local agents in the state and civil society sprang into action and developed viable regulatory tools.

My fieldwork has detected a significant spur for regulation from the housing classes. Tellingly, the mayor of one city said, "We need to have the situation that everyone can enjoy pavements and parks with a safe feeling, while there is an insecure atmosphere, created by homeless people, in which we can't peacefully play in parks" (City of Hiratsuka 2003). This remark was made during a meeting in which the mayor responded to concerns raised by housed citizens about the "insecure" situation reportedly produced by homeless people. In the same meeting, people participating in this dialogue compared homeless people to "dog droppings in a sandbox", which prevent "parents and children" from using a park.

On their part, however, homeless people try to renegotiate this ground-level spur for resocietalisation, in defence of their metabolic spaces. A key part of this trial can be what one might call "hegemony flattering", whereby homeless people try to appear *not* to deeply damage the hegemonic urban imaginaries, partly by using regulatory holes as a potential zone of tacit agreement with regulators and the housing classes. The hope is that homeless people—up to a point—can replace spaces of antihomelessness with spaces with significantly less antihomelessness sentiment (if not prohomelessness). The homeless metabolism, furthermore, prompts homeless people to evade regulation by seeking locations—often in subprime areas—where the pressure of regulation is weak.

The ethnographic inquiry in this book reveals how this process of struggle took place during the widespread cycle of Japanese homelessness in Japan. Cases are taken from the city of Hiratsuka, located in the outlying area of Kanagawa Prefecture (see Chapter 2). This city began to experience intensified homelessness in the late 1990s. During the 2000s, when I was conducting fieldwork, homeless people in this city were strategically renegotiating with, and creatively enduring, the antihomeless regulation and semiosis that were spreading all over the city.

Small Public Parks

In the early 2000s, some homeless individuals were trying to secure their own living space—use values—in Hiratsuka's small public parks and were met with intense policing on the part of neighbourhood communities. By 2003, homeless people in parks such as Shinshuku Park, Sengen Ryokuchi, and Hachiman Yama Park were increasingly seen as a nuisance to the housing classes and their neighbourhood association—the chōnaikai. Homeless people's public drinking, noisy eating, and conspicuous tent pitching were alarming. Figure 4.4 is a notice that a neighbourhood association put up on a bench in one of the most "intolerant" homeless sites. It reads, "Use our park cleanly!!" Feeling that Hiratsuka's municipality was unreliable in maintaining the "safety" of the parks in this early period of homelessness, nearby residents spearheaded antihomeless meaning-making actions for these parks and became the primary agents of policing.

By the summer of 2003, the municipality and the police joined in the policing activity conducted by the housed citizens of this area. The signboard in Figure 4.5, warning against leaving belongings in the park, was the municipality's direct response

Figure 4.4 A bench in Shinshuku Park, 25 August 2004. The message from neighbourhood residents reads "Use our park cleanly!!"
Source: Author.

to homelessness in the area. By these means, homeless individuals were removed from the "worst" encampments in the parks.

In this context of policing dynamics, homeless people who wanted to continue their metabolic life in the parks began to develop new strategies for survival. For one thing, they became very careful about keeping their campsites clean so as to remain unobtrusive to nearby residents and authorities—a common strategy for Japanese homeless people to avoid policing pressure and downright exclusion. Figure 4.6 shows to what extent homeless people in these parks were conscious about cleaning up their encampments.

One homeless group that pitched tents in Hachiman Yama Park deliberately represented itself as "ethical" in order to suggest that the homeless metabolism caused very little disruption to hegemonic societalisation and the housing classes. This homeless group had four members who routinely obtained plastic bags from the public street cleaners to collect fallen leaves and waste on behalf of these cleaners. Maru-san, a homeless man who was engaging in this cleanup activity, said to me, "A cleaner said 'Thank you' to me a few days ago", and he explained that he and the other homeless people were doing this voluntary work "so they will not complain about our sleeping and eating in these parks".[6] Maru-san also mentioned that he and his friends were always "keeping ourselves 'one step behind the general citizens', because we know very well that we're the homeless", adding that

Figure 4.5 A signboard in Shinshuku Park, 28 August 2004. It reads "Don't leave things in the park. Otherwise they will be removed. City of Hiratsuka."
Source: Author.

Figure 4.6 A site of homelessness in Hachiman Yama Park, 28 August 2005.
Source: Author.

they were "remaining very quiet, and so citizens say nothing to us". Yet the possibility of the failure of this "hegemony-flattering" strategy was implied by another homeless individual, Yoshi-san, who said to me, "Perhaps pedestrians will make a claim [to municipal workers]."[7]

A Municipal Sports Park and a Gymnasium

The existence of homeless metabolism was also conspicuous at a municipal sports park and a gymnasium. In the early 2000s, these sites exhibited the contradiction between the metabolisms of homeless people and housed citizens, which in turn drove vigorous antihomeless semiosis and reregulation in this area. The main regulators for this area were security staff hired by the municipality. Faced with the growth of homelessness, these regulators directly controlled homeless people in order to discipline their metabolism—the production–consumption of housing—into highly submissive forms compatible with hegemonic public spaces.

In the case of the city's sports park, homeless people who did not comply with the policing rules were swiftly removed by security staff. The linchpin was this: homeless people were allowed to occupy the space during the night, but in the morning, they had to clear their belongings, hide them in hedges, and stay away. During the period of my fieldwork, around twenty individuals who accepted these rules were pursuing the homeless mode of metabolism. Homeless people's compliance with the rules was checked by security staff on a daily basis, through face-to-face observation. One homeless person, Nakata-san, reported to me that the staff often told them, "Clear up your belongings and get out by nine thirty [a.m.]."[8] This policing rule made the pattern of homelessness highly conformist. Only if homeless people behaved submissively vis-à-vis the security patrol and its rule enforcement on a daily basis (in the manner shown in Figure 4.7) were they allowed to use the site.

A similar pattern of policing emerged at the city's gymnasium, where two homeless people had found a small space in which to sleep. According to them, this formation of a homeless "group" was a means of surviving the reduction in space for homelessness under policing by security staff. This policing could be inferred from a notice put up at the gymnasium: "We spray water every day" (Figure 4.8). The two told me that this forced homeless people to remove their belongings as soon as possible in the morning; they were only allowed to come back in the middle of the night. After a few rule breakers had been removed from the site, these two were still trying to keep up with the strict policing directives in order to continue their metabolic life at this site. These homeless individuals seemed to be cooperatively enduring the pressure of policing by sharing the tools necessary for homeless metabolism—sleeping mats and a gas stove.

A Railway Station

At a railway station, rough sleepers produced and consumed their housing spaces through a minimalised process of homeless metabolism: constructing temporary

Figure 4.7 Belongings of a homeless person at the stadium, 11 August 2004.
Source: Author.

cardboard houses and lying on sleeping mats until the early morning. Around the mid-2000s, this type of homeless metabolism was regulated by passersby—by the "pedestrian circulation" (Lefebvre 2003a [1970], p. 20), which Lefebvre thinks of as a mechanism of urban regulation and as a form of habitat society. In the spring of 2004, the municipality and police dispersed about thirty homeless individuals from this location. The eviction had ousted those using the railway station aggressively—drinking publicly and making noise. Following this eviction, in the summer of 2004, twenty homeless people were still using this site but were obeying some unofficial rules. They gathered only after about 10 p.m. (when the evening rush hour ends); they slept for only a brief period, from midnight until 5 a.m. (when the station was not used by many housed citizens); and they never produced permanent "houses". These were tacit rules, enacted without clear notice, and were enforced by the staff of the railway company and the police.

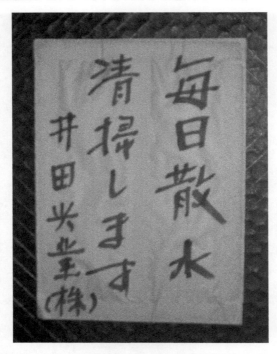

Figure 4.8 A notice at a homeless site beside the gymnasium, 3 April 2004. The notice says, "We spray water every day."
Source: Author.

Homeless people followed these unwritten rules rigorously and submissively, in order that they would not appear to be disturbing passersby and their spatial circulation. In this context of purposeful submissiveness, the flow of pedestrians served as an effective "controller" of the homeless metabolism at the site. At the same time, authorities—the railway employees, municipal workers, and police—could intervene anytime the spontaneous expression of passersby was not enough to maintain the submissiveness of homelessness and the hegemony of this public space. In the winter of 2005, however, a notice displayed by the station personnel and the city told homeless people that their intrusive use of public space would soon be brought to an end (Figure 4.9).

The Coast

Along the city's coast are two boundary lines of trees—pine woods originally planted to control sand erosion. Within these woods are circular boardwalks, provided for the sake of the housed citizens, who use them for recreational purposes. By the

Figure 4.9 A notice at the railway station, 2 December 2005. The notice says, "Remove cardboards and other things from here. We will discard them if they are not removed by 15 December 2005. The Hiratsuka railway station manager and the City of Hiratsuka."
Source: Author.

early 2000s, the coastal area was experiencing an influx of homeless people who were trying to escape the increasing pressure of the antihomeless atmosphere in the main public spaces and to find more tranquil places that were relatively remote from the housing classes. At most, the coastal area hosted around sixty homeless individuals. Initially, homeless people were subject to a lower intensity of policing, as the authorities and housed citizens scarcely intervened. In this context, the homeless metabolism developed more autonomously from this city's regulatory geography of societalisation. Homeless individuals and groups kept relatively permanent houses in this coastal area, and some even farmed the sandy soil to grow vegetables (Figure 4.10).

Hence, during the widespread cycle of homelessness, this coastal area became an emerging niche for homelessness. While state and social sectors began closely monitoring and policing central urban districts, pressure was not as high on the coast. In Hiratsuka, however, this situation changed in 2004, when one homeless person was suspected of having killed another. According to a newspaper report on the murder, the suspect was a fifteen-year-old who was drinking with his homeless friend and stabbed him in the chest with a kitchen knife ("Kōron shi shisatsu" 2004).

Figure 4.10 A house and farm of a homeless person in the coastal area, 18 April 2004.
Source: Author.

After the incident, homelessness received more intensive regulatory pressure, even in this coastal area. The local government started routine policing tours, and notices were pasted on homeless people's houses and tents, stating, "This area of trees is under the control of the prefecture. Remove these possessions." As local authorities began to regulate homelessness even in this coastal area, homeless people were driven to present themselves as submissive and docile. Thus, the "new niches" for the homeless metabolism, having emerged in the 2000s around the central domains of the housing classes, quickly fell under the disciplining arm of the regulators.

Metabolism and Regulation II: Multicity Ethnography

We have seen that the rise of the homeless metabolism during the widespread cycle of homelessness led to the quick dynamism of rescaling reregulation at different locations. This was an attempt to control the presence and movements of homeless people by constricting the spheres of rights, citizenship, and the "welfare state", partly limiting their metabolic life directly and partly eliciting their tacit cooperation. This same dynamic of homeless regulation developed throughout Kanagawa Prefecture during the 1990s and 2000s. In response to the widespread cycle of homelessness, the ground-up production of new regulatory spaces made public spaces unpleasant and dangerous for homeless people in many cities. I now turn to this broader process of public space regulation in Kanagawa Prefecture.

The city of Yokohama was one of the earliest examples. In the JR Yokohama railway station, personnel—with the support of police officers—harshly evicted homeless people. The police went so far as to throw homeless people out of their sleeping places. According to my interview with a movement participant, Yukio Takazawa, the railway station personnel on occasion voiced the belief that the eviction of the homeless people was acceptable because "they don't work and so should be killed". In Yokohama's public parks, including Hēan Park, Chūō Park, and Sawatari Chūō Park, municipal workers were on the front lines of eviction. In Sawatari Chūō Park, municipal officers put up a notice stating that "living in public parks ... is illegal".[9]

In the mid-2000s, the banks of the Nakamura River around the Ishikawa-cho area became a new site of gentrification, multiplying antihomeless evictions (Yamamoto 2008). In this neighbourhood, the developers disliked the sight of homelessness, and an influx of middle-class families further fomented antihomeless semiosis/regulation. The municipality offered homeless people in this area a provisional right to stay in a public shelter, the Nakamuragawa ryō, in exchange for homeless people's total abandonment of the area (City of Yokohama undated). More small-scale instances of eviction and policing were also carried out at various sites in Yokohama in the run-up to the 2000s, in an attempt to preserve the sociometabolic life of the housing classes and to protect the profits accrued by shopkeepers and landowners.

Homelessness also spread to cities and areas outside of Yokohama. Records for Kawasaki, another big city in Kanagawa Prefecture, allow us to interpret how the state and civil society jointly created local webs of homeless regulation in public spaces. There, homeless policing emerged in 1992, when one homeless person at the JR Kawasaki railway station was unreasonably detained by police officers. Tied up, threatened with a pistol, and tortured with boiling water in a police station, he was on the verge of death. This detention took place as a response to housed citizens of the city, who were forcefully calling for the eviction of homeless people from a central business district. This shows the extent to which the city's state and social sectors were alarmed by the loss of hegemony during the early 1990s.

In Kawasaki, antihomeless policing rules and practices quickly materialised after this incident. Police officers began to regularly patrol the homeless-populated areas, in order to interrupt homeless people's "living" in public spaces and to secure the housed citizens' use of those spaces. Housed citizens also started to engage in policing activity in order to protect public spaces themselves. They formed vigilante groups to monitor homelessness, created local policing rules, and evicted some of homeless people whose behaviours were deemed especially unacceptable.[10]

In other municipalities in Kanagawa Prefecture, such as the cities of Sagamihara, Fujisawa, and Hiratsuka, the formation of local policing regimes was delayed because the growth of homelessness came later (see Chapter 8). In these municipalities, the rise of homelessness happened around the late 1990s and early 2000s, which quickly intensified conflicts between homeless people, on the one hand, and local authorities and housed people, on the other. By the early 2000s, new rules of policing had come into being and were applied to sites of homelessness in these middle-size cities.

Compared to big municipalities (such as Yokohama and Kawasaki), in which policing sometimes accompanied big roundups, the medium-size cities often avoided these large-scale evictions. However, the logic and appearance of policing were no different: the state and civil society fomented antihomeless semiosis, jointly developed webs of policing, and coproduced rescaled regulatory fields in which the material–semiotic intrusion of homeless people into habitat was reregulated under the aegis of the integral state, reestablished on the local scale.

Conclusion

A rescaled layer of poverty regulation can emerge from within cities as they negotiate homelessness, and any public space can be a breeding ground for rescaling. Public space, located in the overall public/private matrix, denotes a strategic point of rescaling because, to adopt a Lefebvrian notion, it occupies "the point of delicate balance" (Lefebvre 1984 [1971], p. 32) within the reproduction process of urban everydayness. In defence of this strategic point, public spaces form a local, denationalised, uneven layer of homeless regulation in which homeless people tend to be dissociated from the national standards of citizenship and its "Keynesian" national–local relays. When homeless people continue with their survival economies, their metabolic/sociopolitical impacts might be contained within this layer of rescaled regulation so as to reestablish a well-ordered city of the housing classes—even amid a widespread cycle of homelessness.

The entire regulatory process has a major impact on the welfare state: it drives the rescaling of citizenship from within cities and at the local scale. This rescaling can possibly rehabilitate societalisation from moral panic in a location-specific manner. It does, however, continue to pit homeless people against the housing classes, forming endogenous patterns of urban contradiction that destabilise public spaces as the generative locus of societalisation.

In Japan, these public spaces saw a major influx of homeless people after the early 1990s, at a level incomparable to that of the preceding years. Homeless people's production and consumption of housing in public spaces contradicted "normal" citizens' desire to consume public spaces and infrastructures as common urban amenities and means of transportation. This contradiction at the metabolic level translated to the political level of regulation via the semiotic milieus of the housing classes. Hence homelessness, in producing new metabolic space and "disrupting" the consumption of the housing classes, had an impact on societalisation.

In response, the state and social sectors and their strategic networks/mixtures moved to contain homelessness, to preserve the hegemonic matrix of urban metabolism for the housing classes. At the same time, homeless people who had no immediate place to go continued to live on the streets. In so doing, they often developed a new ability to dodge regulatory pressure and to continue their homeless metabolism by giving it a "prohegemonic" appearance. Homeless people themselves had semiotic (meaning-reshaping) power to minimise antihomeless pressure. When regulation took highly coercive forms, the skilful strategies of homeless people still allowed them to postpone the worst-case scenario of regulation—wholesale eviction and exclusion.

Finally, the gendered character of homelessness in Japanese public spaces must be taken into consideration, though this chapter has not addressed this issue because it approaches the homeless metabolism from the angle of urban class relations. By far the majority of homeless people in Japanese public spaces are men, but there also are homeless women. It is reported that some homeless women in Japan represent themselves as subservient to men in homeless communities (Moon 2006). In other cases, women carefully reconstruct female gender identities in the process of being roofless (Maruyama 2013). This literature suggests that these discursive self-representations of women facilitate their major contribution to street-level survival economies that are highly gendered (on homeless women in Anglo-American cities, see, for instance, May, Cloke, and Johnsen 2007; Watson 1986).

In the context of these discussions, this book's perspective implies a comparative approach to different national regimes of the gender construction of homelessness, which can possibly use a joint analysis of the NSPR and public spaces as an inroad. I have suggested that the gendered experience of poor people can be partly inferred from the gender construction of the nationalised spaces of poverty regulation (Chapter 3). The subaltern strategies of Japanese homeless women reported by these specialists may be understood as women's lifelong renegotiation with the institutionally mediated "domesticity" of impoverished women in Japanese society, historically constructed by Japan's NSPR (Kawahara 2005).

Notes

1 Harvey's 1976 article was included in his *Consciousness and the Urban Experience* (1985a). For reasons unknown to many readers, Harvey did not choose to include the 1976 article when editing *The Urban Experience* (1989b), an easy-to-access abridged version of *Consciousness and the Urban Experience*, and its twin volume *The Urbanization of Capital* (1985b).

2 Soja (1989, p. 95) may be read as critical of this book's use of the housing classes because he emphatically contests the "liberal" social science that makes "efforts to separate consumption from production … to define class, for example, primarily upon consumption characteristics". However, I would raise the possibility that if the *systemic* effect of capitalist urbanisation is to separate the consumption experience from the (value) production experience, as Soja (p. 70) thinks it is, and to *de*politicise consumption on behalf of capitalism as a system, then this experience of urban separation can be powerfully theorised by using the notion of the housing classes (on enduring politics of this separation, see Hayashi 2023a). These classes, I would argue, are an "urban category" of the working class, *not* a category that is theoretically separated out from production (which causes Soja concern due to its possible neo-Weberian consequences).

3 The collective consumption is famously theorised by Manuel Castells (1977 [1972]). To some degree, Castells's heavy reliance on the structuralist metaphors of Althusser was a burden on his major efforts to rethink the collective consumption as a dynamic of hegemony (crisis) and its reregulation. I have tried to rework this "hard shell" of Castells's Althusserian vocabulary in order to conceptually frame an ethnography of homelessness and policing in a Japanese-language paper (Hayashi 2005).

4 West–East dichotomisation is sometimes apparent in *The Prison Notebooks*, as when Gramsci (1971, p. 238) discloses the idea that the theory of hegemony does not apply to Russia, where "the state was everything, civil society was primordial and gelatinous". While the specificity is unquestionable, Japan, particularly after World War II, cannot be understood as an Eastern state in this sense. The present book aims to extend Gramscian theory to Japan while accommodating Japanese contexts and differences.

5 How this administration-oriented form of community (chōnaikai) socially supported and invigorated the initiation of Japan's postwar industrial policy on the local scale, at the level of residential neighborhoods, is richly documented in Nihon Jinbun Kagaku Kai (1956). My knowledge about this little-read book is indebted to Kazushi Tamano.

6 Remarks of a homeless person, 12 November 2003.

7 Remarks of a homeless person, 12 November 2003.

8 Remarks of a homeless person, 8 August 2004.

9 Municipal notice on 2 April 1998, in the archives of the Kotobuki Day Laborers' Union.

10 These descriptions of the city of Kawasaki are entirely based on Kawasaki no Nojukusha Yushi to Kawasaki Suiyo Patororu no Kai (1996), a book published by a movement organisation and found in the archives of the Kotobuki Day Laborers' Union.

Chapter Five
Rescaling Urban Metabolism II: Homeless Labour for Money

Contemporary urbanisation asks deprived people to do something contradictory. On the one hand, their marginalisation in urban labour markets pulls them out of the circuits of capital and this pushes them to the noncapitalist production of use values (see Chapter 4). On the other hand, urbanisation today polices, surveils, and flattens noncapitalist enclaves of use values, especially when they are perceived to encroach on the regulated urban. As a result, deprived people are oriented towards the acquisition of money (exchange values), which can make their material basis multifaceted and resilient. By creatively overlapping these two dimensions of urban metabolism, deprived people can possibly develop their metabolic relations to urban nature into multiple spaces and restrengthen their economic turf. By combining different metabolic strategies in reaction to regulation, they may powerfully broaden the economic space of informality (Roy 2005).

This chapter focuses on the issue of garbage recycling. Recycling activity represents a major exchange value dimension of the homeless metabolism (meaning, in this book, homeless people's labouring processes addressing the pregiven materiality of public spaces for survival and better consumption). Panhandling, another possible approach to exchange values, is associated—if not completely linked—with certain locations and might promote locational surveillance relatively easily (Fooks and Pantazis 1999). Homeless people working as recyclers, in contrast, move more fluidly and ceaselessly around cities in search of valuable materials. This mobility can be a creative reaction of homeless people to dodge locational regulation. However, it subsequently increases the housing classes' concerns about the recyclers' fluidity, promoting a broader, citywide process of rescaling regulation targeting homeless people's value-creating activity.

As such, an exchange value focus on the homeless metabolism offers another informative window through which to decipher the ground-up dynamics of state space rescaling. Enquiries in this direction add to the previous chapter a new argument: when homeless people become "homeless recyclers" to earn money, they present a double challenge to the housing classes, by producing use *and* exchange values against the predominant *form* of public spaces—the socially shared patterns in which public spaces are constructed, used, imagined, and sustained. This chapter retains the core claim of this book, that the use value component of the homeless metabolism (housing) is fundamental.

The "otherness" of homeless people largely originates in their pursuit of "housing goods" against the world of the housing classes. However, this difficult status can be heightened when homeless people engage in recycling activity in public spaces. Their recycling labour contains a series of actions that the housing classes find odd and may perceive as a serious disturbance. In due course, the state and civil society jointly create yet another layer of regulatory codes to ensnare and "contain" the bodies and practices of the recyclers. Homeless recyclers, however, hardly remain passive victims of reregulation. Homeless recyclers try to escape from the webs of regulation in creative ways, while activists seek to negotiate with regulators to change antihomeless regulation.

Homeless Recyclers: A Regulationist Approach

How can homeless people generate cash income while living in public spaces? Why does this activity contradict the sociometabolic scaffoldings of the housing classes? How does this exchange value aspect of the homeless metabolism drive ground-up rescaling? The present chapter continues the book's empirical focus on Kanagawa Prefecture, with particular attention given to concrete ethnographic observation in the cities of Yokohama and Hiratsuka.

Before delving into further details on these two cities, I will focus on homeless recyclers in the international context. Teresa Gowan's (2010) influential volume contains a rich descriptive chapter on homeless recyclers and is thus very helpful. An early version of her ethnographic research on homeless recyclers (Gowan 2000) is compiled in *Global Ethnography*, authored by Michael Burawoy and his students (Burawoy et al. 2000). Addressing Gowan's work at the outset of this chapter is also useful in comparing my regulationist ethnographic approach to the method of global ethnography (see Chapter 2).

Taking instances from San Francisco, Gowan (2010, p. 147) finds that there are homeless individuals who move around the city to collect discarded materials such as "bottles, cans, and cardboard". These recyclers are "self-styled pro can and bottle recyclers" who "[roam] the city for recyclables to exchange for much-needed cash"

(p. 147). The recycling economy includes a cultural dimension. Through this work, homeless people can "struggle to see themselves as ethical subjects" who can overcome "the extreme stigma attached to homelessness" (p. 175). The homeless recyclers can "recover and celebrate the routines, productivity, skill, and solidarity of blue-collar work" (Gowan 2000, p. 78), something that homeless people may otherwise lack in their homeless life. Homeless recyclers suffer the pressure exerted by housed citizens who see them as "public nuisances" (Gowan 2010, p. 173). Yet, in wandering around the city and gathering materials, they do not just frustrate housed citizens but also communicate with them. In Gowan's view, recycling gives homeless people ample opportunities to shake off stigmatisation, strengthen their material lives, and reconstruct their identities; it allows homeless people to be "good citizens" (p. 173).

These descriptions largely apply to the Japanese case as well, and Gowan's ethnography can be used to illuminate some internationally shared elements of the Japanese phenomenon of homeless recyclers. First, most homeless people living on the streets need a modest level of cash income, and recycling—the collection of waste materials—can represent income-generating (exchange value–oriented) labour in the urban setting. Second, homeless recyclers must maintain their physical strength and develop the new skills needed for the recycling work, and this process gives homeless people a rare opportunity to sustain a positive self-image while living in public spaces. Last but not least, through recycling activity, homeless people are thrown into the difficult situation of being seen as disrupting the civic use or notion of public spaces, but at the same time they may communicate with housed citizens while maintaining their economic well-being and staying physically and mentally fit.

All these elements are found in the Japanese case and thus are elements of homeless labour common on both sides of the Atlantic. The extant literature and my own empirical findings enable me to develop a theoretical interpretation of homeless recyclers. It is worth emphasising that my entry point—a regulationist one—differs from Gowan's main focus. My approach is to underscore aspects of regulation, something Gowan perhaps obscured in her ethnography of recyclers, which by and large located the emergent dynamics of regulation in the background of ethnographic narratives. Gowan eagerly highlights the social productivity of the recyclers, the process of *becoming* (through skill formation, identity production, communicative power, and so on). Yet her rich description also implies a more structural understanding of social control, of the process of *being* (e.g., policing, exclusion, compulsion, and the like).

In one instance, Gowan (2010, p. 148) notes, "Outside of legal wage work, homeless survival strategies swarm within a gray area between illicit and licit, between indubitable criminality and street entrepreneurialism." I especially focus on emergent regulatory dynamics found within Gowan's "gray area", which she seems to analyse mainly from the perspective of homeless people. Indeed, I explore the extent to which "becoming"—a growth of homeless people's spaces within "regulated" conditions through making subtle differences to the self and the environment—can or cannot arise within this nuanced middle ground, through advancing conceptual and empirical discussions. Some aspects of "urban becoming" attract the focus of Andy Merrifield (2013) when he redevelops Lefebvrian perspectives into contemporary urban theory; this chapter thus will speak to these ongoing discussions in geography.

The essence of my discussion is visualised in Figure 5.1. It indicates the two types of urban metabolism formed by homeless recyclers, which provide urban administrators the two points of regulation. To begin with, homeless recyclers can suffer the pressure of regulation in their use value–oriented labour, in which they—as homeless people—must primarily produce the use values of housing for consumption (Chapter 4). However, they also can face the pressure of regulation in their exchange value–oriented labour, in which homeless people gather materials from public spaces for income. Homeless people's production of "housing" (and associated consumption) has been conceived in this book as the centre of homelessness and antihomelessness. The mobile process of homeless people's recycling labour is now understood as its possible amplifier.

Hence, recyclers undergo a double-edged experience in which they face various instances of regulation/othering. Given the rescaled conditions, of course, homeless people's ability to escape or negotiate regulation greatly depends on locational parameters—the extent to which a governance field mixes coercion with consensus, and how these elements are geographically distributed in city space. This geography of local homeless regulation in turn can hasten the geographical formation of homeless people's own strategies to avoid the worst scenarios of regulation. My regulationist theory registers these entanglements in these regulatory and counterregulatory geographies of homelessness.

However, my regulationist view also anticipates that these diverse conjunctures of being/becoming tension can converge in similar logical consequences. That is, new regulatory spaces by and large reduce the uncertainties of homeless-populated city space on behalf of the housing classes, managing homeless–housed encounters in acceptable forms for societalisation. In this reregulation process of

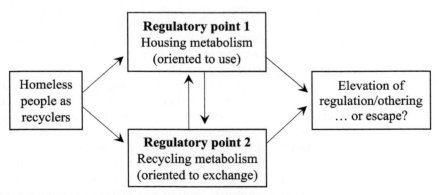

Figure 5.1 Double-edged metabolism of recyclers and its regulation.

metabolic class relations, the recyclers constantly come across new occasions of regulation/othering in the streets; they must manage the pressure of regulation/othering at multiple sites and on multiple levels of metabolism. For Gowan, the recycling activity is a symptom of release, during which the homeless experience of being regulated retreats into the background. Indeed, the busiest zones of US metropolises may allow the most dexterous recyclers some scope for escape. However, serious political tension may exist in US cities, as the tenacious Other status of homeless people can affect every bit of their informal economy, when it becomes the target of exclusion and eviction.

In this respect, it is worth noting that Gowan has depicted her recyclers largely as "professionals" who have skills, capacity, and patience to manage stigmatisation and regulation in the streets. These descriptions suggest that my regulationist view, which emphasises the restricted aspect of homeless labour, can possibly be defended, for it brings spaces of regulation—which are somewhat secondary in Gowan's narratives of the recyclers—to the fore and explains homeless people's diverse economic strategies with reference to new regulatory spaces and their citywide rescaling process.

Homeless Recyclers in Japan

There are Japanese cities in which homeless recyclers experience very acute patterns of othering and regulation. This Japanese experience should be understood as the general difficulty inherent in homeless people's labour when it displays the double-edged pattern outlined in Figure 5.1. Those who produce use *and* exchange values suffer many occasions and logics of being othered and being regulated in cities. However, the Japanese case has some unique features. There is the expectation by Japanese people that streets and parks must be very clean, without the presence of litter. Any litter must be disposed of at public dumping sites, which are operated by neighbourhoods under the strong guidance of the municipality. In Chapter 4, I explained this Japanese type of public space hegemony as a case of hyperconformist societalisation that is highly intolerant of disorder. Because homeless recyclers in Japan collect materials from very regulated public spaces, they become radical disrupters of the sociometabolism of the housing classes.

Around 60% to 70% of homeless individuals in Japan generate income by undertaking some type of labour (Figure 5.2), and the most popular kind of homeless labour is the collection of waste, or recycling (Figure 5.3). In this kind of work, homeless people typically collect empty cans, used books, and broken domestic appliances at public dumping grounds, often using bikes or carts to gather the waste materials (Figure 5.4). The work demands physical strength because they have to circulate among many public dumping sites for extended periods, sometimes for more than eight hours a day. The work requires intellectual ability as

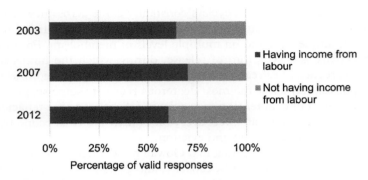

Figure 5.2 Homeless people's cash income from labour, 2003–2012.
Source: Adapted from Ministry of Health, Labour and Welfare, 2017.

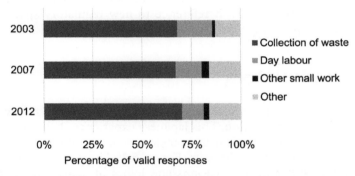

Figure 5.3 Homeless people's income-generating activities, 2003–2012. Multiple answers were allowed.
Source: Adapted from Ministry of Health, Labour and Welfare, 2017.

well, because collectors face various obstacles and uncertainties that constantly have to be resolved.

For Japanese homeless people, income generation, by means of recycling or other means, has increased in importance as their lives have become increasingly subject to "commodification". In the 1990s, homeless life was less commodified. In the important case of nutrition, for instance, time-expired food discarded by small twenty-four-hour *konbini* (convenience stores) was more accessible. As a result, some fundamental part of homeless people's subsistence economies could be maintained less with money and more with the direct acquisition of use values in the streets. However, these stores soon began locking garbage up, which prevented homeless people from taking away expired food, and thus homeless people had to feed themselves in other ways, possibly by *buying* food.

Figure 5.4 Bicycle of a homeless recycler in Yokohama, 1 January 2019.
Source: Author.

This commodification, partly stemming from the loss of the informal use value (food) supply, drove many homeless people to the production of exchange value (money) in public spaces, leading to the rise in recycling activity among homeless people. This activity had long been practised by homeless people, but it increasingly became a matter of life or death.

As many homeless people started to engage in recycling activity in the streets, regulation intensified. The housing classes and the municipality felt an acute "need" for regulation because Japanese cities mostly construct a local (official) system of recycling on the basis of close cooperation between the municipality and residents. This system mobilises neighbourhood associations (chōnaikai) and other groups as a mediator between the municipality and its residents. These neighbourhood associations historically have had a unique hybrid colour within the state–society spectrum; national policy has officially promoted their formation in the locality, while municipal policy has assigned many regulatory tasks to them. As such, neighbourhood associations have been the key arena of Japan's administrative type of societalisation in the city (see Chapter 4).

Homeless people's recycling disturbs this hegemonic construct sustained by state–society collaboration. To collect discarded materials from Japanese public spaces means committing a kind of "theft" from chōnaikai, from the historical centre of Japanese urban societalisation. Yet the *legal* basis of this imagination—"homeless recyclers are thieves"—was shaky until the early 2000s, which drove regulatory evolutions on the local scale. In fact, traditional community forms like chōnaikai have undergone a decline in contemporary Japan; however, my fieldwork has found that they are revitalised, and become local bodies of homeless regulation, when the housing classes encounter homeless people.

We get a glimpse of how rapidly regulation has evolved from this backdrop by looking at formal regulation (ordinances) in the Tokyo–Yokohama metropolitan area. By the mid-2000s, nine out of twenty-six cities in the Tokyo Metropolis, and seventeen out of twenty-three wards, had enacted an ordinance to criminalise nonpublic recyclers. In Kanagawa Prefecture, six out of nineteen cities came to have this type of ordinance during the same period, and the number has since increased to eleven. Table 5.1 offers a list of these cities in Kanagawa Prefecture, my main site of fieldwork, and it is clear how quickly the municipalities drew up such ordinances after the mid-2000s. The ordinances established two legal grounds for the regulation of urban metabolism. First, the ordinances decreed that "recyclable" items discarded in public dumping sites legally belong to the municipality rather than to anyone else. Second, the ordinances decreed

Table 5.1 Ordinances that criminalise nonpublic recyclers in Kanagawa Prefecture.

City	Year of enaction or revision	Name of ordinance	Penalty
Odawara	2004	Ordinance for the Reduction, Recycling, and Appropriate Disposal of Wastes	Yes
Yokohama	2004	Ordinance for the Reduction, Recycling, and Appropriate Disposal of Wastes	No
Zama	2005	Ordinance for the Reduction, Recycling, and Disposal of Wastes	No
Kamakura	2005	Ordinance for the Reduction, Recycling, and Appropriate Disposal of Wastes	No
Chigasaki	2005	Ordinance for the Reduction, Recycling, and Appropriate Disposal of Wastes	Yes
Fujisawa	2006	Ordinance for the Reduction, Recycling, and Appropriate Disposal of Wastes	Yes
Hiratsuka	2006	Ordinance for the Promotion of Delightful and Clean Urban Development	Yes
Sagamihara	2008	Ordinance for the Reduction, Recycling, and Appropriate Disposal of Wastes	Yes
Minamiashigara	2009	Ordinance for the Reduction, Recycling, and Appropriate Disposal of Wastes	Yes
Yamato	2011	Ordinance for the Reduction, Recycling, and Appropriate Disposal of Wastes	Yes
Hatano	2014	Ordinance for the Disposal of Wastes and Cleaning	Yes

that the collection of these waste materials is the responsibility of official recyclers approved by the municipality, and defined nonpublic collectors as committing theft.

I have explained regulation as formal ordinances against homeless recyclers' "nonpublic" urban metabolism in public spaces. This legal aspect is important, but explanations that merely provide such legal information present only a convenient synoptic view of this issue, for the municipality is not the sole actor in local dynamics. As this book has already established, state action is coeval with social action; the complementarities, collaborations, hybrid forms, and knowledge transfers between the two must advance rescaling as the process of *integral* state rescaling. For this reason, the ongoing process of state–society relations must be considered. I will look at Yokohama and Hiratsuka and examine how state and social agents collaboratively produced in each city a localised, rescaled framework of regulation against the recyclers, on the fringes of Japanese citizenship and the nationalised space of poverty regulation.

Regulationist Ethnography I: Regulating the Recycling Metabolism

Regulation in the City of Yokohama

The widespread cycle of homelessness starting in the 1990s brought homelessness to Yokohama's public spaces beyond the inner-city district (Kotobuki). At the beginning of this widespread cycle, homelessness was more "decommodified", that is, the diet of homeless people was maintained with less money. As I have mentioned, small chain stores unwittingly fed homeless people with out-of-date food, as the garbage was often kept unlocked. Yet these stores generally stopped this informal feeding and homeless people came to need more cash than ever before. In this context of commodification, many homeless people in Yokohama started engaging in the collection of discarded materials at public dumping sites, in order to exchange them for money to buy food. In response, Japan's urban project of street-level homeless regulation entered a new phase that targeted the recyclers.

During the period when homeless recyclers were engulfing Yokohama's public spaces by collecting waste materials from public dumping sites, the municipality revised an existing ordinance to outlaw such activity as of April 2004. The title of the ordinance was the Ordinance for the Reduction, Recycling, and Appropriate Disposal of Wastes. The revision of this ordinance established that materials discarded at public dumping sites are the property of the municipality and that nobody—except official recyclers—can take these materials (article 25, clause 4). The city informed citizens and recyclers in advance of the change in the ordinance by putting up a notice at the public dumping sites in February 2004 (Figure 5.5).

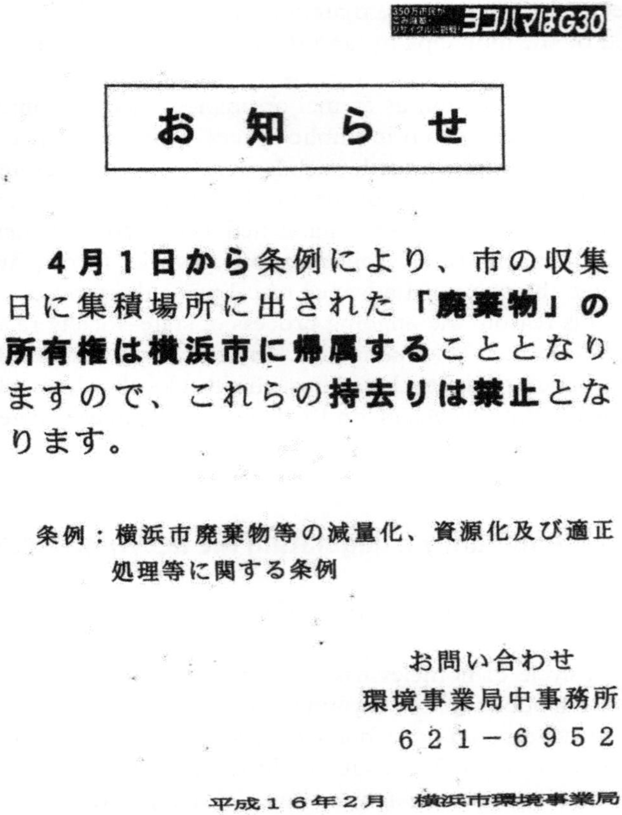

ヨコハマはG30

お知らせ

4月1日から条例により、市の収集日に集積場所に出された「廃棄物」の所有権は横浜市に帰属することとなりますので、これらの持去りは禁止となります。

条例：横浜市廃棄物等の減量化、資源化及び適正処理等に関する条例

お問い合わせ
環境事業局中事務所
621－6952

平成16年2月　横浜市環境事業局

Figure 5.5 Public notice displayed at Yokohama's public dumping sites in 2004. It says, "From April 1 onward, this ordinance defines 'discarded things' left at dumping sites, on municipal collection days, as the property of the City of Yokohama, and it outlaws the act of removal. … February 2004. The Department of Environment Policy. The City of Yokohama."
Source: Archives of the Kotobuki Day Laborers' Union.

This criminalisation of *mochi sari* (taking away)—which redefined homeless recyclers as thieves—did not use the term *homeless*. According to a Yokohama policymaker, the official purpose of the ordinance revision was "to assure collaborative citizens that the city will treat [materials] in proper ways", and a direct reference to homeless people was avoided.[1] Nonetheless, the change and its announcement strongly facilitated the policing of homeless recyclers on the ground. A prominent case happened on 11 January 2004, when Uehara-san, a homeless recycler, was arrested and brought to the Minami police station in the southern area of the city. Uehara-san was fingerprinted, photographed, and detained for two hours before he was forced to pledge never to engage in this "theft" again. The police also began to routinely patrol dumping sites on every collection day.

This reaction of the police was closely connected to residential communities organised by neighbourhood associations. A different homeless recycler, Inagaki-san, said that some neighbourhood leaders in Minami Ward, in the southern part of the city, stood at dumping sites with phones in hand, sometimes telling homeless recyclers, "We will call the police."[2] And homeless recycler Kondo-san was afraid because, after the February 2004 announcement of the ordinance revision, his housed acquaintances no longer brought him aluminium cans, a friendly practice that had continued for quite some time. In Tsurumi Ward, the antihomeless atmosphere led to aggressive antihomeless harassment by housed citizens. For instance, youths overturned bicycles of homeless recyclers at Mitsuike Park, a major site of homelessness in the middle of Yokohama's residential zone.

Regulation in the City of Hiratsuka

In the city of Hiratsuka, the antihomeless atmosphere against homeless recyclers also intensified towards the mid-2000s. Unlike in Yokohama, Hiratsuka's dynamics of regulation were initiated by neighbourhood associations and police officers rather than by the municipality. By early 2004, many public dumping sites in Hiratsuka displayed signs stating that the property rights of waste materials belonged to neighbourhood associations, that homeless people's "taking away" amounted to an act of theft, and that these cases would be reported to the police (Figure 5.6). The municipality produced these signboards and distributed them to neighbourhoods in response to requests from neighbourhood associations and the guidance of the police.

One reason for this antihomeless response among Hiratsuka's neighbourhood associations was its historical commitment to a local recycling programme. Under this programme, the municipality gives each neighbourhood association a small amount of money in return for its compliance with the recycling rules established by the municipality. The City of Yokohama ran the same programme; however, the history of this practice was much older in Hiratsuka, and the residents were more committed to this system.

In October 2006, the city implemented the Ordinance for the Promotion of Delightful and Clean Urban Development. This new ordinance banned "nonofficial" agents from collecting waste from public dumping sites (articles 15, 21). By this time, Hiratsuka had completed the production of its regulatory regime, under which homeless recyclers would be tightly controlled and rejected through state–society collaboration. Even before the enactment of the ordinance, however, neighbourhood residents—united under neighbourhood associations—went as

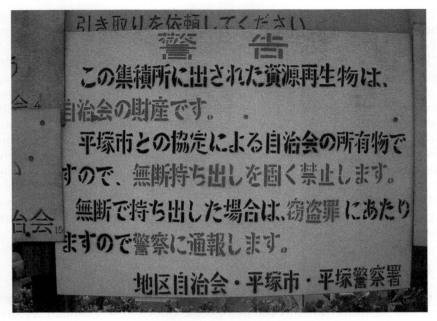

Figure 5.6 Notice board at Hiratsuka's public dumping site, 17 September 2004. It says, "Recyclable waste at this dumping site is the property of our neighbourhood association. It belongs to our neighbourhood association and thus we prohibit unpermitted removal. . . . We report to the police such acts of theft. Neighbourhood Association, City of Hiratsuka, and Hiratsuka Police."
Source: Author.

far as capturing homeless people and taking them to the police. According to official records, one housed resident recounted this story at a municipal committee: "I once caught a homeless person" because the amount of their taking away of discarded materials was "considerable" (City of Hiratsuka 2005). Thus, in Hiratsuka, neighbourhood residents spearheaded the antihomeless regulation and the municipality followed, while in Yokohama the order was reversed.

Hiratsuka's regulation deterred homeless people. The signboard that proclaimed the "criminalisation" of informal recyclers worried and frustrated homeless people. In summer 2004, a homeless individual at a municipal gymnasium, Nakano-san, was nervous because a neighbourhood resident had actually "made a phone call to the police" and "a police officer [had] asked for [his] name and location".[3] The officer eventually left Nakano-san alone after he abandoned all the collected materials, but this experience frustrated Nakano-san, and the frustration boiled up when he heard a similar story about a homeless recycler also detained by the police. A year later, I confirmed that various stories of detention were circulating among many homeless people. Yoshida-san, who slept at a municipal sports ground, told me of a fellow homeless person who suffered policing, emphasising how much this case impacted him: "I completely stopped collecting cans and recyclable materials."[4]

Summary

The two cities' state and social sectors coproduced rules, networks, and working units against the recyclers on the local scale. The urban regulatory complexes in the two cities criminalised and detained homeless people to save the hegemonic framework of urban metabolism and societalisation from the "contamination" of homeless people in search of valuable materials. While the municipality had the formal power of regulation in the form of legislation (ordinance making), local neighbourhoods were capable of producing informal but effective codes; thus, regulation was their joint project. Many homeless people, whose lives had become increasingly commodified in Japan, collected discarded materials to buy food and other necessities. This act of recycling now became criminalised, stigmatised as theft, and condemned as spectacularly "nonpublic" behaviour that derails the "normal" process of recycling metabolism. Thus, Japan's rescaling reregulation controlled the metabolic impact of homeless recyclers by criminalising it.

Regulationist Ethnography II: New Recycling Strategies

Regulation or Escape?

Some homeless people tried to accommodate the regulatory pressure by adapting and evolving their recycling activity. The avoidance of regulatory pressure was difficult even for the most skilful ones. A homeless recycler in Yokohama, Kondo-san, told me that these regulatory dynamics created a harsh local situation: "Even children call me a thief!" Under these conditions, he continued, "we [homeless people] have become tense ... Rough sleepers are now all nervous."[5]

Under the pressure of antihomeless regulation, even the recyclers' most innovative strategies remain prone to failure. Nonetheless, it is incorrect to think that the recyclers readily submitted to regulators and gave up their metabolic space. Some homeless people purposefully tried to survive the regulatory undercurrents by employing new strategies. This section shows three strategies that homeless people employed to sustain their metabolic space of recycling in face of the regulatory pressure. My analysis must now unpack the same regulatory dynamics, not from the side of hegemonic metabolism but from the side of non-hegemonic and counterhegemonic metabolic circuits, and examine how these circuits are strategically reconstructed amid the changing patterns of ground-up homeless regulation.

The First Strategy of Recyclers: Find the Spots

Many recyclers were eager to have location-specific information in order to find regulatory voids, or less-regulated sites, in the city. For instance, a formerly homeless recycler, Yamada-san, found an emerging pattern of regulation in Yokohama. In Kōhoku Ward, in 2003, antihomeless patrols, during which residents and police officers circulated among the public dumping sites, were beginning earlier and earlier in the day. Yamada-san was cautious about this tendency because he wanted to avoid being recognised, for safety reasons. In 2004, another homeless man, Uehara-san, arrested in Yokohama, felt that he could no longer work in Minami Ward, where he had been arrested; however, he still felt that he was safe working in other areas.[6]

Nakano-san, who has already appeared in this chapter, explained that he particularly avoided five districts in the city of Hiratsuka: Matoi, Kawauchi, Tokunobu, Toyoda, and Kaname. Similarly, homeless recycler Kaneda-san recorded the official garbage collection days for different areas of the city (Figure 5.7), so that he could guess the most intensive moments of policing in each area. Inagaki-san suggests another strategy: an increase in working time. He said, "I now need to circulate among more street corners in more districts, and to use much more time, in order to collect the same amount."[7]

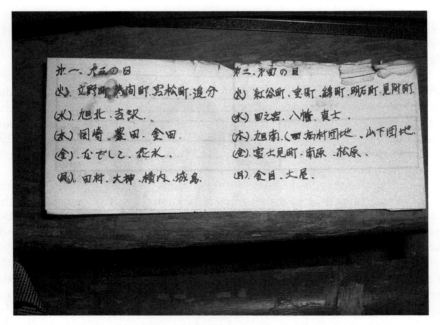

Figure 5.7 Homeless recycler's notes on the days of official garbage collection, 28 August 2005.
Source: Author.

The Second Strategy of Recyclers: Change the Target

A second strategy of recyclers was to avoid regulation by changing the kinds of waste they collected, moving from gathering more valuable things, such as aluminium cans, to less valuable items such as used books and broken domestic appliances. This target change strategy worked because neighbourhoods' antipathy was weaker in the case of less valuable materials, for which neighbourhoods expected less cash return from the municipality. Recycler Nakano-san, in Hiratsuka, had abandoned expensive aluminium cans and was collecting other materials in July 2005 because removal of these materials was better tolerated by residents.

At the same time, however, the target change resulted in a loss of income. Hiratsuka's Kaneda-san, who also avoided collecting aluminium cans, likewise complained about the low income that accompanied this strategy. He would work "day and night ... five days in a week, almost twenty-two days in a month", but it paid him less than 3,000 yen (roughly $24), allowing him only 100 yen (80 cents) for each meal.[8] Because the previous target—aluminium cans—had allowed him to earn about 10,000 yen ($80) per month, the target change had resulted in a significant income loss.

The Third Strategy of Recyclers: Etiquette for Neighbourhoods

The recyclers' third strategy was to purposefully maintain active and good relationships with a few familiar faces in housed neighbourhoods by protecting (or seeming to protect) local etiquette during the process of waste collection. As I have noted, one homeless individual, Kondo-san, had suffered the destruction of friendly relationships with housed citizens who used to bring him cans, after Yokohama outlawed homeless recycling. Thus, the maintenance of friendly ties in housed neighbourhoods was a difficult task, but it sometimes proved helpful. While Nakano-san was at Hiratsuka's public sports park, for instance, a housed friend kindly warned him to be careful when he collected materials from dumping sites and informed him that Hiratsuka was moving towards making homeless recycling illegal. Nakano-san appreciated the friendly warning. Yoshida-san, encamped in Hiratsuka's seaside area, was told by a superintendent of an apartment building, "You can take these books, but only if you clean up the dumping lot every time."[9] The recycler tried to abide by this condition as far as possible.

Summary

Some homeless people developed new strategies to withstand the regulatory undercurrent, but the outcome of these attempts seems inconclusive at best.

Even successful cases were limited and temporary, and the feeling of being subject to regulation discouraged homeless people's painstaking efforts to reconstruct subsistence economies. In short, the recyclers in this chapter experience a constant process of *being* regulated, which is hard to avoid even when homeless people try to reconstruct urban metabolism in innovative ways. In the two cities, the citywide development of rescaled homeless regulation effectively reduced the mobility and intensity of the homeless metabolism. In this context, keeping spirits up, updating survival strategies, and attempting acts of escape should be seen as highly courageous acts of homeless people against the rescaled dynamics of new regulatory spaces.

Regulationist Ethnography III: Movements for Homeless Recyclers

Any Social Movements?

Part 2 of this book has discussed the urban geographies of regulation and of homeless people, revealing that the two sets of geographies interpenetrate each other in public spaces and that the interpenetration may allow for homeless people's circumscribed yet "liveable" economic spaces, around the regulatory limits given by Japan's tight (conformist) societalisation. Against this backdrop, part 3 of the book will explore transformative roles of urban social movements.

While part 3 treats homeless-supporting movements as the "game changer" of regulation, however, the remainder of this chapter will look at how and why these movements could *not* change it. By examining the difficulties inherent in activism on behalf of the homeless recyclers, I want to emphasise the high rigidity of antihomeless policy when it comes to one of the most state-saturated areas of urban metabolism in Japan: recycling. Changing antihomeless regulation was impossible even for experienced activists when the regulation was defending these intensively administered metabolic flows in public spaces. These flows were programmatically reserved for the housing classes by the strict rules and norms of operation/participation and prompted new regulatory actions against homelessness.

A Movement in the City of Yokohama

In Yokohama, activists for the recyclers worked in an inner-city area, the Kotobuki district, which is Yokohama's bastion of prohomeless and homeless-supporting groups. Many of these activists and volunteers belonged to the Kotobuki Day Labourers' Union and/or the Kotobuki Supporters' Gathering Club (see Chapters 6 and 7). Their goal was to argue in favour of the homeless recyclers, and to that end they held discussions with the municipality five times between May 2004 and March 2006; all of these discussions were devoted to the issue of homeless recyclers.

The municipality had just begun to operate the antihomeless ordinance, and activists—sometimes accompanying homeless people to the meetings—claimed that this legal framework destroyed homeless people's life on the streets. Activists also claimed that Yokohama's welfare office during that period would normally tell homeless people, "Live on empty cans as long as your body is okay", with an intention to reduce welfare costs. Activists pointed out that this "street workfarism" in Yokohama contradicted the ordinance that made this type of "work" illegal when it was conducted by homeless people.

A senior policymaker justified the criminalisation by referring to phone calls and letters the city had received from citizens who made accusations against homeless recyclers, which numbered "less than ten in a week".[10] The city also claimed that the revision was necessary in order that waste materials be treated correctly, according to Yokohama's recycling plan, which was known as having strict guidelines for programme operation. Putting aside these justifications, however, Yokohama's senior policymaker confessed, "We didn't have much data for homeless people when we considered the ordinance revision." Moreover, he continued, "We don't want to call homeless people's taking-away an act of theft." It was as if the two sides shared a similar understanding and were moving towards a compromise in which homeless people's recycling would be permitted.

But this compromise never happened. The harsh regulation of homeless recyclers by municipal workers and police officers did not change. As a matter of fact, the policymaker uploaded a link to a now deleted document at the municipality's website that emphasised that the recycling activity of homeless people might be accepted, but only with the "understanding of a neighbourhood" (*chīki no rikai*) (Figure 5.8). Yet this hardly changed the fact of the criminalisation of homeless recyclers on the ground.

Q7：ホームレスの人たちが空き缶（アルミ缶）を持ち去る行為は禁止されるのか。

　　Q5と同様、地域の理解を得た活動であれば、持ち去り行為」にはなりません。
　　ホームレスの人たち以外にも、社会福祉関連の団体等の人たちによるアルミ缶回収など、従来から行われている活動がありますが、このような活動も地域の理解を得て行うようお願いいたします。

Figure 5.8 Yokohama's limited "acceptance" of homeless recyclers. This is a part of a now deleted online document at the City of Yokohama's website. Above is a sample question: "Does this ordinance prohibit empty cans (aluminium cans) collection by homeless people?" Below is the answer: "If ... the collecting activity is permitted by the understanding of a neighbourhood, that activity is not considered as the [criminal] act of 'taking away.'"

A Movement in the City of Hiratsuka

In Hiratsuka, a group called the Hiratsuka Patrol expressed concern for homeless recyclers. Since 2001, this group had engaged in routine discussions with the municipality in order to improve local homeless policy (this will be discussed in Chapter 8). Before homeless recycling was made illegal by ordinance, in 2004, activists told the municipal officials who organised the city's environmental policy that they had grave concerns about the wooden notice shown in Figure 5.6. The claim was that this notice strengthened the negative public image that the "homeless are criminals".[11]

Hiratsuka's officials explained that the notice—which "outlawed" homeless recyclers without showing a clear legal foundation—was produced and provided under the guidance of the police; the municipality merely followed this guidance and distributed the signs to each neighbourhood association. At the same time, the attitudes of Hiratsuka's policymakers were tougher than those of Yokohama's. They clearly stated that the final goal of this regulation was to deter and penalise homeless people who were collecting cans, books, home appliances, and so on from public dumping sites.

In 2005, activists were still thinking that they could slow down—if not stop— the city's move towards criminalisation by presenting a legal argument. This expectation faded. In spring 2006, the city enacted the new ordinance, which made especial reference to the "illegal" recycling activity and the penalty. In the winter of 2005, the Hiratsuka Patrol had a roundtable dialogue with the city specifically on this issue. On this occasion, a policymaker emphasised that the city had received a number of complaints from housed citizens regarding homeless recyclers and that, without making a new ordinance, they could not be certain whether "citizens ever understand our attitude".[12]

The city also said that this "antihomeless" gesture was due to the unique history of local environmental policy, in which community organisations (neighbourhood associations) had long been committed to the local framework of recycling. According to the city, this tradition needed to be protected by ordinance. Finally, the policymaker showed a hawkish opposition to the activists—to their suggestion that the Japanese state's policy might be read as being positive about homeless recyclers. The policymaker objected: "I really don't understand why this [recycling] activity can be interpreted as the 'work' of homeless people."[13]

Four days after the meeting, the members submitted a written statement to the city in which they tried to convey the importance of recycling labour to homeless people, in as formal and yet friendly a manner as possible (Hiratsuka Patororu 2005).

Summary

The reactions of activists resulted in no changes to the regulation of the recyclers. This failure shows how deeply homeless people's economic activity can "disturb" the hegemonic matrix of urban metabolism. The unsuccessful endeavours of activists reveal the *limits* of commoning when it comes to the most state-saturated areas of metabolic circuits. The municipality and neighbourhoods tried to maintain a hegemonic outlook of urban metabolism by excluding the homeless metabolism through legal and nonlegal processes of regulation.

In this context of new regulation, the efforts of social movements to change regulation were likely doomed to fail. The only positive response that activism elicited from the municipality was the City of Yokohama's ambiguous statement on its website, which mentioned the "understanding of a neighbourhood" as a condition for approving the recycling activity. However, even this could be interpreted as a renewal of the hegemonic voice: the "disturbing" actions of homeless recyclers must be thwarted for the sake of the "official" circuits of recycling metabolism, which should be accessed only by the housing classes.

Conclusion

The homeless metabolism is partly commodified. Even homeless people who can create noncapitalist economies—by producing use values—are driven to form a market-participating and exchange value–producing type of subaltern economy. Taking the case of homeless recyclers, this chapter has shown that this exchange value side of the homeless metabolism challenges and compromises urban hegemony and societalisation constructed around the housing classes and augmented by political guardians.

Antihomeless semiosis and politics—othering and reregulation—swelled in response, which represented another ground-up dynamic of rescaling reregulation in public spaces. The regulators were ordinary urban dwellers, police officers, and municipal workers, who jointly materialised local webs of regulatory rules and practices—both formal and informal—against the desocietalising tensions of homeless recyclers. As a result, the recycling activity of homeless people became controlled at the rescaled fringes of citizenship, the housing regime, and public spaces, which all were preserved for the housing classes.

What Chapters 4 and 5 have jointly shown is that when the homeless metabolism frustrated the housing classes in multiple appearances, there arose from within public spaces repetitive, ground-up waves of rescaling regulation. Through these waves, a hegemonic urban society seeks to preserve, against the desocietalising tensions of the homeless metabolism, both the normative construction of public spaces and the effect of societalisation that this public-space construction can bring about in the city.

Notes

1. Remarks of Yokohama's policymaker at the Department of Environment Policy during a municipality–movement meeting, 20 April 2004.
2. Remarks of a homeless recycler, 31 May 2005.
3. Remarks of a homeless recycler, 3 July 2004.
4. Remarks of a homeless recycler, 28 August 2005.
5. Remarks of a homeless recycler, 11 December 2004.
6. Remarks of a homeless recycler, 14 February 2005.
7. Remarks of a homeless recycler, 31 May 2005.
8. Remarks of a homeless recycler, 28 August 2005.
9. Remarks of a homeless recycler, 17 April 2005.
10. Remarks of Yokohama's policymaker in a municipality–movement meeting, 20 April 2004.
11. Remarks of Hiratsuka activists in municipality–movement meetings, 29 March and 31 May 2004.
12. Remarks of a Hiratsuka municipal worker in a municipality–movement meeting, 10 October 2005.
13. Remarks of a Hiratsuka municipal worker in a municipality–movement meeting, 10 October 2005.

Part Three
Urban Social Movements

Chapter Six
Placemaking in the Inner City: Social and Cultural Niches of Homeless Activism

I will now turn to the counterregulatory and postregulatory geographies of social movements under rescaling. In theory, resistive actions of social movement participants can forge a sensitivity to place among the participants (Leitner, Sheppard, and Sziarto 2008; Martin and Miller 2003; Nicholls 2009). However, activists and volunteers working for homeless people can have a hard time constructing places within the geographies of the housing classes. These geographies may be fragmented and "splintered" (Graham and Mervin 2001) yet powerfully rejoined by the matrix of societalisation (i.e., public/private spaces), which may be able to reconstruct these fragmented urban spatialities into more stable geographies of urban encounter, even today, when the notion of urban encounter must include frequent meetings between housed citizens and "outsiders".

As Chapters 4 and 5 revealed, homeless people's *own* appropriations tend to be "masked" and obliterated when these geographies of the housing classes are rehabilitated in the face of rampant homelessness. In this context of *non*homelessness and *anti*homelessness, this chapter finds more favourable spots of prohomeless and homeless-supporting placemaking actions in the margins of the housing classes. In practice, and especially for this book, this means within the inner city. In these margins, participants in homeless activism can possibly construct their places for self-representation, mutual engagement, knowledge production, and critical debate that are crucial to social movements (Routledge 1996).

For these discussions, the initial part of this chapter interrogates the notion of "habitat" in the Lefebvrian sense and links it to Doreen Massey's thesis of "porous" places. The margins of habitat can be a catalyst for various homeless-friendly and even explicitly prohomeless urban views. Most activists and volunteers come from, or belong to, the housing classes. For this reason, activists and volunteers need to divorce their perspectives from their class backgrounds when "in the field", so that they can interpret the homeless–housed divide from the perspective of the homeless subalterns. The margins of habitat can further this redirection through the facilitation of placemaking, which gathers from within and without various sociocultural elements, such as words and vocabularies, ways of speaking up, ways of sharing materials, political and religious beliefs, and *dis*beliefs in "normal" modes of urban encounter. At the margins of habitat, activists and volunteers assemble a local system of places by using these sociocultures and seek to insert these places in the broader geographies of habitat in defence of homeless people.

This chapter uses the empirical case of Kotobuki to show how its "vanguard" activists in the 1970s created a new place that facilitated an early formation of outreach initiatives addressing spaces of homelessness. This early placemaking was followed by the birth of different groups and their placemaking activity towards the 2000s, whereby more diverse kinds of people created their own sociocultural places. Throughout this 1970s–2000s era, different sociocultural elements were mobilised by various activists and volunteers. And projecting them onto the inner-city district helped to navigate the activists and volunteers away from mainstream imaginaries of the urban. Through this local history, the Kotobuki district negotiated the forces and geographies of societalisation.

The Inner City: Beyond Regulation

In part 2, I demonstrated how cities delineate spaces of homelessness by using the public/private matrix of urban space. With recourse to this *dispositif*, which has developed through the modern histories of urbanisation, cities can counterpose homeless people to the housed, filter out homeless people from societalisation, and ignite the ground-up momentum of rescaling for reregulation. Here we see the survival of a historically specific mode of capitalist urbanisation that deploys urban housing regimes as a central framework of society formation and societalisation (for its early history, see Engels 1954 [1872]; see also Hayashi 2015). In the contemporary era, the rescaled maintenance of public/private spaces proliferates the homeless–housed divide and antihomelessness in cities.

Part 3 starts with the recognition that the same regulatory process is acutely felt by social movements. The regulatory pressure against homelessness can be destructive to the social movements discussed in this book because these are movements that seek to mitigate the rampant antihomelessness within the cities of the housing classes. However, even this activism must recruit its members and resources from the world of the housing classes. Without this recruitment, the subaltern geographies of homelessness can be too "fragmented and episodic" (Gramsci 1971, pp. 54–55) and unmanageable for activism.

The question is where and how this mobilisation can be geographically situated. This chapter addresses this key question by focusing on placemaking practices in the inner city. Regulation can make activists/volunteers working for homeless people vulnerable. Yet these activists/volunteers might be able to sidestep the regulatory pressure if they can be placed at the margins of normative habitation. Geoffrey DeVerteuil (2015, pp. 161–162) suggests that the inner city sometimes has offered such favourable environments: "The very concentration of housing and services for low-income and homeless people on Skid Row had encouraged various forms of collective resistance to arise. This included many examples of voluntary-sector organisations working together to help clients, but also banding together when faced with outward threats."

Notably, this passage is directed at the "heartland" of neoliberal capitalism—US cities. Even there, the inner city has played a significant role in preserving progressive/radical politics for homeless people. This chapter shows that this observation of the inner city has wider empirical purchase. The inner city faces the pressure of urban planning and "regeneration", which imposes on it difficult moments of reactionary conflicts, self-closure, and loss. However, the inner city also can play the role of deep urban democratisation for deprived people because even the difficult phase paves the way for the future by preparing for new rounds of placemaking.

In what follows, I shall examine Henri Lefebvre's canonical text *The Urban Revolution* (Lefebvre 2003a [1970]) in order to theorise this dimension from a regulationist angle. This text has been a source of inspiration for generations of urban theorists.[1] This chapter will tease out a new aspect of the text from a perspective on housing. On this basis, this chapter wishes to adapt the book to explore a particular form of urban struggle—urban social movements for homeless people.

Lefebvre in the Inner City

Revisiting Lefebvre

One thread in Lefebvre's *Urban Revolution* runs as follows: the city is an agglomeration of private spaces and their diverse environments, which reproduce well-regulated urban terrains but also incite emancipatory politics beyond the regulated urban. Central to this thesis is Lefebvre's twin conception of habitat and habit*ing*.[2] The first term, *habitat*, refers to existing forms of housing— "large apartment buildings" and "private homes both large and small" (Lefebvre 2003a [1970], p. 80)—as well as to its structural coupling with "parks and open spaces" (p. 27), which are publicly consumed. In this sense, habitat can be considered a grid (matrix) of public *and* private spaces.

In explaining private (housing) spaces themselves, Lefebvre uses some strong descriptors, including "cages", "dwelling machines", and "switching boxes" (pp. 81, 98). Lefebvre pits these labels of conventional housing categorically against habiting (pp. 21, 48, 70, 81–85, 88–89, 100, 178, 182, 188). Habiting is a broad concept that refers to ongoing, nonteleological, antifinalistic struggles against the habitat-based compartmentalisation of urban space, which forms "the dialectical and conflicted movement between habitat and habiting" (p. 85). By participating in and being driven by these habitat/habiting conflicts and dialectics, according to Lefebvre, different kinds of urban residents, who occupy different social positions, can coconstitute the urban as a "virtual object".

In the urban histories of this dialectic, habitat has tended to overwhelm habiting (p. 81). However, habiting still can perform a key role in illuminating, differentiating, and negotiating the normalising effect of the fundamental public/private matrix of urbanisation, which filters out too many irregularities for achieving urban settlement. The city reserves this possibility of being enriched through habiting because habitation is a key metabolic medium of urban imaginaries. "The human being cannot build and dwell, that is to say, possess a dwelling in which he lives, without also possessing something more (or less) than himself: his relation to the possible and the imaginary" (p. 82).

I am invoking this thread of Lefebvre because, throughout part 3, I will show that urban social movements for homeless people represent a likely format in which the ethos and practice of habiting survives and contributes to the flourishing of cities in our age. This or similar approaches to prohomelessness can stir up some uneasy responses within various epistemologies rooted in actual urban communities. However, I hope that the three chapters of part 3 can show in concerted ways that such social movements still retain the important role of rebalancing the regulated urban on behalf of various people—whatever their social ranks. Furthermore, a study that thoroughly subscribes to this fundamental contestation on the urban can powerfully extend the vocabulary of urban theory to its systemic margins and peripheries.

For now, the immediate task is to fully unpack Lefebvre's theory of habitat/habiting. In this discussion, it seems, Lefebvre strongly aspired to resist any atmosphere of euphoria. He identifies habitat with the consumptive side of the "industrial city", and he detects the depoliticising effects of public spaces within it: "The street regulated time outside of work; it subjected it to the same system, the system of yield and profit. It was nothing more than the necessary transition between forced labor, programmed leisure, and habitation as a place of consumption" (Lefebvre 2003a [1970], p. 20).

In this context, public spaces dwindle into "nothing more than a 'passageway'", "pedestrian circulation", "the neocapitalist organization of consumption" (p. 20), "a poor substitute for nature" (p. 27), the hotbed of "myths of the city" (p. 26), and "a degrading form of democratization" (p. 27). Consequently, though Lefebvre conceives emancipation as habiting, and though he wants to find a starting point of "revolutionary events" and "movement[s]" in the streets (pp. 18–19), he has to add that the emancipatory potential has already been damaged, since "habitat, as ideology and practice, repulsed or buried habiting in the unconsciousness" (p. 81). On this ground, he proclaims, "During the reign of habitat, habiting disappeared from thought and deteriorated strongly in practice" (p. 81).

In light of this apparent pessimism, questions abound: How can the city retain transformative voices for urban emancipation? What recourse is there in the face of urban everydayness, colonisation, and occlusion? Is it really possible to get out of this occult-like, almost supernatural situation in which "discontinuities are … masked" and transformative moments are "smoothed over" (p. 41)?

One type of response to these questions is revealed by David Harvey (2012) with regard to commoning, which suggests that neo-Lefebvrian thinkers can expect politics against the regulated everydayness to take root in the middle of the city. As Neil Smith (2003, p. xv) implies, this is the position that must begin with a necessary reshaping of Lefebvre's underpoliticised notion of urban nature into "a venue for political change". In these discussions, Harvey and Smith suggest that capitalist urbanisation can develop new spaces of radical urban politics at the geographical centres of urbanisation.

However, I assert that Lefebvre's text discloses other sites and conduits whereby the city retains radical voices against the regulated everydayness; contemporary Lefebvrian thinkers may have underrated the traction urbanisation can gain from these heterodox spaces of socialisation.[3] In my reading of Lefebvre, the concentration, maintenance, and activation of radical and "wayward" voices, which might revive habiting from a neocapitalist hibernation, is possible in a type of urban niche that Lefebvre (2003a [1970], pp. 53, 109, 113, 118, 170) includes in the category of the "periphery"—a term that denotes subordinate or substandard urban areas that are politically, economically, socially, and symbolically overshadowed by and separated from more privileged areas.

Lefebvre eschews mythologisation of peripheries. They are the products of acute segregation—segregation "by class, by neighborhood, by profession, by age, by ethnicity, by sex" (Lefebvre 2003a [1970], p. 92). Peripheries can breed "violence in its pure state" (p. 145). Elsewhere, Lefebvre (1991 [1974], p. 373) mentions such peripheral spaces as "margins of the homogenized realm" and the "edges of the city, shanty towns, the spaces of forbidden games, of guerrilla war, of war". However, the text constantly keeps a trustful, positively anticipatory eye on these isolated areas of urban marginality. For him, these spaces of the urban periphery can still germinate seeds of transformation because of "what is different is … what is excluded" (p. 373). In the periphery, movements beyond the negativity of urbanisation are accelerated, because real peripheries can "combine the 'negative' forces of revolt against a repressive society with social forces that are capable of 'positivity' resolving the problems of the megalopolis" (Lefebvre 2003a [1970], p. 146).

Thus, in the periphery, Lefebvre seems to find the strategic role of "an other and different place" (p. 118) that can organise habiting and advance it against habitat. He even implies that the periphery might serve as "another center" (p. 118) of urbanisation because it accumulates urban imaginaries in a different way from habitat. I would hypothesise that the positivity of *peripheralised* urban movements hinges upon their ability to translate the negative moments of segregation—the given name of "sick spaces" (Lefebvre 1996 [1967], p. 99)—into more positive notions in defence of the excluded urban and the different urban. At any rate, such a path of urban politics is worth exploring.[4]

Expanding Lefebvre

Contemporary scholars offer topical arguments to expand Lefebvre's discussions. First, Massey's (1994) conflict-based notion of placemaking—that places are founded on "conflictual [space] sharing" (p. 137)—can equip Lefebvre with a useful lens on placemaking (on Lefebvre–Massey links for placemaking analysis, see Brenner 2009). As we have seen, Lefebvre (2003a [1970]) originally conceived habiting as a "dialectical and conflicted movement between habitat and habiting" (p. 85). Massey's notion that placemaking is a conflictual space sharing can be productively dovetailed into this conception of Lefebvre. Through geographically accommodating habitat/habiting conflicts by gathering people's various imaginaries related to habitat, indeed, the periphery of habitat may catalyse, form, and host a *variety* of placemaking strategies for homeless people. This variety in placemaking provides a periphery with the powerful means to thwart or mitigate the antihomeless moments of regulation/segregation in situ, contributing to the possible transformation of a periphery into a new centre of the habiting movement.

This discussion subscribes to Massey's characterisation that different kinds of people can produce places not only through friendship but also through strife—"conflict between interests and views of what the area is, and what it ought to *become*" (Massey 1994, p. 137, original emphasis). The resulting diversity—"meanings and symbolisms which people attach to places" (p. 118)—can make places "porous" (p. 121) and connect them to other places. This inward/outward vitality of porous placemaking strategies will make up an "accumulated history of a place" (p. 156). It seems that Massey thinks of placemaking as a series of sociospatial productions against regulatory power, against its stabilising of "the meaning of particular envelopes of space-time" (p. 5). I contend that multiple histories of placemaking, accumulated in a locality and extending to outer spaces/places/scales, can make the places of homeless activism more porous and less vulnerable to the geographies of regulation/societalisation.

Second, contemporary urbanists remind us that plural urban strata cannot be flattened and reduced to singular forms (Brenner, Marcuse, and Mayer 2012; see also Barnes and Sheppard 2010). It should be noted that Gill Valentine (2008) raises her key conception, "spaces of encounters", against neo-Marxist modes of conceptualisation, suggesting that a structuralist reliance on strong logics reduces urban studies to an oversimplified research field. Arguments under the banner of "spaces of contention" (Nicholls, Miller, and Beaumont 2013) might be read as expressions of analogous awareness by social movement researchers. At no point do I deny the educing power of these works; sociospatial strata will never be singularised, and the plurality is carried into the realm of political economies (Gibson-Graham 2006).

However, I would reinsert in these pluralist views some *structural* tensions, for places of prohomeless encounter/contention are profoundly restricted by the dominant forms and circuits of urban metabolism, its regulatory layers, and its lived experience of the housing classes. As a result, antihomeless divides can swallow up prohomeless encounters, and these divides are acutely felt by activists; *movements themselves are being regulated (and perhaps even flattened)*. In this context, activists' sociospatial investments in the plural urban strata can be understood as their constant attempts at sociocultural production, to endure, postpone, or sidestep the flattening power of regulation and segregation.

Third, specialists on homelessness and urban marginality help to clarify my Lefebvrian ideas for homeless activism and its spatiality. Here, the key characteristic is that homeless-friendly and prohomeless groups question antihomeless NIMBYism (DeVerteuil 2013; Takahashi 1997; Wagner 1993). These anti-NIMBY voices sound very alien to housed citizens when they are voiced in defence of homeless people (Wagner 1993). As Wagner implies, therefore, the geography of homeless activism is not at all congruent with the geography of housed citizens—though today many housed citizens can experience poverty themselves and think that "the poor are us" (Lawson et al. 2015). The corollary is that individuals/groups wishing to work for homeless people might construct their geographical scaffolding—their relatively "safe space" (Tilly 2000)—on the margins of normal housing, and such margins may be the inner city (DeVerteuil 2015), which has historically sustained itself vis-à-vis the homogenising pressure of hegemonic urban space—the "hegemonic mappings and meanings of the city" (Cloke, May, and Johnsen 2010, p. 85)—to which homeless people are inimical. In all, these specialists on homelessness and poverty further this chapter's argument that the geographies of prohomelessness present an avenue for our new understandings of the urban political landscape.

Inclusive Urban Form

Figure 6.1 brings together in one diagram the theoretical, methodological, and epistemological arguments I have presented. The three cells in the diagram—spaces, ruptures, and peripheries—restate my assessments and interpretations of the literature. This diagram offers a map of integral urban form. I would call it "integral" because this form not only includes the better-regulated domains of urban settlement but also covers the "heterodox" spaces of deregulation, desocietalisation, dehomogenisation, and extrahabitat practice.

Ruptures of habitat (homeless people's dwellings)		**Spaces of habitat** (housing classes' dwellings)
• Homeless people's production of space and use values • Formation of the "homeless city" (Cloke, May, and Johnsen 2010) • Homeless people's private things in public as the target of "annihilation" (Mitchell 1997) • Deregulation of habitat through "extrahabitat" moments	Deregulation and desocietalisation → ← Reregulation and resocietalisation	• Housing as "dwelling machines" (Lefebvre 2003a) • Public spaces for "pedestrian circulation" (Lefebvre 2003a) • Habitat as normative public/private experience (Lefebvre 2003a) • Habitat "smoothed over" (Lefebvre 2003a) by rounds of rescaling (Brenner 2004a)

Peripheries of habitat

- Peripheries of habitat can be "another center" (Lefebvre 2003a) for urbanisation through placemaking/commoning/translation
- Sustenance of prohomeless environments in the inner city amid neoliberal trends (DeVerteuil 2015)
- Urban social movements set up imaginaries for habiting, that is, cultures and languages that can discharge habitat (Lefebvre 2003a)
- "Conflictual space sharing" shifts the inner city between "porous" and "nonporous" placemaking (Massey 1994), refashioning peripheral spaces of encounter/contestation

Figure 6.1 Inclusive urban form and its urban effects.

Spaces of habitat are the public and private spaces that become "normal" for the housing classes through the filtering effects of the public/private matrix. These spaces hasten the formation of urban metabolism as "normalised lifestyle"—i.e., shared patterns of material–semiotic consumption. The "grid-like" character of the public/private matrix implies "imposition", but the housing classes live it by enriching public and private spaces through their meaning-shaping and -sharing (semiotic) process of consumption (discussed in Chapter 4). While being delineated by the grid, spaces of habitat accommodate the constructive spirit of the housing classes, who look forward to the meetings, encounters, and reunions in housing, streets, parks, pathways, alleys, and so on, beyond the doctrines of "traffic" and "reproduction" held by policymakers (Castells 1977 [1972]). When the housing classes thus creatively rework the public/private grid, spaces of habitat can envision leaps beyond regulation. Such leaps should be designated as a run-up to habiting, a step towards urban emancipation in search of new metabolic relations. Yet difficulty exists in recognising the ruptures of the public/private grid as a harbinger of new urban politics. Indeed, when the housing classes face such ruptures, these classes often accelerate "masking".

What is being masked here is the *rupture of habitat*, which is perhaps most significantly represented by homeless people. Although homelessness implies the expansion of metabolism with urban nature beyond the public/private matrix, as well as material–semiotic efforts that accompany this expansion, the housing classes often fail to recognise it as habiting. The housing classes can be overwhelmed by the mere presence of homeless people because they see them as "disturbers" of habitat. Homeless people thus induce ruptures of habitat, directing the housing classes and their guardians towards the reregulation of homelessness in defence of urban societalisation based on habitat. Such ruptures are not entirely revolutionary or an unmediated form of habiting. Nonetheless, they tell us that urbanisation is fundamentally contradictory, that cities need deeper democratisation and transformation, and that cities cannot pass off these ruptures simply as negative feeling.

Habitat develops its marginal zone, the *peripheries of habitat*, at the edges of urban housing regimes and their dwellers. Here, the generalisation of the housing classes, the societalisation of metabolism, and the filtering effects of the public/private matrix remain incomplete and can be resisted. Such a periphery might concentrate some negative elements of capitalist urbanisation, and perhaps detonate them in the form of—to invoke Lefebvre—"violence in its pure state". The historicity of such "negativity" should not be downplayed, but a periphery also can use this negativity as a run-up to dialectical democratisation by developing ruptures beyond the mere rejection of habitat. This might happen when a periphery amasses different people and prompts their conflict-prone but facilitating encounters at a relative distance from habitat. This is an emergent form of urban revolution in which a periphery hastens heterodox places of societalisation and "housing". In this way, urban social movements for homeless people can become a likely "format" in which the Lefebvrian habiting movement survives and seeks to impose its relevance in contemporary urbanisation.

Japanese Contexts

Attuning the Theory to Japan

This theorisation of placemaking has much explanatory power for Japan, particularly as it is mediated by my rich experiences with activists, volunteers, and their inner-city-rooted discourses and politics in Japan. At the same time, there are some key elements and tendencies that are relatively unique to Japan and thus cannot be adequately expressed by using only the categories and notions derived from the existing literature. Regarding the three boxes in Figure 6.1, I can highlight three ways in which the Japanese case is unique, in order to contextualise my case study within the theory.

Spaces of habitat in Japan can be understood in relation to its long urban history wherein Japan kept the use value volume of public and private spaces at a highly unsatisfactory level for the everyday consumption of the housing classes, in order to reserve a vast portion of national/urban wealth for industrial expansion in cities (see Chapters 2 and 4). While this developmentalist context of urbanisation could bring the deteriorated metabolic conditions of people into political crises of societalisation at habitat, as it did for a brief moment during the late 1960s, the regulatory strategy of Japan's developmentalist urbanisation was to deflect and disperse the tension by limiting the scope of the adversarial/progressive desires of the housing classes in organisational ways. This Japanese strategy for habitat production confirmed the housing classes in the conformist form of urban settlement by multiplying strict codes/rules of consumption and public behaviour under the leadership of administration-oriented local communities (Matsubara and Nitagai 1976).

In these circumstances, there emerged in Japan a characteristic intolerance on the part of urban dwellers and regulators towards "disturbers" of hegemonic (societalised) metabolism at habitat. *Ruptures of habitat in Japan*, indeed, have been conditioned by the state-saturated form of urban societalisation and its strict codes/rules of consumption, which broadly normalised the processes of urban encounter in public spaces. This translated to the extreme vigilance of urban dwellers and regulators over the "outsiders" who would use public spaces in ways different from the norms of consumption. This typically appeared in the widespread cycle of Japanese homelessness between the 1990s and 2000s. Though Japanese homelessness has perhaps not been noteworthy in terms of numbers, the encounters of the housing classes with homeless people have spawned major disagreements, conflicts, and ruptures within habitat in Japan.

Peripheries of habitat in Japan were inconclusive and unclear in the earlier phase of modern urbanisation due to the delay in building the housing classes and their small use values in public/private spaces. However, after World War II, cities developed clearer geographical borders between the housing classes and their outsiders. As postwar Japan achieved industrial urbanisation with only a few new migrant workers, metropolises materialised peripheries of habitat not as racial/ethnic ghettos but as yoseba zones in which day-labouring people were "pooled" and accommodated on behalf of urban industrialisation. These homeless-prone labourers were gathered in yoseba zones primarily through personal experiences of socioeconomic "failure", which saw people in the housing class arrive in the inner city after suffering unemployment, family breakup, or social dislocation (Eguchi, Nishioka, and Kato 1979). Yoseba zones offered quick access to accommodation and employment and turned homeless-prone individuals into day labourers (Nishizawa 1995). While the local authorities managed the borders of yoseba zones carefully, these areas eventually became a rare site in Japan, where new imaginaries for homeless people took shape.

In terms of gender, yoseba zones have been highly male-dominated spaces and local day labourers have mostly been male workers. In some cases, this gender construction of yoseba zones is a historical result of urban policy that removed female populations from these zones by giving them special treatment that was inaccessible to many males (Nishizawa 1995). In turn, yoseba zones have had a multiethnic character because some day labourers living in these zones had roots in other Asian countries, such as North and South Korea (Aoki 1989) and the Philippines (Ventura 1992; Yamamoto 2008).

However, ethnicity did not become a prime anchor for politicisation in yoseba zones; rather, activists and labourers often used class vocabulary when they conceived solidarity. Exceptional cases did occur in the late 1980s and early 1990s, when some yoseba zones saw a major influx of new foreign labourers (including undocumented workers) during the boom years of the "bubble economy". However, many of these workers left the yoseba zones by the mid-1990s, when local labour markets deteriorated. This yoseba-centred spatiality of Japanese day labourers' politics may be productively compared to day labourers' politics elsewhere, such as in the United States (Theodore 2015).

The Kotobuki District

My site of observation, Yokohama's Kotobuki, is a yoseba zone. The Kotobuki district emerged in the mid-1950s, when the municipality closed previous yoseba-like streets and districts (places of day labourers) scattered throughout the city. The judgement was that these pejoratively imagined streets were too proximate to the main commercial/residential areas of the city, which Yokohama was quickly rebuilding following their wartime destruction. Beginning in the mid-1950s, the newly formed yoseba, constructed in an area just liberated from the US-led occupation force, saw a massive inflow of day labourers working at docks (Figure 6.2). The municipality chose this area for concentrating the facilities serving day labourers on the ground that it was segregated from residential areas and that locating Yokohama's new yoseba zone there was less likely to provoke the negative reaction that was taking place in other areas (Serizawa 1976, p. 53).

Figure 6.2 The Kotobuki district, 1965. Day labourers gather in front of the Employment Security Office in the early morning.

Source: Katsuro Okazawa, originally published in *Yokohamashi no Hyakusanjyūnen* [One Hundred Thirty Years of the City of Yokohama] by Iki Shuppan. © Katsuro Okazawa.

Markedly enough, this concentration of day labourers' facilities in the Kotobuki district coincided with the strengthening patterns of anti–day labourer policing and "environment cleanups" in areas outside of the district—such as in the Sakuragi-chō area, which once had a geography of day labourers but soon became Yokohama's major commercial space (Serizawa 1967, 1976). This suggests that policymakers' calculations of the likelihood of NIMBYism deeply affected the postwar geography of Yokohama's inner-city construction.

In and around the Kotobuki district were three types of day labourers: the privileged and legal, called *aotechō* (bluebooks); the nonprivileged and legal, called *sirotechō* (whitebooks); and the nonprivileged and nonlegal, called *yamikoyō* (shadow employees). The bluebooks who proved their eligibility for unemployment benefits were enrolled in a strict registration system at the employment office, which included skills-assessment tests. They were given preferential treatment with regard to employment and received considerable bonuses twice a year. The whitebooks had the same insurance system and were enrolled only in a very loose registration system at the employment office, with no screening or skills assessment. Whitebooks earned less, had reduced job security, and had a smaller chance of receiving wage increases. The last group, the shadow employees, obtained jobs illegally, outside the purview of the employment office, without labour contracts or unemployment insurance. The whitebook and shadow employee categories were fluid, and individuals frequently moved between the two.

Here, I focus on the whitebooks and shadow employees. Many of them lived in the Kotobuki district and formed the "lowest" strata of day labourers, and homeless people emerged from these two categories. While the Kotobuki district gathered these most disadvantaged labourers from the local day-labouring population, more privileged day labourers—the bluebooks—kept away from the district, viewing Kotobuki as the site of people with no work ethic or skills. Homeless and near-homeless labourers in the district (whether whitebooks or shadow employees) rarely joined in the movements en masse, except during the exceptional time of the mid-1970s, when activism was at its most riotous. Even during these years, the leadership was in the hands of a few activists. Homeless and near-homeless labourers were typically fragmented in politics because their living conditions were harsh and uncertain and because their unpredictable working opportunities made them an itinerant population.

Two kinds of people from outside the group of homeless and near-homeless day labourers assumed lead roles in the Kotobuki district. The first category of activists included those who sporadically engaged in day labour in order to advance their political projects, established a local union for day labourers, identified themselves with day labourers and their homeless-prone living, and produced a vanguard-type of consciousness. I call this category of activists "union activists", and they engaged in "union activism". The second category comprised a band of people more remotely related to day labourers. This group saw themselves simply as "citizens" and they included university students, service providers, and Christians belonging to nearby churches. I term them "citizen activists", engaging in "citizen activism". The union activists originally sought to advance the solidarity of workers who were more active in the labour market (Gill 2001), and their homeless-supporting initiatives were preoccupied with rights to labour rather than with welfare, especially during the 1970s. The citizen activists, however, were more able to pronounce the specificity of the homelessness question that existed outside of the labour market, espousing homeless people's rights to housing and welfare.

These two types of activists evolved different types of local language and identity for placemaking, which is the central focus of this chapter. In theory, there existed a danger that homeless people would remain a fluid "crowd", a mere object of representation, even to the activists. Indeed, authority figures in the Kotobuki district were thinking that "most peripheral day labourers do not say anything, because they can't, as they don't know good ways of self-representation" (*hyōgen hōhō o min'na shiranai*) (Serizawa 1976, p. 225). Nonetheless, by sharing the same district with homeless people and homeless-prone day labourers, activists and volunteers seriously tried to overcome the "othering" effect through the unique "peripheral" placemaking in which subaltern interests were variously reimagined and reconstructed. Within Kotobuki's different areas, different types of activists discursively articulated prohomeless and homeless-supporting forms of urbanisation by using language and identities of their own. Placemaking also strategically strengthened causes and claims against antihomeless regulators. Further, placemaking gave this segregated area a strong capacity to obtain resources and participants from the outside.

Therefore, it is worth noticing that activists and volunteers brought diverse imaginaries—"ideas, representations, images, and even myths" (Lefebvre 2009a [1966], p. 152)—into the Kotobuki district for placemaking. As the placemaking language diverged among activists/volunteers belonging to different social strata, it promoted episodes of "conflictual sharing" of space (Massey 1994, p. 137), which Massey thought of as a spatial catalyst of collaborative struggles. The Kotobuki district showed a remarkable ability to accommodate and appease this duality of conflict and cooperation at the margins of normative urbanisation and the housing classes. This grew into the major geographical resilience of the Kotobuki district and the related urban social movements rooted in this inner-city area.

Placemaking in Yokohama's Inner City: From Run-Ups to the 1970s

After establishing a new yoseba zone in Kotobuki in the late 1950s, the city of Yokohama controlled the area in a patronising, pathologising, and semi-authoritarian way. One "tool" of this disciplinary inner-city policy was the Kotobuki

Chiku Jichi Kai (Kotobuki Self-Management Association, or KSMA). The name suggests that it was a democratic and spontaneous body from the local community; however, that was not the case. From its formation in 1962, the KSMA was, in large measure, under the aegis of the municipality and a platform of state–society collaboration for Yokohama's inner-city control (Serizawa 1967, p. 18, 1976, p. 56). The KSMA board members were local businesspeople—the owners of hotels and restaurants—whom the municipality regarded as "responsible", as they had a vested interest in running the district in line with the municipality (pp. 204, 225; see also Nomoto 1977, 2003).

Before the mid-1970s, the political climate was not ripe for urban social movements claiming the rights of homeless people and near-homeless labourers vis-à-vis the authorities. The prosperous Japanese economy before the severe economic downturn of the mid-1970s was constantly commodifying and "using up" the bodies of many day labourers, absorbing their masculinity into day labour employment and societalising them around local labour markets (though such employment was precarious and intensive and its wages hardly compensated for this condition).

During the world capitalist crisis of the 1970s, homelessness surged among these non-elite day labourers, and the municipality's grip on the inner city via the KSMA weakened. This in turn led to a void in inner-city policy, which could be occupied by a social movement. The local labour market was now unable to send day labourers to the docks as the cargo to be loaded and unloaded had disappeared. This context of crisis fomented a riotous atmosphere among Kotobuki's non-elite day labourers who were on the verge of losing their hotel rooms to live in. This unsettled mood actually led to the rise of activism in 1974.

This movement began in a rather haphazard manner, through the occupation of a municipal building for use as an emergency shelter for homeless labourers. Through this initial phase of placemaking, the movement began justifying its causes for homeless people more confidently, and it quickly became radicalised, widening the local geography of direct action against local authorities, including thronging, occupation, and demonstration. In Chapter 7, I will examine this radical history in its own right, considering how it provoked urban commoning. At present, I analyse this history from the perspective of placemaking, since placemaking paved the way for commoning.

During the five years of the 1970s movement, the leadership was taken on by a few activists, who subsequently established the Kotobuki Hiyatoi Rōdōsha Kumiai (Kotobuki Day Labourers' Union). At the outset, in particular, there was a mass mobilisation of non-elite day labourers, and a few municipal workers also participated in the movement. Yet the leadership continued to be in the hands of a few key activists, whom I have called the union activists. Due to the increasing intervention of the authorities and the difficulty inherent in organising homeless-prone labourers, this relatively large-scale mobilisation was short-lived. After 1976, police intervention was heightened and the mobilisation lost its momentum, dwindling to the occupation of a single municipal building, which ended in 1980. Even in that late phase, however, when activism had lost momentum, the union activists tried to bolster their placemaking activity in innovative ways.

Let's examine the early trials of placemaking. The crisis context precipitated a regulatory void, which was filled by Kotobuki's placemakers. In December 1974, a few people asked the municipality to let them use its four-story building, the Kotobuki Sēkatsu Kan (Kotobuki Livelihood Hall, or KLH), as a temporary shelter. The city reluctantly granted this request on the condition that the KSMA supervise the day labourers who were housed there. At the time, the risk of homelessness was acutely felt by day labourers in the Kotobuki district. Reflecting the crisis context, records and recollections of the event by participants are not positive—they convey grim and tense pictures of death (Endo 1976). Masa'aki Kagoshima, who was a photojournalist and would soon become one of the leaders of the union activism, recalls, "From December 1974 to March 1975, I saw about twenty day labourers die due to illness and malnutrition on sleeping mats spread out [on the floors] ... Even those unemployed who had not lost a hotel room came [to the KLH building] at night, fearful: 'I can die anytime. I'm afraid. I want to be with somebody at least when I die'" (my interview).

Yukio Shinohara, who had worked as a day labourer and lived in the Kotobuki district, and who would later take part in the establishment of the Kotobuki Day Labourers' Union in 1975, recollects that the "atmosphere was good" in the building during the initial phase of occupation. Yet even Shinohara cannot separate this "good" image from death: "I saw a labourer sitting on the floor, dead. I felt something unusual and tried to talk to him, but he was already dead as he sat. We ate poorly, and some drank too much. I often managed funerals on the fourth floor" (my interview).

Another participant in the occupation, Toshio Tanaka, was a municipal worker at the KLH building and briefly took part in the movement until 1975. Tanaka's image is less grim, especially when it comes to the cultural production of solidarity: "We spread sleeping mats [futons] all over the fourth floor and accommodated one hundred [homeless labourers]. Every day, we spread out the sleeping mats, formed a circle, and had a time to introduce the new faces among us. We had so many opportunities for self-introduction: 'I'm somebody, thanks for helping me,' et cetera, et cetera. It was a great experience, because we felt friendship."[5]

The seizure of the building was forming a new sociocultural locus of activism. Activists rejected the city's further intervention and refused entrance to the KSMA staff. Now the KLH building ran into the phase of *jishukanri* (autogestion/self-management). Between 1974 and 1975, this initial course of placemaking pushed many day labourers into riotous acts against the authorities. They engaged in demonstrations, speeches, and riots—on the street, in parks, and in public facilities. Moreover, under the leadership of activists, they together established the Kotobuki Day Labourers' Union. In Chapter 7, I shall further scrutinise these events and consider their impact on Yokohama's homeless policy. Here, my aim is to unpack the sociocultural spectrum of placemaking.

It is important to recognise that the political demands on behalf of homeless people could not begin before a cultural milieu—a place—was safely produced, out of reach of the disciplinary forces. The episode of autogestion was needed to develop the activists' political demands. Through the autogestion process, the intention of participants was to forge the potential "safe space" (Tilly 2000) of activism into a real safe space capable of withstanding the depoliticising efforts of the authorities.

The leaders motivated the day labourers to unite by showing these labourers to be a tough, stubborn, and intellectual collective and by articulating their causes using terms thought to be radical: *class, struggle, rights, self-management, discrimination, monopoly capitalism*. In order to communicate this language to comrades, the movement also produced self-advertising media in the form of handbills. Using mimeograph machines, they produced numerous copies of handbills and leaflets between 1974 and 1980 and circulated them widely inside and outside of the Kotobuki district. Some of the handbills were numbered as a series provocatively entitled *Hiyatoi Kaihō* [The Day Labour Emancipation]. Figure 6.3 shows one edition of such a handbill, in which the union activists are calling for the uprising of day labourers against the authorities.

In sum, the union activists developed new local language of placemaking and practised it at the KLH building to organise homeless labourers beyond the

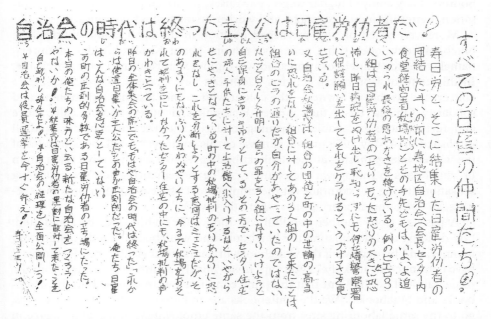

Figure 6.3 Undated handbill distributed in Kotobuki in the mid-1970s. The headline reads, "The time of the KSMA [Kotobuki Self-Management Association] has ended and now day labourers are the protagonist!"
Source: Archives of the Kotobuki Day Laborers' Union.

disciplining reach of the authorities. Through these ideational efforts, the union activists enriched the Kotobuki district and tried to keep the disadvantaged, itinerant day labourers involved in the place-specific activism.

In the late 1970s, when adversarial pressures mounted and began destabilising mobilisations, the cultural struggle for placemaking intensified. The union's placemaking strategy further developed along two lines. First, the union activists tried to form a bond of solidarity between non-elite (unhoused) and elite (housed) sections of day labourers by overcoming—in language—the segregated geography of the Kotobuki district. Second, the union activists created a national coalition of Japan's yoseba zones in order to maintain their momentum against the local pressure of policing and surveillance. Chapter 7 will examine these processes from the perspective of commoning. For now, it is worth noting that Kotobuki's activists were vigorously trying to evolve the placemaking strategy linguistically and geographically along these new lines.

Let's unpack the former line, which is about a new solidarity between non-elite and elite day labourers. In the late 1970s, the union activists pursued an alliance with an elite group of day labourers, the bluebooks, living outside of the Kotobuki district. These labourers rarely faced the risk of becoming homeless and lived in "normal" spaces—in habitat. Especially during downturns, when the local labour market contracted, the bluebooks fared better than Kotobuki's non-elite day labourers. They enjoyed higher wages, pay raises, secure employment, firm unionisation, better insurance coverage, and worker–management meetings.[6]

Moreover, based on this privileged position in the local labour market, the bluebooks developed some pejorative notions about Kotobuki's day labourers, namely, that the whitebooks and shadow employees in Kotobuki were unreliable. In this context, Kotobuki's activists adopted a new strategy of placemaking: to convert the symbol of lowness—the colour white—into a symbol of strength and solidarity. On that basis, they showed Kotobuki's labourers as politically active and, furthermore, as capable of forming solidarity with the bluebooks. A handbill published on 4 May 1978 gives a glimpse of this strategy: "To all the comrades of the whitebooks gathering at the Bankokubashi area! We are the only organisation of whitebooks in Kanagawa Prefecture ... [The movement] is now creating a big sensation among our comrades at the employment office every morning and evening, and at actual labouring sites where they work."

A passage from another handbill (30 June 1978) addressed discrimination: "By dividing and dominating the bluebooks and whitebooks in a discriminatory manner, and by depriving the whitebooks of guaranteed rights, they [capitalists] have continued to suck the 'sweet sap' [*amai shiru*]." A different passage from the same handbill pointed out that the same conditions were imposed on the whitebooks and bluebooks: "We the whitebooks are employed by the same employers, go to the same labouring sites from the same employment office, and engage in the same labouring process." The unvoiced question might have been *Why are we so divided?*

Through this symbolic production and cultural struggle, the union articulated a need to collaborate with the bluebooks, the elite. Practically speaking, the union activists in Kotobuki wanted to learn from the bluebooks how to demand wage hikes and safe working conditions, but they also had an ulterior motive: to form a united body of local day labourers by overcoming their isolation from the bluebooks. This aim was partially successful; Kotobuki's labour unionism won some pay raises by cooperating with the bluebooks. Yet because the economic conditions of the bluebooks were so much better than those of other day labourers, it proved impossible to form a single union body: "The old figures in the Zenkōwan Union are ridiculous because they receive 7,000 and even 8,000 yen, though they don't work as hard as we do", said one Kotobuki day labourer (Serizawa 1976, p. 203).

At any rate, Kotobuki's union activists became highly conscious of the need to connect their place—the putative "lumpenproletariat" fringe of Yokohama—to adjacent areas and people. For that purpose, they developed a strategy and a language of placemaking through rebranding the symbol of lowness as a symbol of strength and solidarity.

Second, Kotobuki's placemaking precipitated trials to produce a new scale for translocal solidarity. Precisely when Kotobuki's activists were seeking to find new comrades in the locality, they were also trying to nationalise the placemaking. In Tokyo's San'ya, Osaka's Kamagasaki, and Nagoya's Sasashima, underprivileged day labourers very similar to those in the Kotobuki district had already developed militant yoseba unionism, but now they were being harshly suppressed. In this context, the Kotobuki district, a "laggard" that was following other yoseba zones, formed a national vortex of day labour unionism, restrengthening similar yoseba movements in Japan. In 1976, the first national assembly of yoseba day labourers was held in the Kotobuki district (Figure 6.4). In 1977, the Day Labourers' United Front, a national coalition of Japan's yoseba zones, was established. In the same year, day labourers and homeless people—gathering from Yokohama, Tokyo, and Osaka—visited the Ministry of Labour and negotiated with national bureaucrats for better working conditions for day labourers.

Summary

In the 1970s, homeless and near-homeless labourers became politicised in Yokohama's inner city under the leadership of union activists. Placemaking activity was central to the process. To escape the reach of the authorities, and to "autonomise" the movement, they occupied the KLH building and established the Kotobuki Day Labourers' Union. After initial riotous events, the movement evolved the placemaking strategy to overcome the rampant pressure of regulation. They tried to share placemaking activity with elite day labourers in Yokohama, and they also tried to incorporate into their circle other yoseba zones across Japan. Translocal connections of activism surged, and placemaking occurred at a wider geographical scale by drawing solidarities across different places/scales.

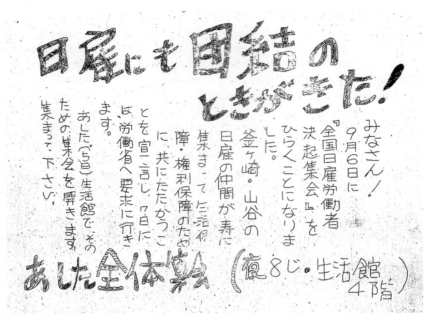

Figure 6.4 Handbill distributed in Kotobuki on 4 September 1976. At the top, it says, "The time has come for day labourers to unite!" In the main body, it calls on Kotobuki's labourers to participate into the Nationwide Meeting of Day Labourers, to be held in the Kotobuki district, and to work with many comrades from Tokyo's San'ya and Osaka's Kamagasaki.
Source: Archives of the Kotobuki Day Laborers' Union.

This nonporous yet extroverted mode of placemaking was based on their invention of local symbolism. The colour white, which previously had been considered a local symbol of lowness with reference to Kotobuki's labourers, was converted into a symbol of strength and solidarity beyond discrimination and segregation. This cultural inversion was intended to show Kotobuki's movement as robust and attractive to (potential) comrades. Throughout, Yokohama developed a sociocultural place of homeless activism in this inner-city area, for the first time in the history of the locality.

Placemaking in Yokohama's Inner City: The 1980s

On the basis of fieldwork in the early 1990s, Stevens (1997, p. 17) reports that "middle-class volunteers in Kotobuki" enjoyed a high level of autonomy in the district. According to this book's materials, however, in the early 1980s the district was still the nonporous, exclusive domain of male day labourers. The union activists were in a position superior to "middle-class" people coming from outside. After the experience of 1970s activism, the inclusion of "old faces" who had participated in the occupation of the KLH building somewhat strengthened local prestige. Under this circumstance, people who did not belong to the union or did not participate in the day labour market were culturally subdued.

The 1980s was thus a situation in which "citizens" started visiting the Kotobuki district but the "old faces" tried to keep the district as their own patch. For activism, this outlook is dangerous, because social movements for and with homeless people—small and weak as they are—need to attract new participants, resources, and worldviews from outside; otherwise, causes and initiatives for homeless people can easily be warped and obliterated by societalisation. The inner city must be connected to the external world, even to the housing classes. And the porous construction of places is vital to that end.

It was ironic—and disturbing—that certain tragic events began to change this nonporous atmosphere in the inner city. In areas adjacent to the Kotobuki district, three homeless people were murdered and five were injured in a series of attacks by junior high school students between 12 January and 10 February 1983. Just after these attacks, furious union activists frequently visited the murder sites and distributed castigating handbills in front of junior high schools in Yokohama. Yet their aggressive reaction led only to the arrest of nine activists at a school gate. At that time, union activism suffered from the lack of a cultural medium to communicate with Yokohama's wider areas, with habitat, and with the housing classes.

In this situation, the "average" people who lived in, commuted to, or visited the district for occupational and religious purposes refashioned the cultural contours of the district. They were self-proclaimed "citizens", the dwellers of Yokohama's habitat. Because of their strong ties with the world of habitat, these citizens had to produce their own place in the Kotobuki district *before* participating in activism. Recognising their origin, the citizens developed a unique set of imaginaries and vocabulary of placemaking when serving homeless people. They formed a new group called Mokuyō Patorōru (Thursday Patrol), with a Baptist church as its hub.

Despite some cooperative relationships with the union, those housed citizens doing voluntary work were culturally marginalised by the union. Union activist Noboru Kondo, who came to Kotobuki in the mid-1980s, describes this intimidating atmosphere from the perspective of the union:

> [In the union] sharp negative opinions existed about those [volunteers] from the churches. Frankly speaking, the union activists looked on volunteers as "unproductive" [*ashi o hipparu*, or literally "pulling the legs"]. That is, they [Christian volunteers] were understood not as partners in struggle but as people who showed up only when they wanted, who did only what they favoured. That was the criticism. It is not that the volunteers actually had such intentions. The union activists just saw them that way. (My interview)

In this atmosphere, Christian activists tried to legitimise their prohomeless actions by using a particular term originally used by the union: *patrol*. This terminology had been integrated into the local idiom of activists during the struggle of the 1970s, when union members appropriated the term from the police and branded their street activities a "people's patrol". When the citizens formed their own prohomeless organisation in 1984, they named the organisation the Thursday Patrol, a culturally ingenious way of rationalising their work vis-à-vis the union. Even after organising themselves in this way, however, the citizens felt the union's dominance. Arriving from habitat, the citizens did not experience severe destitution themselves, and day labourers occasionally grew suspicious.

In this context, everyday encounters with the union members were a source of stress. A veteran member of the Thursday Patrol, Takemaro Sakurai, tells of a unique way they dealt with this situation—by emphasising their ignorance: "When they [day labourers] acted against the murders of homeless people by pursuing patrols, we citizens [*shimin*] had naive questions about homelessness. ... In fact, we argued about what 'citizens' really meant. At any rate, however, we were people who were just interested in homeless people, who periodically gathered, and acted on the streets, in order to know what the real issues were" (my interview).

Here, Sakurai laments that the citizens suffered from ignorance about homelessness, and he states that it led them to the task of information gathering *before anything else*. Sakurai understands that this lack of knowledge continued to stymie their capacity to act for homeless people for quite a long time. As he suggests, citizens—"us"—could hardly overcome this problem, because day labourers and homeless people—"them"—exclusively retained the knowledge about homelessness.

"The people in the union always say that 'We help our comrades.' Their 'side' differed from us. We were, as it were, a 'third party' in terms of homelessness, who merely visited homeless people, asking: 'Could you tell me if you have any suffering?' Some homeless might have felt that we were unpleasant, and some might not have. ... The point is that we and homeless people could never be on the same side" (my interview).

Sakurai's language, distinguishing "us" from "them", seems to deny the ability of housed citizens to overcome the homeless–housed divide in helping homeless people. Only the labourers (the whitebooks and shadow employees) and the union members officially retained this capacity. In fact, the political message communicated by the powerlessness of "citizens" was a weapon for these citizens in protecting their causes and initiatives in the inner city. Of course, such a negative self-image seriously underrated the real power of the citizens; their work was extremely effective in helping out homeless people during the 1980s (see Chapter

7). The point is that the citizens were very careful *not* to identify themselves with homeless people, in word or deed. Sakurai notes:

> [In establishing the organisation], a few members argued that we should bring rice bowls to homeless people. But the conclusion was that we shouldn't. Such a small amount of food, if provided once a week, hardly seemed to cover their diet. This plan of food provision was perfectly meaningless, so long as the intention was to cover someone's nutritional needs. It could even trigger a misunderstanding between us and them. At such moments, our conclusion was: "Don't do that!"
>
> For each homeless person, it [a street corner] is a real "housing space". By any [Japanese] standards, you cannot walk into someone's house with your shoes on. We were risking this danger when we visited homeless people. So we later decided to bring a cup of soup—soup only. And, with the soup, we asked them, "Could you tell me what you suffer from, and why you are here?" The soup was meant to be a trigger for conversation, not a way of feeding them. To feed homeless people was impossible for us. (My interview)

Thus, Sakurai—rather proudly—acknowledges that the Thursday Patrol tolerated the concept of "us" as a given, unquestionable fact of citizen activism. Again, that storyline is partly fictitious, a linguistic construction. It only reproduced— from the perspective of citizens—the union activists' dominating narrative that they had exclusive capacity to communicate with homeless people. The reality, as Sakurai himself recollects, was that the citizens effectively reached homeless people, conversed with them, and provided food. The citizens even brought some specialists to the streets—nurses, doctors, temperance advisers—and gave homeless people rare access to these specialists.

Notwithstanding these actions, which were real acts of commoning (see Chapter 7), the Thursday Patrol continued to emphasise its "uselessness". We find this strategy—*placemaking by self-negation*—in the movement's leaflet, printed in 1985:

> When we started this year's patrol, we discussed many issues, varying from the meaning of our only-once-a-week patrolling activity, to those homeless who expect more support from us. Certainly, these discussions and dialogues developed merely on the side of patrol participants, and never spread to homeless people's side. When we actually visited them, there seemed to be clear dividing lines, which here and there emerged between the participants in patrols and those who received their aid. ... Each of us taking part in the activity has tried to become involved with homeless people as sincerely as possible. But we could never overcome this type of relationship between "people who patrol" and "people who sleep rough". (Mokuyo Patororu 1985, p. 26)

This piece, humbly written by a female contributor, echoes the identity politics and self-negation expressed by Sakurai. People in the Thursday Patrol, arriving from the world of habitat, thus created their place at this fringe of Yokohama's housing classes in a purposefully modest manner. On this basis of placemaking, however, the Thursday Patrol powerfully divorced "citizens" from hegemonic imaginaries about how the city should be. Only in this inverted fashion could they overcome the homeless–housed divide in the Kotobuki district.

Summary

During the 1980s, more average citizens started participating in prohomeless movements. In so doing, they needed their own place in the Kotobuki district. In making a place, their language was humble and even self-denying. Whereas the union activists identified themselves with homeless people, the citizen activists sharply distinguished themselves from such an identification. In one way or another, their language reproduced the borders between "us" (the housed) and "them" (the homeless) and portrayed "us" as powerless to overcome the homeless–housed divide. This linguistic construct paradoxically cultivated their compassion and empathy for homeless people. In practice, this allowed them to cross the homeless–housed divide. Only in this roundabout way could the citizen activists produce their prohomeless place and defend it in the Kotobuki district, where the pressure from the "old faces" was keenly felt by the "citizens".

Placemaking in Yokohama's Inner City: The 1990s

In the 1990s, Japan entered a new cycle of homeless growth, which I call the widespread cycle. In the previous inner-city cycle of homelessness, starting in the 1970s, the distribution of homeless people had been largely restricted to a few metropolitan yoseba zones, so a smaller number of individuals moved around larger public spaces, resulting in a considerably lower density of homelessness in those spaces. We have just seen that even this less dense appearance of homelessness incited antihomeless intimidation and oppression from the world of habitat. However, the new cycle of the 1990s brought far greater metabolic and sociopolitical tensions to public spaces, evoking far stronger dynamics of rescaling reregulation.

Amid widely spreading homelessness and massive rescaling, the Kotobuki district once again developed places for activism. Through this evolution, this inner-city area attracted a range of people from the world of habitat and turned them into activists and volunteers wishing to work for homeless people. This 1990s–2000s pattern of placemaking was characteristic. At last, housed citizens were able to perform self-affirming modes of placemaking in the Kotobuki district. They did not live in the district but frequently visited it. They were not thinking of themselves as homeless but wanted to join in with the activism. They needed a new place that "deserved" them, a place that would bestow the citizens with autonomous and self-affirming positions in the inner city.

In the 1980s, such citizens adopted very humble attitudes. Their language of placemaking was characterised by their self-perception as a powerless "us", although this actually misrepresented their real capacity. In the 1990s, this humble approach was transformed into a more assertive one. This was required, because activism needed more new ideas, participants, and resources in order to conquer the increasing sites of the homeless–housed divide and the rising tension of antihomeless othering, both of which characterised the 1990s and 2000s.

An important part of this placemaking was driven by the Kotobuki Shiensha Kōryūkai (Kotobuki Supporters' Gathering Club). This group was formed in 1993 by university students and social workers. Some founding members had previously engaged in homeless activism in the Kotobuki district, typically as members of the Thursday Patrol, which was the only citizen activist platform before the existence of this club. Participants in the club understood that Kotobuki's activists could no longer indulge in partisan politics, for the pressing need was to spread the prohomeless or homeless-supporting cause from the inner city to the outside, primarily to the world of habitat. For this purpose, the club hoped for a new network of volunteers cutting across the borders of the Kotobuki district. A founding member of the club, Yukio Takazawa, recollects, "Our intention was to create a loose network [*yuruyaka na nettowāku*] that linked the Kotobuki district and a wider society, so as to encourage them [citizens] to visit the district. We wanted 'supporters'—well, perhaps I'd rather say 'citizens' [shimin]—to come up to the Kotobuki district more easily. In the past, we had a situation in which people other than those called 'activists' could seldom visit here" (my interview).

Takazawa was a university student in the early 1990s, and this quote draws a contrast with the mood in the 1980s. Simply put, the normative environment that culturally subdued citizens in the Kotobuki district was weakened. Instead, there came into being a new cultural place in which visiting citizens could justify their homeless-supporting initiatives in more positive and self-affirming ways. A "network", rather than a strict organisation, was an appropriate form for this placemaking. Furthermore, the Gathering Club radically tried to abolish any distinctions or positions that could hint at authoritarian sentiment. A club pamphlet proclaims:

> This [the club] is a peculiar organisation that is somewhat different from conventional movement organisations. We have no representative, no regulation, and of course no qualifications. We also have no fixed membership status. The most important thing is your feelings that "I want to do something" or "I am interested in Kotobuki." We have nothing to do with obligations that "you should do", or with anything like bureaucratic conferences. Once you feel that "I had this or that experience, and so I want to do this or that thing", then, from that moment, you are a member of this "gathering club". (Kotobuki Shiensha Koryukai 1998, p. 13)

This philosophy—no status, no representative, no regulation, no qualifications—was a new cultural tool to construct citizens' positive position in the Kotobuki district. The impending task was to create a space for citizens who wanted to participate in activism outside of what Takazawa refers to as the "class position" (*kaikyū teki ichizuke*). Were such "class consciousness" to prevail, Takazawa feared, "there would be no patrols other than those carried out by left-wing activists" (my interview).

The degree to which the club achieved this promotion of a "loose network" remains an open question. Indeed, the centralised form of mobilisation they ostensibly eschewed continued to play an important role. Two or three foundational figures—Takazawa included—assumed much responsibility for the everyday activity: editing leaflets, printing handbills, setting up gatherings. However, the club's initiative—to let citizens positively affirm their participation in the Kotobuki district—did succeed in attracting new people to the district and in connecting them to the "old faces", even to the union. As we will see in Chapter 7, this new process of placemaking, which increasingly incorporated citizens, promoted new attempts at commoning in the 1990s and 2000s.

The cultural orientation of the club, in which volunteers eschewed strict codes of social relationship, also appears in its attitude towards homeless people. The club frequently held study meetings (*gakushūkai*) in the district and often invited homeless people to these meetings, asking them to speak about their lives—an idea that would have been unimaginable for the Thursday Patrol in the 1980s, when citizens needed to express their submissive position in relation to homeless people. In contrast, the new paradigm of homeless–housed relationships envisaged by the club was to overcome the homeless–housed divide in positive, self-affirming ways. The intended character of homeless–housed relationships is stated in a pamphlet:

> Never do we imagine homeless persons as "the homeless in general", because we favour intimate relationships with them in which faces and names will be known to each other. We will feel what homeless people feel, worry about, are frustrated by, and recollect—without express words. We will grow our power to struggle with homeless people against exclusion. We will ask homeless people to act as they think. We will stay inside of their circles. We will create relationships with homeless people.
> (Kotobuki Shiensha Koryukai 1998, p. 16)

Thus, the Gathering Club offered, and voiced, a more optimistic language of placemaking in which the wall that divides "us" and "them" was purposefully removed. Homeless people asked citizens to do something, but the citizens made requests of homeless people in return. They now invited homeless people to join them for meetings, discussions, lunches, and so on, if at all possible. This aspiration of bilateral communication, the melting away of "us" and "them", perhaps risked a new danger, the danger of romanticising. However, this language functioned as an effective way of placemaking. Even more, it became a powerful cultural weapon of mobilisation in the 1990s and 2000s.

Summary

The 1990s crisis of homelessness deeply engulfed the grid of urban habitat in Yokohama, and this crisis motivated regulators to exclude homeless people. Thus emerged the task of redressing antihomeless terrains in urban policy. Before anything else, the task was to construct sociocultural environments—places—that could advance activism in line with Japan's new cycle of widespread homelessness. New participants, resources, and worldviews were needed.

At this point, citizens produced new places and connected the Kotobuki district to the outside world. Their language of placemaking was increasingly self-affirming, which enabled housed citizens to play more active roles. Citizens were now able to casually divorce ("declass") activism from the hegemonic urban classes and their notions, to communicate with homeless people, and to aspire to go beyond the homeless–housed divide, the public/private matrix, and its societalisation effects. As this porous layer of placemaking was superimposed on prior sociological environments, the Kotobuki district powerfully drove a new cycle of mobilisation for commoning in the 1990s and 2000s, as we will see in Chapters 7 and 8.

Conclusion

The peripheries of the housing classes can be a site of new urban politics that pose fundamental questions about urban societalisation organised by habitat—the matrix of public and private spaces and its meaning-shaping (semiotic) layers of consumption. This movement, which Lefebvre called "habiting", can survive contemporary urbanisation by taking the form of urban social movements for homeless people, which might construct sociocultural places and heterodox societalisation at the margins of habitat. Before anything else, this process needs its own sociological environments running against the societalising pressure of habitat.

By elaborating Massey's notion of placemaking from a Lefebvrian regulationist angle, I have theorised that such places "beyond societalisation" can be created at the peripheries of dominant sociometabolic environments of habitat. Inner-city areas can be transformed into such creative peripheries whenever and wherever people aspire to develop imaginaries and languages free from the dominance of habitat. The imagined distance from hegemonic classes can prompt (would-be) activists towards actions of autogestion. In this sense, the geography of segregation can nurture the places of movements where they can critically decode dominant urban metabolism, societalisation, and habitat for deprived people. The disciplining grip of urban regulation can be weakened, especially in a large-scale socioeconomic crisis, and creative voids can open up. People wishing to work for homeless people might fill these voids with new imaginaries, languages, and placemakings.

By using this theory to collect and analyse ethnographic data, this chapter has narrated the "accumulated history" (Massey 1994, p. 156) of placemaking qua "conflictual sharing" (p. 137) of space, which made for many collaborative events at this periphery of habitat. The Kotobuki district escaped the city's disciplinary policy during the 1970s crisis and became a sociocultural location for an early type of local homeless movement that mobilised activists through the Kotobuki Day Labourers' Union. In the 1980s, new people arrived in the Kotobuki district from the housing classes and embarked on new efforts of placemaking against the backdrop of the older activists, which enriched places of prohomeless activism in Yokohama's urban periphery. In the 1990s, an even newer type of housed citizen started engaging in placemaking activity, which ever vocally targeted the overcoming of the homeless–housed divide from the side of the housed.

Through this local history between the 1970s and 2000s, the Kotobuki district developed different kinds of prohomeless or homeless-supporting places, and overlapped them, at the periphery of the housing classes. This history was necessary for the participants to divorce, declass, and autonomise themselves from the hegemonic classes and their political guardians. The entire history of Kotobuki's placemaking is a history of autogestion from habitat, which led the inner-city district to leap the homeless–housed divide.

Notes

1 *The Urban Revolution* has been widely used when theorists address, for instance, urban capital circuits (Harvey 1989b), collective consumption (Castells 1977 [1972]), urban social movements and appropriation (Castells 1983; Goonewardena 2012; Merrifield 2014; Schmid 2012), sociospatial dialectics (Soja 1989), uneven geographical development (Smith 1984), spatialities of rescaling (Brenner 2004a), or planetary ubanisation (Brenner 2014; Merrifield 2013).

2 Lefebvre develops the notion of habitat in other works (1991 [1974], 1996 [1967], 2003b [1966]). Additionally, I find that the notion of habitat is perhaps most usefully discussed in *The Urban Revolution* as the urban matrix of private *and* public spaces, or the spaces of private housing units *plus* their surroundings (i.e., commonly used environments and amenities).

3 For example, Harvey (1973) seems to have found no positivity in the urban periphery when *Social Justice and the City*—a canonical book that advanced Lefebvrian turns in geography and in his own scholarship—asserted, "Our object is to eliminate ghettos" (p. 137; for his more methodological criticism of ghetto-based research, see Harvey 1972).

4 Elsewhere, Lefebvre (2009a [1966], p. 144) finds political possibilities in the periphery, on the grounds that it denotes ruptures and lacunae within the geography of state space. He says, "Between them [reinforced places of the state] are found zones of weakness or even lacunae. This is where things happen. Initiatives and social forces act on and intervene in these lacunae, occupying and transforming them into strong points or,

on the contrary, into 'something other' than what was a stable existence. Weak parts, voids, are revealed only in practice."

5 Remarks of Toshio Tanaka, at "A Meeting to Hear from Toshio Tanaka", an event held by activists in the Kotobuki district, 6 December 2008.

6 The wages of the bluebooks were generally higher than those of the whitebooks, an underprivileged group of day laborers in the district. According to a record by a chief secretary of the Kotobuki Day Labourers' Union in the mid-1970s, the bluebook labourers commonly received 7,500 to 8,000 yen per day while their whitebook counterparts received only around 6,000 yen—if they were employed at all (Endo 1976, p. 203).

Chapter Seven
Commoning around the Inner City: Whose Public? Whose Common?

This chapter focuses on actions to actualise homeless people's right to the city. I examine this under the banner of commoning. In Chapter 6, I theorised that a variety of homeless activism can congregate at the margins of the housing classes and furnish these margins with urban form–reshaping worldviews. These people may construct a belief system for homeless people as a local system of places in porous and extroverted ways, allowing them to leap the homeless–housed divide and divorce activism from the hegemonic (housing) classes. This chapter shows that effective rules-changing and form-changing initiatives have really progressed from this history of placemaking; placemaking paves the way for commoning.

It should be noted that cities develop regulation and entangle both placemaking and commoning. In Japan, two rounds of rescaling materialised up to the 2000s, though these rounds did not fit perfectly into the cycles of homelessness. The rescaling was experimental, its performance was a matter of chance discovery rather than rational choice on the part of regulators, and the "regulators" themselves had to be discovered, motivated, informed, and set free from national fetters. Subsequently, however, the politics of homelessness became entangled in rescaled webs of rules and practices, which minimised their desocietalising impacts for the housing classes and urban society. These webs of urban regulation can prevent heterodox political actions from outgrowing housing classes–based societalisation. This book therefore cannot discover full-fledged forms of "urban revolution", whereby habiting might outmanoeuvre "urban regulation".

Rescaling Urban Poverty: Homelessness, State Restructuring and City Politics in Japan, First Edition. Mahito Hayashi.
© 2024 Royal Geographical Society (with the Institute of British Geographers). Published 2024 by John Wiley & Sons Ltd.

Thus, this chapter starts with the not-so-optimistic recognition that activists' interests tend to be subdued in the rescaled arenas of governance. Nonetheless, seeds of revolution, steps towards habiting, are implied in the whole process. A wide range of prohomeless/homeless-supporting activists and volunteers can generate "beyond occlusion" effects. These activists and volunteers, through defending spaces for the homeless metabolism (whether as a momentary escape for deprived people or as their more stable basis), reveal that the existing form of urban commons exclusively delineates its borders vis-à-vis homeless people, those who are most dispossessed of urban use values. This power of activism, supported by its cultural dimensions (as discussed in Chapter 6), can be more than cultural in the realm of commoning.

When activism's symbolic references to the homeless metabolism increase, it might lead to viable strategies for reshaping the exclusive rules and forms of the commons. A new form of commons, accessible for homeless people, may result, which this chapter understands as a process of commoning. This way of commoning finds limits in the "normal" mode of urban societalisation based on habitat. Indeed, when the "commoners" critically enunciate this societalisation to make the use value circuits of urban commons (more) accessible for homeless people, urban society can fortify the metabolic and semiotic life of housed citizens against homelessness by tapping into the matrix of public/private spaces.

However, even when the housing classes and guardians did not abandon their majoritarian metabolic relations and their privileged access to urban use values, Yokohama's activists and volunteers cultivated repertoires of commoning and deployed them around the Kotobuki district. These strategies enabled the activists to maximise, and use up, their potential for making urban commons (more) accessible for homeless people within the rescaled arenas of urban governance.

Commoning, Habiting, Othering

Peter Linebaugh (2008, 2014) uses the term *common* as a verb, arguing that people, in creative ways, can enlarge, vitalise, and share "a world of use values" (Linebaugh 2008, p. 43) at the margins of commodity society. A prime example, he says, is European forests. "The woodlands were a reservoir of fuel; they were a larder of delicacies, a medicine chest of simples and cures. As for food, hazelnuts and chestnuts could be sold at market; autumn mushrooms flavored soups and stews" (p. 43). The list of the commons goes on and on. Today's cities include forms comparable to forest commoning, such as "homeless camps". These, he says, "are rarely anyone's idea of utopia yet they meet real needs, they arise from direct actions, they are actual mutualism, they enliven dead spaces, they are cooperative" (Linebaugh 2014, p. 17).

In fact, Linebaugh also submits another, less idealistic view that commoning was *not* completely autonomous from regulatory process, which I find plausible.

European states vigorously enacted the enclosure of forest commons along with property rights, criminalised the commoning populace, and injected them into markets and wage relations by depriving them of their access to commons. But this process of "discommoning" (Linebaugh 2008, p. 49) did not stop the populace. Enclosures turned them into rebellious "commoners" at the margins of class relations and the world of commodity.

Drawing upon Lefebvre's notion of "right to the city", David Harvey (2008) illuminates the role of radical urban politics as something that can make cities into a political arena for radical wealth redistribution. Harvey (2012) develops this view into his thesis of commoning. For him, commoning can be advanced by urban social movements and can have profound power to turn existing "public spaces and public goods" (p. 72) into urban commons that are accessible for everyone, suggesting that homeless people need such commons desperately (pp. 24, 35). The outcome of commoning depends on political conjunctures, in which the rebellious actions of urban social movements must intervene.

As a matter of fact, Harvey thinks that the neoliberal administrator can cunningly exploit the movement's demands for local autonomy (pp. 71, 83–84). Attempts at autogestion—aspiring to turn regulatory decentralisation into "radical decentralization" (p. 84)—face serious difficulty because the movements cannot avoid eliciting the disciplining responses from territorial governance, requiring local activists to develop "overarching" forms of resistance (pp. 121–123, 125). Yet Harvey thinks that urban social movements can forge commoning by reworking territorial governance and creating more autonomous spaces in cities (pp. 16, 85, 153).

These two theories of commoning help this book to avoid the nondialectical (ahistorical, functionalist, deterministic) idea that capitalist relations have subsumed politics of popular classes once and for all and that cities can be a perfect arena for this subsumption. Both cover the case of homelessness. Both suggest that ongoing struggle for subsistent economies politicises the margins of class relations by taking the form of commoning, which tries to wrestle urban use values away from their metabolic integrity with dominant classes.

I amplify this understanding of commoning against the backdrop of this book's general view on social movements for and with homeless people, or habiting. When the politics of the housing classes are embraced within the dominant framework of urban metabolism, semiosis, and encounters, the politics of homelessness reveal those points that are less entangled by the same system. Starting with these ruptures, the commoning of urban use values for homeless people can advance real processes towards habiting as it aims to change the rules, norms, and shape of the commons within and around habitat—initially at each site, then in one city, and then in multiple cities.

The implication is that habiting intrinsically entails multisite, multicity, and cross-scale actions as it seeks to revise or redress the societalisation effect of habitat under rescaling. While the wider spaces/places/scales of commoning will be discussed at length in Chapters 8 and 9, the present chapter aims to address a particular space of habiting and how it took a form of commoning around the inner city.

Commoning against Othering

Commoning occasionally bursts into rebellious acts, as Linebaugh (2008) and Harvey (2012) argue. At the same time, the forced minoritarian nature of prohomeless commoning demands more than "violence in its pure state" (Lefebvre 2003a [1970], p. 145), for the "commoners" in this particular type of commoning suffer deadly effects of othering in urban governance. Because rescaling—a dominant tendency in homeless regulation—further amplifies the effects of othering, the practice of commoning must cultivate new ways to go beyond violence. Otherwise, prohomeless movements dwindle and cease when confronted by regulators.

The notion of "commoning against othering", which I introduce here, is my elaboration of the commoning theories to address this conundrum. The understanding is that for homeless people, commoning must combat the othering–rescaling effects of regulation more or less "directly" in order to make real rules-changing and form-changing impacts over the urban use values (and their extant "commons form") that shape our cities. The difficulty is that homeless people's needs would seem not to *be* needs to the majority (the housing classes)—homeless people's needs do not seem to include the right to the commons, the right to the city, or the right to citizenship. However, the movement's creative mixture of various social movement techniques—intimidation and persuasion, anarchism and collectivism, opposition and collaboration—may make these homeless needs and rights understandable (and even acceptable) for regulators and the housing classes.

Why is it so difficult to recognise, much less guarantee, the needs and rights of homeless people? The difficulty is partly related to the centrality of public and private spaces (as a set) in the extant frameworks of welfare delivery. Nationalised spaces of poverty regulation, and by extension the welfare state itself, advance their societalisation effect by tapping into the society-organising capacity of public and private spaces. In the context of this book, these built environments, which Harvey (1982, 1989b) discussed from geoeconomic perspectives, are the main site of urban societalisation. While this urban process produces and generalises the housing classes in cities, it turns homeless people into a dangerous class, a non-housing class, and the outsiders of societalisation and its housing regimes. Homeless people's everyday needs, and their right to the city, are thus unlikely to be recognised by the hegemonic classes, their guardians, and the rescaled arenas of governance constituted by the two.

The promotion of homeless people's needs and rights demands that social movements expand and develop the strategy of commoning against othering. This commoning can target two immediate goals: the unlocking of existing commons to homeless people and the production of new types of commons suitable/adjusted to homeless people's specific needs. Both meet with the regulatory pressure and must (partially) overcome it. I now explain each in turn.

First, commoning against othering can aim to liberate the use value flows of the commons from their "closed" circulation within the metabolism of the housing classes. That is, commoning against othering seeks to open *existing* public spaces and public provisions to homeless people. Second, commoning against othering tries to establish new versions of urban commons specifically for homeless people. These new commons include various policy and nonpolicy tools and provisions that can address the specific needs that homeless people have on and off the streets, within their survival economies and their post–public space lives.

Located and transfixed on the local scale, these two processes of commoning face the rampant pressure of exclusion, intimidation, and uncertainty because homeless politics are ousted from the secure realm of citizenship and because state and social agents can use a wide range of discretion against the desocietalising "them". While the commoning movement sometimes aspires to overcome the localised situation by upscaling the site of struggle from the local to the national, this upscaling strategy makes things no easier, as the movement still will have to combat the antihomeless atmosphere that takes other formidable forms at the national scale (see Chapter 9).

Nonetheless, even when the movements are enclosed within the local scale, the accumulation of "microhistories" of placemaking in situ can pave the way for commoning—the opening up of the commons to homeless people. In fact, a given form of societalisation always places on this form of commoning certain limits that activists and volunteers cannot outmanoeuvre. However, by accumulating indigenous imaginaries and vocabularies in urban enclaves, and by using these cultural strata for extroverted and porous modes of place-based struggle, whether in the Kotobuki district or elsewhere, commoning against othering can partially change the predominant rules, norms, and imaginaries in terms of how the commons should be used, and by whom, which unlocks the commons to the circuits and spaces of the homeless metabolism.

These discussions can be related and compared to a radical theory of the commons in Michael Hardt and Antonio Negri's (2009) celebrated book *Commonwealth*. People's commons, they argue, are being achieved by many instances of poverty politics—by the "multitude of the poor" (p. 40)—whose biopolitical productivity and local–global ontology outgrow the national. Cities are fundamental because *"the metropolis is to the multitude what the factory was to the industrial working class"* (p. 250, original emphasis). Cities are the "space of the common, of people living together, sharing resources, communicating, exchanging goods and ideas" (p. 250), and they occasion radical urban encounters— "the unpredictable, aleatory encounter or, rather, the encounter with alterity" (p. 252)—that increase the "reservoir of common wealth [which] is the metropolis itself" (p. 153).

Yet I am illuminating these urban encounters and commons from a different angle, that is regulationism, which is neglected in Hardt and Negri's conception. Seen from this angle, the emancipation of urban encounters and commons from existing scales and modes of regulation demands counterregulatory struggles and politics that are aware of, and reveal, the very scales and modes of regulation in practice. Hardt and Negri may have downplayed this counterregulatory dimension of commoning struggle.

Japanese Parameters of Commoning

To tease out the Japanese specification of commoning theory, this chapter will explicate the particular legal character of citizenship in Japan. An important aspect of Japanese welfare statism lies in the way it benevolently legalises the right to livelihood (sēzon ken) as the sacred right of all citizens, regardless of their contributions and social attributes. As I discussed in Chapter 3, the constitution establishes the right to livelihood in a universal manner, declaring, "All people shall have the right to maintain the minimum standards of wholesome and cultured living" (article 25). To realise this right, the Public Assistance Act of 1950 constructed the framework of public assistance: "The minimum standard of living guaranteed by this Act shall be where a person is able to maintain a wholesome and cultured standard of living" (article 3). Essential public assistance benefit programmes—such as income, medical, and housing benefits—are intended to serve as practical tools to maintain the livelihood rights of all Japanese people. Furthermore, the act calls for the flexible mobilisation of assistance. It enumerates the unique problems faced by unhoused people—"the households of persons requiring public assistance who have no home" (article 38)—and provides immediate assistance to such people.

The livelihood right written into the constitution does not, however, contradict my previous discussions about Japan's meagre public provision. As Chapter 3 showed, Japan's nationalised space of poverty regulation has long exhibited weakness in public provision, which contravenes the benevolent legal clauses of the livelihood right. In the wake of World War II, the occupation force was in high democratic spirits and, with progressive Japanese intellectuals, they created the universal legal framework of citizenship for virtually all impoverished people in Japan. However, this democratic state building was soon overshadowed by a developmental state building (see Hayashi 2021), which was a path that fundamentally weakened public provision until today.

Hence, despite the law, postwar Japan failed to realise the livelihood right for many impoverished people, even though that right was (and still is) firmly determined by the legal system. This law–reality gap is, of course, contradictory, but the contradiction is managed in large measure through the assistance of Japan's conservative legal regime. Court cases such as *Asahi v. Horiki* (1967) have established that the benevolent clauses of the livelihood right merely set an effort target—not a real goal—for the Japanese state. With another support being provided by a clause in the Public Assistance Act of 1950 that vaguely implies the program's restricted function (see Chapter 3), local welfare offices have been highly reluctant to extend public assistance to both homeless people and those who have housing and live in poverty (see Eguchi 1979; Iwata 1995; MHW 1962).

Nevertheless, the important fact for activism is that the benevolent clauses have not been changed or eradicated. Despite all the law–reality gaps, the constitutional right to livelihood has continued to exist in law, and activists and volunteers have used it to conceptualise, advance, and justify actions of commoning. The hope is that the idea of the right to livelihood can be used to include the poor and homeless in the realm of citizenship, according to the broadly defined notion in the constitution and other laws, if only they can stop the authorities from ignoring these clauses. This possibility—the utility of the inherent inclusiveness of the livelihood right clauses—has actually inspired many activists, volunteers, and sometimes even public workers to push the local (and national) arenas of governance to acknowledge homeless people's right to the city as part of their right to livelihood. The inclusive idea of the livelihood right was a powerful argument in convincing activists and even some regulators that homeless people's right to urban commons—a radical idea at any time—could be understood positively in postwar Japan.

This is not to say that the gatekeepers of urban commons easily admitted the livelihood right of homeless people. Nonetheless, the benevolent notion of the right to livelihood became the cultural and political pillar of commoning, and the local conditions of homeless people were improved through acts of commoning that echoed and utilised the inclusive idea of this right. In the case of Yokohama, this Japanese parameter of commoning already signalled and inherently supported local movements during the early phase of commoning, in the 1970s. Thereafter, the notion of the livelihood right became further articulated and elaborated in the ongoing processes of activism.

Commoning in Yokohama in the 1970s

The Start of Commoning

The acute growth of homelessness among day labourers in the Kotobuki district was a place-specific manifestation of the 1970s crisis, which significantly damaged Japan's growth pattern and the NSPR's effects of societalisation (see Chapter 3). As Chapter 6 showed, this crisis put a sudden halt to the business conducted at Yokohama's docks. These docks had once attracted a vast number of manual labourers, but the crisis suddenly discontinued this flow of work. Many of Kotobuki's day labourers lost their employment, were stranded in the inner city without money, and ran an increased risk of homelessness.

We saw in Chapter 6 how quickly the unfolding of local crisis promoted an emergent pattern of placemaking in the Kotobuki district. The prime examples were the occupation of a municipality-owned building (the Kotobuki Livelihood Hall) by activists and homeless labourers, and the establishment of the Kotobuki Day Labourers' Union in order to collectivise the radical morale of activism. This initial phase of placemaking was the start of commoning. In the winter of 1974, when the day labourers and activists began occupying the KLH building as a shelter, a soup kitchen, and a distribution centre, the building was already being commoned by these movement participants.

From the beginning, then, commoning in this area took the form of commoning against othering, of reappropriation against exclusion. This Kotobuki district, which was a marginal zone of Yokohama's housing classes, had long been largely depoliticised under the patronising policy of the municipality and its local partners. As a tendency, the "wayward" voices of day labourers had been managed by the municipality's demobilisation efforts. The initial rise of homeless activism had to break down this barrier through creative efforts of commoning, which included these efforts of occupation and organisation within the Kotobuki district.

To depoliticise Kotobuki's day labourers, the municipality had at its disposal a tool of social control: the Kotobuki Self-Management Association. Chapter 6 noted that the KSMA was dominated by local business owners (owners of hotels and restaurants, whose main customers were day labourers). By forming the KSMA, the city officially recognised these business owners as its partners in local policy operation. The KSMA was another example of Japan's traditional community form, strongly tied to authorities, which was in this area bestowed with some autonomous power of regulation over day labourers under the municipality's guidance. In this way, the KSMA helped the city to subdue the everyday discontent and politics of day labourers. By inserting the KSMA between the municipality and the day labourers, the city was able to operate its inner-city policy indirectly but smoothly.

On this basis, regulators indulged in an ideological construction of day labourers as the vulnerable "Other". This is seen, for example, in a remark made by a senior official of the city, who worked as the director of the KLH building: "The [day labourers'] lifestyle, far from being 'stable' and 'willing', can easily be filled with 'discontent' and 'uneasiness', and day labourers do not show efforts to solve these problems. Instead of trying to move out [from this lifestyle], many of them find easy escapes in drinking and gambling, driving these many to a loss of possibility of 'humane life' in consequence" (Nakane 1968, p. 10).

To advance commoning against such pathological discourses of depoliticisation and naturalisation, the movement needed to develop counterhegemonic language and action. In the beginning, this movement of commoning against othering effectively frightened the local authorities, stopped their othering manoeuvres, and even replaced the previous institutions of marginalisation with new institutions of commoning. Activists thought that the best way to overcome the politics of othering was to let the authorities know that the crisis of homelessness was impending and that day labourers and their supporters were capable of solving this crisis by themselves, beyond the patronising policy of the authorities. For this reason, after occupying the KLH building, in November 1974, activists and day labourers began extending the tactic of spatial occupation from the KLH building to various other facilities: the city hall, the prefectural government, and the employment security office, among others. By extending the radical tactic of commoning to these spaces outside of the inner city, they demanded the neglected right of day labourers to livelihood and demonstrated the political autonomy of the movement.

In response to the movement's demands, during the winter of 1974, the authorities created new frameworks for urban commons. In addition to the KLH building itself, Yokohama's new urban commons in this early phase included two other elements: the municipality's system of hotel and food tickets, and the prefecture's framework of year-end annual allowance. First, on 25 November 1974, the municipality established a new rule that it would provide hotel and food vouchers to any homeless labourers in the Kotobuki district. The vouchers were significant because they were intended to accommodate impoverished and homeless people's right to livelihood through a local framework of provision, if not through the national public assistance programme. Then, on 13 December 1974, the Kanagawa Prefectural Government established a framework for a year-end annual allowance for day labourers. This benefit aimed to give day labourers, on a noncontributory basis, a certain amount of cash annually at the end of the year, in order to help them survive unemployment, which generally worsened during the year-end and New Year's holiday due to the closure of day labourers' workplaces. These two progressive frameworks composed the key part of making the urban commons accessible for homeless people, which materialised in the winter of 1974.

From Radicalism to Downright Oppression

Very soon, however, something became clear: commoning was no longer to be tolerated. The authorities now started to launch a new wave of oppression. To understand this quick shift, it is necessary to paint an overall picture of how much the movement had increased its riotous character. Table 7.1 summarises a series of social movement actions carried out towards the late 1970s in and around the Kotobuki district. These were the very dimensions of the movement that surprised—and frightened—the local authorities. Already by 1975, the authorities were drawing the conclusion that the city's "benevolence" was being overused and exploited by the movement, and that this benevolence only heightened the anarchist atmosphere, which would in turn threaten Yokohama's urban societalisation as a whole. In this context, the authorities made the movement choose between two options: to accept the disciplining policy of the authorities, adopt a submissive position, and stop testing the existing urban order, or to continue riotous acts, suffer

Table 7.1 Key movement actions in and around the Kotobuki district in the 1970s.

Date	Site	Action	Demands
21 November 1974	City hall	Occupation	Movement's access to Kotobuki Livelihood Hall (KLH)
22 November 1974	City hall	Occupation	Movement's access to KLH
22 November 1974	KLH building	Beginning of KLH occupation	Food and shelter provision
25 November 1974	KLH building	Negotiation with City of Yokohama	Vouchers
12–15 December 1974	Prefectural office	Occupation	Public sector employment, unemployment insurance, year-end allowance
17–19 December 1974	Public employment security office	Blockage	To prevent provision of an insufficient year-end allowance
19–20 February 1975	City hall	Dissent, sit-in	To protest the municipality's discontinuation of vouchers
23 February 1975	Kotobuki Park	Demonstration	To protest the municipality's discontinuation of vouchers
25 February 1975	KLH building	Start of KLH occupation under illegalisation	To protest against illegalisation
12 April 1975	Outdoor concert hall	Demonstration	Public employment
18 May 1975	Kotobuki Park	Organisation of the union	Sustainable social basis for movement
25 May 1975	NA	Major confrontation with riot police	To protest the police's handling of a dead labourer
3 Aug 1975	City hall	Occupation	To protest the city's decision to cut off gas/water/electric supplies to KLH
6 November 1975	Prefectural office	Negotiation with Kanagawa Prefectural Government	Employment provision and year-end allowance
27 April 1976	NA	Negotiation with the city	Better conditions for discontinuing KLH occupation
30 April 1976	NA	Negotiation with the city	Better conditions for discontinuing KLH occupation
6 September 1976	Kotobuki Park	National assembly of day labourers	To strengthen solidarity among day labourers
24 October 1976	Public employment security office	Occupation	To protest illegally low-paying employment

(Continued)

Table 7.1 (Continued)

Date	Site	Action	Demands
25 November 1976	KLH building	Encountering policemen at KLH	To stop arrests
16 January 1977	Kotobuki Park	Demonstration	To demand employment provision
17 April 1977	NA	Organisation of Day Labourers' United Front	To forge national solidarity of day labourers

Source: Kawase Seji Kun Tsuito Bunshu Henshu I'inkai (1985); Kotobuki Shiensha Koryukai (1998); Nomoto (1977, 2003); Serizawa (1976); and handbills in the Kotobuki Day Labourers' Union Archives.

downright oppression, and abandon any position in the local arena of governance. When day labourers and activists saw the municipality delivering this message, they hardened their attitude and responded with further radicalisation of the movement.

Thus, as early as 18 February 1975, the municipality announced that the movement's use of the KLH building was no longer permitted. On 23 February, the city halted the provision of the hotel and food vouchers, a decision to which the movement reacted by occupying one floor of city hall. On 25 February, the city proclaimed that the occupation was completely illegal and declared—in the name of the mayor—that the KLH building was now closed indefinitely. In response to the criminalising move of the authorities, day labourers declared that they would now "purify" the self-management (jishukanri) of the KLH building, preventing any future involvement by the municipality or the KSMA. The occupation of the KLH building continued.

The confrontation reached its height less than two years later. On 25 November 1976, riot police armed with shields and truncheons stormed the KLH building and arrested union activists. The municipality cut off the gas, water, and electric supply to the KLH building. The movement of commoning against othering lost its former gains in the Kotobuki district and became highly defensive.

A National Scale of Commoning?

As the radicalisation of the commoning movement stepped up, it looked as though the authorities could have stamped it out at any time. At least, that was the fear of the activists. The local authorities no longer accepted commoning in this radicalised, offensive version. In response, they started closing the established urban commons in the Kotobuki district. The riotous nature of the movement, which had been essential in establishing its presence in the initial struggle against othering, had deeply frustrated the urban order, to the degree that the riot police actually intervened and arrested a few key activists. In Chapter 6, I showed that Kotobuki's activists and labourers did not quiet down; they tried to overcome the oppression by evolving their placemaking strategy from an introverted to an extroverted model. Now I want to demonstrate that this new, extroverted pattern of placemaking led to an equally extroverted strategy of commoning.

Most tellingly, the 1977 formation of the Day Labourers' United Front—a national coalition of Japanese yoseba day labourers—found a new channel for negotiation with national regulators at the Ministry of Labour. This opportunity was provided by Sohyō, the biggest body of Japan's working class at that time, which was supporting Kotobuki's movement by providing rice and other supplies. On 25 November 1977, day labourers from various yoseba zones across Japan, gathered under the aegis of the Day Labourers' United Front, held a roundtable discussion with national bureaucrats at the Ministry of Labour. Activists asked the ministry to establish a national hiring centre for day labourers, thinking that such a system could solve the problems of unemployment and homelessness. This demand for a "national" right was rejected, on the grounds that it was beyond the role of bureaucrats. Yet this attempt at national-scale commoning shows how, with a good understanding of the "scales of commoning", Kotobuki's movement creatively tried to conquer the narrowness and saturation of the rescaled political arena in the district.

Disarmament

By the end of the 1970s, Kotobuki's activists were suffering increasing isolation and hardship. They had lost the previously established commons, experienced arrests, and failed in their nationalisation effort. The movement was now barely sustaining itself by retreating into the KLH building. In this context, activists found it difficult to maintain a radical attitude. Indeed, they began informal discussions to seek some realistic conditions to end the occupation of the KLH building.

In winter 1978, discussions started between the City of Yokohama and local people, including members of the union. The union members reached a consensus that they would leave the KLH building on one condition: that the city would guarantee their perpetual access to the KLH building in the future. In response, the municipality proposed to hire one member of the union as a paid worker at the KLH building. The union member would be hired not directly by the municipality but by a semipublic organisation that would manage the building on behalf of the municipality. All parties agreed with this plan, which was subsequently implemented.

This somewhat lukewarm settlement of the riotous 1970s owed much to the calculation on the municipality's side that the union's well-controlled participation in the local political arena would be more helpful for Yokohama's future policy than outright rejection. This anticlimactic ending of the 1970s would mean a lot to the future of commoning as well. In the first place, the ultraradical version of commoning, which was ready to retaliate against even heavily armed police officers, was going to be avoided from this time forward. Any activists in this district were going to seek more communicative strategies and vocabularies of commoning, in an attempt to achieve a democratisation of "government + governance" (Jessop 2002, p. 239). At the same time, however, despite being tamed in this way, the radical spirit of the 1970s was going to be preserved in this inner-city area. The KLH building was going to remain a stronghold of the movement. The contentious history of the 1970s was going to endure as a collective memory, attract new visitors and participants, and inspire a new series of contentious politics.

Summary

In the mid-1970s, the national crisis of poverty regulation was producing a local homeless population in the Kotobuki district—a yoseba zone. There, the inherited policy of othering drove the local dynamics of rescaling reregulation and was trying to contain the tensions of homelessness in the local political arena. The initial phase of commoning started when Kotobuki's activists began to combat this regulatory manoeuvre. Empowered by the ongoing placemaking process, participants threatened authorities and made them respect their political will.

At first, protests elicited positive responses from the authorities, leading them to produce a new catalogue of urban commons on behalf of homeless people's right to livelihood. Soon, however, acceptance turned to rejection. Frightened authorities greeted radicalism with the closure of urban commons and the arrest of participants. These riotous events ended in a somewhat lukewarm manner, which increased the level of communication between the movement and the regulators and put an end to the riotous 1970s. While this was a calculated strategy on the part of the municipality to contain the movement with minimum cost, this course enabled the Kotobuki district to preserve its capacity for future commoning.

Commoning in Yokohama in the 1980s

Between the Two Cycles of Homelessness

This book is based on a cyclical understanding of Japanese homelessness. During the 1970s, homelessness grew among the most disadvantaged segment of day labourers living in the inner-city areas called yoseba. This is what I call the "inner-city cycle" of homelessness. In and after the early 1990s, homelessness grew once again, and to an unprecedented level, taking a more spatially extensive form in which homeless people en masse came to be broadly distributed across public spaces outside of the inner city. This is the "widespread cycle" in my conception of homelessness.

These two cycles of homelessness corresponded to two patterns of social movements addressing urban commons. During the inner-city cycle of homelessness that culminated in the latter half of the 1970s, inner-city activism for homeless people arose in the Kotobuki district and targeted urban commons in and around the district. In the new cycle, beginning in the 1990s, inner-city activism resurged and then outgrew the geography of segregation, mutating into mobile and flux forms able to spread actions of commoning beyond its previous inner-city geography.

This cyclical understanding of homelessness might make the 1980s seem unimportant. Though it lies between the two cycles, however, the 1980s is a highly important period in understanding the commoning movements in this area. This was a time when the housing classes and their urban society—the societalised "us"—began entering into the picture of Kotobuki's commoning projects. During this period, some homeless individuals were already living in Yokohama's "normative" public spaces outside of the inner city. Though the number was small compared to the 1990s, these people were causing tensions in the world of the housing classes. Chapter 6 noted that these tensions took the form of extremely violent reactions on the part of the housing classes—some homeless people were injured or even murdered. I also showed that in this context, a few housed citizens arrived in Kotobuki and made a place for themselves. In short, the 1980s was a highly transformative time for Kotobuki's homeless activism, when the housing classes became both targets of *and* actors in radical urban intervention.

This chapter now shows that the entrance of a few housed citizens into the homeless activism of Kotobuki during the 1980s drove their own action of commoning, along with their placemaking process. Placemaking and commoning are two sides of the same coin—their collaboration may be able to produce the "goods" in the inner city and overturn the "bads" in the regulated city. This commoning by citizens connected Kotobuki's commoning project with Yokohama's wider society in two creative ways: by gathering Yokohama's housed citizens at the Kotobuki district and by using their new power to support homeless people in "normal" public spaces under normative consumption. As we will see, the commoning action of the union also targeted these public spaces, but it failed to achieve its goals due to its narrow ideological base, which inherently antagonised the housing classes. Instead, it was the incorporation of housed citizens that actually helped to overcome this difficulty in the 1980s. The extension of commoning beyond the inner city needed the internalisation of the housing classes within Kotobuki's commoning project.

Commoning by the Union

An escalating series of murders and injuries took place during the one-month period between mid-January and mid-February 1983 (Table 7.2). The sites and

Table 7.2 Murders and injuries of homeless people in Yokohama during winter 1983.

Date	Place	Victims	Injury and (severity)
12 January	An underground passage	A male, age 56	Skull fracture, rib fracture (a month to heal)
15 January	An underground passage	A male, age 66	Face contusion (a week to heal)
15 January	An underground passage	A male, age 55	Face contusion (a week to heal)
16 January	Ōdōri Park	A male, age 38	Rib fracture (two months to heal)
4 February	A bank	A male, age 53	Brain contusion, intercranial bleeding (murdered)
5 February	Yokohama Baseball Stadium	Nine males	Head concussion, skull fracture (severity unknown)
5 February	Yamashita Park	A male, age 60	Rib fracture, organ damage (murdered)
10 February	Matsukage Park	A male, age 43	Brain contusion (murdered)

Source: Korosareru to omotta (1983).

targets of these violent actions were continually changing, which made it difficult for the police to catch the criminals, who remained unidentified until 10 February 1983, when a homeless man was killed at a public park. It was finally discovered that a band of junior high school students in the locality had committed these crimes, and they were eventually detained by the police. The details were disseminated across the city. In response, the union activists spearheaded immediate, furious action against Yokohama's civil society and the housing classes.

To be sure, the union's actions were not just furious but well-conceived. They went to public schools, orated at school gates, and circulated handbills. The diagnosis of the activists was that the students' crimes were a reflection of the warped minds of the adults, for the adults in Yokohama were also involved in antihomeless harassment in those days. Furthermore, the union members thought that the overly competitive environment of the "education mill" in metropolitan Yokohama aggravated antihomeless feeling among the students, as they could easily see homeless people as worthless dropouts from mainstream society. The union activists tried to "emancipate" students and teachers from this "ideological distortion" held by the housing classes, by getting them to realise that they could break the walls of othering only if they *wanted* to communicate with homeless people.

This was the core message that the union activists tried to send to the students and teachers by standing at the school gates in the morning. Figure 7.1 shows a handbill that was handed to students and teachers at Yokohama's junior high schools after the assaults and murders. By circulating these handbills, the union activists sought to address civil society in order to advance the commoning of public spaces for homeless people.

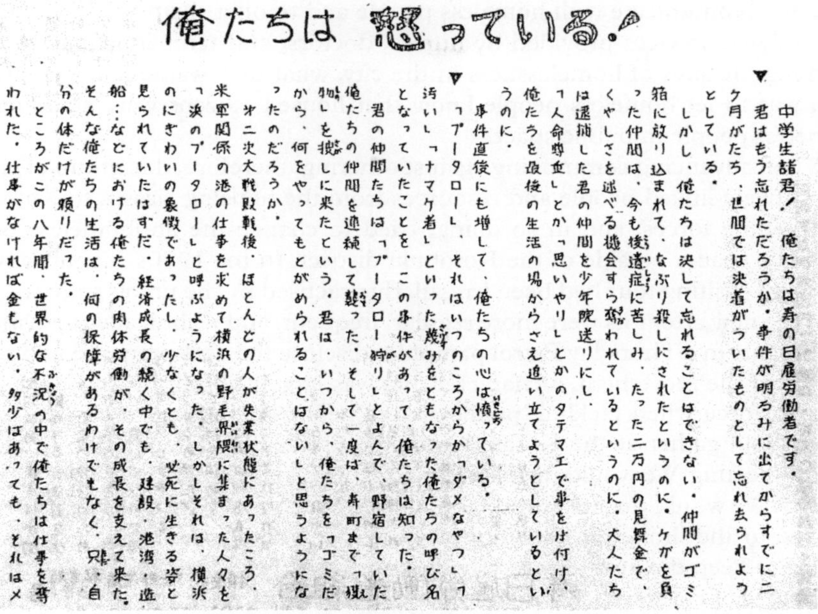

Figure 7.1 Handbill distributed at Yokohama's junior high schools in 1983. With its headline screaming "We are furious!", this handbill groans, "We never forget [the murders and injuries] because our comrades were thrown into garbage cans and bullied to death."
Source: Archives of the Kotobuki Day Laborers' Union.

However, this endeavour hardly bore fruit. Many teachers never understood this action of commoning, and the attempts at commoning by the union ended with the arrest of some activists at one school. Soon, however, citizen activists did manage to instil the commoning ethos, to change Yokohama's civil society and its public spaces. These citizens, following in the footsteps of the union in this realm, mobilised their own interpretational framing, which they were cultivating in the ongoing process of placemaking (see Chapter 6).

Commoning by Housed Citizens

In addressing civil society, the union activists scarcely made any positive inroads. But the task was advanced by citizens who organised a new group, the Thursday Patrol. Forming this group was itself an act to change Yokohama's civil society by connecting the housing classes to the Kotobuki district and promoting prohomeless understanding. The group's formation was a direct response to the murders and injuries of 1983. On this organisational basis, the self-proclaimed citizens started carrying out homeless-visiting tours every Thursday, during which they tried to communicate with homeless people and to offer them food, clothes, and professional services provided by nurses, doctors, and temperance advisers. By roaming the sites of homelessness in the city, what they wanted, above anything else, was to let homeless people know that housed citizens were standing with homeless people in public spaces.

When advancing commoning against othering, therefore, this group of citizens innovatively linked people and resources from the housing classes to Kotobuki's commoning forces, and in so doing, tried to change the antihomeless pattern of public spaces outside of the Kotobuki district. In the 1970s, a similar type of homeless-visiting tour had been irregularly practised by the union activists. However, the new attempts were more regular, frequent, and technically sophisticated. Comments in a Thursday Patrol pamphlet disclose the well-prepared and regular quality of the movement, a character that was largely absent in Kotobuki's commoning force when tackling public spaces before the emergence of this group: "We would gather at the Kotobuki community centre at 7 p.m. We would first have a meeting. We would divide into two groups and prepare soup, blankets, and clothes. We would depart around 9 p.m." (Mokuyo Patororu 1985, p. 6).

Due to the limited availability of participants and resources, the group was forced to keep the area covered by the tours relatively small. This self-limitation in the area of coverage itself demonstrates the conscious efforts of the participants to appear reliable in the eyes of homeless people. The same pamphlet includes further notes: "In light of the [limited] capacity at that time, we would restrict ourselves to visit only the area of the Yokohama baseball stadium (including the city hall) and the area of the Kan'nai underground shopping streets (including the municipal gymnasium). At the end of the patrolling, we would talk with those [homeless individuals] who gathered around the open-air fire in the centre of Kotobuki's yoseba" (Mokuyo Patororu 1985, p. 6).

In Chapter 6, we saw that the Thursday Patrol produced a new sociocultural milieu in the Kotobuki district, in which people arriving from the outside world cultivated a tentative and careful understanding of homelessness. On the basis of this placemaking, I now emphasise, this group effectively advanced real initiatives of commoning against othering, targeting Yokohama's public spaces surrounded by the housing classes. The evil murders and assaults triggered the extensive development of Kotobuki's commoning campaigns.

Summary

The 1980s was not a break for Kotobuki's commoners. Some homeless people existed outside of the inner city, and their lives in public spaces were treated violently by the housing classes. The murders and assaults in 1983 can be understood as another ground-up case of regulation by the housing classes, which now appeared in a renewed violent form. The union started commoning by targeting the education system of the housing classes, but they hardly had any effective medium other than creating and distributing critical handbills.

At this point, housed citizens who were producing their own place in Kotobuki started a more effective process of commoning. Their placemaking in Kotobuki itself represented the creation of a new medium through which housed citizens could access, imagine, and understand homelessness. On this basis, the citizen activists advanced homeless-visiting tours by targeting the city's broader public spaces, seeking to assure homeless people that members of the housing classes were concerned about them and were trying to ameliorate their difficulties.

Commoning in Yokohama in the 1990s–2000s

Commoning Public Spaces

During the widespread cycle of homelessness that began in the 1990s, an even wider range of public spaces in Yokohama grew intolerant of homelessness, which resulted in violent solutions. Webs of regulation restricted and evicted homeless people. As this public space regulation was subsequently associated with new patterns of policy that moved homeless people from public spaces to "off-street" spaces such as shelters, workfarist programmes, and conditional benefits, the visibility and number of homeless people dropped towards the late 2000s in this area as well as in other Japanese cities.

Amid rescaling and the rampant production of new regulatory spaces, the offstreet spaces of homeless policy could be more widely open to renegotiation, while public spaces could remain highly oppressive. Indeed, Yokohama's various parks and streets became the breeding ground for antihomeless regulation in the 1990s because they were the places where the housing classes and their guardians were met with habitat's "repugnant" outsiders. Japan's historical mode of hyperconformist societalisation was being resurrected and revitalised in these public spaces, where the societalised "us" were deeply frustrated by the desocietalising "them".

Nonetheless, Kotobuki's activists continued to believe that Yokohama's local geography of oppression could be alleviated in public spaces. Throughout the 1990s and 2000s, Kotobuki's activists devoted their energy to the mitigation of antihomeless pressure by ensuring homeless people's access to public spaces. If the worst-case scenario of rescaling was a quick closure of parks and streets and a generalisation of harsher methods against homelessness, that scenario was perhaps less conspicuous in the city of Yokohama. Kotobuki's commoning forces contributed a great deal to this less destructive trajectory in Yokohama.

In the 1990s and 2000s, Yokohama's public spaces developed a punitive character. The paradigmatic site was Yokohama Eki, the railway station where antihomeless evictions were rife. Yokohama station comprises not just one but multiple railway stations, as well as many other facilities, including internal streets and corridors, cafés and restaurants, shops and department stores, and various meeting venues. This complex of facilities was increasingly populated by homeless people in the 1990s. Some slept directly on the floor. Others created cardboard houses. In either case, they generated mounds of personal belongings in and around these public spaces.

These homeless people met with violent reactions from personnel and security staff. This was made evident to activists on 28 December 1992, when volunteers directly witnessed their eviction. Immediately, people in Kotobuki visited the manager of the JR Yokohama station and condemned the treatment of homeless people. Figure 7.2 is a handbill distributed after the event, which conveys the politicised atmosphere of the time.

As a result of this initial experience in winter 1992–1993, a new body of commoning was created, Yokohama Suiyō Patorōru (Yokohama Wednesday Patrol), which specifically targeted Yokohama's public spaces. This group attracted participants from Kotobuki's already-existing groups—including the union and the Kotobuki Supporters' Gathering Club, discussed in Chapter 6. In this light, the Yokohama Wednesday Patrol was an issue-specific coalition that directed existing homeless-concerned people in Kotobuki to the issue of public space commoning. Its mission included the distribution of clothes, information, and food; the

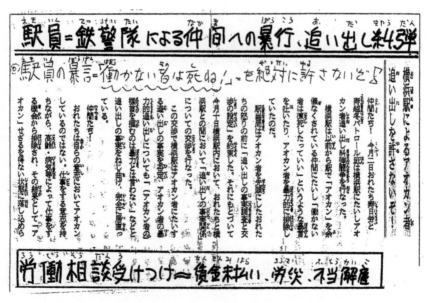

Figure 7.2 Handbill distributed to homeless people in Yokohama on 21 January 1993. It says, "The Yokohama station denied the eviction and justified it ... by saying, 'Don't think it violent because our officer only grabbed his neck.'" The handbill encourages homeless people: "We [homeless people] sleep in the streets not from our choice but due to the advanced age and illness that exclude us from working opportunities."

Source: Archives of the Kotobuki Day Laborers' Union.

observation of policing; the prevention of eviction; and the delivery of encouraging messages to homeless people. Compared to the past patrol groups, this new group was better prepared to combat evictions.

The concern was that intensive policing and eviction of homeless people were spreading everywhere. Indeed, even nonprime areas were fomenting an antihomeless atmosphere, as homeless people were spreading to suburban and nonprime areas in Yokohama. There, housed citizens hardened their hearts, and the municipality and police started evictions. Concerned by this new geography of antihomelessness, activists and volunteers made frequent visits to these nonprime areas to stop new evictions from happening.

For example, in 1994, activists knew that the municipality was trying to remove homeless people from Hēan Park, though it was remote from Yokohama's prime area. Municipal workers told homeless people, "This park will be under construction and dangerous, so you must go away." This "construction plan"—a pretext for the eviction—turned out to be a fabrication of municipal workers, and the activists successfully stopped the eviction. In 1998, another park, Sawatari Chūō Park, was on the verge of similar action. This eviction garnered the special attention of activists because they learned that the city was moving to apply a "no homeless rule" to *every* public park, and this particular park was intended to be a first step. The movement derailed this important case of eviction by arguing that the homeless individuals in this area would do no harm to the neighbourhood.

However, not all evictions were detected, much less prevented. Yokohama covers a large area divided into eighteen wards, and the activists could not keep their eye on all of them during this time. The paucity of information and manpower to monitor remote areas were real obstacles. Difficulties also came from the ideological and legal aspects of urban "beautification" and gentrification. For one thing, in many cases it was private firms, not local authorities, that owned publicly used spaces such as underground passages and alleys. In these cases, evictions were very difficult to prevent due to the difficulty of making a valid legal argument. In addition, even when spaces were publicly owned, evictions for the purpose of gentrification were difficult to stop, because the authorities explained these cases as a necessary part of "urban regeneration", which every citizen (that is, every *housed* citizen) would enjoy. Activists recognised that the gentrification of existing public spaces—which absorbed the glut of capital in the early phase of Japan's postbubble period—was advancing hand in hand with the inherently antihomeless aesthetic of housed citizens (Figure 7.3).

In spite of all these difficulties, Kotobuki's activists and volunteers continued to intervene in public spaces, and they did sometimes "guide" Yokohama's public space regulation in a direction that was less destructive for homeless people and their metabolic relations with public spaces. Crucially, Kotobuki's activists were strongly motivated to cover *all* public spaces. This motivation for extensive commoning can be inferred from Table 7.3, which summarises activists' repeated acts of information gathering in broad areas and at various sites in Yokohama.

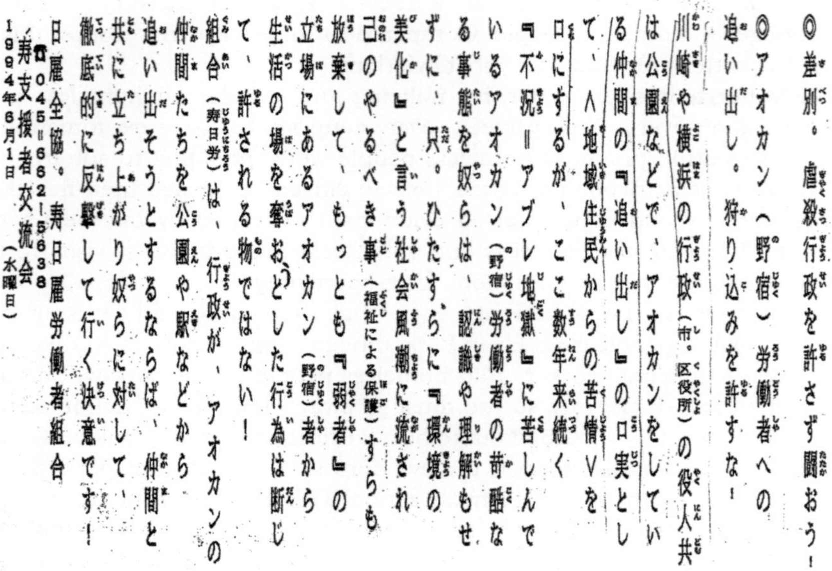
◎差別・虐殺行政を許さず闘おう！
◎アオカン（野宿）労働者への追い出し・狩り込みを許すな！
川崎や横浜の行政（市・区役所）の役人共は公園などで、アオカンをしている仲間の「追い出し」の口実として、＜地域住民からの苦情＞を口にするが、ここ数年来続く「不況＝アブレ地獄」に苦しんでいるアオカン（野宿）労働者の苛酷なる事態を奴らは、認識や理解もせずに、只、ひたすらに「環境の美化」と言う社会風潮に流され己のやるべき事（福祉による保護）すらも放棄して、もっとも「弱者」の立場にあるアオカン（野宿）者から生活の場を奪おうどした行為は断じて、許される物ではない！
組合（寿日労）は、行政が、アオカンの仲間たちを公園や駅などから追い出そうとするならば、仲間と共に立ち上がり奴らに対して、徹底的に反撃して行く決意です！
日雇全協・寿日雇労働者組合
☎045=662-5638
、寿支援者交流会
1994年6月1日（水曜日）

Figure 7.3 Handbill distributed to homeless people in Yokohama on 1 July 1994. It says, "Don't let eviction [*oidashi*] and hunting [*karikomi*] of homeless laborers go on! . . . They are only going along with the trend of environmental beautification [*kankyō bika*]."

Source: Archives of the Kotobuki Day Laborers' Union.

Table 7.3 Information-gathering tours for public space commoning.

Date	Visited area	Observed homeless individuals (*N*)	Participants (*N*)
4 April 1998	*NA*	4	6
29 July 1998	*NA*	43	7
30 September 1998	*NA*	32	9
30 June 1999	Sakuragi-chō	83	7
29 September 1999	Bandōbashi	14	6
1 March 2000	Bandōbashi	17	4
18 April 2000	Nakahara Hēwa Park	8	*NA*
18 April 2000	Tsurumi River	12	*NA*
22 May 2000	Kanazawa Seaside Line	4	*NA*
31 May 2000	Kanazawa Seaside Line	11	5
1 August 2000	Tsuruim Ward	29	5
6 August 2000	Rinkō Park	8	*NA*

Table 7.3 (Continued)

Date	Visited area	Observed homeless individuals (N)	Participants (N)
9 August 2000	Tsuruim Ward	2	NA
30 August 2000	Bandōbashi	20	7
30 May 2001	Bandōbashi	16	5
29 August 2001	Bandōbashi	15	7
14 October 2001	Tsurumi River	44	4
31 October 2001	Kanazawa Seaside Line	15	8
29 May 2002	Hodogaya Ward	11	8
30 October 2002	Bandōbashi	9	5
20 March 2003	Minami Ward	6	4
30 April 2003	Tsurumi Ward	20	6
29 October 2003	Yamashita-chō	3	5
30 June 2004	Yamashita-chō	16	3
29 June 2005	Yamashita-chō	14	4
31 August 2005	Yamashita-chō	8	8
31 May 2006	Yamashita-chō	9	4

Source: Archives of the Kotobuki Day Laborers' Union.

Dubbed *chōsa pato* (research patrol), this type of activity was solely aimed at the acquisition of new knowledge about areas not covered by the regular activity of the commoners. This method of information gathering helped Kotobuki's activists to cast surveillance on the entire city and witness Yokohama's wider geography of antihomelessness. Moreover, based on the newly obtained information, they subsequently created new routes for the homeless-visiting tours. By the early 2000s, five new regular routes were added to an original route that circulated in and around the Yokohama station buildings. As a result, many areas of homelessness came to be covered by the regular activity of the commoners.

Commoning Public Provision

In 1994, Kotobuki's activists and volunteers formed another network that focused on the commoning of public provision and benefits. The network was the Sēzonken o Kachitoru Kotobuki no Kai (Kotobuki Association for Winning the Right to Livelihood). The concern was that homeless people were unreasonably excluded from the framework of social rights determined by Japan's legal system of the right to livelihood (sēzon ken), which Japan's constitution declares to be the right of every Japanese citizen and which is elaborated by the Public Assistance Act of 1950 as a set of housing, food, and medical benefit programmes. With a clear understanding of this legal framework, Kotobuki's activists in this period were able to pronounce homeless people's right to urban commons by using the technical jargon of the livelihood right. Their commoning acts led to two significant outcomes: they persuaded the municipality to use the public assistance programme for old, injured, or sick homeless individuals; and they encouraged the municipality to improve the food and hotel voucher system for those excluded from public assistance.

Initially, the association organised study meetings to elaborate legal grounds for commoning. While having these internal meetings, activists also got the city to schedule formal meetings, which were held three times in summer 1994. The first session took place on 10 June 1994. This was the largest one and lasted four hours. It mobilised approximately 50 activists and volunteers and 100 homeless individuals, who were sitting opposite eight officials from the city. Through the meetings, the petitioners tried to "force the municipality to confirm that the welfare office can accept application to public assistance even by those [homeless people] who have no fixed residential address" (my interview with Noboru Kondo). After the last session, on 23 August 1994, they obtained the city's limited agreement. Though the law does not include any such limits, the city formulated a local rule that homeless people's right to public assistance would be considered when homeless people were old, sick, or injured. What the association achieved was the partial opening of public assistance to homeless people.[1]

Realising that the municipality would not use public assistance for everyone, the association also demanded that the city improve Yokohama's own homeless-relief system. This local system was the programme of food and hotel vouchers, an inheritance from the riotous 1970s. Around 1992, the municipality was already responding to swelling homelessness by employing this old policy, yet it was only a halfhearted attempt. The number of vouchers being issued was insufficient, and the value of the vouchers was low. The association claimed that the municipality should improve the programme in this regard. Under the pressure of the movement, the city began improving the voucher programme, particularly in quantity, by issuing more hotel tickets and, later, food tickets. Figure 7.4 shows the city's letter to the movement, which states that the city will consider the upgrading of the system. Figure 7.5 shows that there were upticks in the number of vouchers issued towards the late 1990s, suggesting that this local system became Yokohama's pillar of public provision for homeless people.

Finally, Kotobuki's activists in the 1990s addressed yet another terrain of public provision—shelters. In this area, too, commoning partially succeeded. In 1993, the city revealed a plan for a public shelter. The idea met the long-standing demand of Kotobuki's activists. The problem was that the city's plan was not enough. The city was announcing that strict behavioural codes would be imposed on the users of the shelter, but activists felt that these rules would make the

平成6年8月9日

医食住を保障せよ！
生存権をかちとる寿の会　様

福　祉　局　長
中　福　祉　事　務　所　長

要　求　書　へ　の　回　答

1，2，3について
　要保護性のある居所のない方に対しては，宿泊券のみですますことなく，居所の確保に
協力し，申請を受理します。
　なお，申請者の状況によってはすみやかに受理します。

4について
　寿診療所からの紹介状は条件ではなく，状態を客観的に判断する参考資料としておりま
す。その際，来所者の身体状況をお聞きし，受診が必要と判断された場合は医療機関を紹
介しております。

5，6について
　パン券・宿泊券の支給については，本市独自の緊急援護対策事業として実施しておりま
すが，昨今，パン券・宿泊券の支給も急増しており，経費上非常に厳しいところです。
　こうした状況の中で，宿泊券については値上げについて検討してまいります。
　また，パン券については，今後，現物給付について検討してまいります。

7について
　緊急一時宿泊所については，本年中の設置に向けて，努力してまいります。

Figure 7.4　Letter from the City of Yokohama to the movement on 9 August 1994. It says that the City of Yokohama will start considering the improvement of its voucher system.
Source: Archives of the Kotobuki Day Laborers' Union.

autonomous life of homeless people impossible and tried to change the internal rules of the shelter (Figure 7.6). In response, when the shelter opened in 1994, the city agreed to impose less restrictive conditions than had been suggested by the original plan.

The success was temporary, however. This shelter, though improved, was soon replaced by a more strictly run shelter, the Nakamura River Shelter. The new shelter accommodated only homeless people evicted from a particular area of the city—a riverside area of the Nakamura River—which became an intensive site of antihomeless evictions in the interests of a locational gentrification programme (City of Yokohama undated; on this location, see also Yamamoto 2008).

210   RESCALING URBAN POVERTY

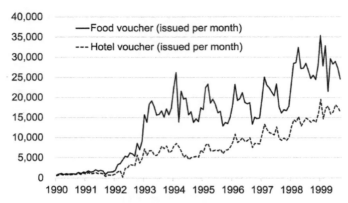

Figure 7.5   Yokohama's food and hotel vouchers issued in the 1990s.
Source: Archives of the Kotobuki Day Laborers' Union.

Figure 7.6   Handbill distributed to homeless people in Yokohama on 21 September 1994. It says that the plan for Yokohama's homeless shelter is a response to activists'"ten-year-long request", but that the city's plan is "highly insufficient to meet the demands of needy people".
Source: Archives of the Kotobuki Day Laborers' Union.

Discommoning

I have shown that rescaling reregulation in Yokohama took a relatively "benign" direction in response to commoning. In the 2000s, however, the city diverged from this previous trajectory in favour of a more neoliberal approach, which was less penetrable by the commoners. Yokohama's new initiatives espoused a systematic plan for workfarist regulation, stating that homeless people should escape poverty by entering the labour market rather than by relying on public provision. In addition, the new policy showed a greater concern for "safe" public spaces.

In many ways, this shift in Yokohama's homeless policy was a response to the Japanese state's rescaling framework that materialised in the early 2000s—what this book has referred to as the 2002/2003 system. As Chapter 3 discussed, the 2002/2003 system steered homeless-prone Japanese cities towards the new picking-off round of rescaling, which replaced the old ground-up round that partially allowed the creativity of the commoners working on the local scale. Previously, municipal governments were able to behave, without effective national "guidance" and "intervention", as almost a sole policymaker for local homelessness. Kotobuki's commoners utilised this informal space of municipal-level autonomy as a space for municipal-level commoning against othering.

Yokohama's commoning strategy, its exploitation of the municipal "anarchism" inherent in the ground-up round of rescaling, now met setbacks under the 2002/2003 system. This national framework included new ideas for the commoners and regulators alike. While Yokohama had formed some useful urban commons through the conflict-riven relationships between the commoners and regulators, this locally radicalised form of "government + governance" (Jessop 2002, p. 239) and its homeless-supporting outcomes were derailed under the 2002/2003 system. This did not mean that local regulators lost autonomy or that they became mere practitioners of the national system. Yet local discretion and autonomy became strictly codified by the new protocols introduced by the Japanese state. As a result, the historical space of commoning was curtailed by the picking-off ethos of the 2002/2003 system.

The system's key characteristics are especially important to understanding Yokohama's *dis*commoning process, which started during this period. First, the 2002/2003 system decreed that the municipality would produce a local system of means-testing and workfarist programmes/institutions, to treat homeless people selectively based on "willingness" and "capacity" to perform as viable and patient wage workers adaptable to fragmented neoliberal labour markets—that is, to wholeheartedly accept the less and less benign societalising requirements and consequences of these labour markets in post-1990s Japan (see Chapter 3). The system established regulatory codes according to which municipalities should create their own workfarist systems, while the details were mostly left to local planning. Through this, the traditional programme of welfarism (public assistance) and the livelihood right became less accessible to homeless people than before. It was also suggested that the municipality could create new institutions to temporarily absorb these "morally inferior" individuals—those deemed not very adaptable to neoliberal labour markets due to their putative lack of work ethic.

Second, the 2002/2003 system legally permitted the municipality to surveil and police homeless people on the grounds of "public safety", to be enjoyed by the housing classes. It thus legalised the hegemonic (societalising) view that homeless people mostly become "dangerous" for urban society when they produce/consume "housing" in public, and the system showed local regulators "legitimate" methods of eviction to remove the threat.

Third, the 2002/2003 system legally justified the incongruence of Japan's homeless regulation with Japan's citizenship framework. It allowed—facilitated, even—the new regulatory spaces of the municipality to dissociate homeless people from the national right to livelihood, which is determined by the constitution to be a benefit of citizenship and accessible for everyone. In so doing, the 2002/2003 system rehabilitated the unity of Japanese state space against its fragmentation by legalising the marginalisation of homeless people from the national right to livelihood; this marginalisation previously had been advanced only in informal and potentially illegal ways.

Under this 2002/2003 system, Japanese cities were asked to review their local policies in light of the new regulatory codes. The 2002/2003 system demanded that municipalities officially declare their homeless policy in a written form—so-called implementation plans (see Chapter 3). Thus, it is relatively easy for us to examine how each metropolitan municipality responded to the 2002/2003 system in official terms. In some cases where homeless policy was historically harsher, the adjustments and interventions made by the 2002/2003 system meant a smooth continuity with the past. Municipal units (wards) of Tokyo, for example, had already developed homeless regulation in a more strongly antihomeless direction than Yokohama (see Kasai 1999). It can be said, therefore, that Tokyo's response to the 2002/2003 system preserved rather than destroyed the previous course. For other cities, which had advanced more "benevolent" types of homeless policy until the 1990s, adaptation to the system led to partial denials of previous pathways. Yokohama was in this category.

Indeed, the 2002/2003 system made it *rational* for the City of Yokohama to break its promises to activists. In response to the system, the city created a new workfarist programme and its facility in 2003. The facility was Yokohama's Self-Help Centre, in the Kotobuki district. This facility served two functions promulgated by the 2002/2003 system: the means-testing and the disciplining of Yokohama's homeless population for their reentry into the labour market (City of Yokohama 2004). As soon as the city situated the Self-Help Centre at the heart of local policy, it began destroying the homeless-friendly framework of the vouchers; the number of hotel and food vouchers issued after the mid-2000s was radically decreased (Figure 7.7). As a result, urban commons accessible from the streets became weaker around the Kotobuki district. This manoeuvre finally abolished the voucher system in 2012, with the move justified as an effort to establish labour-market and workfarist policy, on the local scale, for homeless and near-homeless populations. The municipality claimed, "The provision of the

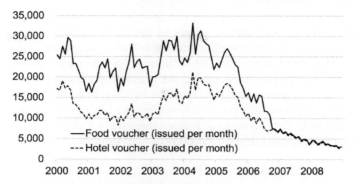

Figure 7.7 Yokohama's food and hotel vouchers issued in the 2000s.
Source: Archives of the Kotobuki Day Laborers' Union.

hotel and food vouchers ... [was] not necessarily linked to the policy of self-help by employment [*syūrō jiritsu*]", and it had to be "replaced by policy that facilitates homeless and other people's self-help life" (City of Yokohama 2006, p. 5).

As the voucher system was disappearing, public spaces became a tougher site for commoning. As outlined in the official guidelines of the Self-Help Act, the 2002/2003 system allowed the municipality to evict homeless people from public spaces when the person threatened the public safety of surrounding neighbourhoods or the "proper use" of a public facility *and* this person was addressed by municipal welfare providers for promoting a self-help life (chapter 3, section 2 of the 2003 guidelines). The problem is that it was unknowable whether these complex conditions were actually met in each case of eviction. Particularly with the matter of eviction from public spaces, therefore, the 2002/2003 system tacitly gave high autonomy to ground-level workers; there was no demand for accountability. In this new context of legal rescaling of urban commons, each eviction could be buried under the secrecy of "local decision-making", as such secrecy was now legalised by the 2002/2003 system. Kotobuki's commoners tried to problematise the worst cases of eviction, but under the 2002/2003 system, the outlook of commoning became ever more defensive in public spaces.

Summary

The city of Yokohama experienced the widespread cycle of homelessness after the early 1990s. In response to the commoning actors, the city's closure of public spaces to homeless people was moderated and its voucher system improved. Furthermore, the national programme of public assistance was made available to the elderly, which was another success of homeless activism in this area. By these means, the constitutional right to livelihood was elaborated and enriched as homeless people's right to urban commons.

Notwithstanding this success in commoning, however, the City of Yokohama made some *dis*commoning moves in the 2000s. The background was the 2002/2003 system, a new rescaling framework that introduced new codes and protocols for homeless regulation. This national system, which initiated the picking-off round of rescaling that replaced the previous ground-up round, redefined municipal homeless policy as a selective and harsh(er) continuum of workfarism plus policing, which virtually revoked homeless people's previous access to urban commons and to livelihood accessible from the streets. Public spaces and benefits thus became less manageable by Kotobuki's commoners.

Conclusion

Employing existing theories of commoning, this chapter has established the interpretive framework of prohomeless commoning that denotes its uniqueness as "commoning against othering". By using this framework, I redeploy the book's regulationist perspective around the rules-changing and form-changing process of activism, in which actors wishing to work for homeless people try to change the prevailing rules, norms, and urban form with regard to the commons—how and by whom public spaces and provisions should be consumed—on behalf of homeless people.

There is a hidden process in urban commons whereby public spaces and services sustain themselves through policing their outer edges vis-à-vis homeless people. Urban social movements for homeless people had to break these effects of othering, which became extremely formidable under the repetitive rounds of rescaling that liberated local regulators from the national fixity of citizenship and rights. The minority interests of the commoners were displaced from the territorially constructed locus of citizenship on the national scale and relocated to its fringe spaces, constructed on the local scale, where initiatives and policies remain highly unstable and inconclusive. In order to continue to be effective in these new regulatory spaces, activists needed to repeatedly update and improve their strategies of commoning in light of changing circumstances—in line with the changing appearance of "fast policy" (Peck and Theodore 2015) that continually metamorphoses in rescaled urban governance.

After the mid-1970s, Kotobuki's activists and volunteers emphatically tried to make Yokohama's public spaces and provisions more pleasant and more accessible for homeless people. Furious actions frightened local authorities and initially led the city to improve urban commons. Soon, however, radicalism hardened the response of the municipality and incited actual oppression. Even so, the local power of commoning never subsided.

In the 1980s, "citizens" arriving from the world of habitat restarted commoning by targeting public spaces and the housing classes. These citizens connected Yokohama's housing classes and their civil society with homeless people and the inner city, and powerfully endorsed homeless people's metabolic life in parks and on the streets.

In the 1990s, commoning evolved in the context of widespread homelessness in Japan. Activists and volunteers improved homeless people's use of public spaces and their access to public provisions, and preserved Yokohama's relatively "benign" approach. The reception of the 2002/2003 system led to some denials of this local benevolence. The new initiative of rescaling deteriorated urban commons by imposing selective, workfarist, policing codes of regulation upon the putatively unworthy and dangerous sections of the homeless population—those who were trying to "live" in public spaces. In this new phase, Kotobuki's commoners—and their attempts to employ the prohomeless potential of new regulatory spaces under rescaling—met with serious limits.

Commoning for homeless people plays the fundamental role of advancing radical urban democracy beyond societalisation, even though this construction of activism finds limits within societalisation per se. The movement seeks to destabilise and change the rules, norms, and forms of urban use values, disclosing that these rules/norms/forms circumscribe the commons to the housing classes in line with societalisation. Commoning is achieved when homeless people—their subaltern metabolism—gain new access to these use values.

This view can usefully revise the two extant theories of commoning from Peter Linebaugh (2008, 2014) and David Harvey (2012) by revealing the importance of focusing on the *margins* of urban class relations, where the politics of exclusion/inclusion are most rampant. This argument can also furnish Michael Hardt and Antonio Negri's (2009) thesis on the commons with a viable perspective on regulation, state space, and rescaling. Overall, the discussions in this chapter have reconsidered the commoning movement as *counterregulation* commoning—"commoning against othering"—under rescaling.

Note

1 In addition, the way that the city accommodated homeless people by using the public assistance programme remained restrictive, as it allowed homeless people applying to the programme to live only in day laborers' small hotel rooms within the Kotobuki district. Chapter 9 will discuss this discrimination against homeless people's right to housing in a more contemporary context.

Chapter Eight
Translating to New Cities: Geographical and Cultural Expansion

This chapter broadens the scope of the social movement research in part 3 from the enclaves of poverty to their outposts and outskirts. This new geographical coverage is important to deciphering the capabilities of prohomeless and homeless-supporting actors during an expansive phase of homelessness. Until now, the main focus of part 3 has been on the spatial niches of poverty—yoseba zones—that morphed into strongholds of the placemakers/commoners. At these locations, activism gained various material and sociocultural resources, which repeatedly reinvigorated prohomeless and homeless-supporting actors amid the rapidly changing context of surveillance and regulation under rescaling.

However, difficulties remain in this construction of activism. If the movement continues this spatially concentrated form of placemaking/commoning, the broader geographical areas of antihomelessness can remain in place and intact. A critical voice might safely argue that this concentrating formation of placemaking/commoning can still be part of the regulating geography of rescaling, which Lefebvre (2009c [1979], p. 128) criticised as "a simulacrum of decentralization" and in which Poulantzas (1978 [1978], p. 83) would detect "a peculiar mechanism of concealment-inversion". To make use of the emancipatory potential of urban governance under rescaling, "prohomeless voices" must perpetually improvise their spatial strategies with reference to a geography of rescaling that continually mutates. Otherwise, activism might end up accepting reregulation and resocietalisation that intensify under rescaling.

Rescaling Urban Poverty: Homelessness, State Restructuring and City Politics in Japan, First Edition. Mahito Hayashi.
© 2024 Royal Geographical Society (with the Institute of British Geographers). Published 2024 by John Wiley & Sons Ltd.

In Japan, the need for this evolution in social movements became pressing during the widespread cycle of homelessness. Activism faced new requirements to broaden its geographical coverage to the outlying cities that were being newly affected by homelessness. In response, activists and volunteers started the expansion of homeless activism by targeting the outlying area of Kanagawa Prefecture's metropolitan centre. I argue that the Gramscian process of cultural transmission, something that neo-Gramscian thinkers understand under the banner of "translation", becomes a key process for this geographical expansion of urban radicalism. By tailoring the Gramscian notion of translation to regulationist interests, this chapter deciphers how the locational strategies and language of placemaking and commoning, which had been practised in and around the Kotobuki district, came to impact the outlying cities of the prefecture's centre.

In both theory and practice, the dissemination of activism to outlying areas was a daunting task, with the new local contexts being challenging and unforeseen by homeless activism. This outlying area had no demarcated enclaves where placemaking could withstand societalisation and where the commoners could outgrow regulators. This situation was not aided by the fact that the hegemonic (housing) classes were susceptible to indulging in the politics of moral panic. Even so, the movement found creative new ways of placemaking and commoning through translation. Cultural migration and rearticulation helped activists and volunteers to revive and enhance the potential of urban politics under rescaling in the 1990s and 2000s.

Outlying Cities

During the widespread cycle of homelessness starting in the 1990s, sites of homelessness became more diversely spread beyond the Kotobuki district (Yokohama's inner-city area), where the manifestation of homelessness had historically been concentrated. Chapters 6 and 7 looked at the city of Yokohama in order to examine the widespread cycle of homelessness and how it elicited regulatory and counterregulatory responses from the municipality, police, housing classes, and activists/volunteers. In the widespread cycle of homelessness, however, numerous cities that hitherto had lacked the acute condition of homelessness also started to experience it (Nishizawa 2000). These new cities in Kanagawa Prefecture are the central concern of this chapter. As these cities are largely located behind the prefecture's metropolitan domains around Tokyo Bay, I term them "outlying" cities.

It is worth emphasising that the context and experience of these outlying cities were different from those of the city of Yokohama. This difference posed unique dilemmas for homelessness and activism. For instance, urban societalisation and its public/private matrix had never been tested by the presence of homelessness.

The outlying area was unaffected by Japan's inner-city cycle of homelessness until the 1980s and then suddenly became exposed to homelessness in and after the 1990s. This made these cities even more susceptible to societal crisis arising from homelessness. In addition, though the situation was eliciting antihomeless reactions from housed citizens and their guardians, the outlying area lacked spaces of homeless activism. Unlike Yokohama, these cities had no enclaves of acute poverty that could defend homeless-friendly imaginaries and nurture prohomeless politics vis-à-vis the hegemonic worldview of the housing classes. Finally, local welfare offices had little past experience with responding to homelessness, either negatively or positively; they were even unaware that homelessness could be a relevant policy issue. All in all, while the case of the outlying cities is not exactly that of rural homelessness (Cloke, Milbourne, and Widdowfield 2002), given that this area is densely populated and commercially integrated into the metropolitan geography, the situation was significantly different from that in the prefecture's metropolitan centre.

For homeless people and activists alike, the entire context of the outlying cities was intimidating. In this light, it is surprising that, towards the 2000s, these outlying cities began hosting new activist groups and their outreach initiatives. While such groups in Kanagawa Prefecture existed only in Yokohama in the early 1990s, these groups came to exist in ten cities by the early 2000s (Table 8.1). Outside of Yokohama, they emerged first in the cities of Kawasaki and Sagamihara (both in 1993). Subsequently, new groups formed in the cities of Fujisawa (1995), Odawara (1996), and Yokosuka (1997). The tide finally reached the cities of Kamakura (2000), Chigasaki (2000), Atsugi (2001), and Hiratsuka (2001). Barring the city of Kawasaki, which should be counted as an integral part of the metropolitan geography around Tokyo Bay, these new cities, like other outlying areas, were characteristically difficult for social movements for and with homeless people.

This diffusion of prohomeless and homeless-supporting groups in Kanagawa Prefecture represents another significant aspect of urban social movements. It is truly remarkable that social movements for those harshly excluded came to cover virtually all homeless-prone cities in the outlying areas, despite the adverse conditions. How was the movement able to advance placemaking and commoning in multiple cities?

In broad terms, two types of resource mobilisation took place. First, the movements stretched old resources. Faced with a scarcity of resources in the outlying cities, activists and volunteers working in the new cities tried to redeploy resources existing in the Kotobuki district. After acquiring food, clothes, blankets, and various types of information from the Kotobuki district, activists and volunteers flew to the outlying cities and communicated with homeless people and regulators. Second, the movement cultivated new resources. Activists particularly succeeded in the stable development of new local resources when they

Table 8.1 Groups for homeless people in Kanagawa Prefecture.

Region	City	Founding year	Name of group
1	Yokohama	1984	Thursday Patrol
		1993	Yokohama Wednesday Patrol
		1997	Totsuka Patrol
2	Kawasaki	1993	Kawasaki Wednesday Patrol
3	Sagamihara	1993	Sagamihara Thursday Patrol
4	Fujisawa	1995	Fujisawa Tuesday Patrol
5	Odawara	1996	Odawara Communicating Patrol
6	Yokosuka	1997	Yokosuka Night Walk
7	Kamakura	2000	Kamakura Patrol
8	Chigasaki	2000	Chigasaki Homeless Supporters
9	Atsugi	2001	Atsugi Patrol
10	Hiratsuka	2001	Hiratsuka Patrol

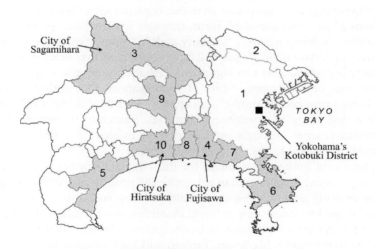

Note: Shaded regions denote the "outlying cities" discussed in this chapter.

cooperated with local Christian churches—key supporters of homeless movements in Japan. This method of resource cultivation became especially useful in cities that were relatively far from the Kotobuki district, such as Atsugi, Chigasaki, Fujisawa, Hiratsuka, and Odawara, which gained support and supporters from local churches.

Brokerage and Translation

In addition to description, my hope here is to theorise and conceptually understand these stretching-out and cultivating efforts of social movement actors within the ambit of the theory of rescaling, urban societalisation, and the public/private matrix. To advance my discussion in this vein, I will invoke two new concepts: brokerage and translation. The joint use of the two concepts can locate this chapter's focus in the overarching theoretical interests of this book.

The concept of brokerage, which has been used and elaborated in social movement theory, helps us to address the spatial diffusion of social movements. Doug McAdam, Sidney Tarrow, and Charles Tilly (2001, p. 68) argue that the concept helps us to understand how a contentious politics can expand its spatial coverage by increasing "*the same or similar shape of forms and claims of contention across space or across sectors and ideological divides*" (original emphasis). To unpack this dynamic, the key concept of brokerage is defined as the "linking of two or more previously unconnected social sites by a unit that mediates their relations with one another and/or with yet other sites" (p. 26). When this brokerage process is happening, it is supposed that the contentious politics is turning from a "contained" to "transgressive" form, through which it can propagate "newly self-identified political actors", "identity shift", "innovative claim making", and "innovative collective action" (pp. 8, 27). It is assumed that these new actors and their identities/innovations can vigorously reshape the pregiven spatial, sectoral, organisational, or ideological limits of mobilisation. The authors characterise this brokerage process as "public" engagement and "public politics", which can entangle a vast range of grievances, identities, frames of reference, and actors/audiences/adversaries through public-oriented modes of communication and claim making (pp. 5, 11, 31).

This notion of brokerage is useful for this chapter. Key activists in the Kotobuki district played a major role in achieving the process of social movement diffusion by creating new linkages among old and new social sites. In so doing, the "brokers" helped to create new political identities, resources, and infrastructures. However, for this book's purpose, this conception of brokerage is only part of the story. Most importantly, McAdam, Tarrow, and Tilly abstract the brokerage process from the urban contexts of metabolism, class relations, societalisation, and overall urban form that make each brokerage programme uniquely challenging. These theorists reserve the notion of "uncertainty", and by extension the "sense of uncertainty", for describing the difficult structural contexts of brokerage and its subjective experience (pp. 45–46, 66, 97, 112, and elsewhere). Yet it seems that their work tends to reduce various theoretical constraints to "uncertainty". As a result, even though they suggest that social movements can redraw their geographical contours "across space or across sectors and ideological divides"

(p. 68), without further theorisation, the key question of how these contentious geographies happen and how these become *limited* can remain an utterly empirical and untheorised matter.

This question can have special meaning for this book's social movements. As I have argued, these are movements for those who seem to be "outsiders"—or even the "repugnant" Other—from the perspective of the housing classes and their sociometabolism. Theoretically speaking, this situation can easily turn urban brokerage for homeless people into a very uncertain series of fragmentary events and discrete episodes without linkages and conduits. Being located in this difficult othering condition, the brokerage actors discussed here can seldom produce or employ coherent models, ample resources, thick organisational fields, trusty master frames, powerful mobilisation structures, reliable political opportunity structures, or a hegemonic social movement sector, all of which are positively discussed by key authors on social movements (Davis et al. 2005; McAdam, McCarthy, and Zald 1996; McAdam, Tarrow, and Tilly 2001; Snow and Benford 1992; Tarrow 1998; for organisational fields, see also Powell and DiMaggio 1991).

Just as crucially, "publics"—which the study of brokerage appraises as a facilitative domain (McAdam, Tarrow, and Tilly 2001)—are not a friendly realm for homeless activism; rather, publics (and public spaces) can be antihomeless because spaces of homelessness stick out from the public/private matrix of urban societalisation. Homeless people, by "surviving" in public spaces in front of publics, almost inescapably increase an antipublic outlook. This can line up various public groups, working within the arenas of governance, against homeless people living in the streets, parks, and so on.

Located in these challenging circumstances, the process of social movement diffusion has been driven by repetitive acts of sociocultural modification—of discursive sophistication and political "disguise"—that reworked the prohomeless frames of reference historically nurtured and accumulated in Yokohama's Kotobuki district. Thus, the linguistic (cultural) reworking of the broker, not just their given sense of uncertainty, must be examined in order to understand how the broker's cultural ingenuity have or have *not* overcome the predominant uncertainty and the metalanguage of metabolism, urban form, urban class relations, and regulation.[1]

The historical niche of poverty in Yokohama has served as a material and semiotic ladder for mobilisation even in the outlying cities. At the same time, the new intensity of placemaking and commoning in the outlying areas was possible when activists became brokering actors and applied linguistic creativity to specific sites. This in turn helped them to open a new action field—a political opportunity—in each of the new cities where no such field had hitherto existed.

I use the critical notion of translation to articulate this linguistic aspect of activism's ideational basis, which empowered homeless activism's migration to the outlying cities. Such thing as "prohomeless brokerage" became possible because it was facilitated by translation. The concept of translation I invoke is a Gramscian one. Contemporary Gramscian thinkers emphasise Antonio Gramsci's interest in language as something that made his own materialism free from dogmatic assumptions of base–superstructure identification (Ekers et al. 2013; Morton 2007; Thomas 2009). His notion of translation is germane to the material–semiotic process of hegemony, counterhegemony, and the philosophy of praxis (Featherstone 2013; Hart 2013; Ives 2004; Ives and Lacorte 2010). Ives (2004, p. 23) thinks that the importance of language derives from the processual aspect of linguistic reformation, and in this chapter I try to grasp the very process through which the vocabularies of prohomeless and homeless-supporting actors—and by implication antihomeless regulators and audiences—get translated.

To be precise, the central cases of translation in Gramsci can be major ones, at the international (or pan-European) scale, which are about translation between "two civilizations [that] must be at a more or less similar level of development" (Boothman 2010, p. 116). At the same time, it seems that translation can also happen in a single civilisation, in a national territory, or even in a rescaled region, when world-sensitising and world-brokering actors try to articulate subtle (but important) differences emerging between different action fields, or between fields and nonfields. It may be that Gramsci, when he examined Italy's north–south divide and city–country gaps, implied that the translating ability of the brokering actor can advance the aerial expansion of social movements working on a "great regional problem": "The close links between urban forces of North and South gave to the latter the strength which came from representing the prestige of the former, and were destined to help the Southern urban forces to gain their autonomy, to acquire consciousness of their historical leadership function in a 'concrete' and not merely theoretical and abstract manner, suggesting the solutions to give to the great regional problem" (Gramsci 1971, p. 99). I argue that a comparable geography of translation transpired in my research field when homeless activism tried to expand itself from Yokohama's inner city to new cities in Kanagawa Prefecture, beyond its west–east divide.

When David Featherstone (2012) revisits Gramsci on the north–south divide, to explore international forms of people's solidarity, he also looks at the concept of brokerage. In fact, Featherstone criticises the concept as having major roots in rational choice theory and argues that it ends up "creat[ing] a limited account of solidarity" (p. 22). Keeping this critique in mind, I nonetheless seek to cross-fertilise the two notions—brokerage and translation—so that the former can be sensitive to the nuanced cultural geographies of prohomeless and homeless-supporting solidarity. Brokerage—which Featherstone rightly thinks is a "goal-based" argument (p. 22)—can be useful in my case because this chapter's aim is to understand a specific geography of prohomeless solidarity and to assess its limits, modification, and migration towards the goal of a more homeless-friendly form of urbanisation. In essence, the chapter attends to a targeted analysis of solidarity, which may call for a research strategy partly different from a general synthesis of solidarity.

On the one hand, preexisting epistemological frameworks were actively reused; this redeployment of inner-city sociocultures was a vital part of the geographical expansion of urban social movements. Similar processes transpired for promoting contesting and supportive geographies in the outlying cities. This type of recurrence can be inferred simply from the names of the new groups enumerated in Table 8.1—all but two have the word *patrol* somewhere in the name. As outlined in Chapter 6, *patrol* was first used in this region during Kotobuki's union activism of the 1970s to justify street-based initiatives against police oppression. Part of a handbill from 1977 indicates an early use of the term (Figure 8.1). In Kotobuki, this term was repeatedly used during the 1980s and 1990s to affirm the importance of homeless-supporting work conducted on the streets and then was reused when the movement spread to the outlying cities. Through this process of recurrence, activists inherited Kotobuki-born epistemological frameworks and transmitted them to the new cities.

On the other hand, however, the recurrence entailed modification and translation, which helped the migration of placemaking and commoning to the outlying cities. First, because civil society was organised around a strong matrix of

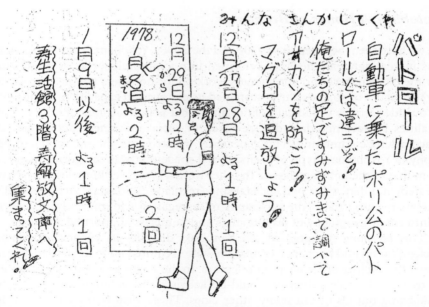

Figure 8.1 Handbill distributed by activists in Yokohama on 27 December 1977. It says, "PATORŌRU [patrol]. We are different from the cops' patrol using cars! Let's search [for homeless people] across the city on foot and prevent rough sleeping! Eliminate street crimes! Please join us!"
Source: Archives of the Kotobuki Day Laborers' Union.

habitat, it was difficult to achieve placemaking. In this hostile sociometabolic context, local churches were the most likely site for placemaking. Yet even when churches could be used, the inherited worldviews and vocabularies brought from the Kotobuki district were sometimes inadequate as they were alarming to local people. Thus, the overt radicalism of Kotobuki-born sociocultures had to be modified before being accepted.

In addition, the inherited strategies for commoning against othering were only partly effective in the outlying cities. Lacking historical lessons and budgetary frameworks, municipalities in the outlying areas were ill-prepared for homelessness, and they also had no ability to steer the local crisis of homelessness in residential neighbourhoods. For their part, the residents and regulators were unnerved by homelessness and initiated early trials of antihomeless eviction. In short, all of the inherited strategies of placemaking and commoning had to be translated to the outlying cities, so that the brokerage of social movements could materialise in the expansive geography of Kanagawa Prefecture.

Placemaking in the Outlying Cities

Kotobuki: A House of Brokerage

As we have seen, between the 1970s and the 2000s, Yokohama's Kotobuki district was increasingly enriched and reformed into a cultural, social, semiotic ladder for the placemakers and commoners working for homeless people. Across these three decades or so, the district sustained its extroverted capacity to connect itself to outside terrains of radical politics and, what is more, it nurtured new porous qualities to accommodate diverse kinds of social movement actors and their placemaking/commoning. This repeatedly injected into the metropolitan geography of Yokohama a type of sociocultural space that was categorically different from that of the housing classes. In other words, places for homeless people were created, and they withstood societalising (regulating) pressure. Activists and volunteers reappropriated the geography of segregation and innovatively converted it into a new geography of prohomeless and homeless-supporting language.

This *becoming* potential of the Kotobuki district—its capacity to outgrow societalisation and to change regulation—also acquired a broader scope, covering the outlying cities of Kanagawa Prefecture. In the 1990s and 2000s, the Kotobuki district received an influx of would-be activists and volunteers not only from Yokohama but also from many other cities. These visitors played a key role in bringing prohomeless and homeless-supporting imaginaries/politics from the Kotobuki district to the outlying cities and in re-rooting them in this new soil. In doing so, the trained activists in the Kotobuki district also gained new understandings about homelessness and homeless regulation in the outlying areas, which motivated them to spread activism to these new cities.

Thus, the Kotobuki district in the 1990s and 2000s developed into a regional mediator of homeless activism in Kanagawa Prefecture, which actually facilitated the proliferation of new groups in the outlying cities (see Table 8.1). In the process, the Kotobuki district endowed the new actors and groups with multiple types of resources—we might call them the "resources of a periphery"—that were useful for brokering and deploying prohomeless and homeless-supporting work in the new geography of the outlying cities. These resources, being accumulated in the inner city and transposed to the outlying cities, included robust interpretational and epistemological frameworks through which the actors became able to read urban landscapes and contours in homeless-supporting and even explicitly prohomeless ways. The Kotobuki district also amassed useful items such as clothes, blankets, food, first aid kits, and so on. Brokerage relied heavily on the resource-rich character of this inner-city area.

Nonetheless, the brokering mobilisation from the Kotobuki district had clear limits. The physical distance was daunting. The paucity of information also was formidable as the location of homelessness in the extended (outlying) areas of Kanagawa Prefecture was often unknown. In addition, the political opportunities for prohomeless and homeless-supporting actions—even when they emerged—were largely separated by municipal boundaries, as these formed the local units of society. For these reasons, simple recourse to the "formula" of the Kotobuki district was not sufficient when expanding the aerial coverage of activism over the prefecture. As we will see, this context prompted the new dynamics of placemaking in the outlying cities. What I will show is the process of *multicity* placemaking that entailed conscious multisite efforts to translate the Kotobuki-born cultures to new circumstances and contexts.

Placemaking in the City of Sagamihara

The first example is found in the city of Sagamihara. The process of brokerage in this city was triggered by Kotobuki's activists, yet the process found new capable actors right from the start, and a new group and sociocultural stronghold (place) in this particular outlying city was thus formed. As such, this case represents one of the "smoothest" cases of extended placemaking in the outlying area.

Part of the background of this process was that the two central figures in this story, who would soon create a new group, frequently visited the Kotobuki district from their hometown of Sagamihara. In fact, the Kotobuki district attracted people from all over the prefecture. When visiting Kotobuki, these two women realised that there were homeless people in their hometown of Sagamihara and that this homegrown homelessness needed attention. A hint was given by a trained activist in the Kotobuki Day Labourers' Union, who would mention something along these lines every time he met them in the Kotobuki district: "Hi, Fujitani-san! Yokohama's homeless people are now catching your attention, and that's very good. But Sagamihara's homeless people should attract you. You know our philosophy, which is the principle of localism [*genba shugi*]" (my interview with Misao Fujitani).

One of the two visitors from Sagamihara—Fujitani—believes that having such regular conversations with Kotobuki's activists influenced her decision. She and her coworker soon realised how big the problem of homegrown homelessness was in their city. "My eyes started discovering Sagamihara's homeless sites. It was like, 'They are here! At this place!' ... I felt like, 'Homeless people are everywhere!' My hometown Sagamihara had so many [homeless people]. Everywhere" (my interview).

This event of "awakening", thus recollected and narrated, should not necessarily be read as an exaggeration. As I have been arguing, the majoritarian sociometabolism of housed citizens is distilled through the public/private matrix of cities, which generalises the predominant pattern of urban epistemology—habitat—that excludes the outsiders of habitat from the societal imaginaries of the urban. Of course, the two figures in Sagamihara—people who have commuted to the Kotobuki district—would have been critical of antihomeless regulation even before this "first contact" with local homelessness. Even for these inherently progressive figures, however, a recognition of local homelessness needed an epistemological turn induced by heterodox social places in the Kotobuki district. Even in this smoothest case of extended placemaking, the Kotobuki district was a sociocultural facilitator for prohomeless semiosis to happen in the outskirts.

A process of translation immediately followed this initial event of brokerage. These figures not only accepted Kotobuki's ideational framework but also improvised a new one based on the old version, thereby remaking the existing ideas into a unique ideational framework for Sagamihara's homelessness. Most fundamentally, Kotobuki's trained activists could not tell them where to meet homeless people or how to communicate with them in the emerging context of the outlying area. Inheritance was not enough. New maps of homelessness had to be created. New ways for homeless–housed communication had to be invented. These two individuals vividly remember the initial encounter with a homeless camp in a public park and how it ended up in the anticlimactic realisation that "intervention" was not needed.

> There was a major homeless site with more than ten people. The site was prominent. ... But the people neglected our "Good evening" greetings. They glanced at us but ignored us. After we visited them for two months in this way, one homeless guy finally informed us, "We are okay. We are all right. Go to Fuchinobe Park. A homeless guy there is not eating. He is ill." And that guy was really ill. He had a rash all over his body. (My interview with Misao Fujitani)

Homeless camps like this were a collective, autonomous model of homeless metabolism, more or less sustainable in their own way. These camps were led by "pros", who were able to sustain the camps by finding better places in terms of policing and regulation. Casual conversations were enough to elicit potential help, though routine visiting might still be necessary because the circumstances could change. The local activists thus learned how to communicate with homeless people who were sustaining "subaltern autonomies", in the streets or elsewhere, vis-à-vis urban hegemony and regulatory power. In turn, closer involvement was needed for isolated individuals who could easily be overwhelmed by discouraging events, a lack of knowledge, or health problems. This sort of visiting practice was a creative translation of Kotobuki's model to the outlying context as it appeared in this city: the space was larger, regulation was less fixed, and access was easier. Sagamihara's actors keenly modified the past strategy of public space commoning in this new setting.

After the initial events, in 1994, the two women dubbed this programme the Sagamihara Mokuyō Patorōru (Sagamihara Thursday Patrol). The two were members of a local church, and the church hosted their placemaking endeavours, offered some support, and never rejected their initiatives. The existence of the church also justified the movement's position to the municipality. Having a basis at the church, it became easier for them to communicate with the City of Sagamihara and to open up a political opportunity in favour of better local policy, as the activists were able to convey their homeless-supporting interests as something deeply rooted in the church's religious mission.

However, they soon learned that the church was not *completely* supportive. Placemaking attracted only a few members of local civil society, even at the church. "We asked church members, 'Please donate blankets to us', and so on. We had a base in a church, and some responded to our requests. When we spoke up, only a few said, 'Okay, I will join.' While some came once a year, others came once in three months" (my interview with Misao Fujitani).

Thus, homeless-supporting placemaking, quick and smooth as it was, remained somewhat inconclusive even in the city of Sagamihara where the brokerage found motivated local actors and where creative translation ensued. This hints at the difficulty of overcoming the sociometabolic walls of the housing classes in the outlying areas.

Placemaking in the City of Fujisawa

The city of Fujisawa is another case of placemaking in an outlying area. In this case, the process of brokerage was started by a young activist from the Kotobuki district. He continued to commute from the Kotobuki district for a year as he followed up with initiatives, until he and his companions secured commitments from a local church. In other words, before achieving placemaking, the members had to engage in the painstaking efforts of stretching Kotobuki's human and non-human resources to this outlying city.

Yukio Takazawa was the central figure in this attempted brokerage that targeted this outlying city. Takazawa has already been mentioned in Chapter 6 as a founder of the Kotobuki Supporters' Gathering Club, a key group that facilitated the participation of housed citizens in central Yokohama. In 1995, he started Fujisawa Kayō Patorōru (Fujisawa Tuesday Patrol), a homeless-visiting programme in Fujisawa.

After a year, Takazawa heard that several homeless people were sleeping at a local church, which seemed to be allowing homeless people to stay. Takazawa's group posted a handbill on the church's bulletin board, and they received a phone call from the church's secretary general, Katsuaki Kawabe, who showed great enthusiasm for the movement and became a regular member, along with his fellows. This influential figure in the church started distributing food to homeless people and created a special facility to keep their belongings at the church. While the church became a new social place for the movement by hosting everyday discussions and internal meetings, it also created new commons accessible from the streets and from the homeless metabolism. In this way, the movement achieved placemaking and (locational) commoning at once.

However, civil society is the locus of the housing classes. At any point, this society can generate constraints to prohomeless imaginaries and initiatives. The city of Fujisawa was no exception. A moment of conflict at the church came when the activists and a few church members unveiled a plan to create a shower room for homeless people on church property. For the activists, it was an idea to produce a homeless-supporting facility in this outlying city—a new version of the Kotobuki Livelihood Hall in Yokohama (see Chapters 6 and 7). But the idea of a shower room incited heated debates. A band of people at the church opposed it, fearing that homeless people would disturb them.

This friction at the church, however, became a major moment of translation. The church's influential figure and now movement participant, Kawabe, helped to translate the Kotobuki-born model of a homeless-supporting facility, using Christian language, saying that the shower room could produce "mutual trust and friendly relationships" between homeless people and "us" (my interview). The opponents themselves also participated in this process of translation. Takazawa, an original member from Yokohama, remembers, "Some opponents participated in our routine patrol activity [in the streets]. That was fascinating" (my interview). The intention was to see the harsh reality of homelessness and to alter opponents' negative attitude if necessary. Through having open meetings at the church and conducting several member surveys, the two sides gradually came to agree with each other about the necessity of creating a shower room for homeless people.[2]

The influential church member explains this reconciliation in a leaflet using religious vocabulary: "In his message—the 'Message on the World Day of Migrants and Refugees'—the Pope gave us a piece of writing entitled 'On the Parish.' In this piece, the Pope says that the parish is a place where there can be no people who are 'outsiders' [*yosomono*]. ... In essence, the Pope said that the parish should never be a mere 'club' of Catholics" (Catholic Fujisawa Church 2001d). This quotation does not mention homelessness, but everyone knew that it referred to the issue of the shower room and the heated debates of the early 2000s. When the shower room opened in April 2002, it had already benefited from many donations from church members.

In this way, through spatially accommodating the debates over the shower room issue, this church was turned into an intensive site of translation at which "old" inner-city strategies for "living with difference" (Valentine 2008) were translated into a form intelligible to local residents in an outskirt area. A (potentially) radical geography of homeless–housed encounters—of "living with *homeless people's difference*"—was produced around this church, allowing both activists and nonactivists to creatively cope with a "structural" geography of the homeless–housed divide.

Placemaking in the City of Hiratsuka

Compared to the previous two cities, the city of Hiratsuka is even farther from the Kotobuki district, but brokerage and group formation were advanced only by Kotobuki's few activists, without local participants. Furthermore, activists had to endure the stretching of manpower and resources over the years, as they did not succeed in placemaking for a considerable time. The group—eventually named the Hiratsuka Patrol—found that homeless people were totally abandoned by the municipality and local society, even though their number was increasing. To solve the problems of homelessness without successful placemaking in the locality, this group framed the issue of homelessness as a problem for the local state. Their strong commitment to having relationships with the municipality was due to the lack of partners in local society. The translation process in Hiratsuka advanced considerably in this way, and this context made the Hiratsuka Patrol a leader of commoning in the outlying areas of Kanagawa Prefecture.

The Hiratsuka Patrol was finally joined by a local church in 2004. After the endeavour of brokerage without a place, they acquired one—the result of a four-year effort to communicate with various local churches. A minister who had just moved to a Baptist church in Hiratsuka grew enthusiastic. This placemaking vitalised the Hiratsuka Patrol. They were now able to store materials such as clothes, blankets, and food at the church. The municipality became more supportive because the movement now included local residents. Furthermore, the activists found that church members were willing to provide food and clothes themselves. The church started holding parties and consultations for homeless people, and these events were run by church members. Such events helped the activists to nurture the trust of homeless people and ultimately testified to the success of the group's placemaking.

Commoning in the Outlying Cities

Early Attempts at Commoning

The various groups in the outlying areas undertook massive efforts to create their own places. While this placemaking is worth noting, it is also fruitful to ask what kinds of commoning activities—"commoning against othering"—followed the placemaking. This brings us to the city of Hiratsuka. We have seen that this city was the least penetrable for placemakers. As I have suggested, this difficulty in placemaking steered the Hiratsuka Patrol to an original pathway to compensate. When the prospect of placemaking looked virtually closed in this city, commoning (rather than placemaking) seemed more promising because the municipality at least gave them opportunities for dialogue. This local circumstance suggested to them an innovative choice—*to be a commoner before being a placemaker*.

Hiratsuka's activism was thus able to spearhead new commoning actions in the outlying cities because their placemaking was *un*successful. Brokerage without placemaking in this city facilitated a vigorous translation of past movement strategies in the realm of commoning. This is why the Hiratsuka case is highly useful in understanding how the brokerage process advanced the translation of Kotobuki-born activism in the realm of commoning.

Initially, the Hiratsuka Patrol castigated the municipality in the strongest possible way, arguing that the lack of positive involvement by the municipality was the largest problem. An activist left a note in 2001: "The problem of Hiratsuka's municipality is that when homeless people visit the city hall in order to apply for the public assistance programme, they get rejected by municipal staff for the reason that they have no fixed address" (*Chōsa Pato Kinkyū*, in the archives of the Kotobuki Day Labourers' Union).

However, the group soon realised that mere condemnation would be far from helpful, since this was not Yokohama's Kotobuki district, where a long history of activism had instilled some prohomeless attitudes and created some sympathisers among municipal workers who could be counted on. After their fruitless critical approaches, this group began trying to communicate with the municipality in more "collaborative" ways. Repeated dialogues with the municipality were a sign of success in this method of translation, though the meetings with the municipality were not the goal. According to Tetsuo Yura, an original member of the Hiratsuka Patrol who also belongs to the Kotobuki Day Labourers' Union, the true aim of the movement–municipality dialogues was to ask the "city to think of the homeless-related issues in a thorough way" (my interview), and to change municipal policy itself. In the early 2000s, achieving that goal seemed remote.

The obstacle faced by this group lay in the extreme difficulty of promoting local improvements. First and foremost, the activists could not persuade Hiratsuka's welfare office workers. The municipality simply kicked homeless people out of the welfare office when they visited it for public assistance and other forms of support. The situation around public spaces was no better. As the number of homeless people increased, housed citizens suddenly grew alarmed and harsh with regard to local homelessness. In movement–municipality meetings, activists asked municipal workers not to remove homeless people, referring to their rights. Yet it was a difficult case of NIMBYism, which tended to express the homeless–housed divide entirely in terms of trade-off relations.

A related matter was the intensification of an exclusive atmosphere in public spaces. For example, in the seaside area, people threw garbage at homeless people, seeing them as a nuisance. After some youths in Hiratsuka reacted violently to homelessness, setting fire to homeless people's belongings, the activists communicated with the Hiratsuka Education Board in order to tell students "to treat [homeless people] as human beings".[3] Yet changing this part of regulation was difficult.

Successes in Commoning

The Hiratsuka Patrol made progress in the realm of commoning, perhaps somewhat surprisingly, *after* the Japanese state created the new framework of rescaling between 2002 and 2003. This book has discussed the 2002/2003 system several times. The understanding has been that the 2002/2003 system gave some national-scale coherence to Japanese rescaling dynamics over homelessness by legalising the relocation of homeless people from the sphere of national citizenship to its margins, where new regulatory spaces had already emerged in ad hoc (ground-up) ways. Through the means-testing and workfarist codes of the 2002/2003 system, the Japanese state promulgated a view that many homeless people were not directly entitled to the benefits of public assistance (a central framework of citizenship in Japan) and could be addressed punitively in the streets and other public spaces. These characteristics of the 2002/2003 system promoted the "picking-off" round of rescaling in Japanese cities (see Chapter 3).

Activists in Hiratsuka and other outlying cities became deeply concerned about possible antihomeless consequences of the 2002/2003 system. This early fear was justified as the system in the city of Yokohama resulted in a deterioration of urban commons accessible from the streets. However, Hiratsuka's activists also realised that the 2002/2003 system could have different results in the outlying cities. In metropolitan municipalities like Yokohama, the 2002/2003 system asked the municipality to build means-testing facilities and programmes to run a local workfarist process. However, the outlying municipalities were unlikely to follow the same path because their financial capacity was more limited and the volume of homelessness was smaller. No viable "homeless policy" nor its social knowledge resources had existed previously in the outlying cities.

Amid repeated ad hoc evictions, Hiratsuka's activists, rather surprisingly, found two characteristics of the 2002/2003 system useful for commoning. These two legal aspects were unfocused in the case of Yokohama, but they were creatively appropriated in the outlying context. First, a particular set of clauses in the 2002/2003 system, heavily utilised in Hiratsuka, asked the municipality to work with nonprofit organisations to operate a local field of governance in the municipality: "Nonprofit organisations and volunteer organisations have developed face-to-face relations with homeless people by assisting their livelihoods, and for this reason these organisations are expected to serve important roles of supporting [homeless people] by taking into account individually different circumstances" (chapter 3, section 2 of the 2003 guidelines; see also article 12 of the Self-Help Act).

Activists in Hiratsuka highlighted these "governance clauses" and argued that the municipality could work closely with the group and make use of its advanced understanding of the issues. In Yokohama, the municipality already had close relationships with activism and a good knowledge of homelessness, so the 2002/2003 system in this particular realm (i.e., the governance clauses) would change nothing in the metropolitan context. In Hiratsuka, however, the municipality's relationships with private actors were weaker, and information was scarce. By creatively highlighting these governance clauses in the 2002/2003 system, Hiratsuka's movement asked the municipality (and other service providers) to give it a firmer position in the emerging arena of rescaled homeless governance.

Second, activists emphasised that the City of Hiratsuka had prepared only scant resources for homeless people and therefore was not actually allowed to advance the eviction of homeless people under the 2002/2003 system. This reading of the 2002/2003 system was theoretically correct, because the removal of homeless people, permitted by the system in favour of public safety, was actually a conditional right for the municipality and would be allowed only when the municipality prepared supportive programmes, according to the official guidelines (see Chapter 7). The "eviction clauses" were vague in terms of what kind of programmes the municipality should have prepared before eviction, but it was clear that the City of Hiratsuka lacked any such programmes. On this ground, the movement argued, the city was not allowed to advance any homeless eviction. Finally, activists stressed that the 2002/2003 system granted considerable discretion to the municipality, with special reference to cities with a "small" homeless population (chapter 3, section 3 of the 2003 guidelines); they affirmed that the welfare office of Hiratsuka was now in a better position than before to offer further support.[4]

A symbolic event took place on 28 November 2005, when the Hiratsuka Patrol was visited by the city's mayor (Figure 8.2). The movement had long asked for the mayor's visit, applying to a formal programme that was aimed to facilitate direct communication between the mayor and citizens. This meeting did not result in a clear understanding with the mayor on polemical issues such as homeless people's collection of aluminium cans, their mistreatment at the welfare office, or their policing by public and private regulators. The mayor listened to what activists said without many signs of agreement—even without many nods, which are frequently made by the Japanese as a sign of listening (though not necessarily of agreement). A handbill distributed by the Hiratsuka Patrol to homeless people on 3 December 2005, five days after the event, described the meeting as:

> not a negotiation or anything like that, but an opportunity to let the city recognise the present conditions of homeless people, such as why, with what intentions, we

visit our comrades forced to sleep rough in Hiratsuka, how homeless people are making ends meet, what kind of policy they wish to have, and so on. This won't change anything soon, but we believe that our activity and the social relations among homeless comrades in Hiratsuka were recognised. Seldom have mayors had such a direct dialogue with a private volunteer organisation. (Archives of the Kotobuki Day Labourers' Union)

As this handbill emphasises, the mayor's visit was thought to be a big step towards mutual recognition and even understanding. While the movement advanced confrontational politics with Hiratsuka's policymakers, it also aspired to materialise more collaborative relations with the municipality. For them, this visit was a long-awaited chance to directly deliver their message to the top officials. That became possible in 2005 at last, after the long effort to better reposition "homeless activism" in Hiratsuka's rescaled local goveranance by using the 2002/2003 system creatively.

In this new context of Hiratsuka's local politics, some municipal workers at the welfare office began to appreciate the homeless-supporting ideas of the Hiratsuka Patrol and to provide food and housing to some homeless people—especially the elderly—by using national and local frameworks, including public assistance. The

Figure 8.2 Mayor of the city of Hiratsuka listening to activists, 28 November 2005.
Source: Author.

emergence of such compassionate public workers was what an original member of the Hiratsuka Patrol had long awaited. "The biggest change was that the city replaced ... a leader [of municipal workers working with poor people]. ... Then, that [new] person started working for homeless people. ... He even travelled to meet those homeless individuals who are willing to apply for public assistance" (my interview with Tetsuo Yura).

Limits loomed, however. Younger homeless individuals and those seen as able to work often were rejected by the welfare office, especially when they went to the office alone, without being escorted by activists. Furthermore, some "benevolent" welfare workers were transferred to different administrative branches after a couple of years, and provision stopped for a time.

The Hiratsuka Patrol could not halt the structural tendency towards antihomeless regulation even at the welfare office. Nonetheless, it did succeed in making key advances in commoning in terms of welfare policy. Moreover, the improved position of the Hiratsuka Patrol in the local governance arena better placed activists vis-à-vis local service providers such as hospitals. In winter 2004, they learned that doctors and nurses at the Hiratsuka Civic Hospital, a public hospital, were treating homeless people badly and discriminatorily. The group made contact. Not only did the hospital meet with the activists, but also the head nurse admitted, "We had a prejudice. That was our failure", and guaranteed improvement in the hospital's treatment of homeless people.[5] This sort of positive acceptance by local service providers was largely unthinkable in the early 2000s.

Solidarity against a New Rescaling

Linking the Cities

In the year 2000, the increasing number and momentum of homeless-supporting groups in Kanagawa Prefecture led to the formation of an intracity coalition, the Kanagawa Zenken Yomawari Patorōru Kōryūkai (All-Kanagawa Assembly of Night-Walk Groups and Patrols). This coalition linked all the groups listed in Table 8.1 with the aim of facilitating their collaborative learning, mutual support, and collective action in the prefecture. While the formation of the All-Kanagawa Assembly was led by the trained activists from the Kotobuki district, the orientation was a highly decentralised one in favour of localism. Those involved had a clear understanding: "We must not end up in a 'metropolitan movement'. We shouldn't have the idea that Yokohama ... [can] represent all Kanagawa Prefecture" (my interview with Noboru Kondo).

The All-Kanagawa Assembly held a monthly internal meeting where the groups learned from one another's initiatives and processes. The groups involved in this new coalition quickly realised that there were differences, as well as commonalities, in municipal policy on homelessness. Most importantly, the zeal with which authorities evicted homeless people from public spaces differed from one city to another, though every outlying city excluded homeless people from public assistance.

To address these gaps, the All-Kanagawa Assembly met with Kanagawa Prefecture on 16 May 2000 to ask the prefectural government to use its power as a leader over the municipality. In May 2000, the groups in four cities—Chigasaki, Fujisawa, Kawasaki, and Sagamihara—reported at a monthly meeting that they were successfully meeting with their municipalities. This type of information exchange at the All-Kanagawa Assembly, and its facilitation of new relationships between activism and the municipality in each city, were among the key outcomes of the coalition.

Such behind-the-scenes facilitation by the All-Kanagawa Assembly, however, was not enough to change the attitude of the municipality in some cases, and local groups had differing abilities to communicate with their municipality. In this context, the All-Kanagawa Assembly became an orchestrator of commoning at the prefectural level. This approach to commoning was called *zenken kōdo* (prefectural action). The idea was to gather activists and volunteers from all over Kanagawa Prefecture to take collective action in one "problematic" city. Such actions would include demonstrations, speeches, and occupation, both inside and outside of municipal buildings, with the help of the coalition.

In the city of Atsugi in the summer of 2000, for instance, activists from the All-Kanagawa Assembly occupied the welfare office to lead and encourage the city to treat homeless people according to the framework of public assistance and to stop evictions of homeless people from public spaces. On 12 January and 8 July 2005, this strategy was deployed to back local negotiations with the City of Sagamihara, where homeless people's applications for public assistance were being rejected.

Learning the Rescaling

The All-Kanagawa Assembly played another key role: advancing collaborative learning about the rapidly evolving rescaling framework, its new (projected) interscalar relations, and its local-scale effects and cosequences. When the Japanese state promulgated the 2002/2003 system, with its seemingly novel ideas, the importance of the system to the outlying cities was unclear to both the movement and the local authority. As we have seen, the 2002/2003 system had large (metropolitan) cities in mind when it asked municipalities to construct temporary shelter facilities to play an official role in "educating" homeless people in the skills, rules, and ethics deemed necessary to engage in wage labour across today's neoliberal labour markets.

Everyone immediately recognised that this central idea of the 2002/2003 system—the encouragement of homeless people's "self-help" by means of workfare-style programmes—was unrealistic for the outlying cities, as these cities generally lacked a comparable budgetary base and had less experience with homelessness.

In addition, the 2002/2003 system granted considerable discretion to municipalities. It enumerated and classified various homeless-regulatory tasks in addition to workfare-style regulation for each municipality, but it was not "imposing" these tasks on municipalities. Outside of the main area of the workfare-style regulation, in particular, the 2002/2003 system was even more flexible.

This structure of the 2002/2003 system was closely scrutinised at the monthly meetings of the All-Kanagawa Assembly. The assembly concluded that any homeless-supporting groups in the outlying cities could use the 2002/2003 system as a weapon to improve local regulation on behalf of commoning. Activists and volunteers thought that the "governance clauses" of the 2002/2003 system would become especially useful. The governance clauses not only justified activists' relationship with the municipality but also implied that the movement, through communicating and collaborating with the municipality, would be able to influence the attitude of local policymakers and municipal staff.

Hence, the 2002/2003 system gave each municipality considerable discretion and allowed nonprofit organisations the potential to act in partnership with the municipality. If they used this framework wisely, the activists thought, further commoning would be possible. We have seen that this very possibility was something that the Hiratsuka Patrol was already seeking to achieve. Following the lead of spearheading groups such as the Hiratsuka Patrol, the activists and volunteers gathering at the All-Kanagawa Assembly collectively gained a locally viable understanding of the rescaling context as it appeared in the outlying cities during the 2000s.

Conclusion

The moving geography of rescaling regulation in the 1990s and 2000s was changing the outlying cities—the municipalities located behind Tokyo Bay—into a new breeding ground for antihomeless politics and epistemology. As the widespread cycle of Japanese homelessness dispersed itself very broadly in Kanagawa Prefecture, the housing classes and their guardians were abruptly alerted. In the outlying areas, local homelessness fomented a high level of moral panic and societal crisis because the sociometabolic process of the housing classes, which must be distilled through the public/private matrix to achieve societalisation, had never been "disordered" by those outside of the housing classes.

This urban hegemony–reducing impact of homelessness led to a series of ad hoc, ground-up reactions of political/social regulators against homelessness in each city. Catching up with this new tide of rescaling reregulation that now reached deep into Kanagawa Prefecture, however, the local history of homeless activism showed a new capacity to transplant the seeds of prohomeless epistemology from the Kotobuki district to these new (outlying) cities.

At the heart of this movement were the twin processes of brokerage and translation, which transposed the Kotobuki-born sociocultures and methods to the outlying cities. The trajectories of brokerage and translation differed from one city to another. When the host society allowed the placemaking of activists, which was most likely to happen at local Christian churches, they modified and translated the inherited sociocultures, in line with this placemaking, alongside the housing classes. Where no such place was found in local society, the new groups extended Kotobuki's human and nonhuman resources to the new cities, through which they actively reworked the inherited models and vocabulary on behalf of movement–municipality collaboration for commoning.

Furthermore, the activists and their groups in Kanagawa Prefecture formed an intercity coalition in the 2000s—the All-Kanagawa Assembly. This body facilitated, at the level of the prefecture, the collaborative learning of the prohomeless and homeless-supporting strategies that would prove most viable under the changing circumstances of rescaling reregulation. The member groups advanced professional readings of the 2002/2003 system and updated local strategies of commoning.

Notes

1 In fact, McAdam, Tarrow, and Tilly (2001) suggest that the cultural process of framing and identity formation can be the central objects of brokerage analysis. However, I would argue that closer examinations of the broker's sociocultural (linguistic) process are needed, with reference to structural contexts, which also can be theoretically articulated in terms of, for example, metabolism, urban form, class relations, and regulation/societalisation.
2 These debates over the shower room issue were publicly shown on the website of the Catholic Fujisawa Church (2001a, 2001b, 2001c) until the site moved to a new domain in 2020. This suggests that the church has long understood these debates about homelessness and thus the locational homeless–housed tensions were resolved creatively.
3 Handbills distributed by the Hiratsuka Patrol to homeless people on 2 February, 2 March, and 17 March 2002, in the archives of the Kotobuki Day Labourers' Union.
4 These creative readings of the 2002/2003 system are clearly shown in the movement's formal query to the City of Hiratsuka (All-Kanagawa Assembly and Hiratsuka Patororu 2003, in the archives of Kotobuki Day Labourers' Union).
5 Remarks of the head nurse of the Hiratsuka Civic Hospital in a meeting between the hospital and activists, 30 November 2004.

Part Four
Towards the Future of Rescaling Studies

Chapter Nine
New Rescalings in Japan

In this chapter I will look at topics and issues that have become observable after the late 2000s. While this newer temporal period has not been covered by the preceding chapters, this more recent phase can provide the latest set of case studies and empirical materials to decipher homelessness from this book's theoretical and methodological perspectives. Events and processes in Japan between the late 2000s and early 2020s—an urban social movement's scale jumping trial, the emergence of a finer workfarist policy, and ramifications of the COVID-19 pandemic—all help this book to reweigh its theoretical understandings in the light of these latest developments.

Upscaling of Homeless Politics in the Late 2000s

In the late 2000s, the previous localising trends of rescaling in Japanese cities saw a reversal, greatly facilitated by a social movement in Tokyo eager to support (nearly) homeless labourers—a movement dubbed the Toshikoshi Haken Mura (Overwintering Village of Dispatched Temporary Workers). The movement's discursive strategy of scale jumping incited a major shift towards nationalisation–upscaling that overturned the historical localisation–downscaling tendency of Japanese homeless politics. In this mobilisation, participants occupied a pivotal area in Tokyo's central business district. Setting up a collective campsite in a public park in front of the national ministries and the diet (the national legislature of Japan), thus positioning themselves opposite the hub of the national state

---

Rescaling Urban Poverty: Homelessness, State Restructuring and City Politics in Japan, First Edition. Mahito Hayashi.
© 2024 Royal Geographical Society (with the Institute of British Geographers). Published 2024 by John Wiley & Sons Ltd.

apparatus, the movement called for the improvement of Japan's homeless and poverty regulation, especially in relation to the livelihood right (sēzon ken). For this commoning to advance on the national scale, the movement employed and evolved a historical movement strategy that hitherto had been practised locally at Japanese yoseba zones.

The critical conjunction was the US subprime crisis, leading on to a global financial crisis, which started negatively affecting the Japanese economy in 2008. It was hurting the labour market, especially at the bottom: manufacturing companies suddenly stopped using temporary staffing agencies to fill job openings, which caused the unemployment of temporary workers, a type of labourer called *haken rōdōsha* (dispatched workers), or simply *haken* (the dispatched). Between late 2008 and early 2009, the mass media reported expectations that a huge number of temporary labourers working in manufacturing lines would soon be unemployed (Hayashi and Ikuta 2008; "Sēzōgyō haken ukeoi" 2009).

This labour market contraction even gained a special noun in the media discourse: *haken giri* (the cutting of the dispatched). This new signifier circulated widely in the media, which turned the term into a near synonym for the Japanese experience of the global financial crisis. This context alarmed activists in Tokyo who were working for poor people and precarious labourers. They took the media discourse about haken giri as a warning sign of upcoming mass homelessness, and reasonably so, because the lowest segments of dispatched temporary workers are often accommodated in dormitories owned by employers, and their job loss could easily mean becoming shelterless (Utsunomiya and Yuasa 2009).

Activists started considering a plan to provide accommodation and other services for the unemployed workers. They selected Hibiya Park, thinking that this would attract public attention (Toshikoshi Haken Mura Jikko I'inkai 2009, p. 26), as indeed it did. This worked because the park is located in front of the key organs of the state, including the Ministry of Health, Labour and Welfare and the diet. This location was considered an ideal place from which to exert political pressure on politicians and bureaucrats to change national regulatory codes (Utsunomiya and Yuasa 2009, p. 54). The leaders had a clear intention to make this event about more than simply providing accommodation for jobless workers. What they planned to do was a creative reappropriation of the *etto* (overwintering) mobilisation model—a model that had been practised in yoseba zones, including Yokohama's Kotobuki, for decades.

In the original conception, the movements in yoseba zones would pitch tents in public parks, occupy public buildings, provide materials and medical treatment, and thereby support the livelihood of day labourers and homeless people during the winter holidays of late December and early January, when government services are closed in Japan. Originally, this type of winter-period mobilisation was intended not just to help impoverished or homeless workers but also to demand improvements in local policy. Tokyo's movement in 2008 intentionally translated this social movement model to the national scale (Utsunomiya and Yuasa 2009; Yuasa 2009).

The leadership of one figure, Makoto Yuasa, helped to propel the movement. Yuasa is an alumnus of an elite university and participated in a pioneering prohomeless group in Tokyo's Shibuya Ward during the 1990s. Before joining the encampment event, Yuasa had already published several books, including the award-winning *Han Hinkon* (Against Poverty), published in 2008, which established him as an intellectual famous in Japan's liberal and progressive publics. The original advocates for the event—lawyers and city union leaders—invited Yuasa to join them when the plan for the encampment was taking off, with the idea that he might have useful knowledge about how to operate the encampment event (Toshikoshi Haken Mura Jikko I'inkai 2009; Yuasa 2009).

On 29 December 2008, in front of volunteers and the unemployed labourers, Yuasa and other leaders gave the opening speeches of the encampment event. While the event itself lasted until 5 January 2009 as intended, it had an immediate impact on national audiences via the mass media. In the media, the crisis of the dislocated workers was framed as a symbol of the global financial crisis hitting Japan at the time. Yuasa was now offering a "legitimate" interpretation of the crisis that focused especially on the plight of the unemployed precarious labourers.

The confluence of these contexts and creative practices in central Tokyo helped the event to enjoy a real resonance with wider audiences in Japanese society beyond the narrow circles of leftist publics. The stories of the unemployed labourers flooded newspapers and TV shows, promulgating the image of unemployed workers as a homogeneous group of "victims" (Jinbo 2009). If this storyline was somewhat simplistic, it was this simplicity that grabbed the attention of a national audience as a counter frame of reference against the conservatives.

Yuasa understood that his public image as an elite patron of poor people was important for the promotion of this nationalisation–upscaling politics. Among his speeches is the one made at the Diet Building, in which he proclaimed:

> In our village, we have welcomed a person who came on foot from faraway Ibaraki Prefecture. We have welcomed a person who had just made a failed attempt at suicide and was brought here by a police officer ... These are people who are struggling to survive. Let us have a society that supports such people. Why were we born to begin with? A society in which we have to question why we were born cannot sustain its power. (Toshikoshi Haken Mura Jikko I'inkai 2009, pp. 82–83)

Promulgating the positive image of homeless people as people "struggling to survive" and insisting that "we" as society are in a good position to assist them, public speeches such as this one popularised the movement's interpretational framing (Snow and Benford 1992). We have seen that similar framing actions have been exercised in homeless politics since the 1970s, but their effects have largely remained on the local scale. The event in Hibiya Park overcame this spatial-scale limitation through its creative process of framing, which succeeded in gaining a national resonance and eliciting regulatory changes from the key national gatekeepers of urban commons.

Improvements took place nationally. On 2 January 2009, the MHLW opened its auditorium as a temporary shelter. This was a delayed response to the movement's request on the part of the ministry, which was increasingly under the influence of positive media coverage (Yuasa 2009, p. 141). The ministry also arranged for four public shelters in Tokyo to accommodate hundreds of people who had nowhere to move to from Hibiya Park (Toshikoshi Haken Mura Jikko I'inkai 2009; Yuasa 2009). In addition, on 18 March, a couple of months after the event ended, the MHLW promulgated to local governments a public circular that was intended to get local welfare offices to more fully support public assistance applications by homeless people and other labourers, insisting that municipalities should use this national framework to maintain the social rights of these people (MHLW 2009b). On 25 December 2009, the MHLW produced and distributed another, similar circular to localities, this one more strongly worded, promoting the use of public assistance for homeless people at local welfare offices (MHLW 2009c).

The magnitude of this national-scale commoning can be inferred from a sharp increase in public assistance recipients, as shown in Figure 9.1, where the category of "Other" households (*sonota setai*) quickly increased after 2008. Government statistics refer to those who had previously been marginalised or excluded from the livelihood right and the welfare state in Japan—those without a fixed address, those who appear to be able-bodied, and unmarried males—as a vague group of unworthy "Other". By contrast, the "Elderly", "Mother and child", and "Disabled/sick/injured" households were clearly and distinctly mentioned. The Japanese state had long considered these groups to be worthy recipients.

It should be noted that this "Other" category in Figure 9.1 grew sharply after 2008, which means that this group of poor people who previously had been seen as undeserving were now covered by public assistance. This inclusion was the result of the MHLW's new legal interpretations, which pushed each municipality to mobilise public assistance even for homeless people. Activists, intellectuals, politicians, bureaucrats, and journalists alike attribute this growth of public assistance to the event in Hibiya Park, which compelled the MHLW to produce its inclusive new rules (Cabinet Office 2011a; Ikeda 2009; Katayama 2012; NHK Shuzai Han 2012; Toshikoshi Haken Mura Jikko I'inkai 2009).[1]

It is reasonable to apply the Gramscian notion of translation to this upscaling (nationalisation) process. I have already elaborated upon the notion when I interpreted the shifting geographies of social movements on the local scale (Chapter 8). In this new case, the translator's audiences were national society and the national state, and the aim of translation was to make these national audiences listen to the commoners fighting against othering. It is true that Yuasa's meaning-making practice hardly touched on the deep-seated uniqueness of the homeless metabolism

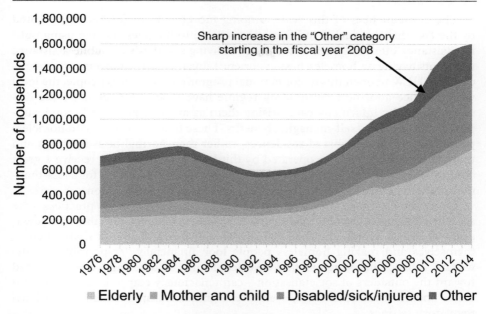

Figure 9.1 Households on public assistance between 1976 and 2014. The years represent Japanese fiscal years, starting in April and ending in March.

Source: Based on data from National Institute of Population and Social Security Research, http://www.ipss.go.jp/s-info/j/seiho/seihoH28/H28-3.xlsx (accessed 30 September 2020).

and its *desocietalising* tension, which is the least comprehensible part of homelessness for audiences. The movement's simplification of homelessness into "understandable homelessness" was the key to the scale jumping process, because it was about bringing the nation and national policymakers to homelessness. Through this translation and simplifying process, the core participants adorned their demand with a charm that resonated with existing national discourses.

However, conflicts and tensions were still rampant, as the movement was inherently radical even after such simplification. Markedly enough, immediately after the 2008 event, authoritarian figures in national politics, such as national diet member Tetsushi Sakamoto, started denouncing the "unethical" nature of homeless people who participated in the event ("Haken mura hatsugen" 2009). Even after gaining national popularity, therefore, the commoning movement faced the ongoing pressure of othering that castigated homeless people's putative lack of work ethic—a claim that was, of course, due to blindness to the homeless metabolism and its *productive* (value-producing) power, concepts not included in Yuasa's simplification. The movement repeatedly counterattacked this ongoing production of antihomeless discourses by the conservatives through an unfolding, reflexive practice of counterdiscourse (Amamiya 2009).

The consequences of this scale jumping movement are further complicated by the fact that the quality of life made available to homeless people using public assistance often has been lower than the living standards of public-assistance recipients having no homelessness experience. Even after the movement prompted the MHLW to open this major national program for homeless people, the local welfare office and the local housing regime have treated homeless people discriminatorily by informally categorising them as an "irresponsible" group, supposedly incapable of self-managing benefits. These treatments can send homeless people to low-quality shared residences, rather than normal housing units, and these shared residences are operated by third-party agencies that receive a great amount of rent and fees from public assistance, often in exchange for a less-than-minimum living space, poor-quality food, and intensive supervision.

Local activists have been trying to mitigate this and similar practices—the so-called "business use of public assistance" (*sēkatsuhogo bijinesu*) that can downgrade homeless people's citizenship in Japan—by operating better shared houses themselves and making homeless people look financially "responsible" at the welfare office. This suggests that rescaled forms of othering—when directed toward the outsiders of societalisation—can tenaciously reappear, at subnational scales and/or in informal ways, even after significant improvements in national regulatory settings.

Despite these aftermaths and ramifications, the Overwintering Village of Dispatched Temporary Workers, in pursuit of the nationwide opening of the commons, effectively combated the long-term, highly systemic moment of antihomeless societalisation in the national arena of politics and public discourses. The nationalisation–upscaling of homeless politics was made ever more possible because the commoning movement skilfully framed and translated "homeless politics" into an understandable form for diverse national audiences in the context of an unfolding global economic crisis.

Neoliberalisation and Workfarist Reform in the 2010s

This nationalisation–upscaling movement of the late 2000s was a feat. The elite symbols and cultural resources were what the local people mostly lacked. With their charm, Tokyo's activists powerfully communicated with national gatekeepers and publics, overcoming the dilemma of local politics. At no point did this result in a "colonisation" of the national scale by the commoners and their discourses. On the contrary, the movement provoked an antipoor backlash from concerned politicians, intellectuals, and publics who wanted to resocietalise Japanese civil society by reacting against the commoners. As of the mid-2010s, they were promoting the building of Japan's new workfarist paradigm of poverty regulation.

Workfarist approaches emerging from this context would show characteristics similar to Japan's homeless regulation in its mature (picking-off) round of the 2000s.

Despite the similarity, a major difference between the 2010s and the 2000s was that the target of rescaling politics was expanded to needy people *in general*. New regulatory spaces were ever more broadly created at the margins of citizenship. Now, needy people in general were to be confined to the limbo between right and non-right—within the institutional spaces tamed, surveilled, and organised by "market efficiency", "policy innovation", and "work ethic". This expansion of new regulatory spaces for needy people has markedly characterised Japan's late neoliberalism.

To begin with, Japan's political, intellectual, and moral leaders were promulgating new discourses about the "destructive" effects of public assistance, with their own framing that public assistance only promotes the "welfare dependency" of people who are "employable" (Peck and Theodore 2000) and produces "parasitic" social classes. For example, an influential welfare economist promoted this agenda at a conference held by a ruling party, where he stated, "After the Lehman shock of 2007, much of the work-capable population ranging from the thirties to the sixties in age has gone on public assistance." This welfare economist, a cabinet adviser, provided his own antipoor interpretation that "some [conservative] citizens, if minorities, are highly discontent" because these citizens wonder "why so many work-capable people are supported [by public assistance] without much intention to get off the welfare rolls" (Cabinet Office 2011a, p. 15).

Even the most influential media conglomerate in Japan, NHK, which is usually considered moderate, expressed similar grave concerns (NHK Shuzai Han 2012), and politicians hardly lagged behind in this discursive trend. For example, a diet member in the Liberal Democratic Party, now a ruling party, summed up her interpretation:

> Public assistance had functioned as a programme only for those who were really unable to work due to advanced age or handicap, and generations of active workers had been prohibited from receiving public assistance because the welfare office employed the so-called extinguishing operation [*mizugiwa sakusen*; for active workers]. However, the event of Toshikoshi Haken Mura posed a threat [to this condition], which I now really think is a threat that millions of workers ... would experience mass homelessness, by losing employment and accommodation at the same time, and by having no functional unemployment insurance. (Katayama 2012, p. 58)

Groups of politicians, intellectuals, and media critics were now lining up against this "threat", a powerful appearance of the "Other" of societalisation, and sharing among themselves new discourses that denounced "welfare dependency" and the "lavish" spending of the government, all using slightly different but mutually understood language (see Ikeda 2009; Takenaka et al. 2010). Furthermore, these new antipoor discourses functioned to elicit civil society support for the state's neoliberal reform of public assistance.

At a policy conference, for instance, bureaucrats used the notion of "work will", tying in a need to cultivate a societal resonance when achieving such a major welfare reform: "The amount of cash assistance provided by public assistance ... should be lowered to a certain level at which the incentive of recipients to work will not be discouraged" (Cabinet Office 2011b, p. 1). At the same conference, MHLW staff suggested that "outsiders" were too easily included in Japanese welfare statism: "Among the [four] household categories of the elderly, mother and child, disabled and injured, and the other, ... we find an especially significant growth in the 'Other' category" (Cabinet Office 2011a, p. 5).

These problem-searching discourses—the language of "sniffing out"—were cultivated in both the state and civil society sectors. While these articulations were not entirely new to Japan, the type of poverty-related political discourses that grew in this period reveal some specificity of Japan's late neoliberalism of the 2010s. Back in the 2000s, the basic mode of poverty discourse was still more fact-finding and was more compatible with scientific forms of statistical analysis advanced by scholars. The newer version of national poverty discourse was more punitive and more inclined towards policymaking against "welfare dependency". This probably reflected the deepening context of Japan's austerity politics and the gloomy prospects of Japanese capitalism, both of which gained momentum in the 2010s. During this period, the discourses posited, the Japanese state was no longer able to spend much money on the "undeserving poor", and the scientific understanding of poverty should now promote a new, effective policy reform against the poor's "indulgence" and "welfare dependency".

Against this backdrop, the language of "sniffing out" has gained real political power in contemporary Japan; the poverty discourse has given rise to a major process of Japan's workfare-state construction. The aim of this politics has been enunciated more clearly than ever before: to reduce the cost of public assistance and relocate the (potential) recipients to a preventive and punitive realm of poverty management, which will be constructed outside of the legal entitlement to citizenship. The belief is that the introduction of new workfarist measures and categories can make public assistance into a more flexible, meagre, time-limited, and conditional space less enjoyable and accessible for impoverished people.

By adding new incentivising and preventive mechanisms to this programme, this reform, starting in the late 2000s, has amounted to a wholesale restructuring of the Japanese citizenship paradigm. If the 2002/2003 system advanced similar initiatives for homeless people, everyone in danger of being poor is now targeted. Some relevant initiatives have been reshaping Japan's citizenship framework and steering it in the direction of workfarist poverty regulation at the national scale.

- In 2011, the Japanese government announced the Final Draft of Comprehensive Tax and Social Welfare Reform, which stated in formal political terms that Japan's public welfare was overloaded and called for radical reform by establishing a "second safety net", meaning in this context more time-limited and conditional provisions of support at the margins of the first safety net of public assistance (Cabinet Secretariat 2011, p. 7).

- Beginning in 2013, the Japanese state started radically slashing the benefit level of public assistance. Between 2013 and 2015, there was a reduction of approximately 6% in benefit spending. In 2017, a further reduction was suggested.
- In 2014, the Act for Promoting Reforms of the Social Security System was enforced, which targets the "best balance of self-help, mutual help, and public help" (article 2), and intends a significant reduction of public assistance by constructing new work-first regulatory principles for needy persons and welfare recipients (article 2, additional clause).
- In 2014, the Public Assistance Act was revised, with an intention to reform the extant public assistance programme by adding to it a new incentive mechanism for the recipients, designed to strongly encourage the job-seeking activity of the recipients after their enrolment in the programme.
- In 2015, the Act for Supporting the Self-Help of Needy Persons began to be enforced, which created a larger space of workfare-style approaches in the Japanese legal framework and thereby "implemente[d] a consultation assistance programme for the self-help life of needy persons" (article 1).

Situated in these new regulatory parameters set by the Japanese state, the municipal welfare offices have started to operate old citizenship frameworks within the new parameters of workfarist poverty regulation. This workfare-state building of Japan has never been a one-time installation of a well-designed framework by the national state. Rather, the process has entailed both careful, step-by-step efforts by national policymakers and an imposition of well-intended but nonetheless uncertain promotion of local policy innovation.

In this development, national policymakers have not lost power. National bureaucrats are still in the powerful position to change, by institutional and legal means, the ways in which "able-to-work age groups" (MHLW 2013, p. 4) fare across Japanese cities. As we will see, however, the Japanese state has been eager to produce another front line in this border-remaking and system-remaking politics within cities and at the local scale. The current workfarist reform has advanced in this highly multiscalar way, and what is more, the "multiscaleness" itself has been an active policy target of national policymakers. Japan's rescaling restructuring of the welfare state has accompanied this somewhat ambivalent invocation of the regulatory muscle of the national state to advance the decentralisation of poverty-related regulatory affairs.

Rescaling for All

In the current political framework, Japanese municipalities are asked to behave as policy innovators capable of advancing a reform best suited to the local contexts of the labour market, needy populations, and urban society. State rescaling has been revived in this context. The regulatory task is formidable: the destabilisation of the existing citizenship paradigm and its partial replacement with urban workfarist regimes, which must assess, address, and "incentivise" needy people in general at the margins of the legal rights to livelihood and public assistance. If the Japanese state's knowledge of how it can achieve this arduous task is limited, it *does* know that this level of reconstruction is fraught with errors, failures, and uncertainties, which national ministries and politicians wish to avoid. To be immune to failures and not risk the legitimacy of the state, this level of workfarist reform is now hastening another new process of rescaling politics in Japan, which keenly emphasises the "policy innovation" of local regulators.

Nowadays, the discourse of the Japanese state tends to promote eager municipalities as central figures in policy innovation beyond the "old" welfarism of public assistance. According to the MHLW (2015, p. 3), the support of needy people must take the new form of "decentral and creative [*sōzōteki*] support", and in this new paradigm "the leading actor is the locality", which is supposed to play the primary role of "creating the local system of support". In this policy innovation, national policymakers are asking municipalities to undertake several difficult tasks at once: to cultivate new relationships with local businesses, to create flexible working opportunities for those who are "rehabilitating" from welfare dependency, and to find helpful supporters in the local community who can decrease the provision of public assistance in neighbourhoods. As for matters *within* the municipality, the Japanese state is asking the welfare office of the municipality to work closely with the public employment security office, encouraging these two hitherto different organs pursuing distinctive functions (welfare and work) to merge and create a new window for workfarist procedures at the welfare office. The MHLW enumerated twelve "creative" examples of this merger on its website, pushing more municipalities towards similar experiments.[2]

Thus, much "policy innovation" is expected to happen locally and in cities. Moreover, this move of decentralisation and rescaling is expanding the role of private firms at the welfare office. Following the policy changes of the 2010s, the welfare office today hires many "employment facilitators" (*shūrō shienin*), who attend to the potential users of public assistance and promote their labour market participation. These facilitators are precarious dispatched employees working under the control of staffing agencies, and we find here a vicious cycle of problem making and problem resolution within the welfare office.

The character of the welfare office as a "public" domain has now been changed. Endemic failures in workfarist regulation, having been transferred from the national to the local scale, are further removed from the public and into the market sphere—a mechanism of *dual* depoliticisation that may hide the endemic failures of Japan's late neoliberalism. The locus of responsibility and accountability is blurred, fragmented, and scattered in the maze of rescaling. Attempts to minimise the welfare rolls are as old as modern Japan, and it has a particular name: the "extinguishing operation" (mizugiwa sakusen). Now this old strategy is innovatively using private actors at the local scale as a stabiliser.

When Public Spaces Are Closed

Since the late 2000s, Japanese public spaces have reduced the visibility of homeless people. The number of homeless individuals apparent to regulators and the housing classes has plummeted (Figure 9.2). It should be noted that this book has characterised Japanese public spaces as spaces that are highly intolerant of homelessness because they were originally constructed under Japan's developmentalist type of capitalist urbanisation—a regime that created only small use values of public spaces/goods for popular consumption. In part 1, I argued that Japanese consumption norms and societalisation on this basis took on a strong colour of cultural conformism, whereby any countering forces could be judged to be seriously threatening to the cohesion of society. Because Japanese capitalist urbanisation was susceptible to "disorder", Japan's two cycles of homelessness historically met with harsh attempts at reregulation. In the context of Japan's conformist type of societalisation, public spaces were prone to moral panic and were likely to amass events of rescaling in bottom-up ways.

In light of this conformist construction of public spaces in postwar Japan, what Japanese cities now witness seems to be explicable; the closure of public spaces to the homeless metabolism seems to be a somewhat "natural" consequence of postwar Japan. However, to achieve this "clean" urbanisation amid the rampant failure of Japanese poverty regulation, public spaces have elevated their preventive capacity against homelessness.

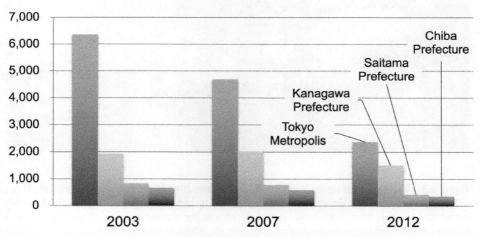

Figure 9.2 Decline in "countable" homeless people in the Tokyo–Yokohama metropolitan region, 2003–2012. Source: Adapted from Ministry of Health, Labour and Welfare, 2020.

The images in Figure 9.3 indicate the most recent pattern of public space management as it appears in the city of Yokohama. The spaces in all these photographs—which were taken at midnight—look recently renovated (except in the fourth photograph) and are brightly lit. This excessive lighting by LED devices is a recent trend in the construction of "safe" and "clean" public spaces against homelessness, which adds a new method of policing to the deployment of surveillance cameras, security staff, and antihomeless obstacles. The lights may make public spaces "homeless free" without resorting to eviction, barricades, or announcing any kind of prohibition (as Japanese municipalities often did to disperse homelessness). Homeless people just cannot sleep well, and may feel uneasy, under these superbright lights and therefore are *spontaneously* driven to

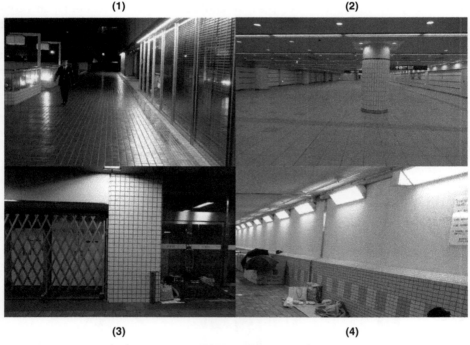

Figure 9.3   Public spaces of central Yokohama, 1 and 2 January 2019. (1) An external passage of Yokohama's railway station complex; this site was once densely populated by homeless people, but not now. (2) A recently renovated, hyperclean street in Yokohama's railway station complex; it shows few signs of homelessness. (3) A small entrance of Yokohama's railway station complex; here, one individual is managing to find a little space beside the barricades. (4) An underground tunnel in the Kannai railway station in the city of Yokohama; it still gathers rough sleepers.

Source: Author.

go away. Hence, less direct coercion is involved in these hyperclean and hyperobjectified public spaces.

Japan's urban regulation has already taken on these sophisticated appearances, which actively manage or fabricate poor people's tacit consent to a societalised urban society, effectively dispelling the homeless metabolism from the facade of urban commons with fewer hints of the classic notion of regulation. Thus, homeless regulation can powerfully depoliticise itself nowadays through the enhanced visibility and "luminosity" of space (Deleuze 1988 [1986]), contributing to the "postpolitical" construction of urban governance (Swyngedouw 2009)—even in Japan, where urban poverty is becoming widespread and in theory can develop highly deregulated appearances inimical to habitat-based societalisation.

This chapter has already examined a similar pattern of depoliticisation in poverty regulation by looking at Japan's workfarist regulation, which eradicated manifest elements of coercion and dispersed needy people from public assistance on the basis of "consent". Today, this trend is broadening and covering another side of urban commons—public spaces. While Japanese poverty regulation has made a long-standing attempt to cultivate and seize the vast, ambiguous area between coercion and consent, this extensive method of poverty regulation is now succeeding in avoiding the sense of coercion and in reaching many different sites of public space. Both of these tendencies are transforming the built environment of the city into a naturalised site of hypersocietalisation without many tinges of eviction.

It should not be forgotten, however, that the growth of poverty is gaining momentum in this era of depoliticisation. As I argued in Chapter 3, the labour market (wages) and social fabrics (family plus community) have lost much of their previous capacity in the Japanese nationalised space of poverty regulation, while the sphere of public provision has systematically watered down its institutional capability due to the workfarist regulatory codes that can position poor people (not just homeless people) outside of public assistance. While these stunted spheres of the NSPR can increase homelessness in Japan, the enhanced luminosity of public spaces is now dispelling potentially homeless people from the facade of public spaces and masking the failures in poverty regulation at the end point of rescaling (see also Hayashi 2023b). Houseless people today are accommodated less by public spaces and more by the "hidden" spaces of homelessness, such as internet cafés that are open twenty-four hours a day, every day (MHLW 2007; TMG 2018).

Repoliticising the Urban

In cities eager to expand the social appearance of conformity and consent even amid mass poverty, urban social movements are still finding new opportunities to reclaim public spaces on behalf of the homeless metabolism. Activists dare to make this hypothetical comparison: if today's public space were subject to the same level of antihomeless policing as it was ten years ago (which was much less intense than it is today), a considerable number of homeless individuals would choose to stay in parks and on the streets rather than leave them. Parks and streets were more "liveable" for homeless people before the 2010s. In this regard, veteran activist Yukio Takazawa states, "There are some homeless people who can do better by living on the streets than by leaving them ... Unfortunately, citizens do not understand this way of living a life. Citizens harshly think that such homeless people are criminals. They castigate homeless people on this ground. ... The job of our movements is to change such society" (my interview).

This statement implies that a new avenue for homeless activism is now emerging. The degradation of the right to livelihood could be politicised and employed by urban social movements that support homeless populations that still appear in public spaces as they are marginalised by mainstream society and its housing regimes/classes. Even in the midst of Japan's late neoliberalisation, which may be closing public spaces to the homeless metabolism, the urban social movements discussed here still can be well-positioned to advance urban commoning, as they can reconceive the regulatory voids in the streets and fill them with new politics and imaginaries. Thus, homeless activism in contemporary Japan still illuminates different ways of urbanisation beyond normalisation and occlusion at the end point of class hierarchies, societalisation, and state rescaling.

At the same time, mired in the antihomeless construction of Japanese society and public spaces, even veteran activists who have long worked for prohomeless causes feel uneasy enunciating these causes to public audiences, in public spheres, and to newcomer volunteers in the strong vocabulary they have long used. The concern is that in the contemporary context of public spaces, in which the homeless metabolism can ever more easily be spotlighted, isolated, and censured, their contestation may lead to a further movement *against* homeless people. In contemporary Japan, urban social movements face this dilemma in relation to the larger sociopolitical environments and public spheres.

The Inner City against Gentrification

As a matter of fact, activists in the Kotobuki district feel that this external pressure has already been much *internalised* to their niches of activism, making their relatively "safe space" (Tilly 2000) unsafe. Especially after the late 2000s, this inner-city area has undergone an increasing pressure of being gentrified, beautified, monitored, and reregulated. This pressure has gnawed at Kotobuki's historical capacity as a vortex of prohomeless and homeless-supporting forces. This process includes the constant replacement of aging buildings—hotels and facilities for day labourers—with new, hyperclean, modern ones whose usage is not restricted to present or former day labourers. The rebuilding of the old hotels and facilities, one after another, has gradually but effectively changed the look of the Kotobuki district.

A related new tendency in the Kotobuki district is the use of existing buildings and surrounding environments for new business purposes. Major real estate companies have been actively redeveloping areas around the district by building relatively expensive condominiums and apartments for middle-class residents, a move that might be seen as the newest example of "colonisation" of the inner city by habitat. In addition, young entrepreneurs have come to the area and started renovating day labourers' hotels for tourists, which nowadays include a lot of foreigners. The Kotobuki district—a historical domain of day labourers and homeless people—might not be an attractive venue for many Japanese people, but foreign tourists may like it, as some of them visit Japan looking for "exciting" experiences.

In short, the Kotobuki district has been experiencing the pressure of gentrification, normalisation, and commodification from different directions. Responding to requests from middle-class residents, the police and the municipality have ramped up antihomeless policing pressure even around the inner city. Antihomeless eviction in one particular area along the Nakamura River, which I discussed in Chapters 4 and 7, was a harbinger. Comparable patterns of gentrification-driven policing patterned on this "successful" removal have already extended as far as the Ishikawa-chō railway station, just north of the Kotobuki district, where homeless people have historically created sites of encampment. This change in the local landscape suggests a loss of Kotobuki's "conspicuous" environment, which has distinguished it from the space of habitat and constituted Kotobuki's potential as a centre of the habiting movement.

This "flattening" of the inner city's unique appearance is joined by the general aging of former and current day labourers and an increase of welfare recipients in the local population, catalysing a loss of momentum for mobilisation around the Kotobuki Day Labourers' Union. Similarly, the decreased attraction of the inner-city area for new volunteers, in light of the changed sociological environment, has somewhat decreased the mobilising power of other organisations, such as the Kotobuki Supporters' Club.

These recent trends, which can promote the demobilisation of Kotobuki's activism, are of concern to local activists. At the same time, Kotobuki's people are not bystanders to the negative pressure—they are struggling to reactivate and renew the historical memories of the Kotobuki district. These memories are a complex set of various placemaking histories of day labourers, homeless people, and activists/volunteers since the 1970s. At one event, held in 2019, activists exhibited old photos and narrative records to a public audience, trying to share the memories with people who had come to the Kotobuki district more recently. Such effort represents the newest terrain of resistance in this area—a culturally nuanced way of reforging the histories of placemaking against the flattening power of the colonisers.

COVID-19, Rescaling, Recommoning

During the course of this writing, the COVID-19 pandemic has put public and private spaces—as "facade effects" (Lefebvre 1991 [1974], p. 275) of urban societalisation—in jeopardy all over the world. In the initial phase, the housing classes retreated en masse from urban consumption in the streets and parks and on public transport. Where did they retreat to? Housing. But a fuller response would be that this retreat into housing was associated with the excessive privatisation of public spaces against the public as an orthodox notion, for public spaces themselves were deemed to be infectious and to be used secretly and privately. This led to the proliferation of quasi-private spaces *in* public spaces, created by individuals who were forced to use the streets, parks, and public transport in highly defensive and private ways. In this respect, the COVID-19 crisis hastened the privatisation of public spaces on the part of the housing classes, tracing a pattern similar to the homeless metabolism—homeless people's "private" space within public spaces.

While capitalist urbanisation has vigorously advanced the twin formation of public and private spaces (into the public/private matrix), this balance was perhaps profoundly damaged in the initial phase of the pandemic, which perhaps tendentiously triggered the crisis of urban societalisation based on habitat. It may be possible to say that the outburst of various kinds of radical politics and public actions in the streets, which we saw all through the pandemic crisis, had something to do with this swift destabilisation of the public/private matrix in the year 2020.

How did this context appear in the spaces of poor and homeless people? First, impoverished urban areas and their dwellers, who had already suffered from a lack of good public and private spaces well before COVID-19, were seriously impacted due to the lack of flexibility in their public and private spaces. If the outpouring of radicalism is related to such urban areas, they perhaps exhibited new possibilities for the habiting movement. The Lefebvrian urban movements of habiting were perhaps revived in this way.

Second, at the end point of urban poverty, homeless people were likely more acutely affected by the pandemic, due to their categorical lack of safe housing units. The increased danger and unpleasantness of urban metabolic relations during the COVID-19 crisis made homeless people's life in the urban outdoors more difficult than ever, because they were surrounded by a high density of potentially infectious materials and elements. As the "public" became a potentially fatal site for everyone and shelters were even worse than the streets in terms of safety, some "powerful" homeless people tried to engage in a new struggle to reopen and reconstruct their circuit of urban metabolism under the threat of infection.

In Japan, the pandemic incited rescaling responses to homelessness. On 20 April 2020, the Japanese state established a special benefit programme that would provide 100,000 yen (approximately US$900) to every individual with an officially registered address in Japan. The Japanese legal system decrees that every citizen should register their residence in a local municipality at birth and reregister every time they move. Education, voting, health care, and other public services are based on the identification of individuals using this registration system. The lack of a registered residence immediately means the exclusion of an individual from public services.

The obvious problem is that homeless people cannot register their residence as "public spaces" at the local municipality. Because homeless people were categorically excluded from the registration system, they were excluded from the emergency benefit programme of 2020. A similar consequence of rescaling also reemerged in the public assistance programme. The number of applications to public assistance soared in many cities, but whether these cases were resolved positively for impoverished people is highly questionable (Ishikawa and Hisanaga 2020; "Sēkatsuhogo shinsē madoguchi" 2020). During the COVID-19 crisis, homeless and nearly homeless people were repeatedly excluded from public assistance (Nakamura 2020; see also Hayashi 2023b).

In the face of this renewed trend of rescaling, social movements in Kanagawa Prefecture are trying to change the consequences of rescaling on behalf of commoning. For instance, activists in Yokohama and other cities are making strong claims for the inclusion of homeless people in the emergency benefit framework. Activists are asking governments to facilitate homeless people's residential registration by permitting shelters and other facilities to be listed as a residence, so that homeless people can receive benefits. Likewise, these activists continue to put pressure on municipal welfare offices to accept homeless people's applications to the public assistance programme and to reduce the number of rejected cases. Finally, activists and volunteers have tried to ameliorate the immediate difficulties that homeless people are experiencing by setting up new, safer shelters. For instance, the City of Yokohama accepted the movement's idea that a municipal gymnasium could be used as a homeless shelter in 2020.

Notes

1 Thus, what the mobilisation realised was not an intercity transfer of regulatory responsibilities, such as from Yokohama to Tokyo. Rather, the achievement was the nationalisation–upscaling of regulatory responsibilities, which had previously been denationalised, fragmented, and localised.
2 This description is based on materials provided by the MHLW at https://www.mhlw.go.jp/stf/seisakunitsuite/bunya/0000054441.html (accessed 27 October 2021).

Chapter Ten
Conclusion

To conclude my discussion, let us revisit the main threads of argument in the book, with particular focus on the seven more "empirical" chapters after part 1. Chapter 3 kicked off part 2 of the book by offering a theory of societalisation, its crisis tendency, and its rescaling from the vantage point of poverty regulation. The notion of nationalised spaces of poverty regulation was used to describe the Gramscian integral state on a national scale, from the perspective of impoverished people. This state space consolidation, usually called the "welfare state", most powerfully evened out the irregular appearances of poverty in society during the golden years of postwar growth periods, often described as Fordism. During these years, the NSPR expanded the scope of societalisation to the lower classes, who were most sensitive to the disruptive tendencies of capitalism. As such, the NSPR acted as a national scaffolding of societalisation that made possible the unification of class-divided society into a (slightly more) cohesive locus for capitalist civilisations.

Societalisation is generally defined as a wider sociological condition of the accumulation regime that supports the capital circuit in its social, cultural, and semiotic outskirts. As such, societalisation can render crisis tendencies inherent in the capital circuit "socially embedded" and immune to self-destruction. By combining the three pillars of public provision, the labour market, and social fabric, the NSPR in the postwar years broadened the scope of normative consumption as a material–semiotic basis of societalisation, which powerfully standardised the process of social reproduction even for impoverished people.

Chapters 4 and 5 showed that cities stabilised this *national* project of societalisation by generating milieus of *urban* societalisation. The backdrop was the stable accumulation regime, the vigorous NSPR, and the material–semiotic inputs from these circuits. Yet the special capacity of cities was that they evolved public and private spaces into a refined urban environmental matrix of societalisation. This matrix of public and private spaces constructed urban dwellers, rich and poor, into the housing classes, that is, into a composite category sharing an important similarity: they had housing units somewhere in the city but *not* in public spaces. This background enabled "housed citizens" to use public spaces according to the consumption norms and rules embedded in each space. The housing classes became the hegemonic actor in urban settlements.

This, of course, did not stop the politicisation of city space, nor the rise of neighbourhood-based coalitions for change. Yet public and private spaces, as a relational system, showed surprising abilities to streamline and integrate urban society beyond antagonism and struggles. In particular, being located in this matrix, the consumption of public spaces became a chief process through which people formed a lot of common ideas about society, life, and the nation, away from "accumulation for accumulation's sake" and its class-dividing tendencies.

Chapters 4 and 5 also discussed the fact that homelessness, once it emerged in this arena of urban societalisation, evoked moments of desocietalisation and deregulation because homelessness was perceived by the housing classes and their guardians as a significant source of moral panic. The reason was that homeless people, after being deprived of housing and thrown into public spaces, necessarily developed spaces of "privacy" within public spaces, which had a major disruptive impact on the rules, norms, and form of urban consumption and, by extension, on societalisation that used urban consumption as a semiotic arena.

On the face of it, political and social agents proliferated new regulatory codes that were practised in specific locations. The hope was that various urban commons would be reserved for the housing classes and for those homeless individuals who would make every effort to appreciate the acculturating demand of the hegemonic classes. The subalternity of homeless people derived from this structural position relative to the housing classes and their guardians, which in large measure made homeless people the Other of urban societalisation that is based on the public/private matrix. This unleashed a torrent of production of new regulatory spaces that propelled the rescaling of Japan's homeless/poverty regulation, initially in ad hoc and then in more systematic ways, precipitating capillary and scaled forms of power around the spaces of homelessness.

However, homeless people were not passive "objects" of regulation who were merely stranded in the rescaled cities where they suffered constant reregulation. Part 2 discussed how homeless people reclaimed (more) autonomous spaces for subsistence and urban metabolism vis-à-vis the housing classes, regulators, and the system of public and private spaces. The postwar expansion of regulated urban spaces had already narrowed what formerly existed as less controlled spaces of homelessness. Yet the homeless people described in this book still sought to open up, and sometimes very successfully unlocked, new spaces of urban metabolism in the face of antihomeless regulators and the housing classes. This metabolic achievement of homeless people was understood in the two dimensions of use and exchange value. Homeless people reworked public spaces in order to produce and consume the use value of housing; they also gathered various materials from public spaces so as to sustain sources of cash income.

What about social movements? In part 3, I argued that activists and volunteers can be real game changers in the rescaled politics of homelessness. I applied Henri Lefebvre's notion of habiting to this aspect of the issue. His seminal work on urban revolution implied that the process of habitat, which is a concept whereby Lefebvre indicated the depoliticising network of public and private spaces, can possibly overcome its own limits as a site of dwelling when it is entered by social movements that are rooted in forms of metabolism other than the "dwelling machine"—the normal mode of housing. This social movement beyond habitat, beyond the dwelling machine, comprises ongoing nonteleological forms of urban-rooted activism struggling with the pregiven form of public and private, towards the urban as a "virtual" goal. Social movements for and with homeless people can be a rare vessel for Lefebvre's habiting movement in our age and a key test case for postregulatory urban politics.

Part 3 also explored three distinguishable subfields in prohomeless and homeless-supporting activism. The first was *placemaking*. Chapter 6 argued that the historical niches of poverty, including the so-called inner-city areas, largely have peripheral positions vis-à-vis the "normal" space of the housing classes and its public/private matrix. Due to this location on the periphery, I contend, the pockets of poverty can be a rare incubator of prohomeless and homeless-supporting imaginaries, which can divorce the activists' existential basis from the hegemonic (housing) classes and thereby emancipate their spontaneous and radical spirits to produce sociocultural places for prohomeless and homeless-supporting work.

The second subfield I looked at was *commoning*. Chapter 7 discussed how social movements for and with homeless people, if they can enjoy these sociocultural places at the margins of habitat, can also nurture strategies and actions to change the regulatory rules over homelessness and its urban environments, against regulators and sometimes against the housing classes, which entails the opening up (commoning) of urban use values to the metabolic circuits of homeless people.

The third subfield is *translating*. Chapter 8 showed that these movements can broaden the geographical coverage of homeless activism, beyond the historical niches of poverty, through remoulding the inherited languages and sociocultures, which this book found originally in peripheral areas, into more adequate forms for far-reaching geographies of homelessness. I argue that this particular aspect can facilitate the cultural migration and relocation of homeless activism to new, broader areas of homelessness that could otherwise be a new locus of rescaling containment. Chapter 9 revealed even newer and broader geographies of homeless activism and rescaling regulation in Japan, showing a broader applicability of my theoretical approach, beyond this book's main cases.

Finally, each chapter from Chapter 3 onward employed a critical methodology of abstraction–concretisation that was elaborated in part 1. In order to avoid a straightforward application of theory to Japan, the more "empirical" chapters in parts 2 and 3 employed the following methodological procedures. First, I characterised the theory and its subcomponents, which the book developed throughout, as a meso-converging abstraction that would be most smoothly applicable to the theoretical birthplace of the concepts: Western Europe and North America (while not denying that this domain is internally diverse, of course). Second, I set about specifying the theory and its subcomponents in Japanese contexts. By using the Japanese "developmental state" as a regional thread of specification, the theory was systematically elaborated, along with the Japanese pattern of integral state formation (political, social, or hybrid), public and private spaces, and urban social movements. Third, the work of ethnography was dovetailed into the abstraction method as a project of regulationist ethnography, which found national territorial space and its historical information to be a still important locus for theory-informing reexplanations.

I conclude with some final thoughts on the book's key theoretical and methodological interventions.

Urban Theory and Ethnography

Both Jennifer Robinson (2006, 2016) and Ananya Roy (2009) have advocated the global dissemination of sites and processes of theory production across the world. Though they approach the question in different ways, this interest has led them to the critical reappraisal of Western concepts. For Robinson (2006, p. 3), what is needed is our decisive "parochialising [of] Western knowledge" against its universalist ethos, because that is a necessary way for us to provoke more cosmopolitan practices of urban research against the problematic shadowing of non-Western geographies by Western concepts. For Roy (2009, p. 820), the matter is perhaps less about "polic[ing] the borders across which ideas, policies, and practices flow and mutate". Rather, Roy frames her strategy as an ongoing management of the paradox inherent in any theoretical approaches, that "theories have to be produced *in* place (and it matters *where* they are produced), but that they can then be appropriated, borrowed, and remapped".

It is hoped that the book's methodological orientations can form a manageable political economy response to these criticisms made by postcolonial urban theorists. There is a possibility of loading new meanings and ontologies of urbanisation upon political economy concepts. In this book, this has been achieved through the "empirical" chapters' deep commitment to theory making and specification that developed extended dialogues between political economy concepts and homelessness (in step 1), for one thing, and the concepts and the Japanese case (in step 2), for another (see Figure 1.2). At the same time, I would also note that this theory–empirics dialogue itself has been advanced by the foreground and background utilisation of ethnography, which has mobilised the local and territorial ontology of the ethnographer who can incite theory making and specification in bottom-up ways.

The deregulation of urban marginality is not nonregulation (Roy 2009, p. 826). Such deregulation, in fact, is a form of urban regulation that has increased in importance during the past few decades of globalisation and neoliberalisation. By drawing new linkages between political economy concepts and these shadowy urban worlds, both topical and geographical, this book has charted an approach that perhaps can respond to Robinson's and Roy's productive relativisations. I have used the ethnographer's role to "sink" political economy concepts in the urban worlds of deregulation (and reregulation) and to enlist them within the epistemologies and even ontologies internal to these worlds. I believe that this theorist–ethnographer comradeship can help us to overcome the myth of deregulation. In this vein, the traditional concepts can be revitalised with reference to *more* urban issues and geographical areas. The unequivocal power of Western knowledge—"the arbitrary character of the concepts" (Escobar 1995, p. 13)—may well be reweighed from this vantage point.

Remapping Urban Political Economy

In the past few decades, urban political economy has been enormously invigorated by David Harvey, and his work has greatly informed the present book. It should be noted that Harvey is a rare "abstractor" whose exemplification covers homelessness (Harvey 2006, 2012). At the same time, Harvey has predominantly used those cases and data that most vividly exemplify his Marxist theory. His favourite cities could be Paris, New York, Baltimore, and the like, to which he would add some southern cities. Other cities—including East Asian cities—have more or less remained at the margins of his empirical scope.

Likewise, even Neil Smith's (1996) and Don Mitchell's (1997, 2003) innovative interpretations of homelessness somewhat identified *local* manifestations of regulation with *global* features of neoliberal urbanisation. The two were in the position to use an intellectually promising domain, New York City, in which gentrification-driven homelessness appeared very acutely. This apparently prompted both Smith and Mitchell to suggest that the extremist neoliberalism in New York City is typical of urban political economy. While New York City could have been understood as just one laboratory of theory (among others), this was not clearly stated. Later works swiftly moved to redefine homelessness as less a product of political economy than a complexity of nuanced, amorphous, mercurial elements. Tendencies like this may have contributed to the general background against which dissatisfactions and counterarguments have arisen, even from political economy approaches and among their sympathisers (Barnes et al. 2007; Brenner 2019; Sayer 1987; Sheppard 2018).

In this context, I would suggest that the survival of abstract categories hinges on how urban political economy can *performatively* show that these categories are still alive, effective, and useful within conjunctural–concrete ("empirical") investigation. In this book, I mobilised the Japanese case in order to practise this performative vindication of the utility of political economy concepts.

This reworking of urban political economy using spaces and politics of homelessness for theory–empirics dialogue implies that political economy concepts can possibly develop productive relations with the threads of contemporary research that seek to revitalise the term *subaltern* by carefully situating it around post-structuralist notions (see Jazeel and Legg 2019). Passing through the prism of Lefebvrian, Gramscian, Harveyan, or other Marxian categories, this book's subaltern materials have disclosed how spaces of homelessness catalyse state/social/hybrid forms of power at the margins of habitat (qua the matrix of public/private spaces), and yet how spaces of homelessness can nurture, in the ambit of these power forms, the various subaltern actions of relative autonomy (autogestion) search by homeless people and social movement participants.

Habitat and Urban Class Relations

The urban social movements discussed here internalise limits, and these limits largely originate from their counterhegemonic enunciation of a hegemonic paradigm of urban societalisation. It may be largely inevitable that homelessness and social movements in this book take on somewhat "dissident" colour insofar as they illuminate the shadows of societalisation around the housing classes. If prohomeless/homeless-supporting activism lacks or negates all such disruptive elements, the unlocking of urban use values beyond the housing classes may be unimaginable. A consistent tracking of such theoretically articulable enunciation and contestation of "habitat form" (qua urban form) may offer an opportunity for urban theorists to disclose the still hidden contours, milieus, and deployments of state space and urban regulation.

Henri Lefebvre's *Urban Revolution* (2003a [1970]) charted a major meso-theoretical picture in which he anticipated both the contemporary role of the habiting movement and its (provisional) decline in neocapitalist urbanisation, largely up until the 1970s. The present book has extended this periodisation to the recent patterns of homeless-related (de)contestation so that Lefebvre's period-sensitive analysis of habitat/habiting can be recontextualised for today's urban process. Further conceptual and empirical investigation—into various forms of urban marginality and contestation—would be helpful.

Homelessness uniquely characterised the early history of modern capitalism in Western cities (Engels 1954 [1872], 1993 [1845]), but contemporary homelessness takes on a different form of appearance (Hayashi 2015). More recently, that is, *urban* parameters influence homelessness, making the (non)housing question into the question of *urbanised* class relations (i.e., relations of and around the housing classes in the city). I observe these parameters in the corrosive survival of the housing classes, on the one hand, and the equally corrosive maintenance of public and private spaces, on the other, which provoke regulation–counterregulation dynamics in the city as a strategic site of societalisation under capitalism.

In turn, this suggests that urban marginality research and social movement research can be more deeply related to the regulationist urban agendas so that (de)contestation around imminent urban marginalisation and poverty can be understood as processes and ramifications of multiscalar regulatory dynamics focusing on cities as a key medium of societalisation and integral state space.

Integral State Rescaling

State rescaling has provided a broad theoretical arena in which urban-focusing scholars can examine their diverse topical interests in relation to the territoriality of state space, with reference to its historicity and restructuring. Key scholars have used the notion of rescaling in autocritical, self-contained ways, by defining it as a meso-level abstraction or by seeing it as a form intrinsic to the West, emphasising the regional–theoretical historicity of Atlantic Fordism and its own transformation. In their case, the conceptual elements of state rescaling theory were effectively collated by their emphasis on a meso-level periodisation that is regionally rooted in North America and Western Europe (N. Brenner 2002, 2004a). In this light, the present book has been keen to appreciate this theorisation from a perspective on integral state rescaling by visiting both the state and social sectors as well as their collaborations and hybrids, which generate various bottom-up efforts for urban poverty governance.

A systematic translation of this theory to non-Western state space can give a full consideration to the meanings of meso-theoretical arguments originally powerfully organised around these Western geographies. On this basis, it would be helpful for us to specify by using regional literatures, and to concretise through multiple ethnographic engagements, state rescaling theory in various contexts outside of the West. In this book, I have used Japanese state space to attempt this vein of theory mobility and translation. This use of the "Japanese laboratory" for the theoretical question of (integral) state rescaling may provide the opportunity for further work within non-Western settings, through which we may translate state rescaling theory and spatialised political economy beyond their theoretical birthplace and birth scale.

References

Books and Journal Articles

Abe, A. (2014). *Kodomo no Hinkon II* [Child Poverty II]. Tokyo: Iwanami Shoten.
Aglietta, M. (1979 [1976]). *A Theory of Capitalist Regulation: The US Experience* (trans. D. Fernbach). London: Verso.
Akimoto, R. (1971). *Gendai Toshi no Kenryoku Kōzō* [The Power Structure of Contemporary Cities]. Tokyo: Aoki Shoten.
Amamiya, K. (2009). "Yowaimono ga yowaimono o tataku" kara dakkyaku dekiruka [Can we escape from the situation in which "the weak beat the weaker"?]. *Subaru* 31 (3): 195–198.
Amaral, D. (2021). Who banishes? City power and anti-homeless policy in San Francisco. *Urban Affairs Review* 57 (6): 1524–1557.
Amin, A. (ed.) (1994). *Post-Fordism: A Reader*. Oxford: Blackwell.
Amix, J.A. (2004). *Japan's Financial Crisis: Institutional Rigidity and Reluctant Change*. Princeton, NJ: Princeton University Press.
Ando, K. and Ishikawa, A. (eds.) (1980). *Nihonteki Keiē no Tenki: Nenkōsē to Shūshin Kōyō wa Dōnaruka* [A Turning Point in Japanese Corporation Management: What Will Happen to Seniority Wages and Lifetime Employment?]. Tokyo: Yuhikaku.
Angelo, H. and Wachsmuth, D. (2015). Urbanizing urban political ecology: a critique of methodological cityism. *International Journal of Urban and Reginal Research* 39 (1): 16–27.
Aoki, H. (1989). *Hiyatoi Rōdōsha no Sē to Shi* [The Life and Death of Day Laborers]. Tokyo: Akashi Shoten.
Aoki, H. (2000). *Gendai Nihon no Toshikasō* [The Lower Classes of Contemporary Japan]. Tokyo: Akashi Shoten.
Appadurai, A. (1996). *Modernity at Large: Cultural Dimensions of Globalization*. Minneapolis MN: University of Minnesota Press.

Arrighi, G. (1994). *The Long Twentieth Century: Money, Power and the Origins of Our Times.* London: Verso.

Arrighi, G. (2007). *Adam Smith in Beijing: Lineages of the Twenty-First Century.* London: Verso.

Bando, M. (2005). Homuresu chīki sēkatu ikō shien jigyō ni okeru apāto no jittai: toyama kōen no baai [Housing conditions of formerly homeless people in the programme to facilitate community-based lives: the case of Toyama Park]. *Shelter-less* 26: 241–247.

Barnes, T., Peck, J., Sheppard, E., and Tickell, A. (2007). Methods matter: transformations in economic geography. In: *Politics and Practice in Economic Geography* (ed. A. Tickell, E. Sheppard, J. Peck, and T. Barnes), 1–24. London: Sage.

Barnes, T. and Sheppard, E. (2010). 'Nothing includes everything': towards engaged pluralism in Anglophone economic geography. *Progress in Human Geography* 34 (2): 193–214.

Baudrillard, J. (1998 [1970]). *The Consumer Society: Myths and Structures* (trans. C. Turner). London: Sage.

Baumohl, J. (1996). *Homelessness in America.* Phoenix, AZ: Oryx Press.

Blau, J. (1992). *The Visible Poor: Homelessness in the United States.* Oxford: Oxford University Press.

Blomley, N. (2009). Homelessness, rights, and the delusions of property. *Urban Geography* 30 (6): 577–590.

Boothman, D. (2010). Translation and translatability: renewal of the Marxist paradigm. In: *Gramsci, Language, and Translation* (ed. P. Ives and R. Lacorte), 107–133. Lanham, MD: Lexington Books.

Boudreau, J., Hamel, P., Jouve, B., and Keil, R. (2007). New state spaces in Canada: metropolitanization in Montreal and Toronto compared. *Urban Geography* 28 (1): 30–53.

Boyer, R. (1990). *The Regulation School: A Critical Introduction* (trans. C. Charney). New York, NY: Columbia University Press.

Boyer, R. (2004). *The Future of Economic Growth: As New Becomes Old.* Cheltenham: Edward Elgar.

Boyer, R. and Saillard, Y. (2002 [1995]). *Régulation Theory: The State of the Art* (trans. C. Shread). Abingdon: Routledge.

Boyer, R. and Yamada, T. (eds.) (2000). *Japanese Capitalism in Crisis: A Regulationist Interpretation.* Abingdon: Routledge.

Bratt, R.G., Hartman, C., and Meyerson, A. (eds.) (1986). *Critical Perspectives on Housing.* Philadelphia, PA: Temple University Press.

Brenner, N. (1998). Between fixity and motion: accumulation, territorial organization and the historical geography of spatial scales. *Environment and Planning D: Society and Space* 16 (4): 459–481.

Brenner, N. (1999). Globalization as reterritorialization: the re-scaling of urban governance in the European Union. *Urban Studies* 36 (3): 431–451.

Brenner, N. (2002). Decoding the newest "metropolitan regionalism" in the USA: a critical overview. *Cities* 19 (1): 3–21.

Brenner, N. (2004a). *New State Spaces: Urban Governance and the Rescaling of Statehood.* Oxford: Oxford University Press.

Brenner, N. (2004b). Urban governance and the production of new state spaces in Western Europe, 1960–2000. *Review of International Political Economy* 11 (3): 447–488.

Brenner, N. (2009). A thousand leaves: notes on the geographies of uneven spatial development. In: *Leviathan Undone? Towards a Political Economy of Scale* (ed. R. Keil and R. Mahon), 27–49. Vancouver: University of British Columbia Press.

Brenner, N. (ed.) (2014). *Implosions / Explosions: Towards a Study of Planetary Urbanization*. Berlin: Jovis.

Brenner, N. (2019). *New Urban Spaces: Urban Theory and the Scale Question*. Oxford: Oxford University Press.

Brenner, N., Marcuse, P., and Mayer, M. (2012). *Cities for People, Not for Profit: Critical Urban Theory and the Right to the City*. Abingdon: Routledge.

Brenner, N. and Theodore, N. (eds.) (2002). *Spaces of Neoliberalism: Urban Restructuring in North America and Western Europe*. Oxford: Blackwell.

Brenner, R. (2002). *The Boom and the Bubble: The US in the World Economy*. London: Verso.

Burawoy, M. (2000). Introduction: reaching for the global. In: *Global Ethnography: Forces, Connections, and Imaginations in a Postmodern World* (ed. M. Burawoy, J.A. Blum, S. George et al.), 1–40. Berkeley, CA: University of California Press.

Burawoy, M. (2009). *The Extended Case Method: Four Countries, Four Decades, Four Great Transformations, and One Theoretical Tradition*. Barkley, CA: University of California Press.

Burawoy, M., Blum, J.A., George, S. et al. (2000). *Global Ethnography: Forces, Connections, and Imaginations in a Postmodern World*. Berkeley, CA: University of California Press.

Burkett, P. (1999). *Marx and Nature: A Red and Green Perspective*. New York, NY: St Martin's Press.

Burnett, P. (1973). Social change, the status of women and models of city form and development. *Antipode* 5 (3): 57–62.

Burrows, R., Pleace, N., and Quilgars, D. (1997). *Homelessness and Social Policy*. Abingdon: Routledge.

Castells, M. (1977 [1972]). *The Urban Question: A Marxist Approach* (trans. A. Sheridan). Cambridge, MA: MIT Press.

Castells, M. (1983). *The City and the Grassroots: A Cross-Cultural Theory of Urban Social Movements*. Berkeley, CA: University of California Press.

Clifford, J. and Marcus, G.E. (eds.) (1986). *Writing Culture: The Poetics and Politics of Ethnography*. Berkeley, CA: University of California Press.

Cloke, P., May, J., and Johnsen, S. (2010). *Swept Up Lives? Re-Envisioning the Homeless City*. Chichester: Wiley-Blackwell.

Cloke, P., Milbourne, P., and Widdowfield, R. (2002). *Rural Homelessness: Issues, Experiences and Policy Responses*. Bristol: Policy Press.

Clump, J. (2003). *Nikkeiren and Japanese Capitalism*. Abingdon: Routledge.

Collinge, C. (1999). Self-organisation of society by scale: a spatial reworking of regulation theory. *Environment and Planning D: Society and Space* 17 (5): 557–574.

Coriat, B., Geoffron, P., and Rubinstein, M. (2000). Some limitations to Japanese competitiveness. In: *Japanese Capitalism in Crisis* (ed. R. Boyer and T. Yamada), 175–191. Abingdon: Routledge.

Cox, K.R. (1997). *Spaces of Globalization: Reasserting the Power of the Local*. New York, NY: Guilford Press.
Cox, K.R. and Mair, A. (1988). Locality and community in the politics of local economic development. *Annals of the Association of American Geographers* 78 (2): 307–325.
Cress, D. and Snow, D.A. (2000). The outcomes of homeless mobilization: the influence of organization, disruption, political mediation, and framing. *The American Journal of Sociology* 105 (4): 1063–1104.
Cresswell, T. (2015). *Place: An Introduction*, 2nd ed. Chichester: Wiley-Blackwell.
Croteau, D. and Hicks, L. (2003). Coalition framing and the challenge of a constant frame pyramid: the case of a collaborative response to homelessness. *Social Problems* 50 (2): 251–272.
Cumings, B. (1999). *Parallax Vision: Making Sense of American-East Asian Relations*. Durham, NC: Duke University Press.
Daly, G. (1996). *Homeless: Policies, Strategies, and Lives on the Street*. Abingdon: Routledge.
Davis, G.F., McAdam, D., Scott, W.R., and Zald, M.N. (eds.) (2005). *Social Movements and Organization Theory*. Cambridge: Cambridge University Press.
Davis, M. (1986). *Prisoners of the American Dream: Politics and Economy in the History of the U.S. Working Class*. London: Verso.
Davis, M. (1992). Fortress Los Angeles: the militarization of urban space. In: *Variations on a Theme Park: The New American City and the End of Public Space* (ed. M. Sorkin), 154–180. New York, NY: Hill and Wang.
Dear, M. and Scott, A.J. (eds.) (1981). *Urbanization and Urban Planning in Capitalist Society*. London: Methuen.
Deleuze, G. (1988 [1986]). *Foucault* (trans. S. Hand). Minneapolis, MN: University of Minnesota Press.
Desai, R. (2013). *Geopolitical Economy: After US Hegemony, Globalization and Empire*. London: Pluto Press.
Development Bank of Japan (2016). Higashinihon Daishinsai kara Gonen: Atarashī Sēchō ni Mukete [Five Years after the Great East Japan Earthquake: Towards New Growth]. Tokyo: Development Bank of Japan. https://www.dbj.jp/pdf/investigate/area/tohoku/pdf_all/tohoku1602_01.pdf (accessed 27 October 2021).
DeVerteuil, G. (2006). The local state and homeless shelters: beyond revanchism? *Cities* 23 (2): 109–120.
DeVerteuil, G. (2013). Where has NIMBY gone in urban social geography? *Social and Cultural Geography* 14 (6): 599–603.
DeVerteuil, G. (2015). *Resilience in the Post-Welfare Inner City: Voluntary Sector Geographies in London, Los Angeles and Sydney*. Bristol: Policy Press.
DeVerteuil, G., Lee, W., and Wolch, J. (2002). New spaces for the local welfare state? The case of general relief in Los Angeles County. *Social & Cultural Geography* 3 (3): 229–246.
DeVerteuil, G., Marr, M., and Snow, D. (2009). Any space left? Homeless resistance by place-type in Los Angeles County. *Urban Geography* 30 (6): 633–651.

DeVerteuil, G., May, J., and von Mahs, J. (2009). Complexity not collapse: recasting the geographies of homelessness in a 'punitive' age. *Progress in Human Geography* 33 (5): 646–666.

Dower, J.W. (1999). *Embracing Defeat: Japan in the Wake of World War II*. New York, NY: W.W. Norton & Company.

Eckstein, D., Künzel, V., Schäfer, L., and Winges, M. (2019). *Global Climate Index 2020: Who Suffers Most from Extreme Weather Events? Weather-Related Loss Events in 2018 and 1999 to 2018*. Berlin: Germanwatch. https://www.germanwatch.org/sites/germanwatch.org/files/20-2-01e%20Global%20Climate%20Risk%20Index%202020_14.pdf (accessed 27 October 2021).

Eguchi, E. (1979). *Gendai no Teishotokusha Sō, Jyō* [The "Low-Income Strata" in the Contemporary Period, 1]. Tokyo: Miraisha.

Eguchi, E. (1980a). *Gendai no Teishotokusha Sō, Chū* [The "Low-Income Strata" in the Contemporary Period, 2]. Tokyo: Miraisha.

Eguchi, E. (1980b). *Gendai no Teishotokusha Sō, Ge* [The "Low Income Strata" in the Contemporary Period, 3]. Tokyo: Miraisha.

Eguchi, E., Nishioka, Y., and Kato, Y. (eds.) (1979). *San'ya: Shitsugyō no Gendaiteki Imi* [San'ya: Contemporary Meanings of Poverty]. Tokyo: Mirai Sha.

Ekers, M., Hart, G., Kipfer, S., and Loftus, A. (eds.) (2013). *Gramsci: Space, Nature, Politics*. Chichester: Wiley-Blackwell.

Ekers, M. and Loftus, A. (2013). Revitalizing the production of nature thesis: a Gramscian turn? *Progress in Human Geography* 37 (2): 234–252.

Elden, S. (2013). *The Birth of Territory*. Chicago, IL: University of Chicago Press.

Endo, K. (1976). 'Kuwasero' kara 'nekasero' e: chīki undo kara rōdōsha kumiai undo e [From "let us eat" to "let us sleep": from a local movement to a day-labourers' movement]. *Hukushi Kiyō* combined issue of numbers 6, 7, and 8: 169–226.

Engels, F. (1954 [1872]). *The Housing Question*. Moscow: Progress Publishers.

Engels, F. (1993 [1845]). *The Condition of the Working Class in England* (trans. D. McLellan). Oxford: Oxford University Press.

Erickson, P.A. and Murphy, L.D. (2013). *A History of Anthropological Theory*, 4th ed. Toronto: University of Toronto Press.

Escobar, A. (1995). *Empowering Development: The Making and Unmaking of the Third World*. Princeton, NJ: Princeton University Press.

Esping-Andersen, G. (1990). *The Three Worlds of Welfare Capitalism*. Cambridge: Polity.

Esping-Andersen, G. (ed.) (1996). *Welfare States in Transition: National Adaptations in Global Economies*. London: Sage.

Esping-Andersen, G. (1997). Hybrid or unique? The Japanese welfare state between Europe and America. *Journal of European Social Policy* 7 (3): 179–189.

Estevez-Abe, M. (2008). *Welfare and Capitalism in Postwar Japan*. Cambridge: Cambridge University Press.

Fairbanks, R.P. and Lloyd, R. (2011). Critical ethnography and the neoliberal city: the US example. *Ethnography* 12 (1): 3–11.

Featherstone, D. (2012). *Solidarity: Hidden Histories and Geographies of Internationalism*. London: Zed Books.

Featherstone, D. (2013). "Gramsci in action": space, politics, and the making of solidarities. In: *Gramsci: Space, Nature, Politics* (ed. M. Ekers, G. Hart, S. Kipfer, and A. Loftus), 65–103. Chichester: Wiley-Blackwell.

Fooks, G. and Pantazis, C. (1999). The criminalisation of homelessness, begging and street living. In: *Homelessness: Exploring the New Terrain* (ed. P. Kennett and M. Alex), 123–159. Bristol: Policy Press.

Foster, J.B. (2000). *Marx's Ecology: Materialism and Nature*. New York, NY: Monthly Review Press.

Foucault, M. (2003 [1997]). *"Society Must be Defended": Lectures at the Collège de France* (trans. D. Macey). New York, NY: Picador.

Fraser, D. (2003). *The Evolution of the British Welfare State*, 3rd ed. Houndmills: Palgrave Macmillan.

Fraser, N. (1990). Rethinking the public sphere: a contribution to the critique of actually existing democracy. *Social Text* 25/26: 56–80.

Fraser, N. and Gordon, L. (1994). A genealogy of dependency: tracing a keyword of the US welfare state. *Signs* 19 (2): 309–336.

Fujii, K. and Tamaki, M. (2003). *Henken kara Kyōsē e: Nagoya Hatsu Hōmuresu Mondai o Kangaeru* [From Prejudice to Coexistence: Considering the Homelessness Question from Nagoya]. Nagoya, Japan: Fubai Sha.

Fujita, H. (2006). *Rojō no Kunigara: Yuragu "Kanson Minpi"* [National Characters in the Streets: Shifts in the "Subjugation of People by Authorities"]. Tokyo: Bungei Shunju.

Gandy, M. (2004). Rethinking urban metabolism: water, space and the modern city. *City* 8 (3): 363–379.

Gardner, K. and Lewis, D. (1996). *Anthropology, Development and the Post-modern Challenge*. London: Pluto Press.

Geertz, C. (1973). Thick description: toward an interpretive theory of culture. In: *The Interpretation of Cultures: Selected Essays*, 3–30. New York, NY: Basic Books.

Gibson-Graham, J.K. (2006). *A Postcapitalist Politics*. Minneapolis, MN: University of Minnesota Press.

Gill, T. (2001). *Men of Uncertainty: The Social Organization of Day Laborers in Contemporary Japan*. Albany, NY: State University of New York Press.

Goffman, E. (1963). *Behavior in Public Places: Notes on the Social Organization in Gatherings*. New York, NY: Free Press.

Goffman, E. (1971). *Relations in Public*. New York, NY: Basic Books.

Goodwin, M. and Painter, J. (1996). Local governance, the crisis of Fordism and the changing geographies of regulation. *Transactions of the Institute of British Geographers* NS 21 (4): 635–648.

Goonewardena, K. (2012). Space and revolution in theory and practice: eight theses. In: *Cities for People, Not for Profit: Critical Urban Theory and the Right to the City* (ed. N. Brenner, P. Marcuse, and M. Mayer), 86–101. Abingdon: Routledge.

Goonewardena, K., Kipfer, S., Milgrom, R., and Schmid, C. (eds.) (2008). *Space, Difference, Everyday Life: Reading Henri Lefebvre*. New York, NY: Routledge.

Gordon, A. (1985). *The Evolution of Labor Relations in Japan: Heavy Industry, 1853–1955.* Cambridge, MA: Harvard University Press.

Gottfried, H. (2000). Compromising positions: emergent neo-Fordisms and embedded gender contracts. *British Journal of Sociology* 51 (2): 235–259.

Gottfried, H. (2013). *The Reproductive Bargain: Deciphering the Enigma of Japanese Capitalism.* Leiden: Brill.

Gough, J. (2002). Neoliberalism and socialization in the contemporary city: opposites, complements and instabilities. *Antipode* 34 (3): 405–426.

Gowan, T. (2000). Excavating "globalization" from street level: homeless men recycle their pasts. In: *Global Ethnography: Forces, Connections, and Imaginations in a Postmodern World* (ed. M. Burawoy, J.A. Blum, S. George et al.), 74–105. Berkeley: University of California Press.

Gowan, T. (2010). *Hobos, Hustlers and Backsliders: Homeless in San Francisco.* Minneapolis MN: University of Minnesota Press.

Graham, S. and Marvin, S. (2001). *Splintering Urbanism: Networked Infrastructures, Technological Mobilities and the Urban Condition.* Abingdon: Routledge.

Gramsci, A. (1971). *Selections from the Prison Notebooks* (trans. Q. Hoare and G.N. Smith). New York, NY: International Publishers.

Gramsci, A. (1992). *Prison Notebooks*, 1 (trans. J.A. Buttigieg and A. Callari). New York, NY: Columbia University Press.

Hague, E., Thomas, C., and Williams, S. (1999). Left out? Observations on the RGS-IBG conference on social exclusion and the city. *Area* 31 (3): 293–296.

Hamnett, C. (2010). The reshaping of the British welfare system and its implications for geography and geographers. *Progress in Human Geography* 35 (2): 147–152.

Hanson, S. and Pratt, G. (1988). Reconceptualizing the links between home and work in urban geography. *Economic Geography* 64 (4): 299–321.

Hanson, S. and Pratt, G. (1995). *Gender, Work, and Space.* Abingdon: Routledge.

Haraguchi, T. (2010). Yoseba "kamagasaki" no sēsan katē ni miru kūkan no sēji: "basho no kōchiku" to "sēdoteki jissen" no shiten kara [Politics of space in the production process of the yoseba "Kamagasaki": from the perspectives of "place construction" and "institutional practice"]. In: *Hōmuresu Sutadīzu* [Homeless Studies] (ed. H. Aoki), 63–106. Kyoto: Minerva Shobo.

Hardt, M. and Negri, A. (2009). *Commonwealth.* Cambridge, MA: Belknap Press of Harvard University Press.

Hart, G. (2013). Gramsci, geography, and the languages of populism. In: *Gramsci: Space, Nature, Politics* (ed. M. Ekers, G. Hart, S. Kipfer, and A. Loftus), 301–320. Chichester: Wiley-Blackwell.

Harvey, D. (1972). Revolutionary and counter revolutionary theory in geography and the problem of ghetto formation. *Antipode* 4 (2): 1–13.

Harvey, D. (1973). *Social Justice and the City.* London: Edward Arnold.

Harvey, D. (1976). Labor, capital, and class struggle around the built environment in advanced capitalist societies. *Politics & Society* 6 (3): 265–295.

Harvey, D. (1982). *The Limits to Capital.* Oxford: Basil Blackwell.

Harvey, D. (1985a). *Consciousness and the Urban Experience: Studies in the History and Theory of Capitalist Urbanization*. Baltimore, MD: Johns Hopkins University Press.

Harvey, D. (1985b). *The Urbanization of Capital: Studies in the History and Theory of Capitalist Urbanization*. Baltimore, MD: Johns Hopkins University Press.

Harvey, D. (1989a). The urbanization of capital. In: *The Urban Experience*, 17–58. Baltimore, MD: Johns Hopkins University Press.

Harvey, D. (1989b). *The Urban Experience*. Baltimore, MD: Johns Hopkins University Press.

Harvey, D. (1989c). The urban process under capitalism: a framework for analysis. In: *The Urban Experience*, 59–89. Baltimore, MD: Johns Hopkins University Press.

Harvey, D. (2006). The political economy of public space. In: *The Politics of Public Space* (ed. S. Low and N. Smith), 17–34. Abingdon: Routledge.

Harvey, D. (2008). The right to the city. *New Left Review* 53: 23–40.

Harvey, D. (2012). *Rebel Cities: From the Right to the City to the Urban Revolution*. London: Verso.

Hasegawa, H. (ed.) (1981). *Gendai Nihon Kigyō to Rōshi Kankē* [Modern Japanese Firms and the Labour–Capital Relationship]. Tokyo: Rodo Junpo Sha.

Hasegawa, M. (2006). *"We Are Not Garbage!" The Homeless Movement in Tokyo, 1994–2002*. Abingdon: Routledge.

Hashimoto, K. (2009). *Kakusa no Sengoshi* [The Postwar History of Social Divides]. Tokyo: Kawade Shobo Sinsha.

Hashimoto, K. (2018a). *Shin Nihon no Kaikyū Shakai* [Japan's New Class Society]. Tokyo: Kodansha.

Hashimoto, K. (2018b). *Andā Kurasu* [The Underclass]. Tokyo: Chikuma Shobo.

Hayashi, M. (2003). Shokugyō kaisō to kazoku [Occupational and familial backgrounds]. In: *Kinkyū Ichiji Hogo Sentā Ōta Ryō Riyōsha Jittai Hōkoku Sho* [Research Report on the Resident Users of the Emergency Shelter Ōta Ryō] (ed. Toshi Sēkatsu Kenkyūkai), 57–72. Tokyo: Tokubetsuku Jinjikosei Jimukumiai.

Hayashi, M. (2005). Toshikūkan ni sumikomu nojukusha: 'tsukaeru jimen' eno shin'nyū to kūkan kanri [Homeless people inhabiting urban space: intrusions into "usable spaces" and spatial control]. *Nenpō Shakaigaku Ronshū* 18: 182–191.

Hayashi, M. (2006). Jakunen nojukusha no kēsē to genzon [The solitude of younger street homeless people]. *Japanese Sociological Review* 57 (3): 493–510.

Hayashi, M. (2007). Sēsē suru chīki no kyōkai: naibuka shita "hōmuresu mondai" to sēdo henka no rōkaritei [Emerging boundaries of regional society: geographical diffusions of homeless street people and institutional changes at the local level]. *Soshioroji* 52 (1): 53–69.

Hayashi, M. (2013a). Times and spaces of homeless regulation in Japan, 1950s–2010s: historical and contemporary analysis. *International Journal of Urban and Regional Research* 37 (4): 1188–1212.

Hayashi, M. (2013b). Kenzō kankyō de tashaka sareru jyūtaku kiki: toshi no shizen o meguru rōdō to kanri to yume [Housing crisis being othered at built environments: labour, control, and myths around urban nature]. In: *Toshikūkan ni Hisomu Haijo to*

Hankō no Chikara [Forces of Exclusion and Resistance Inherent in Urban Space] (ed. T. Machimura), 25–60. Tokyo: Akashi Shoten.

Hayashi, M. (2014a). Urban poverty and regulation, new spaces and old: Japan and the US in comparison. *Environment and Planning A* 46 (5): 1203–1225.

Hayashi, M. (2014b). *Hōmuresu to Toshi Kūkan: Shūdatsu to Ika, Shakai Undō, Kokka–Shihon* [Homelessness and Urban Space: Deprivation through Othering, Social Movements, and the State–Capital Nexus]. Tokyo: Akashi Shoten.

Hayashi, M. (2015). Rescaled "rebel cities", nationalization, and the bourgeois utopia: dialectics between urban social movements and regulation for Japan's homeless. *Antipode* 47 (2): 418–441.

Hayashi, M. (2020). Opening up the welfare state to "outsiders": pro-homeless activism and neoliberal backlashes in Japan. In: *Civil Society and the State in Democratic East Asia* (ed. D. Chiavacci, S. Grano, and J. Obinger), 269–298. Amsterdam: Amsterdam University Press.

Hayashi, M. (2021). Democracy against labor movement: Japan's anti-labor developmental state and aftermaths. *Critical Sociology* 47 (1): 37–58.

Hayashi, M. (2022). Theorizing regulation-in-city for homeless people's subaltern strategy and informality: societalization, metabolism, and classes with(out) housing. *Critical Sociology* 48 (2): 323–339.

Hayashi, M. (2023a). Any labour geographies in urban theory? Workers meet Lefebvre and Harvey (yet again). *Antipode* 55 (2): 415–435.

Hayashi, M. (2023b). Toward "no homeless" public spaces? Homeless policy and a crisis of Japanese urban society. In: *Gender, Safety, Inequality: Key Challenges for Japan* (ed. K. Tanaka and H. Selin), 261–277. London: Springer Nature.

Hayford, A.M. (1974). The geography of women: an historical introduction. *Antipode* 6 (2): 1–19.

Heller, H. (2011). *The Birth of Capitalism: A Twenty-First-Century Perspective*. London: Pluto Press.

Herbert, S. (1997). *Policing Space: Territoriality and the Los Angeles Police Department*. Minneapolis, MN: University of Minnesota Press.

Herod, A. (1997). Labor's spatial praxis and the geography of contract bargaining in the US east coast longshore industry, 1953–89. *Political Geography* 16 (2): 145–169.

Heynen, N. (2009). Bending the bars of empire from every ghetto for survival: the Black Panther Party's radical antihunger politics of social reproduction and scale. *Annals of the Association of American Geographers* 99 (2): 406–422.

Heynen, N. (2014). Urban political ecology I: the urban century. *Progress in Human Geography* 38 (4): 598–604.

Heynen, N., Kaika, M., and Swyngedouw, E. (2006). *In the Nature of Cities: Urban Political Ecology and the Politics of Urban Metabolism*. Abingdon: Routledge.

Hirata, K. (1969). *Shiminshakai to Shakaishugi* [Civil Society and Socialism]. Tokyo: Iwanami Shoten.

Hirayama, Y. and Ronald, R. (eds.) (2007). *Housing and Social Transition in Japan*. Abingdon: Routledge.

Hopper, K. (2003). *Reckoning with Homelessness*. Ithaca, NY: Cornell University Press.

Hou, J. (ed.) (2010). *Insurgent Public Space: Guerrilla Urbanism and the Remaking of Contemporary Cities*. Abingdon: Routledge.
Huber, E. and Stephens, J.D. (2001). *Development and Crisis of the Welfare State: Parties and Policies in Global Markets*. Chicago, IL: University of Chicago Press.
Hudson, R. (2001). *Producing Places*. New York, NY: Guilford Press.
Hutchison, M.M., Ito, T., and Westermann, F. (eds.) (2004). *Japan's Lost Decade: Origins, Consequences and Prospects for Recovery*. Oxford: Blackwell.
Hutchison, M.M. and Watermann, F. (eds.) (2006). *Japan's Great Stagnation: Financial and Monetary Policy Lessons for Advanced Economies*. Cambridge, MA: MIT Press.
Hyodo, T. (1978). Shakai kēyaku rōdō undo to kokumin shuntō [Labor movements in a social contract type and the National Spring Offensive]. In: *Nihongata Shotoku Sēsaku to Kokumin Shuntō* [Japanese Income Policy and the National Spring Offensive] (ed. Rodo Undo Kenkyusha Shudan), 87–111. Tokyo: Nihon Hyōron Sha.
Ibori, T. (2001). *Kokyō Jigyō no Tadashī Kangaekata* [The Correct Understanding of Public Works]. Tokyo: Chuo Koron Shinsha.
Ikeda, N. (2009). *Kibo o Suteru Yūki* [Courage to Abandon Hope]. Tokyo: Diamondo Sha.
Ikuta, T. (2007). *Rupo Saitēhen: Huantē Shūrō to Nojuku* [Report on the Lowest Class: Precarious Labour and Homelessness]. Tokyo: Chikuma Shobo.
Imagawa, I. (1987). *Gendai Kimin Kō* [Thoughts on Modern Abandoned People]. Tokyo: Tabata Shoten.
Ishizuka, H. (1977). *Tōkyō no Shakai Kēzaishi: Shihonshugi to Toshimondai* [The History of Society and Economy in Tokyo: Capitalism and Urban Problems]. Tokyo: Kinokuniya Shoten.
Isogai, A., Ebizuka, A., and Uemura, H. (2000). The hierarchical market-firm nexus as the Japanese mode of régulation. In: *Japanese Capitalism in Crisis* (ed. R. Boyer and T. Yamada), 32–53. Abingdon: Routledge.
Itoh, M. (1990). *The World Economic Crisis and Japanese Capitalism*. Houndmills: Macmillan.
Itoh, M. (2000). *The Japanese Economy Reconsidered*. Houndmills: Palgrave.
Itoh, M. (2009). *Sabupuraimu kara Sekai Kyōkō e: Shinjiyūshugi no Owari to Korekara no Sekai* [From the Subprime Crisis to an International Crisis: The End of Neoliberalism and the Future of the World]. Tokyo: Sedo Sha.
Ives, P. (2004). *Gramsci's Politics of Language: Engaging the Bakhtin Circle and the Frankfurt School*. Toronto: University of Toronto Press.
Ives, P. and Lacorte, R. (eds.) (2010). *Gramsci, Language, and Translation*. Lanham, MD: Lexington Books.
Iwasaki, N., Ajisaka, M., Ueda, T. et al. (eds.) (1989). *Chōnaikai no Kenkyū* [A Study of Chōnaikai]. Tokyo: Ochanomizu Shobo.
Iwata, M. (1995). *Sengo Shakaihukushi no Tenkai to Daitoshi Saitēhen* [The Development of Postwar Social Welfare and the Lowest Groups in Large Cities]. Kyoto: Minerva Shobo.
Iwata, M. (2000). *Hōmuresu/Gendai Shakai/Fukushi Kokka: "Ikiteiku Basho" o Megutte* [Homelessness, Contemporary Society, and the Welfare State: On the "Places for Living"]. Tokyo: Akashi Shoten.
Iwata, M. (2005). Sēsaku to hinkon: sengo nihon ni okeru hukushi kategorī to shiteno hinkon to sono imi [Policy and poverty: poverty as a welfare category and its meaning

in postwar Japan]. In: *Hinkon to Shakaiteki Haijo* [Poverty and Social Exclusion] (ed. M. Iwata and A. Nishizawa), 171–184. Kyoto: Minerva Shobo.

Jappe, A. (2013). Sohn-Rethel and the origin of 'real abstraction': a critique of production or a critique of circulation? *Historical Materialism* 21 (1): 3–14.

Jazeel, T. (2014). Subaltern geographies: geographical knowledge and postcolonial strategy. *Singapore Journal of Tropical Geography* 35: 88–103.

Jazeel, T. and Legg, S. (eds.) (2019). *Subaltern Geographies*. Athens, GA: The University of Georgia Press.

Jessop, B. (1982). *The Capitalist State*. Oxford: Basil Blackwell.

Jessop, B. (1990). *State Theory: Putting the Capitalist State in Its Place*. Cambridge: Polity.

Jessop, B. (2002). *The Future of the Capitalist State*. Cambridge: Polity.

Jessop, B. (2004). The gender selectivities of the state: a critical realist analysis. *Journal of Critical Realism* 3 (2): 203–237.

Jessop, B., Bonnet, K., Bromley, S., and Ling, T. (1988). *Thatcherism: A Tale of Two Nations*. Cambridge: Polity.

Jessop, B. and Sum, N. (2006). *Beyond the Regulation Approach: Putting Capitalist Economies in Their Place*. Cheltenham: Edward Elgar.

Jinbo, T. (2009). Medeia hihyō, dai 15 kai [Media critique no.15]. *Sekai* 788: 126–133.

Johnsen, S. and Fitzpatrick, S. (2010). Revanchist sanitation or coercive care? The use of enforcement to combat begging, street drinking and rough sleeping in England. *Urban Studies* 47 (8): 1703–1723.

Jonas, A.E.G. (1994). The scale politics of spatiality. *Environment and Planning D: Society and Space* 12 (3): 257–264.

Jonas, A.E.G. (1996). Local labour control regimes: uneven development and the social regulation of production. *Regional Studies* 30 (4): 323–338.

Johnson, C. (1982). *MITI and the Japanese Miracle: The Growth of Industrial Policy, 1925–1975*. Stanford, CA: Stanford University Press.

Jones, M. (1997). Spatial selectivity of the state? The regulationist enigma and local struggles over economic governance. *Environment and Planning A* 29 (5): 831–864.

Jones, M. and MacLeod, G. (1999). Towards a regional renaissance? Reconfiguring and rescaling England's economic governance. *Transactions of the Institute of British Geographers* 24 (3): 295–313.

Kamata, T. (ed.) (1999). *Hinkon to Kazoku Hōkai* [Poverty and Family Breakdown]. Kyoto: Minerva Shobo.

Kamata, T. and Kamata, T. (1983). *Shakai Shokaiso to Gendai Kazoku* [Social Classes and the Contemporary Family]. Tokyo: Ochanimizu Shobo.

Kariya, Y. (2006). *Hurachi na Kibō* [Immoral Hope]. Kyoto: Shorai Sha.

Kasai, K. (1999). *Shinjuku Houmuresu Funsen Ki: Tachinoke do Kiesarazu* [Records of How Homeless People Resisted in Shinjuku: Retreat, Not Disappearance]. Tokyo: Gendai Kikaku Shitsu.

Kasai, K. (2005). Chīki sēkatsu ikō shien jigyō no kon'nichi nani o hatten sase nani o kadai to subeki ka? [What should we improve and what should we question today with the Programme to Facilitate Community-Based Lives]. *Shelter-less* 25: 70–81.

Kase, K. (1997). *Syūdan Shūshoku no Jidai: Shūsan Shūshoku no Ninaite Tachi* [The Era of a Collective Employment System: Participants in the System]. Tokyo: Aoki Shoten.

Katayama, S. (2012). *Shōjiki Mono Ni Yaruki o Nakusaseru? Hukushi Izon no Inmoraru* [Discouraging Honest People? The Immorality of Welfare Dependence]. Tokyo: Okura Shuppan.

Kato, T. and Steven, R. (eds.) (1993). *Is Japanese Management Post-Fordist?* Tokyo: Mado Sha.

Kawahara, K. (2005). Hukushi sēsaku to josē no hinkon: hōmuresu jyōtai no hinkon ni taisuru shisetsu hogo [Welfare policy and women's poverty: the institutional protection of the homeless poor]. In: *Hinkon to Shakaiteki Haijo* [Poverty and Social Exclusion] (ed. M. Iwata and A. Nishizawa), 195–222. Kyoto: Minerva Shobo.

Keil, R. and Mahon, R. (eds.) (2009). *Leviathan Undone? Towards a Political Economy of Scale*. Vancouver: University of British Columbia Press.

Kiener, J. and Mizuuchi, T. (2018). Homelessness and homeless policies in the context of the residual Japanese welfare state. In: *Faces of Homelessness in the Asia Pacific* (ed. C. Zufferey and N. Yu), 9–27. Abingdon: Routledge.

Kitagawa, Y. (2001). Nojukusha no shūdan kēsē to iji no katē [The process of group formation and sustenance among homeless people]. *The Liberation of Humankind: A Sociological Review* 15: 54–74.

Kitagawa, Y. (2006). Nojuku sha no saisenbetsu katē [The reselection process of homeless people]. In: *Hurachi na Kibō* [Immoral Hope] (ed. A. Kariya), 119–160. Kyoto: Shorai Sha.

Kitagawa, Y., Kawahara, K., and Hayashi, M. (2003). *Kinkyū Ichiji Hogo Sentā Ōta Ryō Riyōsha Jittai Chōsa (Siryō Hen)* [Actual Report on the Users of the Emergency Shelter Ōta Ryō (Data Edition)]. Tokyo: Tokubetsu Ku Jinji Kose Jimu Kumiai.

Kohn, M. (2004). *Brave New Neighborhoods: The Privatization of Public Space*. New York, NY: Routledge.

Konno, H. (2012). *Burakku Kigyō: Nihon o Kuitsubusu Yōkai* [The Evil Enterprise: A Monster that Destroys Japan]. Tokyo: Bunge Shunju.

Krätke, S. (1999). A regulationist approach to regional studies. *Environment and Planning A* 31 (4): 683–704.

Kwon, H. (ed.) (2005). *Transforming the Developmental Welfare State in East Asia*. Houndmills: Palgrave Macmillan.

Lawson, V., Elwood, S., Canevaro, S., and Viotti, N. (2015). "The poor are us": middle-class poverty politics in Buenos Aires and Seattle. *Environment and Planning A* 47 (9): 1873–1891.

Lefebvre, H. (1976 [1973]). *The Survival of Capitalism* (trans. F. Bryant). London: Allison and Busby.

Lefebvre, H. (1984 [1971]). *Everyday Life in the Modern World* (trans. P. Wander). New Brunswick, NJ: Transaction Publishers.

Lefebvre, H. (1991 [1974]). *The Production of Space* (trans. D. Nicholson-Smith). Malden, MA: Blackwell.

Lefebvre, H. (1996 [1967]). Right to the city (trans. E. Kofman and E. Lebas). In: *Writings on Cities* (ed. E. Kofman and E. Lebas), 61–181. Malden, MA: Blackwell.

Lefebvre, H. (2003a [1970]). *The Urban Revolution* (trans. R. Bononno). Minneapolis, MN: University of Minnesota Press.

Lefebvre, H. (2003b [1966]). Preface to the study of the habitat of the 'pavillion'. In: *Henry Lefebvre: Key Writings* (ed. S. Elden, E. Lebas, and E. Kofman), 121–135. New York, NY: Continuum.

Lefebvre, H. (2009a [1966]). Theoretical problem of autogestion (trans. G. Moore, N. Brenner, and S. Elden). In: *State, Space, World: Selected Essays* (ed. N. Brenner and S. Elden), 138–152. Minneapolis, MN: University of Minnesota Press.

Lefebvre, H. (2009b). *State, Space, World: Selected Essays* (ed. N. Brenner and S. Elden). Minneapolis, MN: University of Minnesota Press.

Lefebvre, H. (2009c [1979]). Comments on a new state form (trans. V.S. Johnson and N. Brenner). In: *State, Space, World: Selected Essays* (ed. N. Brenner and S. Elden), 124–137. Minneapolis, MN: University of Minnesota Press.

Legg, S. (2016). Empirical and analytical subaltern space? Ashrams, brothels and trafficking in colonial Delhi. *Cultural Studies* 30 (5): 793–815.

Leitner, H., Sheppard, E., and Sziarto, K.M. (2008). The spatialities of contentious politics. *Transactions of the Institute of British Geographers* NS 33: 157–172.

Li, Z., Xu, J., and Yeh, A.G.O. (2014). State rescaling and the making of city-regions in the Pearl River Delta, China. *Environment and Planning C: Politics and Space* 32 (1): 129–143.

Lim, K.F. (2017). State rescaling, policy experimentation and path dependency in post-Mao China: a dynamic analytical framework. *Regional Studies* 51 (10): 1580–1593.

Linebaugh, P. (1976). Karl Marx, the theft of wood, and working-class composition: a contribution to the current debate. *Crime and Social Justice* 6: 5–16.

Linebaugh, P. (2008). *The Magna Carta Manifesto: Liberties and Commons for All*. Berkley, CA: University of California Press.

Linebaugh, P. (2014). *Stop, Thief! The Commons, Enclosures, and Resistance*. Oakland, CA: PM Press.

Lipietz, A. (1994). The national and the regional: their autonomy vis-à-vis the capitalist world order. In: *Transcending the State-Global Divide: A Neostructuralist Agenda in International Relations* (ed. R.P. Palan and B. Gills), 23–43. Boulder, CO: Lynne Rienner.

Loftus, A. (2015). Violent geographical abstractions. *Environment and Planning D: Society and Space* 33 (2): 366–381.

Logan, J.R. and Molotch, H.L. (1987). *Urban Fortunes: The Political Economy of Place*. California, CA: University of California Press.

Low, S. (2003). *Behind the Gates: Life, Security, and the Pursuit of Happiness in Fortress America*. Abingdon: Routledge.

Low, S. and Smith, N. (eds.) (2006). *The Politics of Public Space*. Abingdon: Routledge.

Lowe, S. (1997). Homelessness and the law. In: *Homelessness and Social Policy* (ed. R. Burrows, N. Pleace, and D. Quilgars), 19–34. Abingdon: Routledge.

Luxemburg, R. (2003 [1913]). *The Accumulation of Capital*. Abingdon: Routledge.

MacKenzie, S. and Rose, D. (1983). Industrial change, the domestic economy and home life. In: *Redundant Spaces in Cities and Regions? Studies in Industrial Decline and Social Change* (ed. J. Anderson, S. Duncan, and R. Hudson), 155–200. London: Academic Press.

MacKinnon, D. and Show, J. (2010). New state spaces, agency and scale: devolution and the regeonalisation of transport governance in Scotland. *Antipode* 42 (5): 1226–1252.

MacLeavy, J. and Harrison, J. (2010). New state spatialities: perspectives on state, space, and scalar geographies. *Antipode* 42 (5): 1037–1046.

MacLeod, G. (1999). Entrepreneurial spaces, hegemony, and state strategy: the political shaping of privatism in Lowland Scotland. *Environment and Planning A* 31 (2): 345–375.

MacLeod, G. and Goodwin, M. (1999). Space, scale and state strategy: rethinking urban and regional governance. *Progress in Human Geography* 23 (4): 503–527.

Marcus, G.E. (1998). *Ethnography through Thick and Thin*. Princeton, NJ: Princeton University Press.

Marcuse, P. (1996). Space and race in the post-Fordist city: the outcast ghetto and advanced homelessness in the United States today. In: *Urban Poverty and the Underclass* (ed. E. Mingione), 176–216. Oxford: Blackwell.

Marr, M.D. (2015). *Better Must Come: Existing Homelessness in Two Global Cities*. Ithaca, NY: Cornell University Press.

Marshall, T.H. (1964). *Class, Citizenship, and Social Development: Essays by T.H. Marshall*. Garden City, NY: Doubleday Anchor.

Martin, D. and Miller, B. (2003). Space and contentious politics. *Mobilization: An International Journal* 8 (2): 143–156.

Maruyama, S. (2013). *Josē Hōmuresu to shite Ikiru* [Living as Homeless Women]. Kyoto: Sekai Shiso Sha.

Marx, K. (1973). *Grundrisse* (trans. M. Nicolaus). London: Penguin Books.

Marx, K. (1976 [1867]). *Capital: A Critique of Political Economy*, 1 (trans. B. Fowkes). London: Pelican Books.

Marx, K. (1996 [1842]). *Proceedings of the Sixth Rhine Province Assembly. Third Article. Debates on the Law on Thefts of Wood* (trans. C. Dutt). https://www.marxists.org/archive/marx/works/download/Marx_Rheinishe_Zeitung.pdf (accessed 27 October 2021).

Massey, D. (1994). *Space, Place, and Gender*. Minneapolis, MN: University of Minnesota Press.

Masuda, H. (2014). *Chihō Shōmetsu* [The Demise of the Locality]. Tokyo: Chuo Koron Shinsha.

Matsubara, H. (ed.) (1974). *Jyūmin Sanka to Jichi no Kakushin* [The Participation of Residents and the Reform of Self-Government]. Tokyo: Gakuyo Shobo.

Matsubara, H. and Nitagai, K. (eds.) (1976). *Jūmin Undō no Ronri: Undō no Tenkai Katē to Tenbō* [Logics of Residents' Social Movements: Development Processes and Prospects of Movements]. Tokyo: Gakuyo Shobo.

May, J., Cloke, P., and Johnsen, S. (2007). Alternative cartographies of homelessness: rendering visible British women's experiences of 'visible' homelessness. *Gender, Place and Culture* 14 (2): 121–140.

Mayer, M. (1994). Post-Fordist city politics. In: *Post-Fordism: A Reader* (ed. A. Amin), 316–337. Oxford: Blackwell.

McAdam, D., McCarthy, J.D., and Zald, M.N. (eds.) (1996). *Comparative Perspectives on*

Social Movements: Political Opportunities, Mobilizing Structures, and Cultural Framings. Cambridge: Cambridge University Press.

McAdam, D., Tarrow, S., and Tilly, C. (2001). *Dynamics of Contention.* Cambridge: Cambridge University Press.

McCann, E. and Ward, K. (eds.) (2011). *Mobile Urbanism: Cities and Policymaking in the Global Age.* Minneapolis, MN: University of Minnesota Press.

McDowell, L. (1983). Towards an understanding of the gender division of urban space. *Environment and Planning D: Society and Space* 1 (1): 59–72.

McDowell, L. (1991). Life without father and Ford: the new gender order of post-Fordism. *Transactions of the Institute of British Geographers* 16 (4): 400–419.

Merrifield, A. (2013). *The Politics of the Encounter: Urban Theory and Protest under Planetary Urbanization.* Athens, GA: University of Georgia Press.

Merrifield, A. (2014). *The New Urban Question.* London: Pluto Press.

Miller, B. (2000). *Geography and Social Movements: Comparing Antinuclear Activism in the Boston Area.* Minneapolis, MN: University of Minnesota Press.

Mingione, E. (ed.) (1996). *Urban Poverty and the Underclass: A Reader.* Oxford: Blackwell.

Mitchell, D. (1997). The annihilation of space by law: the roots and implications of anti-homeless laws in the United States. *Antipode* 29 (3): 303–335.

Mitchell, D. (2003). *The Right to the City: Social Justice and the Fight for Public Space.* New York, NY: Guilford Press.

Miyamoto, K. (1976). *Shakai Shihon Ron, Kaitē Ban* [The Theory of Social Capital, rev. ed.]. Tokyo: Yuhikaku.

Mizuuchi, T. (2002). Nojukusēkatsusha eno undo jigyō no kēi to kēfu [Background and genealogy of movements and projects for self-reliance support of homeless people: the case of Osaka prefecture and city]. *Shelter-less* 15: 49–61.

Moon, J. (2006). Josē nojukusha no sutorīto aidenteitei: kanojo no muryokusa wa tēkō dearu [Street-level identities of the female homeless: their powerlessness is resistance]. In: *Hurachi na Kibō* [Immoral Hope] (ed. K. Ayumi), 198–233. Kyoto: Shorai Sha.

Moore, B.W. (1967). *Social Origins of Dictatorship and Democracy: Lord and Peasant in the Making of the Modern World.* Boston, MA: Beacon Press.

Moore, Joe. (1983). *Japanese Workers and the Struggle for Power, 1945–1947.* Madison, WI: University of Wisconsin Press.

Moore, Jason.W. (2015). *Capitalism in the Web of Life: Ecology and the Accumulation of Capital.* London: Verso.

Morioka, K. (2013). *Karōshi wa Nanio Kokuhatsu Shiteiru ka: Gendai Nihon no Kigyō to Rōdō* [Who Is to Blame for the Overwork-to-Death? The Firm and Labour in Contemporary Japan]. Tokyo: Iwanami Shoten.

Morton, A.D. (2007). *Unravelling Gramsci: Hegemony and Passive Revolution in the Global Political Economy.* London: Pluto Press.

Mugikura, T. (2006). *Hōmuresu Jiritsu Shien Shisuytemu no Kenkyū* [Research of the Support System for Homeless People's Independent Life]. Tokyo: Daiichi Shorin.

Nagayama, T. (ed.) (2000). *Rōdō Kēzaigaku* [Labour Economics]. Kyoto: Minerva Shobo.

Nakagawa, I. (ed.) (2011). *Komyunitei Saisē no Tameno Shikumi to Jissen* [Systems and Practices of Local Autonomy for Community Regeneration]. Tokyo: Gakugē Shuppan Sha.

Nakagawa, K. (1985). *Nihon no Toshi Kasō* [Urban Lower Classes in Japan]. Tokyo: Keso Shobo.

Nakagawa, K. (2000). *Nihon Toshi no Sēkatsu Hendō* [Changes in Lifestyle in Japanese Cities]. Tokyo: Keso Shobo.

Nakamura, I. (ed.) (2011). *Komyunitei Saisē no Tame no Chīkijichi no Shikumi to Jissen* [Practices and Mechanisms of Local Self-Government for Community Regeneration]. Kyoto: Gakuge Shuppan Sha.

Nakamura, T. (1993). *Nihonkēzai: Sono Sēchō to Kōzō*, Dai San Pan [The Japanese Economy: Its Development and Structure, 3rd ed.]. Tokyo: University of Tokyo Press.

Nakane, A. (1968). *Huryō Kankyō Chitai ni Okeru Kyojyū Kankē ni Tsuite: Yokohama Shi Naka Ku Maichi Doyagai ni Tsuite* [On Housing Relations in a Delinquent Environment: Day Labourers' Hotel District in the Reclaimed Land of Nakawa Ward, Yokohama]. Yokohama: City of Yokohama's Study Group of Slums.

Nakane, M. (1999). Gendai nihon shakai ni okeru toshikasō no henbō [Changes in contemporary Japan's lower classes]. *The Annals of Japan Association for Urban Sociology* 17: 39–54.

Newell, J.P. and Cousins, J.J. (2015). The boundaries of urban metabolism: towards a political–industrial ecology. *Progress in Human Geography* 39 (6): 702–728.

NHK Shuzai Han (2012). *Sēkatsuhogo Sanchōen no Shōgeki* [Shocking Facts in the Three-Trillion-Yen of Public Assistance]. Tokyo: Takarajima Sha.

Nicholls, W. (2009). Place, networks, space: theorizing the geographies of social movements. *Transactions of the Institute of British Geographers* NS 34: 78–93.

Nicholls, W., Miller, B., and Beaumont, J. (2013). *Spaces of Contention: Spatialities and Social Movements*. Farnham: Ashgate.

Nihon Jinbun Kagaku Kai (ed.) (1956). *Kindai Sangyō to Chīki Shakai* [Modern Industry and Local Society]. Tokyo: University of Tokyo Press.

Nikkeiren (1971). *Tenki o Mukaeta Chingin Mondai to Nihon Kēzai* [The Wage Problem and the Japanese Economy at a Turning Point]. Tokyo: Nihon Keiēsha Dantai Renmē Kōhōbu.

Nikkeiren (1995). *Shinjidai no nihonteki kēei: chōsen subeki hōkō to sono gutaisaku* ["Japanese management" in the new era: a direction we should challenge and its concrete plans]. *Nikkeiren Taimusu* 2302: 226–239.

Nishizawa, A. (1995). *Inpē Sareta Gaibu: Toshikasō no Esunogurafui* [The Concealed Externality: An Ethnography of the Urban Lower Class]. Tokyo: Sairyu Sha.

Nishizawa, A. (2000). Toshi kasō no kashika to henyō: nojukusha o megutte [The visualisation of homelessness and its alteration: on homeless people]. *Yoseba* 13: 27–37.

Nomoto, S. (1977). *Kotobuki Sēkatsukan Nōto: Shokuba Dakkan eno Tōi Michi* [Notes on the Kotobuki Livelihood Hall: A Long Way to the Regaining of a Workplace]. Tokyo: Tabata Shoten.

Nomoto, S. (2003). *Kojinshi Seikatsusha* [A Personal History of an Ordinary Person]. Tokyo: Shakai Hyoron Sha.

Offe, C. (1996). *Modernity and the State*. Cambridge: Cambridge, MA: MIT Press.

Ohmae, K. (1995). *The End of the Nation State: The Rise of Regional Economies*. New York, NY: Free Press.

Pahl, R.E. (1988). Some remarks on informal work, social polarization and the social structure. *International Journal of Urban and Regional Research* 12 (2): 247–267.

Painter, J. (1997). Regulation, regime and practice in urban politics. In: *Reconstructing Urban Regime Theory: Regulating Urban Politics in a Global Economy* (ed. M. Lauria), 122–143. London: Sage.

Panitch, L. and Gindin, S. (2012). *The Making of Global Capitalism: The Political Economy of American Empire*. London: Verso.

Park, B.-G. (2005). Spatially selective liberalization and graduated sovereignty: politics of neo-liberalism and "special economic zones" in South Korea. *Political Geography* 24 (7): 850–873.

Park, B.-G. (2008). Uneven development, inter-scalar tensions, and the politics of decentralization in South Korea. *International Journal of Urban and Regional Research* 32 (1): 40–59.

Park, B.-G. (2013). State rescaling in non-Western contexts. *International Journal of Urban and Regional Research* 37 (4): 1115–1122.

Park, B.-G., Hill, R.C., and Saito, A. (2012). *Locating Neoliberalism in East Asia*. Chichester: Wiley-Blackwell.

Peck, J. (1996). *Work-Place: The Social Regulation of Labor Markets*. New York, NY: Guilford Press.

Peck, J. (2001a). *Workfare States*. New York, NY: Guilford Press.

Peck, J. (2001b). Neoliberalizing states: thin policies/hard outcomes. *Progress in Human Geography* 25 (3): 445–455.

Peck, J. (2002). Political economies of scale: fast policy, interscalar relations, and neoliberal workfare. *Economic Geography* 78 (3): 331–360.

Peck, J. (2003). Geography and public policy: mapping the penal state. *Progress in Human Geography* 27 (2): 222–232.

Peck, J. (2013). For Polanyian economic geographies. *Environment and Planning* A 45 (7): 1545–1568.

Peck, J. and Miyamachi, Y. (1994). Regulating Japan? Regulation theory versus the Japanese experience. *Environment and Planning* D 12 (6): 639–674.

Peck, J. and Theodore, N. (2000). Beyond 'employability'. *Cambridge Journal of Economics* 24: 729–749.

Peck, J. and Theodore, N. (2015). *Fast Policy: Experimental Statecraft at the Thresholds of Neoliberalism*. Minneapolis, MN: University of Minnesota Press.

Peck, J. and Tickell, A. (1992). Local modes of social regulation? Regulation theory, Thatcherism and uneven development. *Geoforum* 23 (3): 347–363.

Peck, J. and Tickell, A. (1995). The social regulation of uneven development: 'regulatory deficit', England's South East, and the collapse of Thatcherism. *Environment and Planning* A 27 (1): 15–40.

Peck, J. and Tickell, A. (2002). Neoliberalizing space. *Antipode* 34 (3): 380–404.

Pekkanen, R. (2006). *Japan's Dual Civil Society: Members Without Advocates*. Stanford, CA: Stanford University Press.

Pele, M., Bellut, C., Debergue, E. et al. (2017). Cultural influence of social information use in pedestrian road-crossing behaviours. *Royal Society Open Science* 4 (2): 1–16.
Pierson, C. (2006). *Beyond the Welfare State? The New Political Economy of Welfare*, 3rd ed. Cambridge: Polity.
Piven, F.F. and Cloward, R.A. (1971). *Regulating the Poor: The Function of Public Welfare*. New York, NY: Pantheon Books.
Pleace, N., Burrows, R., and Quilgars, D. (1997). Homelessness in contemporary Britain: conceptualisation and measurement. In: *Homelessness and Social Policy* (ed. R. Burrows, N. Pleace, and D. Quilgars), 1–18. Abingdon: Routledge.
Polanyi, K. (1957). *The Great Transformation: The Political and Economic Origins of Our Time*. Boston, MA: Beacon Press.
Poulantzas, N. (1973 [1968]). *Political Power and Social Classes*. London: New Left Books and Sheed & Ward.
Poulantzas, N. (1978 [1978]). *State, Power, Socialism* (trans. P. Camiller). London: New Left Books.
Powell, W.W. and DiMaggio, P.J. (eds.) (1991). *The New Institutionalism in Organizational Analysis*. Chicago, IL: University of Chicago Press.
Relph, E. (1976). *Place and Placelessness*. London: Pion.
Rex, J. and Moore, R. (1967). *Race, Community, and Conflict: A Study of Sparkbrook*. Oxford: Oxford University Press.
Rinji Gyose Chosakai (1981). *Gyosē Kaikaku ni Kansuru Daiichiji Tōshin* [The First Report on the Administrative Restructuring]. Tokyo: Prime Minister's Office.
Robinson, J. (2006). *Ordinary Cities: Between Modernity and Development*. Abingdon: Routledge.
Robinson, J. (2016). Comparative urbanism: new geographies and cultures of theorizing the urban. *International Journal of Urban and Regional Research* 40 (1): 187–199.
Robinson, T. (2019). No right to rest: police enforcement patterns and quality of life consequences of the criminalization of homelessness. *Urban Affairs Review* 55 (1): 41–73.
Roelvink, G., Martin, K.S., and Gibson-Graham, J.K. (eds.) (2015). *Making Other Worlds Possible: Performing Diverse Economies*. Minneapolis, MN: University of Minnesota Press.
Rossi, P.H. (1989). *Down and Out in America: The Origins of Homelessness*. Chicago, IL: University of Chicago Press.
Routledge, P. (1996). Critical geopolitics and terrains of resistance. *Political Geography* 15 (6/7): 509–531.
Roy, A. (2005). Urban informality: toward an epistemology of planning. *Journal of the American Planning Association* 71 (2): 147–158.
Roy, A. (2009). The 21st-century metropolis: new geographies of theory. *Regional Studies* 43 (6): 819–830.
Saito, M. (2015). *Shinsai Hukkō no Sēji Kēzai Gaku* [The Political Economy of Disaster Recovery]. Tokyo: Nihon Hyōron Sha.
Sakokawa, N. (2013). *Shinjuku Danbōru Mura: Sasakawa Naoko Shashinshū 1996–1998* [Shinjuku Cardboard Houses: Naoko Sakokawa's Photo Collection, 1996–1998]. Tokyo: DU Books.

San'ya Rodosha Fukushi Kaikan Unei I'inkai (1992). *Yoseba ni Hirakareta Kūkan o* [Let Us Have Open Space in Yoseba]. Tokyo: Shakai Hyoron Sha.
Sassen, S. (2001). *The Global City: New York, London, Tokyo*, 2nd ed. Princeton, NJ: Princeton University Press.
Sayer, A. (1987). Hard work and its alternatives. *Environment and Planning D: Society & Space* 5 (4): 395–399.
Sayer, A. (1989). Postfordism in question. *International Journal of Urban and Regional Research* 13 (4): 666–695.
Sayer, A. (2010). *Method in Social Science: A Realist Approach*, rev. 2nd ed. Abingdon: Routledge.
Schmid, C. (2012). Henri Lefebvre, the right to the city, and the new metropolitan mainstream. In: *Cities for People, Not for Profit: Critical Urban Theory and the Right to the City* (ed. N. Brenner, P. Marcuse, and M. Mayer), 42–62. Abingdon: Routledge.
Schmitter, P.C. and Lehmbruch, G. (eds.) (1979). *Trends Toward Corporatist Intermediation*. London: Sage.
Schwartz, A.F. (2010). *Housing Policy in the United States*, 2nd ed. Abingdon: Routledge.
Serizawa, I. (1967). *Doyagai no Hassē to Kēsē* [The Origin and Formation of a Day Labourers' Hotel District]. Yokohama: City of Yokohama.
Serizawa, I. (ed.) (1976). *Hukushi Kiyō*, a combined issue of No. 6, No. 7, No, 8 with the special title of *Kotobuki Doya Gai: Mōhitotsu no Siminshakai to Hukushi* [The Kotobuki Doya Streets: Another Civil Society and Welfare]. Yokohama: Kanagawa Ken Kyōsai Kai.
Sharp, J. (2011). Subaltern geopolitics: introduction. *Geoforum* 42: 271–273.
Sheppard, E. (2018). Heterodoxy as orthodoxy: prolegomenon for a geographical political economy. In: *The New Oxford Handbook of Economic Geography* (ed. G.L. Clark, M.P. Feldman, M.S. Gertler, and D. Wójcik), 159–178. Oxford: Oxford University Press.
Shimoyama, H. (1982). *Gendai Nihon Kigyō to Chingin Kanri* [Modern Japanese Firms and the Management of Wages]. Tokyo: Rōdō Junpō Sha.
Shinjuku Renraku Kai (1997). *Shinjuku Danbōru Mura: Tatakai no Kiroku* [The Shinjuku Cardboard Village: A Record of Struggle]. Tokyo: Gendai Kikaku Shitsu.
Shinkawa, T. (2005). *Nihon Gata Fukushi Rejīmu no Hatten to Hen'yō* [Developments and Transitions in the Japanese Welfare Regime]. Kyoto: Minerva Shobo.
Shoji, H. and Miyamoto, K. (1964). *Osorubeki Kōgai* [Fearful Pollution]. Tokyo: Iwanami Shoten.
Skocpol, T. (1992). *Protecting Soldiers and Mothers: The Political Origins of Social Policy in the United States*. Cambridge, MA: Belknap Press of Harvard University Press.
Smith, N. (1984). *Uneven Development: Nature, Capital, and the Production of Space*. Oxford: Blackwell.
Smith, N. (1993). Homeless/global: scaling places. In: *Mapping the Futures* (ed. J. Bird, B. Curtis, T. Putnam et al.), 87–119. Abingdon: Routledge.
Smith, N. (1996). *The New Urban Frontier: Gentrification and the Revanchist City*. Abingdon: Routledge.
Smith, N. (2000). What happened to class? *Environment and Planning A* 32 (6): 1011–1032.

Smith, N. (2003). Foreword. In: *The Urban Revolution* (ed. H. Lefebvre), vii–xxiii. Minneapolis, MN: University of Minnesota Press.

Snow, D.A. and Anderson, L. (1993). *Down on Their Luck: A Study of Homeless Street People*. Berkeley, CA: University of California Press.

Snow, D.A. and Benford, R.D. (1992). Master frames and cycles of protest. In: *Frontiers in Social Movement Theory* (ed. A.D. Morris and C.M. Mueller), 133–155. New Haven, CT: Yale University Press.

Soja, E.W. (1989). *Postmodern Geographies: The Reassertion of Space in Critical Social Theory*. New York, NY: Verso.

Sonn, J.W. (2010). Contesting state rescaling: an analysis of the South Korean state's discursive strategy against devolution. *Antipode* 42 (5): 1200–1224.

Sorensen, A. (2002). *The Making of Urban Japan: Cities and Planning from Edo to the Twenty-First Century*. Abingdon: Routledge.

Stanek, Ł. (2011). *Henri Lefebvre on Space: Architecture, Urban Research, and the Production of Theory*. Minneapolis, MN: University of Minnesota Press.

Stevens, C. (1997). *On the Margins of Japanese Society: Volunteers and the Welfare of the Urban Underclass*. Abingdon: Routledge.

Stoner, M.R. (1995). *The Civil Rights of Homeless People: Law, Social Policy, and Social Work Practice*. Hawthorne, NY: Aldine de Gruyter.

Stuart, F. (2014). From 'rabble management' to 'recovery management': policing homelessness in marginal urban space. *Urban Studies* 51 (9): 1909–1925.

Sum, N. and Jessop, B. (2013). *Towards a Cultural Political Economy: Putting Culture in Its Place in Political Economy*. Cheltenham: Edward Elgar.

Sumiya, M. (1964). *Nihon no Rōdō Mondai* [Labour Problems in Japan]. Tokyo: University of Tokyo Press.

Swyngedouw, E. (1996). The city as a hybrid: on nature, society and cyborg urbanization. *Capitalism Nature Socialism* 7 (2): 65–80.

Swyngedouw, E. (1997). Neither global nor local: "glocalization" and the politics of scale. In: *Spaces of Globalization: Reasserting the Power of the Local* (ed. K.R. Cox), 137–166. New York, NY: Guilford Press.

Swyngedouw, E. (2009). The antinomies of the post-political city: in search of a democratic politics of environment production. *International Journal of Urban and Regional Research* 33 (3): 601–620.

Swyngedouw, E. (2015). *Liquid Power: Contested Hydro-Modernities in Twentieth-Century Spain*. Cambridge, MA: MIT Press.

Swyngedouw, E. and Heynen, N.C. (2003). Urban political ecology, justice and the politics of scale. *Antipode* 35 (5): 898–918.

Tachibanaki, T. (1998). *Nihon no Kēzai Kakusa: Shotoku to Shisan kara Kangaeru* [Japan's Economic Divides: Considering Income and Assets]. Tokyo: Iwanami Shoten.

Tachibanaki, T. (2005a). *Confronting Income Inequality in Japan: A Comparative Analysis of Causes, Consequences, and Reform*. Cambridge, MA: MIT Press.

Tachibanaki, T. (2005b). *Kigyō Hukushi no Shūen: Kakusa no Jidai ni Dō Taiō Subeki ka*

[The End of Company-Based Welfare: How Can We Respond to the Age of Divisions?]. Tokyo: Chuo Koron Shinsha.

Takahashi, L.M. (1997). The socio-spatial stigmatization of homelessness and HIV/AIDS: toward an explanation of the NIMBY syndrome. *Social Science and Medicine* 45 (6): 903–914.

Takeda, H. (2008). *Kōdo Sēchō* [High Economic Growth]. Tokyo: Iwanami Shoten.

Takenaka, H., Ikeda, N., Doi, T., and Suzuki, W. (2010). *Nihon Kēzai "Yomē San'nen": Zaisē Kiki o Dō Norikoeru ka* [The Japanese Economy Has "Three Years Left": How Can We Overcome a Financial Crisis?]. Tokyo: PHP.

Tamano, K. (1993). *Gendai Nihon no Toshika to Chōnaikai no Sēritsu* [Urbanisation in Modern Japan and the Establishment of Chōnaikai]. Tokyo: Kojin Sha.

Tamano, K. (2005). *Tokyo no Rōkaru Komyunitei: Aru Machi no Monogatari 1900–80* [Local Community in Tokyo: The Story of a Town, 1990–80]. Tokyo: University of Tokyo Press.

Tarrow, S. (1998). *Power in Movement: Social Movements and Contentious Politics*, 2nd ed. Cambridge: Cambridge University Press.

Theodore, N. (2003). Political economies of day labour: regulation and restructuring of Chicago's contingent labour markets. *Urban Studies* 40 (9): 1811–1828.

Theodore, N. (2015). Generative work: day labourers' Freirean praxis. *Urban Studies* 52 (1): 2035–2050.

Thomas, P.D. (2009). *The Gramscian Moment: Philosophy, Hegemony and Marxism*. Leiden: Brill.

Tickell, A. and Peck, J. (1992). Accumulation, regulation and the geographies of post-Fordism: missing links in regulationist research. *Progress in Human Geography* 16 (2): 190–218.

Tilly, C. (2000). Spaces of contention. *Mobilization: An International Journal* 5 (2): 135–159.

Toscano, A. (2008). The open secret of real abstraction. *Rethinking Marxism: A Journal of Economics, Culture & Society* 20 (2): 273–287.

Toshikoshi Haken Mura Jikko I'inkai (2009). *Haken Mura: Kuni o Ugokashita Muika Kan* [Haken Mura: The Six Days that Changed the State]. Tokyo: Mainichi Shimbun Sha.

Trattner, W.I. (1999). *From Poor Law to Welfare State: A History of Social Welfare in America*, 6th ed. New York, NY: Free Press.

Tsukamoto, T. (2012). Neoliberalization of the developmental state: Tokyo's bottom-up politics and state rescaling in Japan. *International Journal of Urban and Regional Research* 36 (1): 71–89.

Tuan, Y.-F. (1977). *Space and Place: The Perspective of Experience*. Minneapolis, MN: University of Minnesota Press.

Uemura, H. (2000). Growth, distribution and structural change in the post-war Japanese economy. In: *Japanese Capitalism in Crisis: A Regulationist Interpretation* (ed. R. Boyer and T. Yamada), 138–161. Abingdon: Routledge.

Ui, J. (1974). *Kōgai Jyūmin Undō* [Residents' Social Movements Against Environmental Pollution]. Tokyo: Aki Shobo.

Ushikusa, H. (1988). *Kamagasaki: rōdōsha zōka no jittai to sono kōzō* [Kamagasaki: the reality of an increase in workers and its structure]. *Yoseba* 1: 152–168.
Utsunomiya, K. and Yuasa, M. (eds.) (2009). *Haken Mura: Naniga Towarete Irunoka* [A Village of Dispatched Workers: What Is Questioned?]. Tokyo: Iwanami Shoten.
Valentine, G. (2008). Living with difference: reflections on geographies of encounter. *Progress in Human Geography* 32 (3): 323–337.
Ventura, R. (1992). *Underground in Japan*. London: Jonathan Cape.
Vogel, S.K. (2006). *Japan Remodeled: How Government and Industry are Reforming Japanese Capitalism*. Ithaca, NY: Cornel University Press.
Wachsmuth, D. (2012). Three ecologies: urban metabolism and the society–nature opposition. *The Sociological Quarterly* 53 (4): 506–523.
Wacquant, L. (2008). *Urban Outcasts: A Comparative Sociology of Advanced Marginality*. Cambridge: Polity.
Wagner, D. (1993). *Checkerboard Square: Culture and Resistance in a Homeless Community*. Boulder, CO: Westview Press.
Wallerstein, I. (1979). *The Capitalist World-Economy*. Cambridge: Cambridge University Press.
Ward, K. and Jonas, A.E.G. (2004). Competitive city-regionalism as a politics of scale: a critical reinterpretation of the new regionalism. *Environment and Planning* A 36 (12): 2119–2139.
Watson, S. (1986). *Housing and Homelessness: A Feminist Perspective*. Abingdon: Routledge and Kegan Paul.
Wilson, W. (1997). *When Work Disappears: The World of the New Urban Poor*. New York, NY: Vintage.
Woo-Cumings, M. (ed.) (1999). *The Developmental State*. Ithaca, NY: Cornell University Press.
Woodward, R. (1995). Approaches towards the study of social polarization in the UK. *Progress in Human Geography* 19 (1): 75–89.
Woon, C. (2011). Undoing violence, unbounding precarity: beyond the frames of terror in the Philippines. *Geoforum* 42: 285–296.
Wu, F. (2016). China's emergent city-region governance: a new form of state spatial selectivity through state-orchestrated rescaling. *International Journal of Urban and Regional Research* 40 (6): 1134–1151.
Yamada, M. (2004). *Kibō Kakusa Shakai* [Divides in Hope Within Society]. Tokyo: Chikuma Shobo.
Yamada, S. (2005). Sēsaku ga hito o korosu toki [When a policy kills people]. *Shelter-less* 26: 228–233.
Yamaguchi, K. (1998). Shinjuku ni okeru nojukusha no ikinuki senryaku: nojukusha kan no shakai kankē o chūshin ni [Survival strategies of homeless people in Shinjuku: social relationships among homeless people]. *The Annals of Japan Association for Urban Sociology* 16: 119–134.
Yamakita, T. (2006). Nojukusha ni okeru nakama to iu komyunikēshon [Comradeship within communities of homeless people]. *Japanese Sociological Review* 57 (3): 582–599.

Yamamoto, H. (2005). Chiiki sēkatsu ikō shien jigyō (yoyogi kōen) [The programme to facilitate community-based lives (Yoyogi Park)]. *Shelter-less* 26: 214–219.

Yamamoto, K. (1977). *Sengo Kiki ni Okeru Rōdō Undo* [Labour Movement in the Postwar Crisis]. Tokyo: Ochanomizu Shobō.

Yamamoto, K. (2008). *Yokohama Kotobuki Chō to Gaikokujin: Gurōbaruka suru Daitoshi In'nā Eria* [Yokohama's Kotobuki Town and Foreigners: An Inner-City Metropolitan Area under Globalisation]. Tokyo: Fukumura Shoten.

Yamamura, T. (1996). *Huyu no Machi: San'ya no Madoguchi Nikki* [A Winter City: *A Diary from a Window in San'ya*]. Tokyo: Kindai Bunge Sha.

Yamaoka, K. (1996). *Yama: Yararetara Yarikaese* [Yama: When You Get Hit, Hit Back]. Tokyo: Gendai Kikaku Shitsu.

Yamasaki, K., Inatsuki, T., Morimatsu, N. et al. (2006). *Hōmuresu Jiritsu Shien: NPO, Shimin, Gyōsēkyōdō ni Yoru "Hōmu" no Kaihuku* [The Support of Homeless People's Self-Help Life: The Restoration of "Home" by NPO, Citizens, and their Collaboration with the Municipality]. Tokyo: Akashi Shoten.

Yokoyama, G. (1994 [1903]). Kasō shakai no shingenshō kyōdō nagaya (A new phenomenon of lower-class society: the collective nagaya). In: *Meiji Tokyo Kasō Sēkatsu Shi* [Lives of Tokyo's Lower Class in the Meiji Era] (ed. K. Nakagawa), 195–217. Tokyo: Iwanami Shoten.

Yokoyama, G. (1994 [1912]). Kakyū rōdō shakai no ichidai mujyun [A significant contradiction in lower-class labourers' society]. In: *Meiji Tokyo Kasō Sēkatsu Shi* [Lives of Tokyo's Lower Class in the Meiji Era] (ed. K. Nakagawa), 281–292. Tokyo: Iwanami Shoten.

Yoshihara, N. (1989). *Sengo Kaikaku to Chīki Jyūmin Soshiki: Senryōka no Toshi Chōnaikai* [Postwar Reforms and the Neighbourhood Residential Organisation: Urban Neighbourhood Associations during the Occupation Period]. Kyoto: Minerva Shobo.

Yuasa, M. (2008). *Han Hinkon* [Against Poverty]. Tokyo: Iwanami Shoten.

Yuasa, M. (2009). Haken mura wa nani o toikake te irunoka? [What does the village of dispatched workers question?]. *Sekai* 788: 138–156.

Zhang, S. and He, S. (2021). From dissensus to consensus: state rescaling and modalities of power under the Belt and Road initiative in western China. *Annals of the American Association of Geographers* 111 (5): 1519–1538.

Government Publications

Cabinet Office (2011a). *Gyōsē Sassin Kaigi Wākingu Gurūpu "Tēgengata Sēsaku Shiwake" WG-B* [The Government Revitalisation Unit, the Working Group B of "The Recommendation Type of Policy Reorganisation"]. Tokyo: Cabinet Office.

Cabinet Office (2011b). *'Teigen Gata Sēsaku Shiwake' Teigen o Uketa Kakuhucho no Torikumi Gaiyo* [Ministries' Outlines of Response to the Policy Reorganisation Conference]. Tokyo: Cabinet Office.

Cabinet Office (2018). *Shōshika Taisaku Hakusho* [White Paper on Policy for the Declining Birthrate]. Tokyo: Cabinet Office. https://www8.cao.go.jp/shoushi/shoushika/white paper/measures/w-2018/30pdfhonpen/30honpen.html (accessed 27 October 2021).

Cabinet Office. (2019). *Reiwa Gan'nen Ban Shōshika Shakai Taisaku Hakusho* [2019 Annual Report on the Measures for Declining Birthrates]. Tokyo: Cabinet Office. https://www8.cao.go.jp/shoushi/shoushika/whitepaper/measures/w-2019/r01pdfhonpen/r01honpen.html (accessed 27 October 2021).

Cabinet Secretariat. (2011). *Shakai Hoshō Zei Ittai Kaikaku Sēan* [A Comprehensive Final Plan for the Total Reform of Social Insurance and Tax]. Tokyo: Cabinet Office. https://www.cas.go.jp/jp/seisaku/syakaihosyou/kentohonbu/pdf/230630kettei.pdf (accessed 27 October 2021).

City of Hiratsuka (2003). *Simin to Shichō no Idobata Kaigi (Hēsē 15 Nen 11 Gatsu 1 Nichi) Kaigi no Gaiyō* [A Meeting Between the Mayer and Residents (1 November 2003): A Summary]. Hiratsuka: City of Hiratsuka.

City of Hiratsuka (2005). *Hēsē 17 Nendo Dainikai Hiratsukashi Haikibutsu Taisaku Sshingikai Gijiroku* [Proceedings of the Second Conference on Waste Disposal Policy in Fiscal Year 2005]. Hiratsuka: City of Hiratsuka.

City of Kawasaki (2004). *Kawasaki Shi Hōmuresu Jiritsushien Jissi Kēkaku* [Kawasaki's Implementation Plan to Support the Self-Help of Homeless People].

City of Nagoya (2004). *Nagoyashi Hōmuresu no Jiritsu no Shien Nado ni Kansuru Jissi Kēkaku* [Nagoya's Implementation Plan to Support the Self-Help of Homeless People]. Nagoya: City of Nagoya.

City of Osaka (2004). *Ōsakashi Nojuku Sēkatusha (Hōmuresu) no Jiritsu no Shien Nado ni Kansuru Jissi Kēkaku* [Osaka's Implementation Plan to Support the Self-Help of Homeless People]. Osaka: City of Osaka.

City of Yokohama (2004). *Yokohamashi Hōmuresu no Jiritsu no Shien Nado ni Kansuru Jissi Kēkaku* [Yokohama's Implementation Plan to Support the Self-Help of Homeless People]. Yokohama: City of Yokohama.

City of Yokohama (2006). *Hēsē 18 Nendo Kenko Hukushi Kyoku Unē Hōshin* [Fiscal Year 2006 Management Principle of the Department of Health and Welfare]. Yokohama: City of Yokohama.

City of Yokohama (undated). *Yokohama Shi Hōmuresu Kinkyū Ichiji Shukuhaku Shisetsu Nakamuragawa Ryō* [Yokohama's Emergency Shelter for Homeless People: The Nakamuragawa Dormitory]. Yokohama: City of Yokohama.

MHA (1983). *Komyunitei Taisaku no Suishin ni Tsuite* [On the Advancement of Community Policy]. Ministry of Home Affairs.

MHLW (2003). *Hōmuresu no Jittai Nado ni Kansuru Zenkoku Chōsa Hōkokusho* [Research on the Actual Conditions of Homeless People]. Tokyo: Ministry of Health, Labour and Welfare.

MHLW (2007). *Jyūkyo Sōsitsu Huantē Syūrōsha no Jittai nado ni Kansuru Chōsa Hōkokusho* [Report on the Actual Conditions of Precariously Housed Temporary Labourers]. Tokyo: Ministry of Health, Labour and Welfare. https://www.mhlw.go.jp/houdou/2007/08/dl/h0828-1n.pdf (accessed 27 October 2021).

MHLW (2009a). *Hēsē 21 Nendo 'Rikon ni Kansuru Tōkē' no Gaikyō* [Fiscal Year 2018 Overview of the Statistic on Divorce]. Tokyo: Ministry of Health, Labour and Welfare.

https://www.mhlw.go.jp/toukei/saikin/hw/jinkou/tokusyu/rikon10/index.html (accessed 27 October 2021).

MHLW (2009b). *Shoku ya Sumai o Usinatta Katagata e no Shien no Tettē ni Tsuite* [On the Appropriate Enforcement of Assistance for People Who Have Lost Employment and Housing]. Tokyo: Ministry of Health, Labour and Welfare. https://www.mhlw.go.jp/content/000608930.pdf (accessed 27 October 2021).

MHLW (2009c). *Shitsugyō Nado Niyori Sēkatsu ni Konkyū Suru Katagata eno Shien no Ryūijikō ni Tsuite* [On the Matters of Consideration When Using Assistance for People Who Have Lost Employment and Housing]. Tokyo: Ministry of Health, Labour and Welfare. https://www.mhlw.go.jp/content/000608930.pdf (accessed 27 October 2021).

MHLW (2013). *Shakai Hoshō Shingikai Sēkatsu Konkyūsha no Sēkatsu Shien no Arikata ni Kansuru Tokubetsu Bukai Hōkokusho* [Report on the Livelihood Support of Needy Persons, from the Special Committee of the Social Security Advisory Council]. Ministry of Health, Labour and Welfare. http://www.mhlw.go.jp/stf/shingi/2r9852000002tpzu-att/2r9852000002tq1b.pdf (accessed 27 October 2021).

MHLW (2015). *Sēkatsu Konkyūsha Jiritsushien Sēdo ni Tsuite* [On Policy for the Self-Help of Needy Persons]. Tokyo: Ministry of Health, Labour and Welfare. https://www.mhlw.go.jp/file/06-Seisakujouhou-12000000-Shakaiengokyoku-Shakai/2707seikatukonnkyuushajiritsusiennseidonituite.pdf (accessed 27 October 2021).

MHLW (2016). *Hēsē 28 Nen Kokumin Sēkatsu Kisochōsa no Gaikyō* [2016 Overview of the Comprehensive Survey of Living Conditions]. Tokyo: Ministry of Health, Labour and Welfare. https://www.mhlw.go.jp/toukei/saikin/hw/k-tyosa/k-tyosa16/dl/16.pdf (accessed 27 October 2021).

MHLW (2017). *Hēsē 29 Nendo Kōsē Rōdō Hakusho* [Fiscal Year 2017 Annual Report on Health, Labour and Welfare]. Tokyo: Ministry of Health, Labour and Welfare. https://www.mhlw.go.jp/wp/hakusyo/kousei/17/index.html (accessed 27 October 2021).

MHLW (2019). *Hōmuresu no Jittai ni Kansuru Zenkoku Chōsa (Gaisū Chōsa) Kekka ni Tsuite* [Result of National Research (Round Numbers) on the Actual Conditions of Homeless People]. Tokyo: Ministry of Health, Labour and Welfare. https://www.mhlw.go.jp/content/12003000/000505478.pdf (accessed 27 October 2021).

MHW (1962). *Shōwa 37 Nendo Ban Kōsē Hakusho* [Fiscal Year 1962 White Paper on Health and Welfare]. Tokyo: Ministry of Health and Welfare.

MLIT (2003). *Hēsē 14 Nendo Matsu Toshi Kōen tō Sēbi no Genkyō ni Tsuite* [Fiscal Year 2015 Report on the Actual Situation of Green Space Improvement]. Ministry of Land, Infrastructure, Transport and Tourism. https://www.mlit.go.jp/kisha/kisha03/04/040828_.html (accessed 27 October 2021).

MLIT (2014). *Kokudo no Grando Dezain 2050: Tairyū Sokushin Gata Kokudo no Kēsē* [The Grand Design of the National Land Toward 2050: The Creation of Japan's Convection-Facilitating National Territory]. Tokyo, Ministry of Land, Infrastructure, Transport and Tourism. https://www.mlit.go.jp/common/001047113.pdf (accessed 27 October 2021).

MLIT (2015). *Hēsē 27 Nendo Matsu Toshi Kōen tō Sēbi Oyobi Ryokuchi Hozen Ryokuka no Torikumi no Genkyō (Sokuhōban) no Kōhyō ni Tsuite* [Fiscal Year 2015 Update Report on the Actual Situation of Policy Activity for Creating and Preserving Green Space].

Tokyo: Ministry of Land, Infrastructure, Transport and Tourism. https://www.mlit. go.jp/common/001174177.pdf (accessed 27 October 2021).

MLIT (2018). *Toshi no Ryokuka Hozen Ryokuka Suishin ni Kansuru Sesaku Nado* [Policies and Others for Preserving Green Space and Facilitating Greening in the City]. Ministry of Land, Infrastructure, Transport and Tourism. https://www.env.go.jp/content/900399463.pdf (accessed 27 October 2021).

TMG (2004). *Hōmuresu no Jiritu Shien Nado ni Kansuru Tōkoto Jissi Kēkaku* [Tokyo's Implementation Plan to Support the Self-Help of Homeless People]. Tokyo: Tokyo Metropolitan Government.

TMG (2007). *Tokyo no Hōmuresu Hakusho II* [White Paper on Tokyo's Homeless II]. Tokyo: Tokyo Metropolitan Government.

TMG (2009). *Kōen tō Sēkatsusha Chīki Sēkatu Ikō Shien Jigyō* [The Programme for the Facilitation of Community-Based Lives in Support of People Living in Parks and Other Areas]. Tokyo: Tokyo Metropolitan Government. https://www.zaimu.metro.tokyo.lg.jp/syukei1/zaisei/21jimujigyohyoka/jigokensho/037.pdf (accessed 27 October 2021).

TMG (2014). *Tokyoto Chōki Bijon: "Sekaiichi no Toshi Tokyo" no Jitsugen o Mezashite* [Tokyo's Long-Term Vision: Toward "Tokyo as a Number One City in the World"]. Tokyo: Tokyo Metropolitan Government. https://www.seisakukikaku.metro.tokyo.lg.jp/tokyo_vision/vision_index/index.html (accessed 27 October 2021).

TMG (2018). *Jyūkyo Sōshitsu Huantē Shūrousha Nado no Jittai ni Kansuru Cyōsa Hōkoku Sho* [Research Report on the Actual Conditions of Precarious Homeless Workers]. Tokyo: Tokyo Metropolitan Government. https://www.metro.tokyo.lg.jp/tosei/hodohappyo/press/2018/01/26/documents/14_02.pdf (accessed 27 October 2021).

Newspaper Articles

Adachi, K. and Wada, H. (2019). Tamagawa no hōmuresu tonai yuiitsu no shisha ni sukuenakatta ka [A homeless person at the Tama river became the only victim: we could rescue him] *Mainichi Shimbun* (10 October) https://mainichi.jp/articles/20191019/k00/00m/040/075000c (accessed 27 October 2019).

Aoki, M. (2019). Taito ku no jishuhinanjo hōmuresu dansē no hinan kotowaru [An evacuation centre of the Taito ward declined homeless men's refuge] *Asahi Shimbun* (10 October) https://www.asahi.com/articles/ASMBF3RVWMBFUTIL01K.html (accessed 15 October 2019).

Haken mura hatsugen sakamoto sēmukan ga tekkai, "jittai ha'aku sitenakatta" [Sakamoto political official retracts statement on the Village of Dispatched Temporary Workers, saying "I didn't understand the reality"] (2009). *Asahi Shimbun* (6 January) http://www.asahi.com/special/08016/TKY200901060105.html (accessed 27 October 2021) [Article by anonymous author].

Hayashi, K. and Ikuta, D. (2008). Shinsotsu naitē torikeshi 331 nin, hisēki sanman nin shisshoku mo [331 students face job-offer retraction, and 30,000 non-regular workers

are in danger of dismissal] *Asahi Shimbun* (28 November) http://www.asahi.com/spe cial/08016/TKY200811280032.html (accessed 27 October 2021).
Ishikawa, H. and Hisanaga, R. (2020). Sēkatsuhogo tetsuzuki ni ikkagetsu [Taking one month to finish the paperwork of Public Assistance]. *Asahi Shimbun* (2 July) https://www.asahi.com/articles/ASN722RRHN71UTFL00B.html (accessed 27 October 2021).
Kōron shi shisatsu yōgi: nojuku sēkatsusha taiho [A murder suspect after quarrels: a homeless man arrested] (2004). *Asahi Shimbun, Shōnan ed* (13 March) [Article by anonymous author].
Korosareru to omotta [We thought we would be killed] (1983). *Kanagawa Shimbun* (13 February) [Article by anonymous author].
Nakamura, M. (2020). Chionagasu shika nai: korona ka de konkyū suru sēkatsu hogo no shinsē sha: jichitai no oikaeshi ōkō [We have to shed blood: public-assistance applicants declined by the municipality and impoverished during the coronavirus pandemic]. *Tokyo Shimbun* (1 August) https://www.tokyo-np.co.jp/amp/article/46380 (accessed 27 October 2021).
Sēkatsuhogo shinsē madoguchi taraimawashi kencho: korona ka shiendantai ga hihan [Public assistance applications kept prevented: a support group's criticism during the coronavirus pandemic] (2020). *Asahi Shimbun* (2 July) https://www.asahi.com/articles/DA3S14533790.html (accessed 27 October 2021) [Article by anonymous author].
Sekiya, S. (2017). Higashinihon shinsai 6 nen: hukkō yosan dō tsukawareta? [Six years after the 2011 Great East Japan Earthquake: what was the purpose of the reconstruction budgets?] *Mainichi Shimbun* (2 February) https://mainichi.jp/articles/20170221/ddm/010/040/015000c (accessed 27 October 2021).
Sēzōgyō haken ukeoi 40 man nin sitsugyō mitōshi, gyōkai dantai shisan [400,000 temp/contract workers in manufacturing are in the danger of dismissal, say officials] (2009). *Asahi Shimbun* (27 January) http://www.asahi.com/special/08016/TKY200901270287.html (accessed 27 October 2021) [Article by anonymous author].

Materials in the Archives of Social Movements

All-Kanagawa Assembly and Hiratsuka Patororu (2003). The movement's formal query to the City of Hiratsuka entitled Hōmuresu tokuso hō no kaishaku ni tsuite no kenkai [Our understanding of the Homeless Self-Help Act] (dated 28 February 2003). Material kept in the archives of the Kotobuki Day Labourers' Union.
Catholic Fujisawa Church (2001a). *Shyawā Rūmu Setchi o Kangaeru Tsudoi* [The Meeting to Consider Setting Up a Shower Room] (dated 26 August 2001). Material kept in the archives of the Catholic Fujisawa Church.
Catholic Fujisawa Church (2001b). *Shyawā Rūmu Setchi Kentō Dai Nikai Zentai Shūkai Hōkoku* [A Report on the Second Overall Meeting to Consider Setting Up a Shower Room] (dated 26 August 2001). Material kept in the archives of the Catholic Fujisawa Church.

Catholic Fujisawa Church (2001c). *Hōmuresu Kanren Shawā Rūmu Setchi ni Tsuite Ankēto Shūyaku Kekka* [Setting Up a Shower Room Related to Homelessness: The Overall Result of Inquiries] (dated 13 November 2001). Material kept in the archives of the Catholic Fujisawa Church.

Catholic Fujisawa Church (2001d). *Sankō Siryō (Shawā Rūmu o Kangaeru Tameni)* [Supplementary Material (on Considering Setting Up a Shower Room)] (dated 26 August 2001). Material kept in the archives of the Catholic Fujisawa Church.

Chōsa Pato Kinkyū Pato Kiroku [Records of the Research Patrol and the Emergency Patrol] (undated). Material kept in the archives of the Kotobuki Day Labourers' Union. [Handwritten notes by anonymous authors].

Hiratsuka Patororu (2005). *"(Kashō) Hiratsukashi Sawayaka de Sēketsu na Machizukuri Jyōrē" ni Taisuru Iken* [Our Opinion on the "Ordinance for the Promotion of Delightful and Clean Urban Development" (Tentative Name)]. Material kept in the archives of the Kotobuki Day Labourers' Union.

Kawasaki no Nojukusha Yushi to Kawasaki Suiyo Patororu no Kai (1996). *Fuyu o Ikinuki Haru o Yobikome* [Let Us Survive the Winter and Welcome the Spring]. Material kept in the archives of the Kotobuki Day Labourers' Union.

Kawase Seji Kun Tsuito Bunshu Henshu I'inkai (1985). *Kotobuki ni Ikite* [Living in Kotobuki]. Yokohama: Kawase Seji Kun Tsuito Bunshu Henshu I'inkai. Material kept in the archives of the Kotobuki Day Labourers' Union.

Kotobuki Shiensha Koryukai (1998). *Dai 25 Ji Kotobuki Ettō Noto: Ettō Shihansēki Tokubetsugō* [Notes on the 25th Kotobuki Overwintering: A Special Issue on the Quarter-Century History of Overwintering]. Material in the archives of the Kotobuki Supporters' Gathering Club.

Mokuyo Patororu (1985). *Kotobuki 1985 Huyu: Mokuyō Patorōru Hōkoku* [Kotobuki 1985, Winter: The Thursday Patrol Reports]. Material in the archives of the Wednesday Patrol.

Laws, Ordinances, and Legal Guidelines

City of Hiratsuka. *Sawayaka de Sēketsu na Matizukuri Jyōrē* [Ordinance for the Promotion of Delightful and Clean Urban Development]. http://www.city.hiratsuka.kanagawa.jp/common/000061499.pdf (accessed 27 September 2020).

City of Yokohama. *Haikibutsu Nado no Genryōka Shigenka Oyobi Tekisē Shori ni Kansuru Jyōrē* [Ordinance for the Reduction, Recycling, and Appropriate Disposal of Wastes]. https://cgi.city.yokohama.lg.jp/somu/reiki/reiki_honbun/g202RG00000771.html (accessed 27 October 2021).

Government of Japan. *Sēkatsu Hogo Hō* [The Public Assistance Act]. https://www.mhlw.go.jp/web/t_doc?dataId=82048000&dataType=0&pageNo=1 (accessed 27 October 2021).

Government of Japan. *Hōmuresu no Jiritsu no Shien Nado ni Kansuru Tokubetsu Sochi Hō* [Act on Special Measures Concerning Support for Homeless People's Self-Help]. https://elaws.e-gov.go.jp/search/elawsSearch/elaws_search/lsg0500/detail?lawId=414AC1000000105 (accessed 27 October 2021).

Government of Japan. *Shakaihoshō Sēdokaikaku Suishin Hō* [The Act for Promoting Reforms of the Social Security System]. https://elaws.e-gov.go.jp/search/elawsSearch/elaws_search/lsg0500/detail?lawId=424AC1000000064 (accessed 27 October 2021).

Government of Japan. *Sēkatsu Konkyūsha Jiritsu Shien Hō* [The Act for Supporting the Self-Help of Needy Persons]. https://elaws.e-gov.go.jp/document?lawid=425AC0000000105 (accessed 27 October 2021).

Ministry of Health, Labour and Welfare. *Hōmuresu no Jiritsu no Shien Nado ni Kansuru Tokubetsu Sochi Hō* [The Act on Special Measures Concerning Support for Homeless People's Self-Help].

Ministry of Health, Labour and Welfare. *Hōmuresu no Jiritsu no Shien Nado ni Kansuru Kihon Hōshin* [Guidelines Concerning Support for Homeless People's Self-Help].

Interviews

Fujitani, M., a member of the Sagamihara Wednesday Patrol, 28 August 2006.

Kagoshima, M., a member of the Kotobuki Day Labourers' Union, 14 August 2012.

Kawabe, K., a member of the Fujisawa Tuesday Patrol, 14 May 2013.

Kondo, N., a member of the Kotobuki Day Labourers' Union, 18 June 2006, 23 July 2006, and 23 February 2016.

Sakurai, T., a member of the Wednesday Patrol, 17 October 2006.

Shinohara, Y., a member of the Kotobuki Day Labourers' Union, 3 August 2003 and 23 February 2016.

Takazawa, Y., a member of the Kotobuki Supporters' Gathering Club, 23 July 2006 and 21 February 2018.

Yura, T., a member of the Kotobuki Day Labourers' Union and The Hiratsuka Patrol, 11 February 2006.

Index

Note: References in *italic* and **bold** refer to figures and tables. References followed by "n" refer to notes.

2002/2003 system, 17, 40, 211, 215, 236
  characteristics, 231–232
  defining public spaces, 97
  encouraging municipalities, 97
  governance clauses, 232, 236
  and homeless regulation, 96–97
  implementation plans, 97–98, 212
  integration of nongovernmental organisations and activist groups, 99
  means-testing and workfarist codes, 231
  query to City of Hiratsuka, 237n4
  regulatory codes, 211–212
  response from municipalities, 98
  secrecy of "local decision-making," 213
  Tokyo's "self-help system," 98
  workfarist programme, 212–213
  see also commoning around inner city
2003 guidelines, 96–97, 232

abstract–concrete spectrum/linkages, 9, 26
abstraction, 29, 30, 46, 261
  and concretisation, 261
  meso-level, 28, 31–32, 35, 46, 264
  methodological, 8–9, 27, 31, 47
  urban, 107

accumulation
  of capital, 111
  crisis, 31, 39, 69, 76
accumulation regime, 12, 67–68, 78
  during economic growth in Japan, 79–80
  and normative consumption, 65
  and NSPR, 75–76
  during postbubble crisis in Japan, 87
  during world financial crisis and mass disasters in Japan, 89–90
Act for Promoting Reforms of the Social Security System, 249
Act for Supporting the Self-Help of Needy Persons, 249
Act on Special Measures Concerning Support for Homeless People's Self-Help *see* Self-Help Act
Aglietta, Michel, 12, 65–66
All-Kanagawa Assembly of Night-Walk Groups and Patrols, 234–236, 237
antihomeless
  gentrification, 19
  NIMBYism, 163
  policing in public spaces, 104
  regulation, 34
  semiosis and politics, 153

INDEX 295

situation in public spaces, 20
antihomelessness, 123, 157, 158
   Yokohama's geography of, 205, 207
antipoor campaigns to rescale
   poverty, 99–100
applicationism, 28, 35
asset-inflated economy of Japan, 85–87
Atsugi city
   groups for homeless people in, 218, **219**
   welfare office ouucpation by
      activists, 235

bluebooks, 169, 174, 185n6
Boyer, Robert, 12, 65
Brenner, Neil, 9, 31, 106
   meso-level theory, 77–78
   ontologically prejudge, 10
   about state rescaling, 9–11
   about state space, 48
British homelessness, 16
British rescaling, 16
brokerage for homeless people, 220–221
   in Kotobuki district, 224–225
   prohomeless, 221
   in Sagamihara city, 225
   and translation, 222–224
bubble economy and NSPR, 85–87
Burawoy, Michael, 48, 136
"business use of public assistance," 246

Capital (Marx), 101n2
capitalist urbanisation, 10, 134n2, 256
"capturing" (*hosokusē*) principle, 80
Castells, Manuel, 106, 134n3
"catching-up" economy, 39
Catholic Fujisawa Church, 237n2
central business district (CBD), 50
Chigasaki city
   All-Kanagawa Assembly, 235
   groups for homeless people in, 218, **219**
chōnaikai (neighbourhood associations),
   42, 60n1, 82, 85, 119–120
"circuits of capital" thesis, 109–110
citizen activists/activism, 169–170
City of Nagoya v. Hayashi case, 102n8
civil society, 113, 114, *115*, 228
class position, 182

"class struggle on Avenue B," 7
Cloke, Paul, 7, 9
coast, homeless people in, 128–130
collective consumption, 114, 119, 121, 134n3
"colour white" symbolism, 174, 176
commoning against othering, 189, 215
   discommoning, 25, 118,
      210–213, 214
   early attempts outlying cities at, 229–231
   inherited strategies for, 224
   in Kotobuki district, 190, 193
   regulationism, 191
   social movement of, 189–190, 193–194,
      195–196
   successes in outlying cities at, 231–234
   in Yokohama city, 192–193
commoning around inner city,
   186–187, 215
   framework of prohomeless
      commoning, 214
   and habiting, 188–189
   Harvey's thesis of, 188
   Japanese parameters of, 191–192
   of urban use values for homeless
      people, 188
   see also placemaking in inner city
commoning in Yokohama city
   commoning against othering, 192–193
   commoning by union, 199–201
   disarmament, 197–198
   frameworks for urban commons, 194
   by housed citizens, 201–203
   movement of commoning against
      othering, 193–194
   nationalisation of commoning, 196–197
   public provision, 207–210
   public space, 203–207
   from radicalism to downright oppres-
      sion, 194–196
   between two cycles of homeless-
      ness, 198–199
   see also placemaking in inner city
commoning of urban use values for
   homeless people, 24, 25, 188, 260
commons, 4, 6, 24, 214
   commons accessible from streets, 228, 231
   commons form, 24, 189, 191

borders of commons, 34, 187
gatekeepers of commons, 192
new commons form production, 24, 224
rescaling of commons, 213
see also commoning
Commonwealth (Hardt and Negri), 190
composite theory of state rescaling, 37
concrete, 9, 26, 30–31, 45, 48, 53
see also abstraction
"conflictual sharing" of space, 170, 184
conjuncture, 35, *35*
consumption-intensive metabolism, 109
consumption of public spaces, 259
COVID-19 pandemic impact in Japanese public spaces, 256–257
Cresswell, Tim, 23
cultural transmission, Gramscian process of, 217
cyclical spatialisation of homelessness, 6

day labourers
  Japanese homeless people living among, 121
  in Kotobuki district, 167–170, *168*
  uprising Yokohama city, 171–175
  as vulnerable "Other," 193
Day Labourers' United Front, 175, 197
dehomogenising, 19
Department of Housing and Urban Development, 43
deprived people, 135
desocietalisation, 15, 17, 19, 72, 76, 87, 89, 91, 94, 259
developmental state, 32, 33, 39, 59, 77–78, 86, 94, 101n3, 261
  Johnson's arguments on, 37
  homelessness, data on, 54
  meso-theoretical construction, 64
  national states, 38–40
  public and private spaces, 40–43
  regulation, data on, 55
  regulationist ethnography, 45–49, 59
  sites of participatory observation, 49–53
  social movements, data on, 55–56
  subaltern materials, 56–59
  urban social movements, 44–45

DeVerteuil, Geoffrey, 7, 8, 25, 159
disarmament of commoning, 197–198

economic growth and NSPR in Japan, 79–83, 91, **92**
ethnography, 261–262
  locational, 122–130
  multicity, 130–132
  regulationist, 37–38, 45–49, 59
etto-mobilisation model, 242
Euro-American geographical conceptions of homelessness, 9
exchange value, 135–136
  exchange value–oriented income-generation, 137
  production of Japanese homeless recyclers, 141
"extinguishing operation," 247, 250
extremist neoliberalism in New York City, 262–263

fast policy, 49, 100, 104, 214
Featherstone, David, 56, 222
  about brokerage, 222
Final Draft of Comprehensive Tax and Social Welfare Reform, 248
"first-order" regulation, 49, 65, 72
Fordist/Fordism, 38, 258
  Fordist–Keynesian urbanisation, 43
  Fordist public provision, 70
forest regulation, 111, 113
form-destabilising, 22
Foucault, Michel, 69
Fujisawa city
  All-Kanagawa Assembly, 235
  groups for homeless people in, 218, **219**
  local policing regimes, 132
  placemaking in, 227–229
Fujisawa Tuesday Patrol, 56, 227

garbage recycling issue, 135–136
Geertz, Clifford, 46–47
gentrification, 7
  antihomeless, 19
  destruction of affordable housing, 7
  inner city against, 254–255

INDEX 297

ghettoisation, 15, 16, 71
 homelessness without, 78, 89, 91, 93, 100
 inherited spaces in yoseba zones, 89
 new urban poverty, 15
ghettos, 23, 93
 racial/ethnic, 167
Gill, Tom, 60n2
Global Ethnography (Burawoy), 136
globalisation, 48
global warming, 4
Goffman, Erving, 110
Gowan, Teresa, 136–138, 139
Gramsci, Antonio, 60n1, 221–222
 hegemony concept, 113–114
 "integral state" concept, 66, 104
 linguistic theorisation, 34
 philosophy of praxis, 24
 theory of state and civil society, 113
 "translation" concept, 221–222
ground-up rescaling in Japan, 6, 73, *74*, 75, 95–96, 120–122
growth patterns, 67
 during bubble economy in Japan, 85
 national, 67, 91, **92**
Guidelines Concerning Support for Homeless People's Self-Help *see* 2003 guidelines
gymnasium, homeless people in, 126, *128*

habitat, 157, 159, 184n2, 260
 Japanese urban matrix, 107–108
 margins of, 157–158
 peripheries of, *164*, 165–166, 167
 ruptures of, *164*, 165, 166
 spaces of, *164*, 165, 166
habiting, 22–23, 44, 160, 183, 188–189
 commoning, 24, 25, 44–45
 placemaking, 23, 25, 44
 translating, 24–25, 26, 44, 45
Hachiman Yama Park, 123, 124, *125*
haken giri, 242
Han Hinkon (Yuasa), 243
Hardt, Michael, 190, 191, 215
Harvey, David, 133n1, 184n3, 215, 262
 arguments on public/private spaces, 106–107

"circuits of capital" thesis, 109–110
 about commoning, 161, 189
 about role of radical urban politics, 188
 theory of urban public spaces, 114
 use value enlargement under Keynesian urbanisation, 105–106
hegemony, 113–114
Hibiya Park, 242, 244
Hiratsuka city, 53, 54
 groups for homeless people in, 218, **219**
 homelessness, data on, 54
 local policing regimes, 132
 Mayor of, *233*
 municipality's relationships with private actors, 232
 notice board at public dumping site, *146*
 placemaking in, 229
 recycling metabolism regulation in, 145–147
 regulation, data on, 55
 scant resources for homeless people, 232
 social movements, data on, 55–56
 social movements for homeless recyclers, 152
 urban regulatory complexes, 147
Hiratsuka Patrol, 54, 56, 152, 229, 230–234, 236
home/house, 23
homeless-driven public space, *115*, 116
"homeless-friendly"—policies, 122
homeless activism, 34, 54, 186, 199, 233
 cultural migration and relocation, 260
 expansion in outlying area of Kanagawa Prefecture, 217
 geography of, 163
 in Kotobuki district, 225
 lacking spaces in outlying area for, 218
 national programme of public assistance, 213
 publics and, 221
 rescaling reregulation in Kanagawa Prefecture, 236
 sociocultural place in Yokohama, 176
 transformative moments, 99

urbanisation beyond normalisation and occlusion, 254
see also placemaking in inner city
homeless–housed divide, 6, 111
  formidable, 22–23
  proliferation of, 103–104, 107
  in public spaces, 20
homeless–housed relationships, 182
homeless labour for "housing"
  locational ethnography, 122–130
  metabolism and societalisation, 107–111
  multicity ethnography, 130–132
  rescaling and reregulation, 111–116
  theory specification, 116–122
  urban matrix and housing classes, 104–107
homeless metabolism, 21, *112*, 126, 127, 130, 131, 254
  closure of public spaces to, 251–252
  commodification, 153
  exchange values, 135–136
  frustration with housing classes, 153–154
  value-producing aspect of, 104
homelessness, 5, 259
  challenges Japanese pattern of societalisation, 120
  cyclical spatialisation of, 6
  data of Kanagawa Prefecture on, 54
  decreasing probability of societalisation, 66
  gendered character in Japanese public spaces, 133
  without ghettoisation, 78, 89, 91, 93, 100
  and habiting, 22
  inner-city cycle of, 6, 39, 51, 52, 85, 198
  Lefebvre–Harvey line of discussion, 107
  Marx's metabolism theory, 109
  neo-Marxist approach to, 8
  new urban poverty, 15
  during postbubble crisis in Japan, 88–89
  regulatory situations and tension of, 17
  urban abstraction, 107

urban hegemony–reducing impact of, 236
  in urban Japan, 5–6
  urban political economy for, 7–9
  widespread cycle of, 6, 39–40, 198–199, 203, 213, 217
homeless people, 3–4
  cash income from labour, 139–140, *140*
  along coastal areas, 128–130
  commoning of urban use values for, 188
  emergency centres for, 102n9
  filtration from public and private spaces, 108
  along gymnasium, 126, *128*
  handbill distribution in Yokohama city, *204*, *206*
  hegemonic imaginaries and forms, 114, 116
  in homeless-policing dynamics context, 124
  as homeless recyclers, 135–136
  income-generating activities, *140*, 140–141
  living among day labourers in Japan, 121
  marginalisaton in societalisation process, 103
  metabolic circuits in public space, *112*
  minimalist approach to accommodation, 21
  minoritarian pattern of urban metabolism, 108–109
  along municipal sports park, 126
  murders and injuries in Yokohama city, **200**
  new use value of housing, 104
  in New York City, 26
  non-citizenship, 33
  "otherness" of, 136
  during postbubble crisis in Japan, 89
  production and consumption of housing, 132–133
  public spaces for, 259–260
  along railway station, 126–128, *129*
  "right to the city," 24
  along small public parks, 123–126
  societalisation in Japan, 40–43

spaces and cycles of urban social movements, 6
special "outsiders," 19
subalternity of, 259
subaltern struggles, 58
subsistent economies, 33
in urban Japan, 5–6
urban social movements for, 214
use of public spaces, 21
use values of housing in public, 33
homeless recyclers
by changing kinds of waste, 149
disturbing hegemonic construct, 141–142
double-edged metabolism by, 138, *138*
etiquette for neighbourhoods, 149
finding regulatory voids, 148
Gowan's ethnographic research, 136–138, 139
handling regulation/othering issue, 139
homeless people's cash income from labour, 139–140, *140*
homeless people's income-generating activities, *140*, 140–141
notes on days of official garbage collection, *148*
ordinances for criminalising, **142**, 142–143
social movements for, 150–153
see also recycling metabolism
homeless regulation, 64, 65, 66
affinities with Marx's forest regulation, 111, 113
localised forms of, 66
rescaling formation of, 19–20
throughout Kanagawa Prefecture, 130–131
Homeless Vehicle, 26
housed circuit of metabolism, *112*
housed citizens, commoning by, 201–203
housing, 24
and contestation as perspective, 263–264
new use value of, 104
standardized housing, 65–66
see also homeless labour for "housing"
housing classes, 103

civil society, 228
during COVID-19 pandemic, 256
late formation in Japan, 116–117
"liberal" social science, 134n2
peripheries of, 183
urban consumption, 110
urban matrix and, 104–107
Weberian theory of, 106
"housing first" programme, 98
hyperconformist societalisation, 120

impoverished people, 4, 13, 15, 35
"defensive" reformation of neighbourhoods against, 77
filtering out deregulating appearances, 66
labour market for, 69
new spatial strategies, 72
saimin, 41
social fabric for, 81
social reproduction, 258
subsumption into the capital circuit, 70
universal legal framework of citizenship, 191
inclusive urban form, 163
peripheries of habitat, *164*, 165–166, 167
ruptures of habitat, *164*, 165, 166
spaces of habitat, *164*, 165, 166
inner-city cycle of homelessness, 6, 39, 51, 52, 85, 198
integral state, 13, 48, 60n1, 66, 104, 114, 143

Japan-targeting theory specification, 35, *35*
Jazeel, Taric, 58
Jessop, Bob, 31
"growth patterns" formulation, 67
neo-Gramscian state theory, 60n1
about societalisation, 13, 14, 68
state unity conception, 11
Johnsen, Sarah, 7, 9
Johnson, Chalmers, 37, 83

Kamakura city, groups for homeless people in, 218, **219**
Kanagawa Prefecture, 32, *51*
groups for homeless people in, **219**

Hiratsuka city, 53, 54–56
homeless regulation, 130–132
Kawasaki city, 52, 54–56
Kotobuki district, 51–52, 53, 60n2
ordinances for criminalising nonpublic recyclers in, **142**, 142–143
participatory observation in, 49–50
rescaling reregulation, 236
social movements in, 257
Yokohama city, 50, 52, 53
Kawasaki city, 52, 134n10
All-Kanagawa Assembly, 235
groups for homeless people in, 218, **219**
homelessness, data on, 54
regulation, data on, 55
social movements, data on, 55–56
Keynesian deficit spending, 83
Keynesian–Fordist national states, 33
Kotobuki Association for Winning the Right to Livelihood, 207
Kotobuki-born activism, 34
Kotobuki Day Labourers' Union, 54, 56, 150, 171, 172, 175, 184, 185n6, 193, 225
Kotobuki district, 51–52, 53, 60n2, 167
brokering mobilisation from, 225
citizen activists/activism, 169–170
commoning against othering, 190, 193
day labourers in, *168*, 168–169
history of placemaking, 184
middle-class volunteers's role, 176–177
NIMBYism, 169
placemaking in, 224–225
places for activism, 180–181
pressure of gentrification, 254–255
social movement of commoning against othering, 194, **195–196**
social movements for homeless recyclers, 150
union activists/activism, 169
Kotobuki Livelihood Hall (KLH), 172, 175, 193, 194, 196–198
Kotobuki Self-Management Association (KSMA), 170–171, 193
Kotobuki Supporters' Gathering Club, 54, 56, 150, 181–182, 204, 255

labour market, 13, 69, 71, 258
during 1970s world crisis in Japan, 84
during bubble economy in Japan, 86
during postbubble crisis in Japan, 88
in postwar Japan, 81
during world financial crisis in Japan, 90
Lefebvre, Henri, 10, 68, 159, 216, 263
examination of peripheries, 33–34
habitat/habiting conflicts and dialectics, 22, 159–162, 183, 184n2
justification and support for homeless people, 36n4
material–semiotic demarcation of urban space, 106
mechanism of urban regulation, 127
political possibilities in periphery, 184n4–5
space of reproduction, 18
treating public and private spaces, 105–106
Legg, Stephen, 58
Linebaugh, Peter, 187, 189, 215
about commoning and discommoning, 187–188
liveable wages, 65, 81
locational ethnography
background for ethnographic narratives, 122–123
coast, 128–130
municipal sports park and gymnasium, 126
railway station, 126–128
small public parks, 123–126
Logan, John R., 106
Luxemburg, Rosa, 111

Marcus, George E., 47
Marr, Matthew, 57
Marshall, T. H., 71
Marxist crisis theory, 83
Marx, Karl, 21
forest regulation, 111, 113
about labour metabolism, 109
about urban consumption, 110
wage relations, 68
mass disasters and NSPR in Japan, 89–91
Massey, Doreen

INDEX 301

"conflictual sharing" of space, 162, 170
notion of placemaking, 183
"porous" places, 157
material–semiotic consumption in Japan, 118–120
May, Jon, 7, 9
McAdam, Doug, 220, 237n1
McKinney–Vento Homeless Assistance Act, 40
Merrifield, Andy, 138
meso-level
  abstraction, 28, 31–32, 35, 46, 264
  theorisation, 30–31
  theory, 35, *35*, 77–78
metabolism, 21, *112*
  normative, 104
  and societalisation, 107–111
  see also homeless metabolism; recycling metabolism; urban metabolism
Ministry of Health, Labour and Welfare (MHLW), 43, 250
minoritarian metabolism, 108–109
Mitchell, Don, 104
  analytic view of homeless regulation, 7, 8
  antihomeless gentrification, 19
  interpretations of homelessness, 262
  mobilisation of theory for Japan, 77–79
mochi sari, criminalisation of, 144
"mode of regulation," 12, 65
Mokuyō Patorōru *see* Thursday Patrol
Molotch, Harvey L., 106
moral panic, 77, 94, 103, 132, 217, 236, 251, 259
Motomachi area, 50
multicity ethnography, 130–132
  see also locational ethnography
multiscalar dynamics of state space (re)construction, 101n1
municipal sports park, homeless people in, 126

Nakamura River Shelter, 209
nationalisation
  of commoning, 196–197
  of welfare statism, 16

nationalisation–upscaling
  politics, 241, 243
  of regulatory responsibilities, 257n1
nationalised spaces of poverty regulation (NSPR), 13, 38, 63, 67, 91, **92**, 189, 258
  1970s world crisis in Japan, 83–85
  arguments on societalisation, 13–15
  bubble economy in Japan, 85–87
  comparisons to Brenner's meso-level theory, 77–78
  crisis of, 70–72
  decoupling local initiatives for homeless people, 20
  economic growth in Japan, 79–83, 91, **92**
  gender selectivity of, 101
  ground-up restructuring of, 64
  historical dynamics of, 13
  meso-abstracted theory, 64
  mobilisation of theory for Japan, 77–79
  national growth patterns, 67
  postbubble crisis in Japan, 87–89
  poverty-regulating capacity, 39
  process of restructuring poverty growth, 16
  rescaling of, 40, 72–76
  societalisation and, 67–69, 100
  spheres of poverty regulation, 69–70
  world financial crisis and mass disasters in Japan, 89–91
Negri, Antonio, 190, 191, 215
New State Spaces (Brenner), 9
new urban poverty (NUP), 15, 16, 33, 38, 85, 91, 93, 100
  bottom-up eruptions of new regulatory spaces, 78
  crisis formation in societalisation, 71
  formation in postwar Japan, 94–95
  haphazard eruptions, 73
  in meso-level theorisation, 76–77
  normative consumption, 65
  North American and Western European geographies, 64
NIMBY *see* "not in my backyard"
NIMBYism, 19, 77, 110, 230

antihomeless, 163
  in Kotobuki district, 169
"normal" public space, *115*, 116
normative consumption, 65–66, 199, 258
"not in my backyard" (NIMBY), 19
NSPR *see* nationalised spaces of poverty regulation
NUP *see* new urban poverty

Odawara city, groups for homeless people in, 218, **219**
Odawara Communicating Patrol, 56
"off-street" spaces, 203
Ordinance for the Promotion of Delightful and Clean Urban Development, 145
Ordinance for the Reduction, Recycling, and Appropriate Disposal of Wastes, 143
Other(s), 58, 105, 193, 244
  of habitat, 22
  of hegemonic urban consumption, 121
  of normative urban settlements, 33
  repugnant, 221
  of societalisation, 247, 259
Othering, 187–189
  see also commoning against othering
"otherness" of homeless people, 136
outlying cities of homelessness, 52, 217
  commoning in, 229–234
  groups for homeless people in Kanagawa Prefecture, **219**
  placemaking in, 224–229
  resource cultivation, 219
  resource mobilisation, 218–219
outsiders *see* Other(s)
Overwintering Village of Dispatched Temporary Workers, 241, 246

Peck, Jamie, 8, 15, 103
  fast policy, 49
  rollout neoliberalism, 22
  "scale manager" role of national states, 11, 20, 39, 64, 78
  social movements, 21–22
  workfare theory, 73

people's commons, 190–191
period-defining feature of Japanese society, 91
peripheries, 23
  of habitat, *164*, 165–166, 167
  of housing classes, 183
  Lefebvre's examination of, 33–34
  mythologisation of, 161
  resources of, 225
picking-off rescaling, 6, 73, *74*, 75, 96–98
placemaking in inner city, 23, 25, 157–159, 183, 260
  accumulated history of, 184
  antihomeless NIMBYism, 163
  day labourers in Kotobuki district, 167–170
  inclusive urban form, 163–166, *164*
  Lefebvre's habitat/habiting conflicts and dialectics, 159–162
  Massey's conflictual space, 162
  theorisation to Japan, 166–167
  Valentine's "spaces of encounters" concept, 162–163
  in Yokohama city, 170–183
  see also commoning in inner city; commoning in Yokohama city
placemaking in outlying cities
  in Fujisawa city, 227–229
  in Hiratsuka city, 229
  in Kotobuki city, 224–225
  in Sagamihara city, 225–227
Polanyi, Karl, 69–71, 81
postbubble crisis and NSPR in Japan, 87–89
Poulantzas, Nicos, 68, 216
poverty
  historical niche in Yokohama, 221
  rampant deregulation of, 39
  regulation in Euro-American countries, 100
  regulatory space of, 71
  spatialisation of, 82–83, 91, **92**, 93
  spatial niches of, 44
  urban, 11, 39, 63, 93
  see also nationalised spaces of poverty regulation (NSPR); new urban poverty (NUP)

The Prison Notebooks (Gramsci), 134n4
private spaces, 17, 160
   Lefebvre's treatment of, 105
   remoulding working class, 106
   rescaling formation of homeless regulation, 19–20
   societalisation through, 17–18
The Production of Space (Lefebvre), 105
prohomeless
   activism, 263
   actors, 216
   brokerage, 221
   placemaking theory, 34
   social movements, 23
Public Assistance Act (1950), 45, 80, 95, 191, 192, 249
public assistance programme in Japan, 247–248
   "business use of public assistance," 246
   during closure of public spaces, 251–253
   Japanese citizenship paradigm initiatives, 248–249
   national programme of, 90
   "sniffing out," language of, 248
   state rescaling, 249–250
public provision, 13, 69, 70, 71, 258
   during 1970s world crisis in Japan, 84
   during bubble economy in Japan, 86
   commoning, 207–210
   during postbubble crisis in Japan, 87–88
   in postwar Japan, 80–81
   role in preventing Japan's economic crisis, 89–90
public spaces, 17, 19, 33, 40–43, 107–111, 158, 256–257
   antihomeless gentrification, 19
   commoning, 203–207
   comparative view of Japan, *118*
   decline in countable homeless people, *251*
   developing societalisation effect, 104
   difficulties for commoning, 213
   homeless–housed divides in, 20
   influx of homeless people in Japan, 132
   information-gathering tours for public space commoning, **206–207**
   in inner city, 160
   Lefebvre's treatment of, 105
   new regulatory spaces, 103–104
   pattern of homeless regulation in, 122
   people's metabolic circuits in, *112*
   privatisation of, 19
   public assistance programme during closure of, 251–253, *252*
   public space–centred approach, 33
   regulation of urban encounter and societalisation, 114, *115*
   remoulding working class, 106
   rescaling formation of homeless regulation, 19–20
   role in societalisation, 108
   societalisation through, 17–18
pure coercion, 114

radical decentralization, 188
radicalism of commoning movement, 194–196
railway station, homeless people in, 126–128, *129*
recurrence process, 223–224
recycling metabolism
   Hiratsuka city, regulation in, 145–147
   new homeless strategies, 147–150
   social movements for homeless recyclers, 150–153
   Yokohama city, regulation in, 143–145
   see also homeless recyclers
regulationism, 191
regulationist ethnography, 37–38, 45, 59
   ethnographer's goal, 47–48
   ethnographic engagement, 45–46
   theory–ethnography linkages/partnership/comradeship, 49, 262
   theory–ethnography rapprochement, 47
   "thickness" of description, 46–47
regulation theory, 15, 26, 33
   normative consumption, 65–66
   objectives, 64
   Parisian school of, 64–65

societalisation, 66
  unproblematic applicability to Japan, 66–67
rescaling regulation, geography of, 216, 236
  brokerage and translation, 220–224
  commoning in outlying cities, 229–234
  homeless activism, 216–217
  outlying cities of homelessness, 217–219
  placemaking in outlying cities, 224–229
  solidarity against new rescaling, 234–236
  see also state rescaling
resource mobilisation of urban social movements, 218–219
right to livelihood, 192, 212
Robinson, Jennifer, 30, 261, 262
rollout neoliberalism, 8, 22
Roy, Ananya, 30, 261, 262
ruptures of habitat, *164*, 165, 166

Sagamihara city
  All-Kanagawa Assembly, 235
  groups for homeless people in, 218, **219**
  local policing regimes, 132
  placemaking in, 225–227
Sagamihara Thursday Patrol, 56, 227
Saillard, Yves, 65
Sawatari Chūō Park, 205
Sayer, Andrew, 31, 46
scale concept, 36n3
"scale manager," theoretical role of, 75, 78, 94
"second-order" regulation, 49, 65
Self-Help Act, 96, 213
self-help assistance centres for homeless people, 98, 102n9
Sengen Ryokuchi, 123
shadow employees, 169, 174
Shinshuku Park, 123, *124*, *125*
small public parks, homeless people in, 123–126
small use values
  attached to Japan's urban matrix, 117–118
  of public spaces, 120

Smith–Mitchell line of argument, 7, 8
Smith, Neil, 18, 26, 104, 161
  antihomeless gentrification, 19
  interpretations of homelessness, 262
  revanchist urbanism, 7, 8
"sniffing out," language of, 248
social cohesion, 13–14, 66
social fabric, 13, 69–70, 71, 258
  during 1970s world crisis in Japan, 84
  during bubble economy in Japan, 86–87
  during postbubble crisis in Japan, 88
  in postwar Japan, 81–82
Social Justice and the City (Harvey), 184n3
social movements, 21–26, 33–34, 44–45, 218–219, 253–254, 260, 263
  of commoning against othering, 194, **195–196**
  data of Kanagawa Prefecture on, 55–56
  diffusion, 221
  for homeless people, 44
  for homeless recyclers, 150–153
  in Kanagawa Prefecture, 257
  need for evolution in Japan, 217
  prohomeless, 23
  during rounds of rescaling, 75
  subaltern solidarities for homeless people, 57
societalisation, 13, 40–42, 66, 67–68, 258–259
  contingency of, 14, 15
  dynamics of, 14, 15
  failure in, 70
  family production, 68
  effect of habitat under rescaling, 188
  Japanese state-permeated, 118–120
  metabolism and, 107–111
  national, 15
  NSPR's role in, 15
  regulation in public space, 114, *115*
  spatial-scale selectivity of, 68–69
  see also nationalised space of poverty regulation (NSPR)
societalising spheres, 38
Soja, Edward W., 134n2
solidarity against new rescaling
  learning rescaling, 235–236
  linking cities, 234–235

INDEX   305

Sorensen, André, 119–120
standardized housing, 65–66
"state" concept, 113, 114, *115*
  see also state rescaling
state-saturated societalisation in
    Japan, 118–120
state rescaling, 5, 9, 28, 35, 36n3, 249–250
  antihomeless situation in public spaces, 20
  and commoning, 189
  composite theory of, 37
  devolutionary politics of, 10, 16
  dynamics of Japan, 100–101
  dynamism around homelessness
    in Japan, 94
  formation of homeless regulation, 19–20
  ground-up, 6, 73, *74*, 75,
    95–96, 120–122
  integral, 13
  new state capacity, 10, 11–12
  new urban dynamics of, 63–64
  and non-western state space, 264
  of NSPR, 72–76
  picking-off, 6, 73, *74*, 75, 96–98
  and reregulation, 111–116
  reregulation, 66
  rescaling theory, 10–11
  rounds of, 6, 33, 73, *74*, 75, 186
  spaces and processes within
    Euro-American world, 12
  unfolding, 99–100
state theory, 32–33, 50
  neo-Gramscian, 60n1, 66
state unity conception, 11
Stevens, Carolyn, 25, 60n2, 176
"streetisation" of societalisation crisis, 20
subaltern materials in Japanese develop-
    mental state, 38, 56–59
Sum, Ngai-Ling, 13, 14, 67

Tamano, Kazushi, 134n5
Tarrow, Sidney, 220, 237n1
Theodore, Nik, 49
theory–ethnography
  linkages/partnership, 48, 49
  rapprochement, 47
theory making, 26, *27*, 28
theory specification, 26, *27*, 28–29

comparative view of Japanese public
    space, *118*
  ground-up rescaling in Japan, 120–122
  late formation of housing classes in
    Japan, 116–117
  national states, 38–40
  public and private spaces, 40–43
  small use values attached to Japan's
    urban matrix, 117–118
  state-permeated societalisation and
    consumption in Japan, 118–120
  theory for Japan, 116
  urban social movements, 44–45
Thursday Patrol, 56, 177–180, 181
Tickell, Adam, 8, 15, 22
Tilly, Charles, 220, 237n1
Tokyo Metropolitan
    Government (TMG), 98
Toshikoshi Haken Mura *see*
    Overwintering Village of Dispatched
    Temporary Workers
translating/translation, 24–25, 26, 34, 217,
    221, 260–261
  brokerage and, 222–224
  Gramscian concept of, 220, 222
  in Sagamihara city, 226
  to upscaling of homeless politics, 244, 245

unfolding rescaling, 73, *74*, 75, 99–100
union, commoning by, 199–201
upscaling of homeless politics in Japan, 241
  consequences of scale jumping
    movement, 246
  etto–mobilisation model, 242
  Gramscian notion of translation
    to, 244, 245
  growth of public assistance
    recipients, 244, *245*
  labour market contraction, 242
  nationalisation–upscaling
    politics, 241, 243
  role of MHLW, 244
  impact of US subprime crisis, 242
  see also state rescaling
urban encounter, 18, 157, 158
  emancipation of, 191
  "normal" public spaces, 116

radical, 190
regulation in public spaces, 114, *115*
urbanisation, 17–18, 22, 135
urban matrix/grid, 18, 105, 114, 159, 165
  and housing classes, 104–107
  small use values attached to Japan, 117–118
urban metabolism, 33
  double-edged metabolism by homeless recyclers, 138, *138*
  image-generating process in consumption, 110
  in public spaces, 109
urban revolution, 22, 165, 186, 260
The Urban Revolution (Lefebvre), 159, 184nn1–2, 263
"us" and "them" concept in Yokohama city, 178–179, 180, 182

Valentine, Gill, 162–163

wage–labour nexus, 65
  Parisian concept of, 65
  wage relations, 68
Wagner, David, 25
Weberian theory of housing classes, 106
West–East dichotomisation, 134n4
whitebooks, 169, 174, 185n6
widespread cycle of homelessness, 6, 39–40, 198–199, 203, 213, 217
Worker Dispatch Law (1985), 88
workfarist regulation of Japan
  depoliticisation in poverty regulation, 253
  endemic failures in, 250
  workfarist reform, 246–249
workhouse regime, 73
"work will," 247–248
world crisis (1970s) and NSPR in Japan, 83–85
world financial crisis (2000) and NSPR in Japan, 89–91

Yokohama city, 50, 52, 53, 54, 170
  1990s crisis of homelessness, 183
  discommoning in, 210–213, 214
  groups for homeless people in, **219**
  handbill distribution, *172, 176, 201*
  historical niche of poverty in, 221
  KLH role in placemaking, 172
  Kotobuki Day Labourers' Union, 171, 172
  Kotobuki district, 25, 26, 34
  KSMA role in placemaking, 170–171
  limited "acceptance" of homeless recyclers, *151*
  municipal gymnasium as homeless shelter in, 257
  municipality's relationships with activism, 232
  murders and injuries of homeless people in, **200**
  placemaking by self-negation, 179–180
  politisation of day labourers, 175–176
  prohomeless movements, 176–177, 180
  public assistance programme, 215n1
  public notice at public dumping sites, *144*
  recycling metabolism regulation in, 143–145
  Sakurai's "us" and "them" concept, 178–179, 180
  social movements for homeless recyclers, 150–151
  Thursday Patrol and, 177–178
  union activists' placemaking strategy, 171–175
  urban regulatory complexes, 147
  widespread cycle of homelessness, 180–182, 213
  see also commoning in Yokohama city
Yokohama Wednesday Patrol, 204
Yokosuka city, groups for homeless people in, 218, **219**
yoseba zones, 3, 39, 51, 82, 198, 216
  developmentalist urbanisation in, 120–121
  gender construction of, 167
  homelessness of day labourers in, 198
  Kotobuki district, 167–170
  reduction of homelessness in, 89–90